WILLIAM M. HARNETT

WILLIAM M.

PUBLISHED BY

AMON CARTER MUSEUM · THE METROPOLITAN MUSEUM OF ART

HARRY N. ABRAMS, INC., NEW YORK

HARNETT

EDITED BY

DOREEN BOLGER, MARC SIMPSON,

AND JOHN WILMERDING

With the assistance of Thayer Tolles Mickel

This volume has been published in conjunction with the exhibition *William M. Harnett,* which was co-organized by The Metropolitan Museum of Art, New York; Amon Carter Museum, Fort Worth; and The Fine Arts Museums of San Francisco.

THE METROPOLITAN MUSEUM OF ART, NEW YORK
March 14–June 14, 1992

AMON CARTER MUSEUM, FORT WORTH
July 18–October 18, 1992

THE FINE ARTS MUSEUMS OF SAN FRANCISCO
November 14, 1992–February 14, 1993

NATIONAL GALLERY OF ART, WASHINGTON
March 14–June 13, 1993

The exhibition has been made possible by grants from the National Endowment for the Humanities and the National Endowment for the Arts, federal agencies. Additional funding for the publication was provided by the William Cullen Bryant Fellows of The American Wing at The Metropolitan Museum of Art.

Alamo Rent A Car, Inc., is the corporate sponsor of the exhibition in New York and San Francisco.

LIBRARY OF CONGRESS
CATALOGING-IN-PUBLICATION DATA

William M. Harnett /edited by Doreen Bolger, Marc Simpson, and John Wilmerding, with the assistance of Thayer Tolles Mickel.
    p.   cm.

"Published in conjunction with the exhibition *William M. Harnett,* which was co-organized by The Metropolitan Museum of Art, New York; Amon Carter Museum, Fort Worth; and The Fine Arts Museums of San Francisco"—T.p. verso.

Includes bibliographical references and index.
ISBN 0-8109-3410-8 — ISBN 0-88360-069-2 (pbk.)
1. Harnett, William Michael, 1848–1892—Exhibitions.
2. Harnett, William Michael, 1848–1892—Criticism and
    interpretation.

I. Bolger, Doreen, 1949–   . II. Simpson, Marc, 1953–
III. Wilmerding, John, 1938–   . IV. Amon Carter Museum
of Western Art. V. The Metropolitan Museum of Art (New
York, N.Y.)

ND237.H315A4   1992   91-26675
759.13—dc20   CIP

The poetry of Emily Dickinson quoted in John Wilmerding's "Notes of Change: Harnett's Paintings of the Late 1870s" is reprinted by permission of the publishers and the Trustees of Amherst College from *The Poems of Emily Dickinson,* Thomas H. Johnson, ed., Cambridge, Mass.: The Belknap Press of Harvard University Press, Copyright 1951, © 1955, 1979, 1983 by the President and Fellows of Harvard College.

Published in 1992 by Amon Carter Museum, Fort Worth; The Metropolitan Museum of Art, New York; and Harry N. Abrams, Incorporated, New York. A Times Mirror Company

Edited by Pamela T. Barr, The Metropolitan Museum of Art

Designed by Tom Dawson and Bill Maize, Duo Design Group, Fort Worth

Printed and bound in Japan by Nissha Printing Co., Ltd.

Cover/Jacket: *Still Life—Violin and Music* (pl. 43)
Title page: *Job Lot Cheap* (pl. 9)
Frontispiece: *Ease* (detail, pl. 41)

LENDERS TO THE EXHIBITION

Addison Gallery of American Art,
Phillips Academy, Andover, Mass.

Mr. and Mrs. Garett Albert

Albright-Knox Art Gallery,
Buffalo, N.Y.

Amon Carter Museum, Fort Worth

The Armand Hammer Museum
of Art and Cultural Center,
Los Angeles

The Art Institute of Chicago

Berry-Hill Galleries, New York

Brandywine River Museum,
Chadds Ford, Pa.

The Brooklyn Museum

The Butler Institute of American
Art, Youngstown, Ohio

The Carnegie Museum of Art,
Pittsburgh

The Chrysler Museum, Norfolk, Va.

City Art Galleries, Sheffield, England

The Cleveland Museum of Art

Columbus Museum of Art, Ohio

The Corcoran Gallery of Art,
Washington, D.C.

Dallas Museum of Art

The Fine Arts Museums of
San Francisco

Flint Institute of Arts, Mich.

Frye Art Museum, Seattle

Jo Ann and Julian Ganz, Jr.

High Museum of Art, Atlanta

Honolulu Academy of Arts

Kennedy Galleries, Inc.,
New York

The Manney Collection

Manoogian Collection

James H. Maroney, Jr.

The Metropolitan Museum
of Art, New York

Munson-Williams-Proctor Institute
Museum of Art, Utica, N.Y.

Museum of Fine Arts, Boston

Museum of Fine Arts, Springfield,
Mass.

The Newark Museum, N.J.

Philadelphia Museum of Art

Reynolda House, Museum of
American Art, Winston-Salem

Santa Barbara Museum of Art

Wadsworth Atheneum, Hartford,
Conn.

Westmoreland Museum of Art,
Greensburg, Pa.

Wichita Art Museum

Private collectors

CONTENTS

THE MAJOR THEMES

▼

▼

FOREWORD

▼

William M. Harnett celebrates the achievements of one of America's most accomplished still-life painters. The first retrospective devoted to Harnett since his death exactly one hundred years ago, the exhibition brings together forty-nine of his most important pictures and offers visitors an opportunity to experience firsthand the artist's incredibly deceptive realism.

The exhibition was organized by the Amon Carter Museum, The Fine Arts Museums of San Francisco, and The Metropolitan Museum of Art. The show and the accompanying publication are the result of a close collaboration among curatorial staff members—Doreen Bolger, Curator of Paintings and Sculpture, Amon Carter Museum; Marc Simpson, The Ednah Root Curator of American Paintings, The Fine Arts Museums of San Francisco; and John Wilmerding, Visiting Curator, Department of American Art, The Metropolitan Museum of Art, and Christopher Binyon Sarofim '86 Professor, Princeton University. They were greatly assisted by Thayer Tolles Mickel, Research Assistant at the Metropolitan and, later, Curatorial Assistant at the Amon Carter, who coordinated the research and photography for the publication. The book has been significantly enriched by contributions from distinguished scholars of the museum and university communities: Henry Adams, Samuel Sosland Curator of American Art, The Nelson-Atkins Museum of Art, Kansas City, Mo.; Maria Chamberlin-Hellman, Associate Professor of Art History, Marymount College, Tarrytown; Nicolai Cikovsky, Jr., Deputy Senior Curator and Curator of American and British Paintings, National Gallery of Art, Washington, D.C.; Elizabeth Jane Connell, Curator, Columbus Museum of Art, Ohio; William H. Gerdts, Professor of Art History, Ph.D. Program in Art History, Graduate School and University Center of The City University of New York; Elizabeth Johns, Silfen Term Professor of American Art History, University of Pennsylvania, Philadelphia; Judy L. Larson, Curator of American Art, High Museum of Art, Atlanta; David M. Lubin, Associate Professor of Art and American Studies, Colby College, Waterville, Maine; Chad Mandeles, Adjunct Assistant Professor, Fashion Institute of Technology, New York; Roxana Robinson, independent scholar; and Paul J. Staiti, Associate Professor, Art Department, Mount Holyoke College, South Hadley, Mass. Five of Professor Wilmerding's students in the Department of Art and Archaeology at Princeton have written essays—Laura A. Coyle, Jennifer Hardin, Jennifer Milam, Douglas R. Nickel, and Paul Raymond Provost—as have Andrew Walker and Sylvia Yount, students of Professor Johns's.

The exhibition was realized through the generosity of public and private lenders who made their works available for an extended national tour. Without them, we would not have been able to bring together these beautiful paintings.

The William Cullen Bryant Fellows of The American Wing, who sponsor Metropolitan Museum publications devoted to the exploration of major themes and issues in American art, helped defray the cost of the catalogue.

Alamo Rent A Car, Inc., generously sponsored the exhibition at the Metropolitan and at The Fine Arts Museums of San Francisco. A grant from the National Endowment for the Humanities supported the publication and enabled participating institutions to develop an ambitious educational program to accompany the exhibition. Additional support from the National Endowment for the Arts contributed to registration expenses for the project.

PHILIPPE DE MONTEBELLO
Director
The Metropolitan Museum of Art

JAN KEENE MUHLERT
Director
Amon Carter Museum

HARRY S. PARKER III
Director
The Fine Arts Museums
of San Francisco

J. CARTER BROWN
Director
National Gallery of Art

ACKNOWLEDGMENTS

▼

The exhibition *William M. Harnett* has a long and rather complicated history. The artist has not been accorded a retrospective since 1892, nor has he been the subject of a monograph since Alfred Frankenstein's *After the Hunt: William Harnett and Other American Still Life Painters, 1870–1900,* first published nearly forty years ago. In 1987, Marc Simpson of The Fine Arts Museums of San Francisco, and Linda Ayres, former Curator of Paintings and Sculpture at the Amon Carter Museum and now Deputy Director of the Wadsworth Atheneum, began to plan an exhibition on the artist. In 1988, John Wilmerding, Visiting Curator, Department of American Art, The Metropolitan Museum of Art, and Christopher Binyon Sarofim '86 Professor, Princeton University, and Doreen Bolger, then Curator of American Paintings and Sculpture at the Metropolitan, conceived a similar project. They saw this as a forum for the educational initiative that began between Princeton and the Metropolitan with Wilmerding's appointment—graduate students were to undertake scholarly projects that would involve them with the Museum's collections and activities. When Dr. Bolger was appointed Curator of Paintings and Sculpture at the Amon Carter in 1989, the two exhibitions came together, with the Amon Carter, the Metropolitan, and The Fine Arts Museums of San Francisco as organizers. The three curators—Bolger, Simpson, and Wilmerding—enlisted Thayer Tolles Mickel to assist with the extensive research required.

In determining the format and content of this volume, the curators were guided by the state of the existing literature. Frankenstein had unearthed what remains the main body of information on the artist, reconstructed the outlines of his biography, compiled a critical catalogue, and revived interest in Harnett's trompe-l'oeil followers. *American Still-Life Painting* (1971) by William H. Gerdts and Russell Burke and *Painters of the Humble Truth: Masterpieces of American Still Life, 1801–1939* (1981) by Dr. Gerdts had placed Harnett's work in the context of other examples of the genre. After some discussion with colleagues, particularly Professor Jules Prown of Yale University, the curators decided to assemble a team of writers to contribute interpretive essays investigating Harnett's work thematically and exploring wider cultural issues. The authors were drawn from the university and museum communities, from the fields of art history and American studies.

We would like to acknowledge the many staff members of the organizing institutions who have contributed so generously to our progress over the last five years. Directors Philippe de Montebello, Jan Keene Muhlert, and Harry S. Parker III made this project a priority at their active institutions. Emily Kernan Rafferty, Vice President for Development and Membership at the Metropolitan, and her very competent staff, particularly Terri A. Constant, Nina Diefenbach, Erin Durkin, Carol Ehler, Nancy McLaughlin, and Lynn Winter, worked to secure corporate funding for the exhibition. Judith Gibbs, Development Coordinator at the Amon Carter, skillfully compiled lengthy applications submitted to the National Endowment for the Humanities and the National Endowment for the Arts on behalf of the organizers. Irvin Lippman, Assistant Director at the Amon Carter, and Sharon H. Cott, Associate Counsel at the Metropolitan, cooperated in the development of an agreement among the participating institutions. Melissa G. Thompson, Registrar at the Amon Carter, ably coordinated the traveling arrangements for the exhibition. John Buchanan, Chief Registrar at the Metropolitan, offered much appreciated advice on matters of shipping and insurance. At the Amon Carter, Allison Perkins, Senior Educator, and at the Metropolitan, Kent Lydecker, Deputy Director for Education, and Stella Paul, Assistant Museum Educator, collaborated with the curators on the development of shared educational programs and materials.

The book accompanying the exhibition was published by the Amon Carter Museum, The Metropolitan Museum of Art, and Harry N. Abrams, Inc. The text was prepared for publication by the editorial staff of the

Metropolitan Museum. John P. O'Neill, Editor in Chief and General Manager of Publications; Barbara Burn, Executive Editor; and Teresa Egan, Managing Editor, supervised the endeavor. Pamela T. Barr edited the volume with immense skill and good grace and organized the efforts of bibliographer Jayne Kuchna and proofreader Renée Gernand. Carol Fuerstein and Joanna Ekman lent their expertise in the early stages of the project. Connie Harper and Erik La Prade tended to innumerable details. The book was designed under the direction of the Amon Carter, where Nancy Stevens, Editor; Jane Posey, Editorial Assistant; and Carolyn LeMaster, Curatorial Secretary, assisted with the final stages of production. The clear and elegant design is the work of Tom Dawson and Bill Maize of DUO Design, Fort Worth. Margaret Kaplan of Harry N. Abrams supervised the production of the publication. The authors are indebted to all these individuals for their substantial contributions to the content and appearance of the volume.

A number of individuals assisted with research for the project. With determination and cheerfulness, Andrew Walker unearthed valuable information on Harnett's Philadelphia career. Beate Hirsch read German-language newspapers published in New York during the artist's lifetime and documented his years in Munich. Kathleen Bennewitz, formerly Curatorial Assistant at the Amon Carter; Betsy Boone; Lisa Chalif; Laura A. Coyle; David B. Dearinger; Sally Mills, formerly Associate Curator at The Fine Arts Museums of San Francisco; Joy Mitchell; and Lesley Wright scoured newspapers and exhibition catalogues nationwide for lists and reviews of exhibitions in which the artist participated. Paul S. Barr, M.D., and John Richardson, M.D., graciously offered advice regarding Harnett's medical condition and its impact upon his art. We are most grateful for all these efforts.

At the Metropolitan Museum of Art, the administration of the exhibition was overseen by Mahrukh Tarapor, Assistant Director, with the help of Martha Deese, Senior Assistant for Exhibitions. Linda M. Sylling, Manager for Operations, helped plan the installation in New York and prepare the budget that served all participants; her involvement was crucial to the success of the project. Marceline McKee helped arrange replacement loans. Designer Daniel Kershaw developed the installation of the exhibition and Sophia Geronimus, its graphic materials. John Ross, Manager of Public Information, and Richard J. Lombard, Assistant Public Information Officer, coordinated press matters and public information. Maryan W. Ainsworth and Dorothy Mahon in Paintings Conservation were valued contributors to the research and implementation phases of the exhibition. William B. Walker and the staff of the Thomas J. Watson Library deserve special notice; we particularly thank Patrick Coman, Katria Czerwoniak, and Ronald Fein. Also acknowledged with gratitude are: Kathleen Arffman, Department of Visitor Services; Deanna Cross and Diana F. Kaplan, Associates for photograph and slide-library orders; Barbara Bridgers, Manager, Photograph Studio; and Walter Liedtke, Associate Curator, European Paintings. In The American Wing, Kevin Avery, Assistant Curator of American Paintings and Sculpture, supervised the installation with the advice of John Wilmerding. John K. Howat, Lawrence A. Fleischman Chairman of the Department of American Art; H. Barbara Weinberg, Curator of American Paintings and Sculpture; Peter M. Kenny, Assistant Curator of American Decorative Arts and Assistant for Administration of The American Wing; and Carrie Rebora, Assistant Curator of American Paintings and Sculpture and Manager of the Henry R. Luce Center for the Study of American Art, offered their unflagging support. Administrative Assistants Elisabeth R. Agro, Catherine Hiller, and Audrey Irwin, as well as former Associate Coordinator Pamela Hubbard, willingly took time from their busy schedules to assist with various aspects of the project.

At the Amon Carter Museum, Doreen Bolger coordinated loans for the exhibition with the assistance of Melissa G. Thompson; Julie Causey, Assistant

Registrar; and Carolyn LeMaster. Milan Hughston, Librarian, and his staff, particularly Sherman Clark, kindly answered innumerable research queries. Rynda Lemke prepared many photographs for the publication. Christopher Rauhoff, Coordinator of Preparation and Installation Services, designed the installation.

At The Fine Arts Museums of San Francisco, Marc Simpson was responsible for the development and installation of the exhibition. Steven A. Nash, Associate Director and Chief Curator, and James Forbes, Deputy Director, Development, lent their support to the realization of the project. Debra Pughe, Exhibitions Manager; Kathy Baldwin, Operations Manager; Therese Chen, Exhibitions Registrar; Virginia Kelly and the Art Handlers/Technical Staff; William White, Exhibition Designer; and Connie King, Graphic Designer, oversaw and installed the exhibition. Lois Gordon, Curator of Education and Programs, and Jean Chaitin, Programs Officer, developed accompanying educational programs and materials. Linda Jablon and Robin Koltenuk, Public Information, coordinated local press and publicity matters.

At the National Gallery of Art, Nicolai Cikovsky, Jr., Curator of American and British Paintings, coordinated the installation with the help of Charles Brock, Exhibition Assistant. Dodge Thompson, Chief of Exhibition Programs, and Cameran Castiel, Exhibition Officer, handled the many details of the exhibition, and Mary Suzor, Registrar, its packing and shipping. Gaillard Ravenel, Mark Leithauser, Gordon Anson, and Barbara Keyes saw to the installation with good sense and good taste. Ruth Kaplan, Press and Public Information Officer, and Deborah Ziska, Publicist, provided an effective liaison with the communications media. Elizabeth A. C. Perry, Corporate Relations Officer, and her assistant, Elisa Buono Glazer, attended to the funding of the exhibition.

Many museums, libraries, and historical societies assisted us by making their research collections accessible, answering numerous inquiries, and offering useful suggestions. We would like to thank our colleagues in New York at the Frick Art Reference Library, Geneological and Biographical Society of New York, The New-York Historical Society, and The New York Public Library; in Philadelphia at the Free Library of Philadelphia and the Historical Society of Pennsylvania; and in Washington, D.C., at the Archives of American Art and the Inventory of Paintings at the Smithsonian Institution, and the Library of Congress.

The following organizations and their staff members deserve special acknowledgment: William P. Cressler, American Irish Historical Society, New York; Milo M. Naeve, formerly of The Art Institute of Chicago; Sinclair Hitchings and Karen Shafts, Boston Public Library; Barbara Dayer Gallati, The Brooklyn Museum; Irene Roughton, The Chrysler Museum; Bruce Robertson, The Cleveland Museum of Art; Ulla Voulk, Cooper-Union for the Advancement of Science and Art, New York; Franklin Kelly, formerly of The Corcoran Gallery of Art and now at the National Gallery; James W. Tottis, The Detroit Institute of Arts; Judith A. Neiswander and Phoebe Peebles, Fogg Art Museum, Harvard University, Cambridge, Mass.; Helen Sanger, Frick Art Reference Library, and Charles Ryskamp, The Frick Collection, New York; Jennifer Saville, Honolulu Academy of Arts; Kenneth Finkel, Library Company of Philadelphia; Bonnie L. Conway and Patricia L. Serafini, Munson-Williams-Proctor Institute Museum of Art, Utica, N.Y.; Carol Troyen, Museum of Fine Arts, Boston; Heather Haskell and Martha Hoppin, Museum of Fine Arts, Springfield, Mass.; Rona Roob, The Museum of Modern Art, New York; Barbara S. Krulik and Thérèse Diamond-Rosinsky, National Academy of Design, New York; Adele A. Lerner, Medical Archives, New York Hospital–Cornell Medical Center; the late Gary A. Reynolds, The Newark Museum, N.J.; Susan Danly, Cheryl Leibold, and Jeanette M. Toohey, Pennsylvania Academy of the Fine Arts, Philadelphia; Darrel L. Sewell, Philadelphia Museum of Art; Martin E. Petersen, San Diego Museum of Art; Anne Goodchild, Sheffield City Art Galleries; Linda Ayres and Elizabeth Kornhauser, Wadsworth Atheneum, Hartford, Conn.; George W. Ambrose, John

Wanamaker and Company, Phildelphia; Paul A. Chew, Westmoreland Museum of Art, Greensburg, Pa.; Betty Monkman, The White House, Washington, D.C.; Marion Goethals, Williams College Museum of Art, Williamstown, Mass.; and Helen Cooper, Yale University Art Gallery, New Haven.

We were assisted by many in the complex endeavor of securing photographs and transparencies for the publication. We would like to thank especially Anne Potter, Archives of American Art; Paula Pergament, formerly at The Art Institute of Chicago; Lisa Luedtke, The Corcoran Gallery of Art, Washington, D.C.; Jody Cohen, High Museum of Art, Atlanta; Monica Crystal and Janice Dockery, Historical Society of Pennsylvania; Susan Oyama, The Library Company of Philadelphia; Elliot M. Shirwo, Los Angeles County Museum of Art; Barbara De Silva, The Manney Collection; Joan Barnes and Cheryl M. Robledo, MASCO Corporation; Karen L. Otis, Museum of Fine Arts, Boston; Judith H. Moore, Pennsylvania Academy of the Fine Arts; Meg Perlman; John B. West, Reynolda House, Museum of American Art, Winston-Salem; Cathy Ringewald Cirina, University of California Press, Berkeley; Raymond Petke, Wadsworth Atheneum; and William Cuffe, Yale University Art Gallery.

Among the many auction houses and commercial art dealers who cooperated with our research, we thank in particular Glenn C. Peck, Allison Gallery, New York; Frederick Hill, James Berry Hill, and Bruce Weber, Berry-Hill Galleries, New York; Butterfield and Butterfield, San Francisco; Christie, Manson and Woods International, Inc.; Jerald Fessenden, Coe Kerr Gallery, Inc., New York; Thomas Colville; William Doyle Galleries, New York; Stuart P. Feld and M. P. Naud, Hirschl and Adler Galleries, Inc., New York; Henry B. Holt; Lawrence A. Fleischman, Lillian Brenwasser, and Lynn Bettman, Kennedy Galleries, Inc., New York;

Marcey Hladik, Litchfield Auction Gallery, Conn.; James H. Maroney, Jr.; Alan Pensler, Washington, D.C.; Gerald Peters; Skinner, Inc., Bolton, Mass.; Holly Goetz, Sotheby's; Gerold Wunderlich; and Richard York and Eric Widing, Richard York Gallery, New York.

A number of individuals merit our gratitude for their enthusiastic support of diverse aspects of the project: Herbert and Susan Adler; Loranne Carey Block; Dr. Irving F. Burton; Geoffrey Clements; Mr. and Mrs. Morton Funger; Jo Ann and Julian Ganz, Jr.; Dr. Walter Goldfarb; Robert McNeil, Jr.; Gloria and Richard Manney; Richard Manoogian; Mr. and Mrs. Meyer P. Potamkin; Joy Peto Smiley and Blossom S. Bejarano, the granddaughters of John F. Peto; and Harriet and Mortimer Spiller.

Scholarly exhibitions and publications entail great expenses for preparation and implementation. Our plans for *William M. Harnett* would not have become a reality without the funds generated by the cooperation of private, federal, and corporate sponsors who supported different aspects of the project. The William Cullen Bryant Fellows of The American Wing of the Metropolitan Museum contributed funds for the publication. The National Endowment for the Humanities supported the publication as well as the development of various shared educational programs and materials. Registration expenses for the first three venues were defrayed by the National Endowment for the Arts. Through the corporate sponsorship of Alamo Rent A Car, Inc., the exhibition was brought to audiences in New York and San Francisco. Our gratitude to these generous sponsors is enormous.

Finally, the contributors to this volume join with the participating institutions in thanking the lenders, public and private, who have shared their paintings with the many visitors who will attend the exhibition.

INTRODUCTION

William M. Harnett commemorates the hundredth anniversary of the death of an artist who pioneered a highly realistic style and fostered a school of American still-life painting. Comprised of a selection of his best works, the exhibition brings together his most important pictures and outstanding examples of his smaller, more private studies. Revealed are the full range of his subjects and the evolution of his trompe-l'oeil style, chronicling his remarkable artistic achievement.

The accompanying publication enriches our appreciation of the works by examining them in a broader social and cultural context and in light of recent scholarly developments in the field of American art history. These considerations determined the format of the book—a series of thematic essays rather than a biographical account with catalogue entries on individual paintings. We have sought diverse viewpoints and authors utilizing different methodologies to reach conclusions that are sometimes mutually reinforcing, sometimes contradictory.

The opening section of the book, "Approaches to Still-Life Painting," examines Harnett in relation to his contemporaries and explores the significance of trompe l'oeil in the American artistic tradition. In the late nineteenth century, the status of illusionism, debated since ancient times, remained at the heart of an ongoing dialogue about the purpose and meaning of art. American artists, critics, and the general public pondered the relationship between the observed world and the expression of ideas and emotions. Harnett's paintings reflect many of the concerns of his contemporaries—fascination with change; nostalgia; obsession with reality, imitation, and deception. Because Harnett's works mirror the more mundane values of the burgeoning middle class (as opposed to the refined aesthetics of the cultural elite), they illuminate the preoccupations of his age more completely than the works of more "high-brow" still-life painters such as John La Farge and William Merritt Chase.

The essayists contributing to the second section, "Elements of Artistic Development," have considered Harnett's formative training and experiences, necessarily relying as much on knowledge of his artistic and social milieu as on factual information about Harnett himself. Virtually no primary documentation (except newspaper reviews and a few uninformative letters and postcards) on the artist has survived. Other than painter John Frederick Peto, Harnett's close friends were relatively unknown artisans and tradesmen. Most of his patrons, while wealthy and prominent during the 1880s and 1890s, remain obscure today. Even after exhaustive research, only the barest outlines of Harnett's biography are known.

The final group of essays, "The Major Themes," focuses on Harnett's paintings by subject matter—fruit, newspapers, books, bric-a-brac, hunting equipment, vanitas imagery, literary motifs, and music. These writings explore meanings that contemporary viewers might have found in the artist's images.

Despite Harnett's current reputation as one of the greatest nineteenth-century American painters, his work rarely received thoughtful consideration during his lifetime. Many of his pictures were shown at industrial expositions, and reviews of his paintings, even those in exhibitions at the art academies, were summarily descriptive. The majority of commentators marveled at the impression of reality the artist was able to replicate but rarely, if ever, discussed the possible meanings of his art. The critical response to *Still Life with the Toledo Blade* of 1886 (fig. 100) was typical:

> The subject is a plain one, but the artist has made it so perfect—so like the real—that in looking upon it you are liable to forget that it is a picture and feel that you are looking upon a true violin, a genuine candle, etc. The highest triumph of artistic genius is in approaching the actual—in the perfect reproduction of the subject presented.[1]

A year after Harnett's death, even his friend, painter and writer Alfred Trumble, asserted that Harnett possessed no "imaginative quality" and concluded, "He could not create, he could simply imitate."[2] Only a review published in Germany in 1882 acknowledged the possibility that Harnett's humble models merited more than superficial interpretation. The writer commented that the artist's representations of sheet music and musical instruments "provide more food for thought than any of your wooden, badly executed human figures."[3]

Until recently, writers remained convinced that searching for messages hidden in Harnett's compositions would be futile. As the painter Marsden Hartley observed in 1939:

> Harnett invested all his paintings with the reality of things, having nothing to do with interpretations. . . . Because there is no interpretation in Harnett, there is nothing to bother about, nothing to confuse, nothing to interpret, there are in the common sense no mind-workings—there is the myopic persistence to render every single thing, singly.[4]

Harnett's first modern biographer, Alfred Frankenstein, laid the groundwork for reintroducing Harnett to twentieth-century art historians with his pioneering monograph in 1953. Like Hartley, Frankenstein maintained that Harnett "is fascinated by books, but he has no interest in their literary implications. Any book will do so long as its shape, color, and texture are right for his pictorial purposes."[5]

Harnett, on the other hand, had taken a rather different position, claiming that subject matter held great importance for him. "I always group my figures, so as to try and make an artistic composition. I endeavor to make the composition tell a story," he asserted on the one occasion he is known to have articulated his artistic philosophy.[6] In recent years, scholars have begun to address the expressive potential of Harnett's paintings: Carol J. Oja has explored the musical subjects; William H. Gerdts, the bric-a-brac compositions; Edward Nygren and Bruce W. Chambers, the depictions of money; Barbara S. Groseclose and Chad Mandeles, the vanitas themes derived from Dutch and Flemish traditions; and Robert F. Chirico, the language and imagery involving texts.[7] Clearly, there is more to Harnett's elaborate groupings than a striving after formal effects. An interest in his own Irish-Catholic background, as well as the subtle traces of humor and irony that recur in his works, testify to the creativity of Harnett's imagination and his urge to convey a story. The many words that find a place in his paintings—titles of books and musical compositions, printed cards, and newspaper banners—move the narrative forward.

The essayists contributing to this volume have sought large patterns—biographical, social, and cultural—in Harnett's choice of objects. In many respects this quest has been more successful in illuminating the character of Harnett's era than in revealing his personality, which remains a mystery. But the paintings and the responses they generated abound with clues about American life, art, and thought during the last quarter of the nineteenth century. We are grateful to the contributors for their exploration and elucidation of these issues and hope the volume will further a deeper understanding of Harnett's achievement.

DOREEN BOLGER
*Curator of Paintings
and Sculpture,
Amon Carter Museum*

MARC SIMPSON
*The Ednah Root Curator of
American Paintings,
The Fine Arts Museums
of San Francisco*

JOHN WILMERDING
*Visiting Curator,
Department of American Art,
The Metropolitan Museum
of Art*

THAYER TOLLES MICKEL
*Curatorial Assistant,
Amon Carter Museum*

1. Clipping from the *Philadelphia Catholic Standard,* October 1892 (otherwise unidentified), Blemly scrapbook, Alfred Frankenstein Papers, Archives of American Art, Smithsonian Institution, Washington, D.C., microfilm, roll 1374, frame 323.

2. [Alfred Trumble], "The Awakening of the Giant," *Collector* 4 (October 1, 1893), p. 294.

3. "Neues aus dem Kunstverein," clipping from the *Münchner Neueste Nachrichten und Münchner Anzeiger,* August 1882 (otherwise unidentified), Blemly scrapbook, frame 335, quoted in Alfred Frankenstein, *After the Hunt: William Harnett and Other American Still Life Painters, 1870–1900,* rev. ed. (Berkeley and Los Angeles: University of California Press, 1969), p. 62, n. 34.

4. Marsden Hartley, *On Art by Marsden Hartley,* ed. Gail R. Scott (New York: Horizon Press, 1982), pp. 178–79.

5. Frankenstein, *After the Hunt,* p. 40.

6. "Painted Like Real Things: The Man Whose Pictures Are a Wonder and a Puzzle," interview in *New York News,* probably 1889 or 1890, quoted in Frankenstein, *After the Hunt,* p. 55.

7. Carol J. Oja, "The Still-Life Paintings of William Michael Harnett (Their Reflections upon Nineteenth-Century American Musical Culture), *Musical Quarterly* 63 (October 1977), pp. 505–23; William H. Gerdts, "The Bric-a-Brac Still Life," *Antiques* 100 (November 1971), pp. 744–48; Edward J. Nygren, "The Almighty Dollar: Money as a Theme in American Painting," *Winterthur Portfolio* 23 (Summer–Autumn 1988), pp. 129–50; Bruce W. Chambers, *Old Money: American Trompe l'Oeil Images of Currency,* exhib. cat. (New York: Berry-Hill Galleries, 1988); Barbara S. Groseclose, "Vanity and the Artist: Some Still-Life Paintings by William Michael Harnett," *American Art Journal* 19, no. 1 (1987), pp. 51–59; Chad Mandeles, "William Michael Harnett's *The Old Cupboard Door* and the Tradition of *Vanitas,*" *American Art Journal* 18, no. 3 (1986), pp. 51–62; and Robert F. Chirico, "Language and Imagery in Late Nineteenth-Century Trompe l'Oeil," *Arts Magazine* 59, no. 7 (March 1985), pp. 110–14.

EXPLANATORY NOTE

If the current location of a work by Harnett is known, a figure or plate number or owner is given within each essay. If we can no longer determine the identity and/or location of a Harnett painting that is mentioned in the nineteenth-century literature, only the title is provided. Paintings included in the exhibition are designated as plates. In dimensions, height precedes width.

Pl. 1. William M. Harnett, *A Wooden Basket of Catawba Grapes,* 1876.
Oil on canvas, 22 x 27¼ in. Frye Art Museum, Seattle

Pl. 2. William M. Harnett, *Still Life with Ginger Jar,* 1876. Oil on canvas, 18 x 24 in. The Manney Collection

Pl. 3. William M. Harnett, *Mortality and Immortality,* 1876. Oil on canvas, 22 x 27 in.
Wichita Art Museum, The Roland P. Murdock Collection

Pl. 4. William M. Harnett, *A Smoke Backstage,* 1877. Oil on canvas, 7 x 8⅛ in.
Honolulu Academy of Arts, Gift of John Gregg Allerton, 1964 (3211.1)

Pl. 5. William M. Harnett, *Still Life,* 1877. Oil on canvas, 9 x 12 in.
The Chrysler Museum, Norfolk, Va.

Pl. 6. William M. Harnett, *The Banker's Table,* 1877. Oil on canvas, 8 x 12 in.
The Metropolitan Museum of Art, New York, Purchase, Elihu Root, Jr., Gift, 1956

Pl. 7. William M. Harnett, *A Man's Table Reversed,*
1877. Oil on canvas, 12 x 10¼ in.
Collection of the Brandywine River Museum,
Chadds Ford, Pa., Gift of Amanda K. Berls

Pl. 8. William M. Harnett, *Still Life—Writing Table,* 1877. Oil on canvas, 8 x 12 in.
Philadelphia Museum of Art, Alex Simpson, Jr., Collection

Pl. 9. William M. Harnett, *Job Lot Cheap,* 1878. Oil on canvas, 18 x 36 in.
Reynolda House, Museum of American Art, Winston-Salem

Pl. 10. William M. Harnett, *Music and Literature,* 1878. Oil on canvas, 24 x 32⅛ in.
Albright-Knox Art Gallery, Buffalo, N.Y., Gift of Seymour H. Knox, 1941

Pl. 11. William M. Harnett, *Attention, Company!,* 1878. Oil on canvas, 36 x 28 in.
Amon Carter Museum, Fort Worth

Pl. 12. William M. Harnett, *Memento Mori—"To This Favour,"* 1879. Oil on canvas, 24 x 32 in.
The Cleveland Museum of Art, Mr. and Mrs. William H. Marlatt Fund (65.235)

Pl. 13. William M. Harnett, *Secretary's Table,* 1879. Oil on canvas, 14 x 20 in.
Santa Barbara Museum of Art, Gift of Mrs. Sterling Morton to the Preston Morton Collection

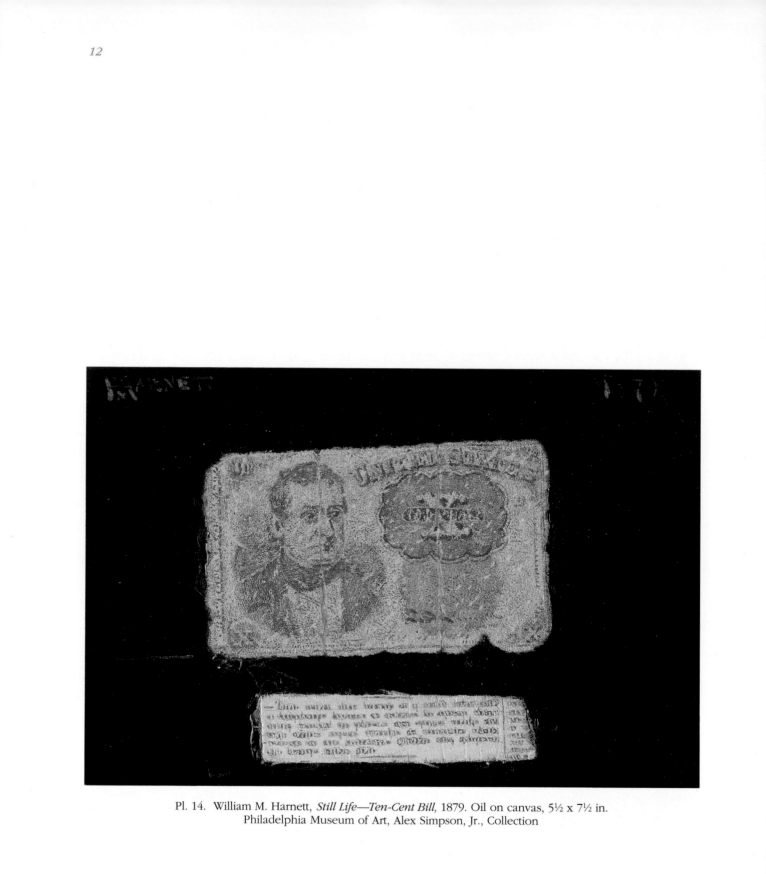

Pl. 14. William M. Harnett, *Still Life—Ten-Cent Bill*, 1879. Oil on canvas, 5½ x 7½ in.
Philadelphia Museum of Art, Alex Simpson, Jr., Collection

Pl. 15. William M. Harnett, *Still Life with Letter to Thomas B. Clarke*, 1879. Oil on canvas, 11 x 15 in.
Addison Gallery of American Art, Phillips Academy, Andover, Mass., Gift of Harold Clarke Durrell (1941.71)

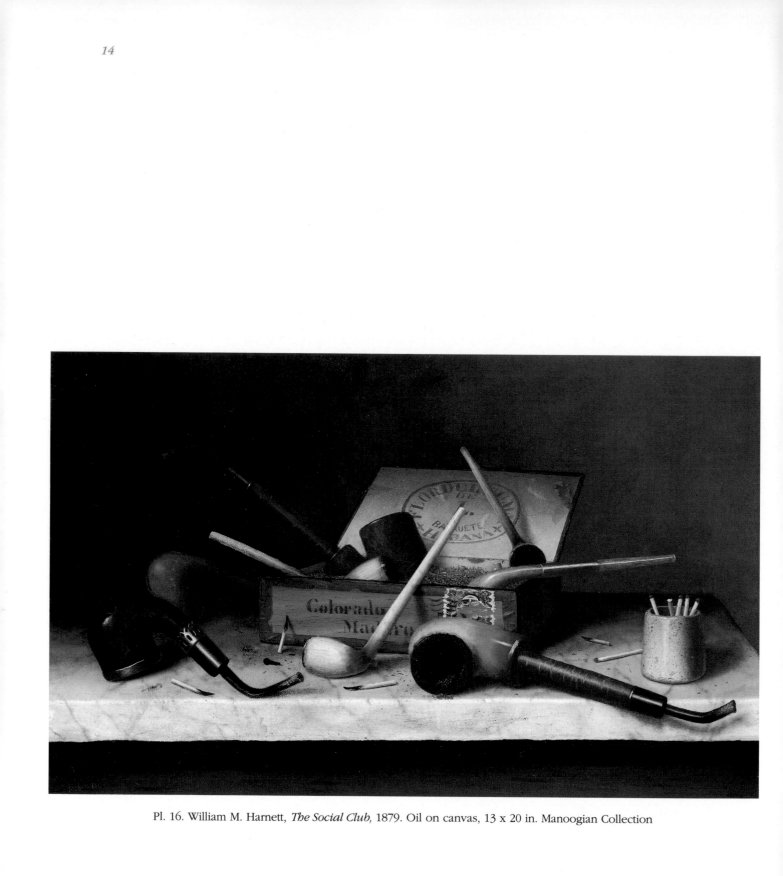

Pl. 16. William M. Harnett, *The Social Club,* 1879. Oil on canvas, 13 x 20 in. Manoogian Collection

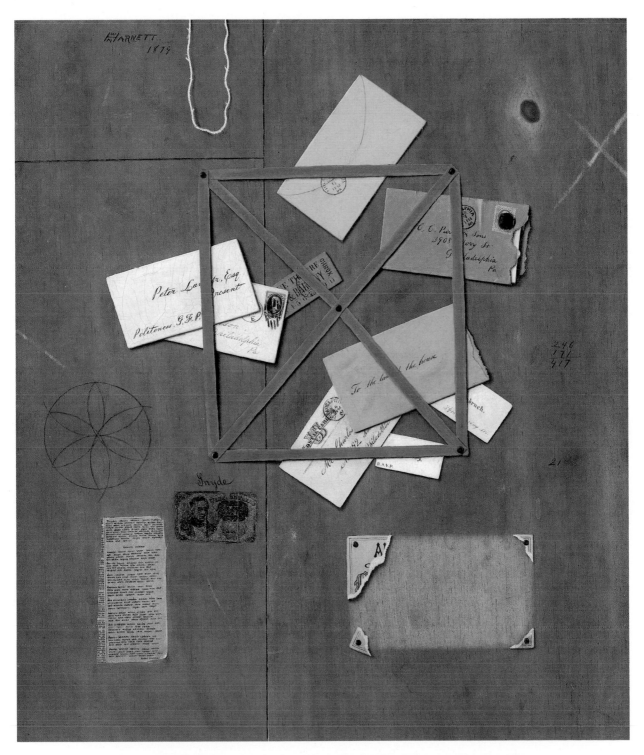

Pl. 17. William M. Harnett, *The Artist's Letter Rack*, 1879. Oil on canvas, 30 x 25 in.
The Metropolitan Museum of Art, New York, Morris K. Jessup Fund, 1966

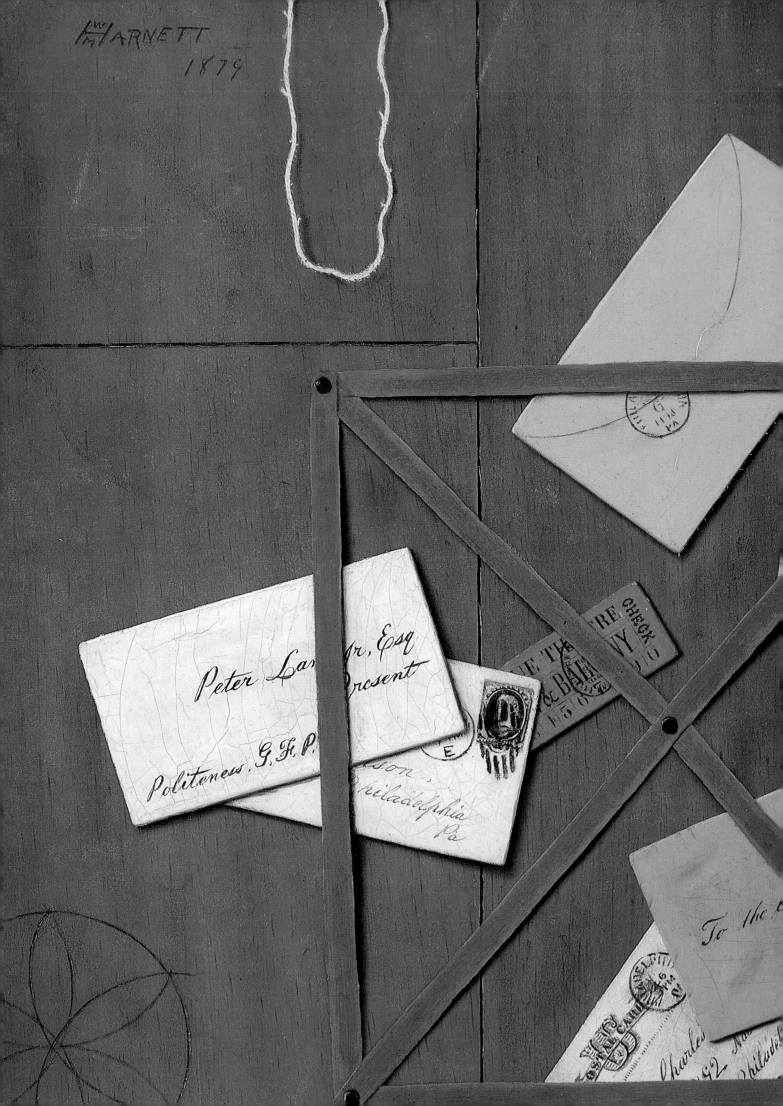

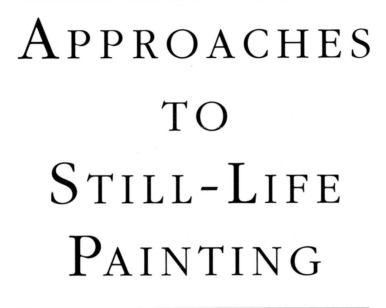

APPROACHES TO STILL-LIFE PAINTING

"SORDID MECHANICS" AND "MONKEY-TALENTS"

The Illusionistic Tradition

NICOLAI CIKOVSKY, JR.

The truth is, quite simply, that we do not know exactly what inspired William Michael Harnett to become a still-life painter or what artistic issues and experiences determined the particular type of painter he became. One explanation is based upon the extraordinary resemblance Harnett's work has to that of Raphaelle Peale (1774–1825), America's first known still-life painter. As the principal modern Harnett scholar, Alfred Frankenstein, put it, "Place a Harnett still life of the middle 1870's [fig. 1] next to a Raphaelle Peale of 1815 [fig. 2] and it is impossible to believe that they are separated by two generations, that the one belongs to the era of James Madison and the other to that of U. S. Grant." Frankenstein accounted for this similarity by a "direct line of descent" from Peale to Harnett but added, "If there are any intermediate links between them, they have yet to be discovered."[1]

There are, it is true, certain circumstantial possibilities of linkage between the two Philadelphia painters, and there was something of a continuous tradition of still-life painting in the city that might have transmitted Peale's example to Harnett.[2] When looked at more strictly, however, that possibility begins to diminish and dissipate.

When Harnett, as he put it, "went wholly into painting" about 1875, Peale had been dead for fifty years, had been dropped completely from the historical record, and was, for all intents and purposes, unknown.[3] As early as 1852, when Peale's *Wine and Cake* was shown in the annual of the Pennsylvania Academy of the Fine Arts, someone noted "amateur" in a copy of the catalogue, indicating how greatly memory of the artist had faded and how his reputation had declined. And when Harnett spoke of his artistic beginnings he did not mention Peale or, for that matter, the influence of any other artist.

Accounting for the resemblance between Peale and Harnett by the influence of one upon the other or by a tradition that connected them is not, it turns out, terribly successful. What is more, to do so is really to succumb to certain art-historical habits of thought and assumptions of method—the habit of accounting for an artist's style mainly by what might have influenced it, and the assumption that all influences are visual ones. Harnett's paintings look, in certain respects, like Peale's; therefore, in the typical formulation, Harnett "must have known them." But direct or traditional visual influences alone may not explain the similarities we are considering.

Fig. 1. William M. Harnett, *Still Life,* 1877.
Oil on canvas, 11½ x 13½ in.
Collection of Dr. Herbert and Elizabeth Sussman

Opposite: William M. Harnett, *The Social Club* (detail, pl. 16)

Fig. 2. Raphaelle Peale, *Still Life with Dried Fish* (*A Herring*), 1815.
Oil on wood, 9⅝ x 14¼ in. Historical Society of Pennsylvania, Philadelphia

Yet that resemblance remains. What it seems chiefly to consist of, though, is not a compellingly close similarity of style or subject matter—no one can really mistake a Harnett for a Peale in either of those respects—but, instead, a common practice of illusionism or, more exactly, the most extreme form of illusionism, trompe l'oeil.

Illusionism and still life are, to a very considerable extent, inseparable. Of course, there are many forms of illusionistic art besides still life, just as the still lifes of different artists and periods may vary greatly in the degree of illusion they are able, or choose, to achieve. But the believability of painted imitation—the convincing illusions of texture and volume, substance and space, reflected and refracted light—is more essential to the success of still life than it is to the success of any other subject of art; it is also more completely its *purpose*. However, trompe-l'oeil illusionism—illusionism carried beyond convincingness to deception—was not the ambition of most still-life painters. On the

contrary, it was a special and historically infrequent occurrence. Trompe l'oeil is the rarest form of "traditional" still-life painting. It is the form that is the least likely, therefore, to be transmitted directly by its precedents; and the one, moreover, that is less a matter of individual style than of the stylistically depersonalizing requirements of verisimilitude and strategies of visual deception. It is, though, mostly in their practice of illusionism that the resemblance between Harnett and Peale exists. Indeed, it was specifically because of their trompe-l'oeil paintings that their long-lost artistic identities were recaptured at about the same time, in the 1930s—Peale through *Venus Rising from the Sea— A Deception* (also called *After the Bath*) of 1822 (fig. 3), and Harnett through *The Faithful Colt* of 1890 (pl. 48).[4]

A high point of trompe-l'oeil painting in America occurred about 1800. In the 1795 Columbianum exhibition in Philadelphia, there were five "deceptions" among the two dozen still lifes exhibited, including two by Raphaelle Peale and the most ambitious of all

American trompe-l'oeil paintings, *The Staircase Group* of 1795 (fig. 4) by Charles Willson Peale (1741–1827), which depicts full-length portraits of his sons Raphaelle and Titian mounting a flight of stairs set in a real door frame with a real step attached to it.[5] In the 1812 annual of the Pennsylvania Academy, Raphaelle exhibited *Catalogue for the Use of the Room, a Deception;* in 1817 (and for the next three years as well), he exhibited *Still Life—A Catalogue and Papers Filed;* and in 1822, he showed *Venus Rising from the Sea.*[6]

During this episode of "deceptionism" in Philadelphia, then unquestionably one of the most cultivated cities in America, trompe-l'oeil illusionism occupied an unusually important place in the enterprise of serious artists and was welcomed in the exhibition of the Columbianum and at the Pennsylvania Academy. After about 1825 (the year of Raphaelle Peale's death) it was no longer as valued. *Venus Rising from the Sea* was the last deception exhibited at the Pennsylvania Academy, and no residual tradition of such openly deceptive illusionism remained, at least as may be measured by the appearance of deceptively illusionistic painting titles in professional exhibitions.

Fig. 3. Raphaelle Peale,
Venus Rising from the Sea—A Deception, 1822.
Oil on canvas, 29¼ x 24⅛ in.
The Nelson-Atkins Museum of Art,
Kansas City, Mo., Nelson Fund (34-147)

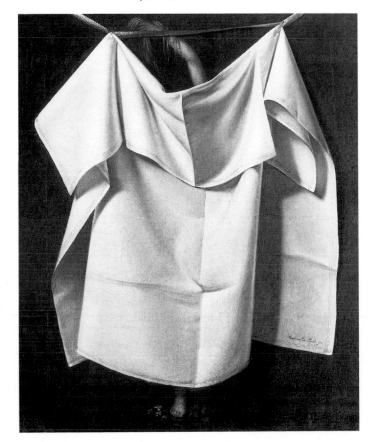

Fig. 4. Charles Willson Peale, *The Staircase Group:*
Raphaelle and Titian Ramsay Peale I, 1795.
Oil on canvas, 89 x 39½ in. Philadelphia Museum of Art,
The George W. Elkins Collection

Venus Rising from the Sea, Peale's only known surviving trompe-l'oeil painting, the only visible remnant of his practice of deception, was not rediscovered until a hundred years after his death—and forty after Harnett's.[7]

Of course, trompe-l'oeil paintings were not made only by the Peales in Philadelphia (though they were never made anywhere else in such numbers).[8] Charles Bird King (1785–1862) painted them in Baltimore and Washington, D.C.; Charles Fraser (1782–1860) and William Aiken Walker (1838–1921) painted them in Charleston, South Carolina; and mapmaker Joseph Goldsborough Bruff (1804–1889) and George Washington Sully (1816–1890) executed them in watercolor in Washington, D.C., and New Orleans, respectively.[9] It is possible, in other words, that the practice of trompe l'oeil survived elsewhere, in such places as Washington, Charleston, and New Orleans, after it had ceased among professional artists in major artistic centers.

If illusionism did survive, it was very much as a marginal enterprise. Provinciality—geographical separation—is one obvious form of marginality. Indeed, to the extent that Philadelphia had undeniably lost much of its earlier artistic importance to New York by the time Harnett and his friend John Frederick Peto (1854–1907) painted their trompe-l'oeil paintings there, beginning roughly about 1880, that too was a provincial phenomenon. The other major trompe-l'oeil painter of the late nineteenth century, John Haberle (1856–1933), worked in New Haven. And taking a larger view of the matter, it is even possible to regard the American propensity for trompe-l'oeil painting, to which there was nothing of comparable degree in Europe or England, as a function of provincial marginality as well.

Marginality was arguably the most essential and distinctive condition of the production of trompe-l'oeil painting. And if marginality—a geographical, ideological, or social position outside the prevailing currents and standards of artistic practice, belief, and influence—was the essential situation and condition of illusionistic painting, then perhaps the discussion of a tradition of illusionism needs to be refocused. Rather than being concerned with stylistic transmission and resemblance, it should instead focus on those traditions of belief, those artistic ideas and social attitudes, that fixed the place of illusionism and set the price of its practice. From this point of view, what illusionistic painters may have had most in common was not, or was not only, their language of style but their marginal artistic existence: the loneliness, alienation, and poverty that were the social, artistic, and economic costs of the undertaking of illusionistic still-life painting. The recurrence of those conditions from Raphaelle Peale to Harnett was, perhaps, the truest tradition of illusionism.

It is a necessary commonplace in the discussion of still-life painting to point out the low regard in which it was almost universally held; that it was assigned the lowest rank in the academic classification of subject matter first decreed in the seventeenth century and still accepted two centuries later. According to this hierarchy, its "low and confined" subject matter lacked the human interest, moral force, and intellectual substance possessed in highest form by depictions of heroic historical events based on the models of classical antiquity.[10]

At issue in this classification was the insignificance and inarticulate nature of still-life subjects. Equally implicated in this ranking, however, though it is less frequently noticed, was the *style* of still life. In a discourse he delivered to the students of the Royal Academy of Arts in London in 1770, Sir Joshua Reynolds said the "highest ambition" of the still-life painter "is to give a minute representation of every part of those low objects which he sets before him."[11] Some forty years later, Benjamin Robert Haydon, a British history painter and fierce champion of high art, again linked the subject and style of still life: "To hear terms that would be applicable to the highest beauties of Art applied to a tame, insipid, smooth, flat, mindless imitation of carrots—Good God, is this the end of Art, is this the use of Painting?"[12] Still life was inferior, in other words, not only because of the "low objects" it depicted but because of the style it employed to depict them. And it is clear that to Reynolds and Haydon, that style was objectionable because of its degree of illusionism, its "minute representation" and "smooth" imitation.

In the theoretical literature that guided artistic practice and critical thinking, nothing was censured as severely as imitation that deceptively copied particular objects—"the mere imitation of individual ordinary nature," as the nineteenth-century British painter James Barry put it in one of his Royal Academy lectures. Equally contemptible was the artist whose aim was to please by painting such deceptions—a "mere sordid mechanic, divested of intellectual capacity," declared Barry; or, in the words of fellow artist John Opie, a "petty kind of imitative, monkey-talent."[13]

The lower class to which imitative artists were consigned was not simply a matter of artistic, but of social, inferiority as well. The language used to condemn illusionism is rife with terms of social significance—words such as *mechanical* and *servile*—that are traceable to the belief that the making of such art properly belonged to a laboring class of servants and mechanics. Lower forms of painting, Reynolds said, were a "mechanical trade," and a Boston critic wrote in 1831 that the painter who copies such things as brass kettles and dead game is only "somewhat more refined than the tinker or cook who handles the originals."[14]

The most threatening thing about illusionism, however, was not the kind of artist who made it but those for whom it was made or to whom it appealed.

Illusionism was a *popular* style, not merely in the sense that it was widely liked, but that it was widely liked by the common people, the populace. Haydon wrote in 1808, "With the People of England, all their ambition and all their delight, and all their ideas of art go not beyond the immediate object of their senses; the exact copy of a pound of butter, or a capitally touched china cup." What also troubled him was that illusionism appealed to those who should, by their social position, know better: "Uneducated People might be forgiven—but Noblemen, . . . the ministers of the Country, the government of England, . . . instead of being ambitious of having their Souls elevated, and their minds expanded . . . [utter] exclamations of ravishment and rapture, at a smutty crock, or a brass candlestick."[15]

We do not know from Raphaelle Peale himself why—that is, with what purpose or by what policy—he painted illusionistic still lifes. But we can assume with a certain amount of confidence that he knew that painting still lifes professionally rather than as an amateur pastime and painting them in a deceptively imitative way disregarded and even openly defied the canons of belief that guided artistic thought and practice at the turn of the century. We cannot determine with the same degree of assurance whether his deeply troubled life—beset by poverty, illness, derangement, alcoholism, and thoughts of suicide—was the price he paid for that defiance. Of course, defiance cannot have been wholly the cause of his suffering, but Peale's life was so much more troubled than the merely difficult lives of contemporary artists who painted more orthodox subjects that his chosen genre and style were surely contributing factors. What is most telling, though, is Peale's dedication to his choices in the face of such adversity. He continued to paint still lifes and to represent himself in professional exhibitions by, for the most part, still lifes and deceptions.

In order to paint still lifes, Harnett seems to have accepted or, at any rate, to have endured extreme marginality and an utterly alienated social and professional life as the necessary, unavoidable cost. He spent much of his early life in poverty and neglect. He lived with "hermit-like modesty," wrote critic Alfred Trumble, and "died as he had lived, alone."[16] Harnett also engendered the contempt of other artists. "'Imitation is worthless,'" wrote the nineteenth-century American landscape painter George Inness, citing what was clearly Harnett's *After the Hunt* of 1885 (pl. 34) as his example.[17] Harnett's work was rarely shown in exhibitions at the National Academy of Design in New York or at the Pennsylvania Academy, and when it was, it was hung in inferior, marginal places (what a critic, referring to the trivial popularity of illusionism, meant when he wrote about Harnett's "paintings of familiar objects of still life [that] are so familiar in the corridor

at the [National] Academy each year").[18] Harnett did not receive the prizes and awards by which academies recognized merit or rewarded achievement, and he experienced the scorn or, more often, the silence of critics.

The canons of belief ranged against Peale about 1800 determined Harnett's artistic station just as forcefully. They resound, for example, in the criticism of Harnett's art. In 1879, a critic for the *New-York Daily Tribune* referred to his *Social Club* of 1879 (pl. 16), "in which the skill of the human hand is ostentatiously displayed working in deceptive imitation of Nature," as a low form of art to which "very few artists of merit have ever condescended to apply their skill."[19] They are audible, too, in the words of a reviewer for the *Studio,* who wrote in 1887 of "Mr. Harnett's popular success in cheating the untrained eye, following the earlier example of other mechanic painters. . . . Only children and half-taught people take pleasure in such tricks of the brush as Mr. Harnett has lately made the fashion."[20]

Since what Reynolds, Haydon, and others seemed to fear most about illusionism was its popularity or, more exactly, the threat its popularity posed to the dignity and decorum of high art, nothing would have revolted them more, or more fully justified their fears, than the way Harnett's art was seen and appreciated. He showed his paintings in such places as jewelry shops, drugstores, department stores, saloons, and industrial expositions as often as he did in academies, art galleries, and museums, which were by convention licensed—and, in the late nineteenth century, increasingly sanctified—for that purpose. And the transactions between Harnett's audience and his painted objects were often fundamentally different from the decorous distance that was traditionally expected (and increasingly enforced at museums founded during the period, such as the Metropolitan Museum of Art in New York) in the presence of serious art.[21] When *The Old Violin* of 1886 (pl. 37) was shown at the Thirteenth Cincinnati Industrial Exposition, for example, a guard was stationed to prevent people from touching it and "attempting the removal of the newspaper scrap with their finger-nails."[22] And in Theodore Stewart's saloon on Warren Street in New York, where *After the Hunt* was hung (unguarded), disputes about illusion and reality were often settled by touching the painting.[23]

Reynolds located the chief defect of the imitative artist in a lack of intelligence and imagination: "A mere copier of nature can never produce any thing great. . . . The wish of the genuine painter must be more extensive: instead of endeavouring to amuse mankind with the minute neatness of his imitations, he must endeavour to improve them by the grandeur of his ideas; instead of seeking praise, by deceiving the superficial sense of the spectator, he must strive for fame, by captivating the imagination. . . . As this principle is observed or neglected, our profession becomes either a liberal art, or a mechanical trade."[24]

It was precisely such a lack of imagination, according to Alfred Trumble, that made Harnett an illusionistic still-life painter. Harnett was convinced, Trumble thought, that "he possessed none of the imaginative quality which is the prime factor of an artist's creations. He could not create, he could simply imitate. . . . He said that he could not think of anything, that he did not believe he had any inventive faculty whatever, so that willy-nilly he had to stick to his still life. . . . He painted what he could best paint, and making no pretensions to anything beyond."[25]

Harnett's artistic choices may not have been totally free, wholly undetermined by poverty or native ability. But in choosing to paint illusionistic still lifes, and in pursuing that choice to the radical extreme of trompe-l'oeil illusionism, he must have known that he was setting himself against conventional belief and placing himself at the margins of acceptability and respectabil-

ity to a degree that would not have been the case had he painted other subjects in other ways. That act has about it a sense not simply of failure or a deficiency of will or wit, as it appeared to Trumble, but of a more consciously different purpose, which accepted alienation and oblivion as its unavoidable condition—a consequence that, in other cases in the late nineteenth century (Albert Pinkham Ryder and Winslow Homer in America and, to a greater extreme, Paul Cézanne, Vincent van Gogh, and Paul Gauguin in France), appears more clearly to have been a virtual requirement of art that was in advance of its time or dissented from its orthodoxies.[26]

It may seem ridiculous to think of Harnett this way (though his rediscovery in the 1930s largely depended on the resemblances his paintings seemed to bear to modernist abstraction and Surrealism). In relation to the advanced painting of his time, which variously argued the claims of nonrepresentational expression and aestheticism, the art he practiced seemed posi-

Fig. 5. John Haberle, *Reproduction,* ca. 1886. Oil on canvas, 10 x 14 in.
Courtesy of Hirschl & Adler Galleries, Inc., New York

tively backward (hence Inness's derision of illusionistic imitation) and to belong to a type of painting that traced its roots directly to antiquity (hence the citations, in discussions of Harnett, of the story in Pliny's *Natural History* of the contest between the Greek painters Zeuxis and Parrhasius to decide who could produce the most perfectly deceptive illusion).[27] Since there was no active tradition of illusionism in America when Harnett began to make illusionistic paintings, his illusionism was not simply the survival of an uninterrupted though dormant practice but more a reinvention of it. Therefore, Harnett and other American trompe-l'oeil painters did not paint as they did because of the imperatives of a stylistic tradition. On the contrary, their undertaking so openly defied long-standing conventions and widely held beliefs and so inevitably entailed marginality and its consequences of poverty and oblivion, that it was in some significant measure a willed and—to the extent that there was in it a defiant stubbornness of purpose—a willful act.[28]

This is most openly expressed, perhaps, by a type of painting that, as far as we know, Harnett invented: the painting of money.[29] Harnett executed the first trompe-l'oeil money picture in 1877 and made a total of six known paintings of the subject before 1880.[30] Money often appears in earlier still lifes as an ingredient of vanitas iconography, but Harnett's money paintings differ in their concentration upon money itself and in the assertive directness of its depiction. Money paintings may be interpreted on many levels,[31] but one meaning that has a particularly interesting bearing upon the enterprise of trompe l'oeil is their criminality. The title of one of Harnett's money pictures, *A Bad Counterfeit—Panel,* which he exhibited at the National Academy in 1878, openly raised the issue of criminality. In 1886, his *Still Life—Five-Dollar Bill* (fig. 68), which hung in one of Theodore Stewart's New York saloons, was probably the painting confiscated by Treasury agents as a counterfeit, and the Secret Service paid a visit to Harnett's studio with the intention of arresting him and seizing other spurious bank notes.

Harnett's money pictures are criminally harmless, of course, but in a sense they bear an aspect of criminality. In them, illusionism is expressed as deception carried to the illicit extreme of a counterfeit. Counterfeiting, in other words, is a metaphor not only for the full power of illusionism to deceive but—according to laws of art that Harnett certainly knew and was aware (if only from his critics) he had transgressed—for the artistic "illegality" of illusionistic deception as well.

Harnett did not pursue this issue, did not drive home the point of his money paintings. Numerically, they occupy only a small part of his subject matter as a whole and even of his illusionistic paintings, and he abandoned them completely when threatened with legal action. In fact, it must be said that, in general, Harnett tempered the full impact of illusionism. He gave his trompe-l'oeil paintings literary titles—*The Old Violin, An Old-Fashioned Colt* (now called *The Faithful Colt*), *Old Models, After the Hunt, For Sunday's Dinner*—that soften or distract from the issue of illusionism. In his only public discussion of his life and work, Harnett said, "In painting from still life I do not closely imitate nature. Many points I leave out and many I add. Some models are only suggestions."[32] Thus, he conventionalized illusionism by making its method less precisely—that is, less "mechanically" and "servilely"—imitative and brought it more into conformity with the exercise of imagination that, for someone like Reynolds, most fully characterized the difference between high art and "mere" imitation.

John Haberle, one of Harnett's colleagues in the enterprise of trompe-l'oeil illusionism, seems to have recognized the implications of Harnett's money pictures more clearly than Harnett himself did, and with more aggressiveness, Haberle made his own images of the subject into virtual manifestos of illusionism. Haberle may have hoped to capitalize upon the notoriety of Harnett's money pictures (Haberle's earliest dates from 1886 or 1887), but he also may have regarded his own as a continuation and perhaps, to some extent, a critique of Harnett's in the sense of carrying them to higher degrees of explicitness than Harnett cared to and flirting with criminality as the condition and the metaphor of illusionism more than Harnett dared. Although Haberle was also threatened with arrest, he continued to paint bank notes and, what is more, made the entire issue of counterfeiting, the counterfeit, and the counterfeiter part of the meaning of his paintings. In *U.S.A.* of about 1889 (Jo Ann and Julian Ganz, Jr.), he flaunted illegality by including the text of the warning against imitating money that was printed on the reverse of all United States currency at the time: "Counterfeiting, or altering this note," that warning read, in part, "is punishable by $5000 fine or 15 years at hard labor or both."[33] Another of Haberle's money paintings, *Reproduction* of about 1886 (fig. 5), includes at the lower left (as painted imitations, of course) a small tintype photograph—a self-portrait— that overlaps a clipped newspaper text that in turn overlaps a larger clipping that includes both a text and an engraving (fig. 6). The headline of the first clipping is *A Counterfeit,* and part of the legible fragment of the larger clipping reads: *John Haberle the Counter*[*feiter*]*/*[*de*]*ceives the eye into the belief that.* The engraving depicts a bearded man, who looks very much like Haberle (as the "photograph" enables one to see), bent over a table and working by the light of a lamp; on the wall behind him hang what Frankenstein nicely described as "a ludicrously criminal pistol and dagger."[34] This painting amounts to an extremely witty yet deliberately serious commentary on illusion-

Fig. 6. John Haberle, *Reproduction* (detail, fig. 5)

istic deception and the status of the illusionistic artist. *Reproduction* announces itself to be a "counterfeit" made by the artist, who included within his illusion not only an image of himself but also the projection of his self-invented persona—"John Haberle the counterfeiter," the illusionistic painter who "deceives the eye" and the criminal, identified by obvious attributes of criminality, furtively at work at his artistic crime. There is no clearer expression of the social marginality—to the point of self-proclaimed and willingly assumed illicitness—of the enterprise of illusionistic art.

Haberle's work is the clearest access we have to the self-awareness and sense of purpose—the consciousness—of an illusionistic painter. We may attribute this consciousness to Harnett or Raphaelle Peale or infer it circumstantially. But the pains Haberle evidently took to show and explain what the enterprise of illusionism entailed leave no doubt about his consciousness nor any need to infer it. And if tradition implies—or in its truest sense *is*—consciousness, then this awareness, not apparent resemblances of style, may be the truest form of illusionism in America.

NOTES

▼

1. Alfred Frankenstein, *After the Hunt: William Harnett and Other American Still Life Painters, 1870–1900,* rev. ed. (Berkeley and Los Angeles: University of California Press, 1969), pp. 31, 32.

2. According to Frankenstein (*After the Hunt,* p. 31), "The Philadelphia of the 1850's and 1860's swarmed with daughters and granddaughters, nieces and grand-nieces of Raphaelle and [his uncle] James, and these venerable ladies emitted still lifes of their own with remarkable frequency and rapidity."

3. "Painted Like Real Things: The Man Whose Pictures Are a Wonder and a Puzzle," interview in *New York News,* probably 1889 or 1890, quoted in Frankenstein, *After the Hunt,* p. 29.

4. The Peale was given the title *After the Bath* by the New York dealer Edith Gregor Halpert, who acquired it in 1931; she sold it the same year to the William Rockhill Nelson Trust in Kansas City, Mo., from which it passed to the William Rockhill Nelson Gallery of Art and Mary Atkins Museum of Fine Arts, in 1934. Halpert bought *The Faithful Colt* in 1935 and sold it the same year to the Wadsworth Athcneum in Hartford, Conn. (see Elizabeth Johns, "Harnett Enters Art History," pp. 101–2).

5. *The Exhibition of the Columbianum, or American Academy of Painting, Sculpture, Architecture, &c. established at Philadelphia, 1795,* exhib. cat. (Philadelphia: Francis & Robert Bailey, 1795). This was the only exhibition of the Columbianum.

6. See Dorinda Evans, "Raphaelle Peale's *Venus Rising from the Sea:* Further Support for a Change in Interpretation," *American Art Journal* 14, no. 3 (Summer 1982), pp. 62–72. Peale's *Catalogue for the Use of a Room* is now lost; *Catalogue of the Peale Museum* of 1813 (private collection) by Raphaelle's cousin Margaretta Angelica Peale may be a copy (illustrated in Nicolai Cikovsky, Jr., *Raphaelle Peale Still Lifes,* exhib. cat.[Washington, D.C.: National Gallery of Art, 1988], p. 48).

7. Two deceptions once thought to be by Peale have now been reattributed: *Patch Picture for Dr. Physick* (see Frankenstein, *After the Hunt,* pl. 43) and *A Deception* (see William H. Gerdts, "A Deception Unmasked: An Artist Uncovered," *American Art Journal* 18, no. 2 [1986], pp. 4–23).

8. Still lifes were exhibited with some frequency at National Academy of Design exhibitions and a few were shown at Boston Athenaeum exhibitions, but none, judging from their titles (which is a fairly good way of judging), were trompe-l'oeil deceptions.

9. See King's *Poor Artist's Cupboard* of about 1815 (The Corcoran Gallery of Art, Washington, D.C.), *Landscape with Catalogue* (*Environs of Milan, Italy*) of 1828 (Redwood Library and Athenaeum, Newport, R.I.), and *Vanity of an Artist's Dream* of 1830 (Fogg Art Museum, Harvard University, Cambridge, Mass.). King had been in Philadelphia about 1813 and his trompe-l'oeil paintings, the first of which he made only a year or two later, may reflect his experience there. See Andrew J. Cosentino, *The Paintings of Charles Bird King (1785–1862),* exhib. cat., National Collection of Fine Arts, Smithsonian Institution, Washington, D.C. (Washington, D.C.: Smithsonian Institution Press, 1977).

See Fraser's *Still Life with Playing Card, Silhouette Newspaper Clipping* of about 1796 (Carolina Art Association, Charleston, S.C.) and *Still Life: Ducks and Snipe* of about 1840 (Carolina Art Association, Charleston, S.C.). The checklist of an 1857 exhibition of his paintings at the Fraser Gallery, Charleston, lists *Imitation of Wood, with a Nail Painted on It.* See Martha R. Severens and Charles L. Wyrick, Jr., eds. and comps., *Charles Fraser of Charleston: Essays on the Man, His Art and His Times* (Charleston, S.C.: Carolina Art Association, 1983), pp. 83, 96, 97.

See Walker's *Dollarfish and Sheepshead* of 1860 (Museum of Fine Arts, Boston); Bruff's watercolor *Assorted Prints* of about 1845 (private collection); and Sully's watercolor *New Orleans Rack Picture* of about 1836 (Morris Museum of Art, Augusta, Ga.). See M. L. d'Otrange Mastai, *Illusion in Art: Trompe l'Oeil, A History of Pictorial Illusionism* (New York: Abaris Books, 1975), fig. 314; and Bruce W. Chambers, *Art and Artists of the South: The Robert P. Coggins Collection,* exhib. cat., Columbia Museum of Art (Columbia, S.C.: University of South Carolina Press, 1984), p. 64.

10. "Low and confined" is the phrase employed by Sir Joshua Reynolds, speaking of what was almost as bad as still life, the "low and vulgar characters" of Hogarth (*Discourses on Art,* ed. Robert R. Wark [New Haven and London: Yale University Press, 1975], p. 51).

11. Ibid., p. 52.

12. *The Diary of Benjamin Robert Haydon,* 5 vols., ed. Willard Bissell Pope (Cambridge, Mass.: Harvard University Press, 1960–63), 1, p. 7.

13. *Lectures on Painting, by the Royal Academicians: Barry, Opie, and Fuseli,* ed. Ralph N. Wornum (London: Henry G. Bohn, 1848), pp. 93, 97, 248.

14. Reynolds, *Discourses,* p. 57; and "Exhibition of Pictures at the Athenaeum Gallery: Remarks upon the Athenaeum Gallery of Paintings for 1831," *North American Review* 33 (October 1831), p. 512.

15. Haydon, *Diary,* 1, p. 5.

16. [Alfred Trumble], "The Awakening of the Giant," *Collector* 4 (October 1, 1893), p. 294.

17. Quoted in George Inness, Jr., *Life, Art, and Letters of George Inness* (New York: Century Co., 1917), p. 124.

18. "The National Academy," *Sun* (New York), April 13, 1879, p. 2.

19. [Clarence Cook], "Academy of Design: Fifty-fourth Annual Exhibition," *New-York Daily Tribune,* April 26, 1879, p. 5.

20. "The Society of American Artists: Ninth Exhibition," *Studio,* n.s. 2, no. 12 (June 1887), p. 217.

21. See Lawrence W. Levine, *Highbrow/Lowbrow: The Emergence of Cultural Hierarchy in America* (Cambridge, Mass., and London: Harvard University Press, 1988), pp. 182–86.

22. "A Wonderland," *Cincinnati Enquirer,* September 19, 1886, p. 12.

23. See, for example, Paul Staiti, "Illusionism, Trompe l'Oeil, and the Perils of Viewership," pp. 32–34. In Dawn Powell's 1954 novel *The Wicked Pavilion* (New York: Vintage Books, 1990), an official at what is clearly the Metropolitan Museum refers to what is surely Harnett's *Faithful Colt:* "You should have been here when we showed Harnett and some early American primitives. We caught a screwball trying to get a revolver out of one painting to shoot himself right here" (p. 197).

24. Reynolds, *Discourses,* pp. 42, 57.

25. [Trumble], "Awakening of the Giant," p. 294.

26. There may appear to be more romanticism than modernity in Harnett's life—Trumble wrote of the "whole pathetic romance" of Harnett's career ("Awakening of the Giant," p. 294)—yet neither Harnett nor other American trompe-l'oeil painters of the late nineteenth century seem to have been given to romantic posturing or bohemian behavior.

27. "In our school-days we used to read with admiration the story of the contest between the Athenian painters: how Zeuxis having depicted a bunch of grapes so cunningly that the birds pecked at them challenged Parrhasius to draw aside the curtain from his picture, and then discovered that he himself had been deceived by his rival's painted drapery. The late W. M. Harnett, of New York, was a worthy successor of the celebrated Grecians in his ability to represent inanimate objects with such fidelity as to produce an effect of reality" (Louisa Trumbull Cogswell, "Art in Boston," *Arcadia* 1 [December 1, 1892], pp. 305–6). Earlier, a critic for the *Sun* had written of "what true and absolute literalness and realism always have been able to effect ever since the time the birds flew at the grapes that the painter of tradition had

put on his canvas, down to the period of Mr. Harnett" ("The National Academy," April 13, 1879, p. 2).

28. William H. Gerdts senses this quality in Joseph Decker's "aggressively realistic works" and claims that, in painting them, Decker assumed "the role of *peintre terrible*" ("Joseph Decker—New Revelations," in *Joseph Decker (1853–1924): Still Lifes, Landscapes and Images of Youth,* exhib. cat. [New York: Coe Kerr Gallery, 1988], unpaginated).

29. See Bruce W. Chambers, *Old Money: American Trompe l'Oeil Images of Currency,* exhib. cat. (New York: Berry-Hill Galleries, 1988), passim; and Edward J. Nygren, "The Almighty Dollar: Money as a Theme in American Painting," *Winterthur Portfolio* 23 (Summer–Autumn 1988) pp. 129–50. Raphaelle Peale's *Bill* of 1895 may have been the precursor of Harnett's painting, but only if it depicted money, as Frankenstein suggests (*After the Hunt,* pp. 31–32); there is, however, no assurance that it did.

30. Chambers, *Old Money,* p. 100, n. 12.

31. See ibid., passim; and Nygren, "Almighty Dollar," passim.

32. "Painted Like Real Things," quoted in Frankenstein, *After the Hunt,* p. 55.

33. Frankenstein, *After the Hunt,* p. 117.

34. Ibid., p. 116.

ILLUSIONISM, TROMPE L'OEIL, AND THE PERILS OF VIEWERSHIP

PAUL J. STAITI

A painting [*The Old Violin*] has been added to the Art Gallery, which has created a furore. It has . . . a crowd of bewildered gazers continually about it. It represents an old violin hanging on an old time worn door. By it hangs the bow, and under the violin is a sheet of music with dog-eared corners. A blue envelope is stuck in the warped lower corner of the door, and above it is a newspaper clipping, that a man wanted to bet $10 last evening, was pasted on the board. . . . An old gentleman stood and gazed at it last night, through his spectacles, and finally said: "By Jove, I would like to play on that violin," enthusiastically judging that many a touching melody had been wafted from its well resined strings. The gentleman never noticed the deception until he went closer to it and he was "completely got." A policeman stands by it constantly, lest people reach over and attempt to see if the newspaper clipping is genuine by tearing it off. They want to pull at the envelope as well.

Cincinnati newspaper, 1886

Whatever excites and stimulates our interest is real; whenever an object so appeals to us that we turn to it, accept it, fill our mind with it, or practically take account of it, so far it is real for us, and we believe it.

William James, *Principles of Psychology* (1890)

What was the experience of viewing an illusionistic still-life painting by William Michael Harnett in the nineteenth century? As the first passage above[1] and others like it indicate, the body of evidence points to a crisis over the status of representation. It was usually a crisis in epistemology as well as perception, and it was often experienced in a public space and in the company of other viewers. The dimensions of the crisis varied—between social classes, from picture to picture, from one venue to another. But the essential questions raised by viewing the pictures were exceptionally consistent. What was it that was being seen? Were the objects unquestionably representation? Did they playfully mimic actual objects? Or were they perceptually indistinguishable from actual objects? And, through what processes and by what criteria did a viewer measure and verify the authenticity of his experience?

In the literature on American art, Harnett's still lifes are traditionally studied in terms of his mechanical proficiency and exacting formal methods insofar as they contradicted the predominant artistic authority of late-nineteenth-century aestheticism and classicism. This essay moves in a different direction, toward a phenomenology of viewing Harnett's visual fictions. What, in other words, did it feel like to experience Harnett's illusionism in late-nineteenth-century America?[2] In such an expanded purview, Harnett's illusionism might be seen as part of the cultural poetics of an era that obsessively and seemingly everywhere

Opposite: William M. Harnett, *The Old Violin* (detail, pl. 37)

called reality into question.[3] Although isolated from the academic mainstream of American art, Harnett's pictures, especially the riveting trompe-l'oeil still lifes, participated in a prevailing cultural discourse of illusion, deception, fraud, and humbug. His artistic enterprise was closely connected to the tricks of the confidence man as he appeared in literature and on the streets, to the showmanship of P. T. Barnum and the spectatorship he constructed, and to the controversy over the flimsy representative power of paper money.[4] Because his pictures engrossed viewers in an arbitrary, persuasive system of reality, Harnett—like all popular illusionists—could hold an audience, guide its response, or even provoke uncharacteristic physical behavior. Nineteenth-century viewers, especially those from a middle class newly enfranchised as consumers of culture, delighted in debates over what was real or unreal in art. Vocally participating in a world in which the perception of objects was corrigible instead of fixed, the viewing circle around Harnett's pictures was a populist outpost of the new phenomenological psychology, posited in the epigraph from William James, in which reality is a mere mental construction built on the fragile foundations of "belief."[5]

So real is it [*The Old Violin*], that one of Captain Wise's specials has been detailed to stand beside the picture and suppress any attempts to take down the fiddle and the bow. . . . The writer being one of those doubting Thomases who are by no means disposed to believe their own eyes, was permitted to allay his conscientious scruples by feeling of it, and is prepared to kiss the book, and s'help me, it is painted. Mr. Harnett is of the Munich school, and he takes a wicked delight in defying the possibilities.

                                        Cincinnati Commercial Gazette, September 16, 1886

Crowds still stand doubtingly before the famous Harnett violin hanging on the old door, uncertain as to how much is painting and how much reality.

                                        Cincinnati newspaper, 1886

*T*he Old Violin of 1886 (pl. 37) attracted intense specular interest during its exhibition at the Thirteenth Cincinnati Industrial Exposition. Viewers lavished praise on the instrument's "perfect finish, matchless color and absolute correctness of detail";[6] on the "marvelous" iron hinges, ring, and staple; and on the "miracle" of the newspaper clipping.[7] In other cities, where different Harnetts were on exhibition, viewers responded much as had their counterparts in Cincinnati. Confronted with *After the Hunt* of 1885 (pl. 34), New Yorkers were "enraptured" (a verb, like *engrossed* and *enthralled,* that carries the sense of lapsed volition). They were thrown "into ecstasies over the feathery plumage of the birds and the furry coat of the rabbit, over the wonderful representation of the butt end of an old snap-lock gun, over the extraordinary imitation of the brass work of the horn."[8] Viewing an earlier version of the same theme in Munich, a newspaper critic observed, "There is not a tiny splinter, not a nailhead, nothing that is not depicted to perfection, so that one does not know which to admire more—the artist's gigantic patience or his astonishing powers of observation and imitation."[9]

These commentaries record the responses of viewers who admired Harnett's achievement while retaining the sense that what they were seeing was no more than an extraordinarily accurate pictorial representation of familiar objects. But the critics introduced in the epigraphs above did not close their responses with feelings of admiration.[10] They were so challenged by illusion that they entered a state of cognitive bewilderment in which a representation was seemingly a reality. Viewers might discern some depicted items as painted (the iron hinges, ring, and staple), but other items, such as the newspaper clipping that people wanted to tear or the violin that a gentleman wanted to play, were not conclusively representations. As signifiers of indeterminate signification, anxiously indicating both object and representation, these items were so deceptively painted that viewers were impelled to abandon the etiquette of passive spectatorship by actively moving near the picture or even touching it in an effort to determine what it was they were seeing. Similar tales were told about a hanging committee that was about to soak the illusionistic label off *Shinplaster with Exhibition Label* of 1879 (fig. 7) until they "saw that it was a part of the picture," or about the Treasury agents who arrested Harnett because it was thought his *Still Life—Five-Dollar Bill* of 1877 (fig. 68) was actual counterfeit money (a double deception), or about the bets wagered in Stewart's saloon on Warren Street in

Fig. 7. William M. Harnett, *Shinplaster with Exhibition Label,* 1879. Oil on canvas, 5 x 7 in. Private collection

New York that the objects in *After the Hunt* were "real until proved by examination."[11] One viewer was so frustrated over determining the authenticity of that picture that he "wickedly stuck his cane into the painting and slightly damaged it."[12] Inevitably, it was proven to all unharnessed viewers that everything in these framed pictures was flat, painted representation. Having been fooled by illusion, they were forced to retreat into lame invocations of astonishment ("By Jove"; "S'help me"; "Gee whittikers!"; "Marvellous! The most remarkable thing I ever saw") and into the concession—as if galleries were competitive gaming arenas—that the artist's pictorial skills were superior to their reading skills (Harnett took "wicked delight" in the deceit; he "completely got" one viewer).[13]

Yet even when a viewer's guilelessness was exposed publicly, it seems no one was angered by the deception, however indecorously or even disruptively the viewer may have behaved. If anything, the deception had enlivened the experience of viewing; there

was both animation and pleasure derived from the mental game of doubt played with Harnett's pictures. And, not only was the deceived-but-astonished viewer amused, so were the viewer's viewers. A correspondent for the *Star* described the theater of spectatorship he encountered on a visit to Stewart's. In the chaotic interior, hundreds of prominent citizens daily gathered around *After the Hunt* to wager wildly and express opinions as to its being an optical illusion or a real painting. One saloon patron was challenged by the crowd to "feel it," whereupon he "found that it was a flat panel." The duped viewer—in effect, the active agent of the saloon's inquiring viewership, brokering the transaction between picture and public, representation and reality—still refused to relinquish his belief in the visual deception. Although he had touched the canvas and admitted that the rabbit and birds could immediately be taken for painted, he was nonetheless persuaded by "the hanging up of that bottle, because [he] could see in a moment that the string was real."

Fig. 8. Photograph of William M. Harnett's *Ease* (pl. 41)

Having egged on the man, the crowd "burst into a roar of laughter" before he "made a dash for the bottle; but his hands met only the flat surface of a panel. He was dumbfounded. 'Gee whittikers!' at last broke from his lips."[14]

This viewer's behavior was made possible, in part, by the saloon on Warren Street for which owner Theodore Stewart purchased *After the Hunt*. Dedicated to uninhibited consciousness and sensual pleasure, Stewart's was an unorthodox site for viewing the many works of art kept on permanent display. It was a place where viewership was liberated and democratized, where one found, as one would never find it at the National Academy of Design, a *communal* imagination composed of enthralled men "riveted before it [Harnett's picture] in groups."[15] Although it was extraordinary and atypical in the way it encouraged a theater of response, Stewart's display of *After the Hunt* nonetheless revealed, in exaggerated form, that however still and innocuous the objects in Harnett's trompe-l'oeil pictures looked, they were so illusionistic

that spectators acted out a debate, either mentally or physically, over what it was they were perceiving. Their response, in other words, was about how to respond. Instead of pondering iconography, viewers thought about phenomenology—that is, what it felt like to experience the objects in the picture. For example, one reviewer writing in heightened response to the table cover and lit cigar in *Ease* of 1887 (fig. 8) claimed that "the eye feels its texture" and "one smells the fragrance of the smoke that rises." The "immediate impulse" of the spectator, revealing not only his effort to make the representation real but also his urge to participate in the reality he was manufacturing, "is to step forward and remove the lighted cigar which has just been laid down upon a newspaper, and which has already burned a circle in the paper."[16]

There is little overt narrative in still-life pictures, but narrative activity evolved nonetheless and was made conscious in the transactions between picture and viewer; the reviewer, for example, feeling that an actual cigar was burning and that the whole still life was about to go up in flames. These transactions over what it was that was being seen, actual objects or their representation, could be quietly speculative or, as in the case of the cane-wielding viewer of *After the Hunt,* aggressively physical, leading to the collapse of the phenomenological discourse. In either case, there was a partnership between persuasive pictures and viewers willing to enter into a cognitive debate over what they were experiencing. Harnett's pictures did not simply appeal to their consciousness; they also appealed to their willingness to assent to—to have confidence in—the untrustworthy matter of pictures.

Of course, there were also extrapictorial ways of heightening the transaction between picture and viewer. For instance, the police guards standing next to *The Old Violin* with the stated responsibility of protecting the painting, could be read a second way, as guards protecting an actual violin. The same is true of the railings erected in front of the picture. The newspaper accounts also helped manufacture and enhance spectatorship by perpetuating the expectation of an irresistible illusion, as only the more sensational responses were printed.

Although that makes the journalistic record a distorted lens for viewing the full spectrum of viewership, the newspaper reports did set the standard for public response; in effect, training thousands of their own readers how to read a Harnett. Like shills, the papers multiplied desire as they predisposed an audience to become vividly engaged in the illusionistic discourse. Whether or not the reviewers themselves were deceived, they validated the ritual of being deceived and were thus, however unwittingly, part of the con game. To use the language of psychologist James Sully, the media might be said to have "bribed" viewer attention; they created in the minds of viewers an "intellectual preadjustment" powerful enough to obliterate the "undeceiving circumstances" of the illusion (the flat picture surface, the gallery setting, and so forth).[17]

The gallery guards and promotional journalism were peripheral elements in the large rhetorical enterprise of an illusionistic art painted during an era in which there was a national preoccupation with trust and its companion, doubt.[18] Like the confidence games that proliferated across the country in the middle and late nineteenth century, Harnett's illusionism created a brokered space that partitioned the viewer from the picture and, at the same time, joined him to it.

Trompe-l'oeil painting shares a number of characteristics, both aesthetic and psychological, with the con game, whether it is in the form of three-card monte played on the wooden slats of a barrel top or the elaborate deceptions performed by Herman Melville's shifty protagonist in *The Confidence-Man* (1857). For instance, in a con game, there is typically a premium on seamless techniques that achieve a naturalness of effect but that are, in fact, the product of artifice and chicanery. This is particularly true in the game called count and read, in which a con artist has to be exquisitely deft as he examines a mark's perfectly authentic money under the guise of benevolently helping him identify counterfeit bills. In the process of so doing, he substitutes his own counterfeit bills and fleeces the mark.

Like the viewing of trompe-l'oeil painting, cons are also typically conducted in closed spaces. Although the setting may be public, the "outer" world of the city or the street collapses into the self-contained "inner" world of the transaction. For example, chapter 7 of Horatio Alger's *Ragged Dick; or, Street Life in New York* (1867) opens with its savvy, adolescent hero, Dick Hunter, walking up Broadway at Fifth Avenue with his naive friend Frank. They comment on the urban space and on the architecture of the Fifth Avenue Hotel. But two pages later, their visual experience is reduced to the examination of a wallet, seemingly stuffed with bills, as they begin an exchange with a con artist whom Dick eventually out-cons. Only in the next chapter, after the end of the con, does the cityscape open up again.[19]

Equally like a viewer's experience before a trompe-l'oeil still life is a mark's visual access to a con, which is usually unhindered and undisturbed. In fact, the con artist sustains belief either by encouraging close inspection of the objects being manipulated or by persuading the mark to participate in the con through handling fake objects substituted for real ones. Con games were conducted on the street, in trains, at fairs, and, significantly, in light of the exhibition site of *After the Hunt,* in saloons. They often focused on objects that Harnett painted: paper currency, coins, books, pistols, and calling cards. And because cons are so strictly choreographed, those objects were carefully composed to appear naturalistic and randomly positioned. What all cons do to their marks—and what Harnett's illusionistic pictures do to many of their viewers—is to generate their own internally consistent systems of reality. Blocking out the claims of the outer world, where a person's normal analytical judgment is operational, the successful con game rivets the mark's attention onto a substitute reality, similar in appearance to the outer world but often more compelling for the easy riches, both material and visual, that it offers.[20]

Harnett's pictures are also like con games in the way they motivate the viewer to participate in an illusionistic discourse controlled by the illusionist; a successful con artist has to show trust that will produce trust in return. The pictures draw in the viewer with a generous, hospitable, but ultimately gratuitous pitch in the form of tantalizingly "real" and immediately accessible sheet music, swelling bugles, popped violin strings, unglued papers, and flopping book covers.[21] In

Fig. 9. William M. Harnett, *Still Life with Bric-a-Brac,* 1878. Oil on canvas, 31 x 41 in. Fogg Art Museum, Harvard University, Cambridge, Mass., Gift of Grenville L. Winthrop (1942.220)

an overture to viewing and believing in the pictorial illusion, these objects invitingly spill out of the picture into the viewer's space. But they are only "teases" that precede a more troubled experience. (One writer categorized Harnett's pictures as "Vexir" art, a term derived from the German verb *vexieren,* which means "to tease.")[22] Actual con artists open in similar fashion. In the rocks game, for example, a mark is shown or even allowed to hold a few authentic diamonds that are for sale, cheap. Once hooked by such a show of good faith, however, the mark is then sold a bag containing a few real diamonds mixed in with many paste ones.

Like con games, Harnett's pictures make an opening gesture of good faith only in order to ask the same of the viewer. But the preliminary openness of the pictures soon turns to concealment, as they deploy a battalion of strategies to deter deeper readings: objects overlap other objects; papers are often folded in half, rolled, ripped, rotated, or illegible; music disappears in mid-bar. Hospitality turns demanding, as the inquisitive viewer must move closer to the pictures, crane his

neck, and resort to unconventional tactics to see what is there. When, for example, a viewer attempts to penetrate *Still Life—Writing Table* of 1877 (pl. 8), his eyes can initially glide over the spine of the *U.S. Gazette,* two coins, and a ceramic inkwell, but elsewhere he sees only the end of a closed roll of paper money and a few words on an envelope that is partially covered by the inkwell. In the picture's biggest con, he clearly sees a legible letter, but it is folded as well as upside down, requiring the enterprising viewer to come close and practically stand on his head to read what turns out to be an unilluminating message.[23] In other tabletop still lifes—*Still Life with Bric-a-Brac* of 1878, *Reminiscences of Olden Time* of about 1881, and *Still Life* of 1884 (figs. 9, 113, pl. 32)—some objects are positioned close to the viewer, but knives and swords are threateningly placed in such a way as to guillotine the threshold between the viewer and the inner objects.

The objects in the trompe-l'oeil paintings may be more accessible than those in the tabletop still lifes

Fig. 10. William M. Harnett, *The Artist's Letter Rack* (detail, pl. 17)

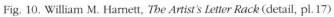

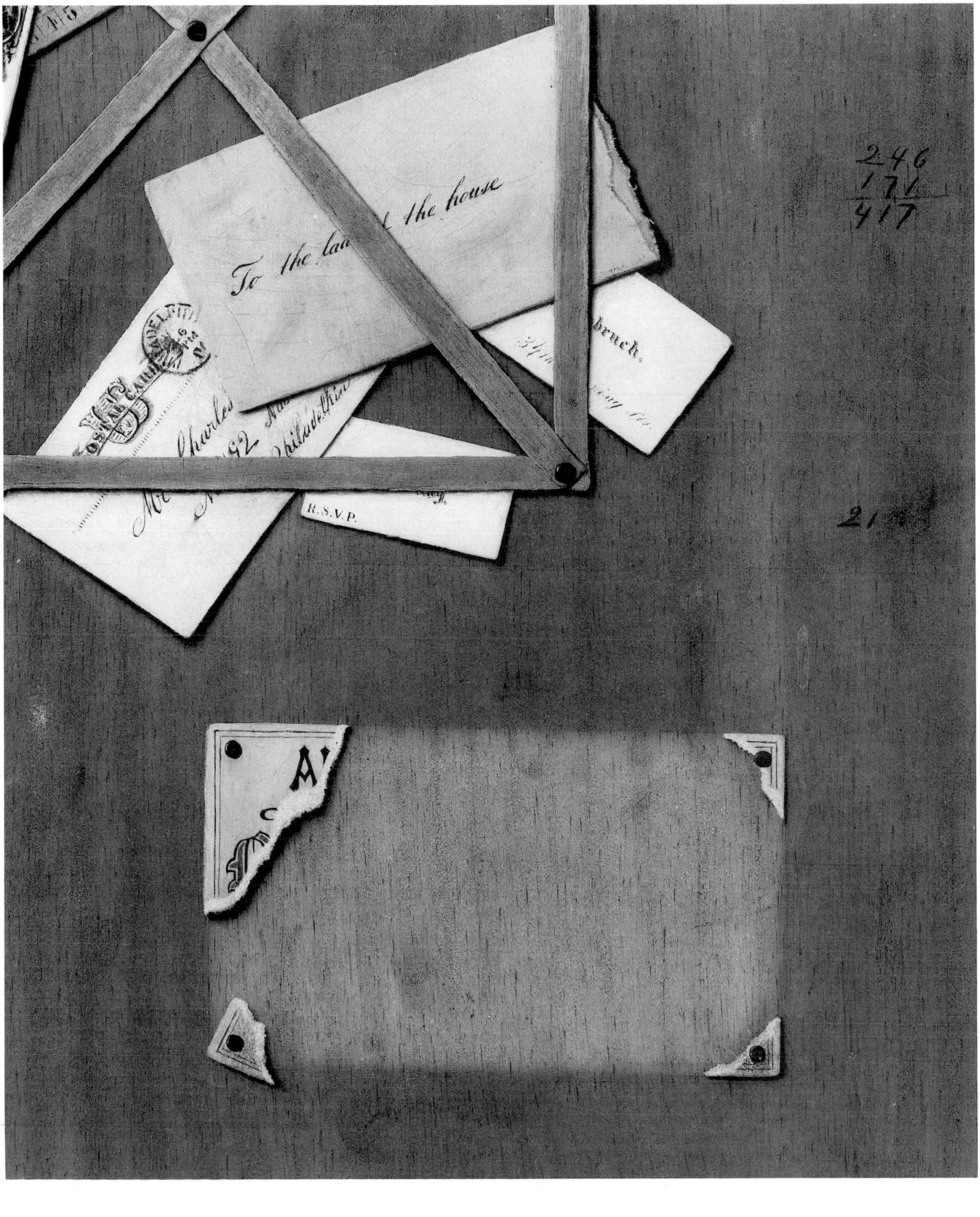

Fig. 11. William M. Harnett, *Old Models* (detail, pl. 49)

because of the shallowness of the pictorial space. But in a work such as *The Artist's Letter Rack* of 1879 (pl. 17), the levels of illusion are bewildering, as one encounters a staggering array of painted illusions on canvas of *other* media on *different* supports: handwriting in ink on paper, ink stamps on envelopes, engraved cards, cardboard labels, printed stamps glued onto envelopes, tape on paper, chalk on wood, and pencil on wood (fig. 10). For the intimate viewer, there is such a web of entangling illusions, so many thresholds of deceit to be crossed, that he can lose his mental bearings. He can be drawn so deeply into Harnett's discourse that after a while he loses his footing in reality and moves instead from one illusion to another.

What all these pictures invite viewers to do (and what the newspaper accounts claim that viewers did do) is to engage in a cycle of reading in which response is a steady movement toward the picture. Viewing begins with a distanced, genteel, dispassionate sighting of an entire painting: the ensemble of objects in it, their shapes, formal pattern, and position in a shallow space. Response is held in check at first, but it leads to a more proximate, lively, and, finally, more troubled encounter with a surrogate reality. Teased closer by an

ingratiating display of objects, the viewer moves to a new discourse. Leaving the large compositional issues behind, a viewer of *Old Models* of 1892 (pl. 49), for example, begins to constrict attention to irresistible details: the rosin dust beneath the violin strings, the ragged edges of ripped paper, the individual coils of violin strings, the broken green threads wriggling out of a ripped leather bookbinding, the crisp hairline crack in a ceramic pitcher on which the original painted design is indistinct beneath a thick glaze (fig. 11). He can believe, as one person wrote of *After the Hunt,* that "the wood *is* wood, the iron is iron, the brass is brass, the leather is leather."[24] Without knowing it, the viewer might find himself at the mercy of the picture, an unwitting conspirator in an illusionistic transaction. He may have begun his visual experience from a viewer's sovereign space, but he eventually ruptures or "brackets" it, then accepts, enters, and consensually participates in the illusionistic theater.[25] In the case of the most accomplished trompe l'oeil and the most inexperienced viewer, his defenses crumble. He loses command over his controlled, polite response. He may doubt the picture, doubt himself, and begin to flounder anxiously in a fictive world.[26]

If the engrossed viewer is not suffering from doubt but is instead lodged in the *certitude* of the reality of what he is seeing (for example, that he is seeing an actual piece of paper glued to a surface), he may continue to believe in it even when confronted by evidence that is contradictory.[27] Recall the man who insisted that the hanging bottle in *After the Hunt* was a real object even after he had touched the picture and concluded that the rabbit and birds were painted. Or consider reports of other committed viewers who, even after discovering that all the objects in *After the Hunt* are painted, "will often protest that the painting has been done on an actual door."[28] Once invested in an illusion, the viewer who is deeply committed to being right about what is going on has difficulty extricating himself from the deception. His tenacity is similar to a phenomenon that occurs in con games. When a con man completely "gets" a mark's confidence, it is not uncommon for the mark to continue to believe in the validity of a deal even after he is told he has been swindled.[29] Like a con man, Harnett must have understood intuitively that engrossment consciously achieved is consciously sustained, for he seems to toy with a viewer's reluctance to disbelieve. This is pointedly apparent in the bold use of impasto in otherwise seamless picture surfaces. In *Old Models,* for instance, pigment swirls liquidly in the highlights of the pitcher and on the upturned rips in the sheet-music cover and gathers three-dimensionally on the horn of the bugle (fig. 12). All these painterly passages declare the fictiveness of the painting by showing brushwork to be a truth more elemental than illusion.[30] But by that point in the experience, the viewer has so thoroughly

Fig. 12. William M. Harnett, *Old Models* (detail, pl. 49)

adjusted himself to the cognitive premises proposed by the picture that he cancels the dissonant information provided by the impasto and, in fact, intensifies belief.[31]

So spellbound by voluptuous illusion at this juncture, the most aggressive and complicit viewer, even if he knows that most of what he is seeing is

painted, might violate the line that is ordinarily maintained between picture and observer in his unsatiated desire for explicit conclusiveness. In the case of at least one picture, *Attention, Company!* of 1878 (pl. 11), viewer contact is encouraged by the inclusion of painted illusionistic fingerprints on a painted illusionistic wood fence, a clever way of establishing precedent—and also giving authorization—for touching the picture surface. When the viewer touches a painting, he abrogates the polite rules of conventional response that give him neither the obligation nor the privilege to participate. As soon as he makes contact, however, he "breaks frame," to use Erving Goffman's terminology. Having worked himself into a frame of mind in which he has "come to terms with all events in that activity," his contact with the paint surface is the kind of "occurrence which cannot be effectively ignored and to which the frame cannot be applied."[32] The illusion is instantaneously discredited and its place as a reality is wiped from his mind. Realizing his mistake with chagrin or amazement, he ends his bondage and returns to the outer world. The picture, meanwhile, though unmasked for what it is, nonetheless continues to insist with quiet authority on its original claim to reality. "The illusion even then persists," wrote one observer about this phenomenon.[33] Unlike even the most accomplished con artist, painted illusions never flinch, never break stride, never flee; they continue, instead, to demand belief.[34]

The nineteenth-century newspaper accounts of viewer response testify to the partnership between picture and viewer. But the partners were never truly equal, for it was always Harnett, in absentia, who set the terms of the social and narrative negotiations, who threw representation and reality into question, at least provisionally, and who ultimately, through his deceptive practices, held imaginative authority for himself.[35] Harnett quietly declared that authority in many ways. In *The Artist's Letter Rack*, for example, he ironically calls for *Politeness* on a white envelope on the left; yet, in the center, he encourages response with the letters *R.S.V.P.* written on a calling card. In *Attention, Company!*, he announces that he is taking his viewers on a *Gr[and] Excur[sion]*. Harnett's messages on cards are telling of his mastery: in *Still Life—Violin and Music* of 1888 (pl. 43), the calling card inscribed *W. M. Harnett* magically lifts toward the viewer as if it were, literally, the agent of the viewer's introduction to the picture; in *Mr. Hulings' Rack Picture* of the same year (pl. 44), one card reads [M]ary Commandery, a reference to a secret order. Harnett's habit of depicting calling cards is significant, for they were instruments of entry in the nineteenth century.[36] A visitor submitted a card to a doorkeeper, who gave it to the mistress of the house, who, after assessing it for authenticity, usefulness, and class, may or may not have assented to a meeting. Calling cards, in other words, marked the first stop in a ritual of penetration; the cards that collect in Harnett's rack pictures are records of the efforts of callers—in effect, viewers—to peel away the sedimentary layers separating them from some partially concealed inner world.

The accounts of viewer response also offer evidence that persuasive trompe-l'oeil painting traded on the ability of a picture to manufacture belief in itself. In order to deceive a viewer into believing that a painted object was real (especially when a flat, framed picture hanging on a wall seemed to be an overwhelmingly literal situation), it was necessary to acquire the consent of the person to be fooled. Harnett achieved that in his pictures by risking what he hoped to win: trust. That is, he had to offer, at least conditionally, a painted image that was more compelling as a reality than any reality the viewer had known. Harnett presented the viewer with a "gift": the privilege of seeing common objects in a hyperbolic state—more precise, detailed, focused, and accurate than those objects ordinarily would have been seen outside the picture frame. Harnett specifically referred to this effect in one of his rare public statements: "In painting from still life I do not closely imitate nature. Many points I leave out and many I add."[37] In order to make viewers believe that what they were seeing was an unvarnished truth, Harnett resorted to a heightening of visual experience that, examined closely, actually varnished the truth. By doubling surface effects in a self-assured tour de force, Harnett was able not only to solicit interest but then to shepherd the viewer into a fictively charmed zone in which seduction commenced. Thereafter, Harnett could be more stingy, diffident, and challenging to the viewer by requesting that he not only suspend disbelief in an avowed fiction, but that he actually believe that painted paper was paper; in other words, that what he was seeing was a truth more compelling than reality.

At that point in experiencing one of Harnett's pictures, what was at stake for the viewer was not merely an interpretation to be won, for the work at hand was more than a picture; it was a generative force that pulled its audience into a phenomenological crisis, into an anxious experience in which what was being seen was, as was never so self-evident before, a construction of belief.[38] Like the con men and tricksters who populate Melville's *Confidence-Man*, Harnett worked on the assumption that he could alter the viewer's perception of reality. Armed with extraordinary rhetorical abilities, the con man appeals to anyone who, as Melville perceived, "sufficiently shows that he is not unwilling to drop real life, and turn, for a time, to something different." Con artists gifted at illusion can count on finding many people who "look not only for more entertainment, but, at bottom, even for more reality, than real life can show." Victims want "nature," but, like the nature offered by Harnett, they want it "unfettered, exhilarated, in effect transformed."[39]

Harnett's pictures—as well as the games of the confidence man—would not have been so successful at manufacturing belief had reality not been such an indeterminate thing in late-nineteenth-century America. The philosophical questions being posed toward a definition of reality were not based on Kantian theories of the "itselfness" of an object. Instead, it was the experiential theories of William James and his colleagues that became the American philosophical template for adducing reality.[40] Although there is no evidence for believing that Harnett and his viewers were active followers of James's philosophy, there is every reason to believe that in his writings, James captured contemporary American doubt over what constituted reality and in so doing created philosophical space for an entire culture to wonder whether a piece of paper was depicted in a picture or glued to it. The operational question about whether something is real, in James's phenomenological terms, is: under what circumstances does one *think* something is real? Reality is a matter of one's sense of realness—of a belief, in other words, that what is being experienced is real. And belief is nothing more than what James calls the "degree of assurance," the "possible certainty" of an object's existence.[41] Instead of being fixed, absolute, and eternal, the existence of an object hinges on the shifting sands of trust—a *"sort of feeling more allied to the emotions than to anything else."*[42]

It was precisely in the philosophical opening provided by "possible certainty" that Harnett's illusionistic objects acquired their power to persuade, to insinuate themselves as reality.[43] In late-nineteenth-century America, a willing viewer, in transaction with a persuasive artist, could believe, perhaps playfully, that a painted envelope was an actual envelope and could continue to posit it *"as absolute reality"* until "contradicted by some other thing of which we think" (for example, it could also be simply a painted envelope).[44] The reversibility of object and representation may have caused "mental unrest," to use a Jamesian term, among the viewers at Stewart's and in Cincinnati, but it was also a source of *pleasure* in experiencing a Harnett picture, for it placed in the foreground, as few pictures do, the viewer's ability to *"choose which way of thinking to adhere to and which to disregard."*[45] This was evident when an artist for *Puck*, seeing *After the Hunt*, was convinced that "he could very fairly resist the artist's endeavor to cheat him" because, after all, he too was an artist. But the keyhole in the picture was "so natural that it was hard to believe that it was not there." Captured by illusion, this experienced viewer then played with the picture as he "looked at it [the keyhole] in different ways; first from a front near view, then from a side view, then from a distance," before he "placed his hand close to the nearest of the side lights, and flashed a shadow upon the poor key hole, which at once showed itself to be a deception."[46] This story and others record the delight in debating over which reality to choose; viewing was a form of entertainment. Whether an object seen in a picture was read as something surely pictorial or wonderfully mimetic or real was all in the play of a mentally enthralling game.

For an illusion to work, Harnett needed to have only the viewer's normal visual cognition in operation, aided by the expectations encouraged by the media. Again, James explains why:

> Visual sensations [do not necessarily have] any inward affinity with the things of whose presence they make us aware. Those things are *tangibles;* their real properties, such as shape, size, mass, consistency, position, reveal themselves only to touch. But the visible signs and the tangible significates are by long custom so "closely twisted, blended, and incorporated together, and the prejudice is so confirmed and riveted in our thoughts by a long tract of time, by the use of language, and want of reflection" that we think we *see* the whole object, tangible and visible alike, in one simple indivisible act.[47]

As James makes clear, people habitually fill in the missing tactile properties of objects merely seen. One is most likely to believe that something is the real object one thinks it is when the experience is restrictedly visual, because of all the senses, sight is "pregnant with illusions"; with no other sense are people "so apt to treat the sensations immediately given as mere signs."[48] The inherent corrigibility of a visual sign is doubled, according to James, when the referent is known "by long custom"; that is, when it is a common, familiar object—like an envelope, a bugle, a calling card, or sheet music—that requires minimal "reflection" to fill in its tangible attributes. The inferring of tangible properties and three dimensions to flat, painted representations of common objects is the result of the great lengths to which Harnett went to stimulate what James calls *"sensational and reproductive brain-processes"* that *"give us the content of our perceptions."*[49] The exquisite details and reflections in Harnett's pictures, the true sizes and shapes, and the nuanced colors (that is, the classic stylistic elements of trompe l'oeil) comprise a field of signs that trigger the other unfelt properties of those familiar objects. It takes the perception of only a "few qualities or attributes" before they are "shot into various paths which habit has already organized in the hemispheres," the result being a "consciousness of that more complex 'object,' the whole 'thing.'"[50]

Illusion, according to James, is thus not the result of reading false information; instead, "in every illusion what is false is what is inferred." The problems viewers had in determining what it was they were seeing in Harnett's pictures were not situated in the pictures or in their perception of what was in the pictures, but in their leaping to false conclusions. James clarifies: *"The so-called 'fallacy of the senses', of which the ancient sceptics made so much account, is not fallacy of the senses proper, but rather of the intellect, which interprets wrongly what the senses give."*[51] What was occurring between viewers' first, distant, disengaged, passive reading of *The Old Violin* and *After the Hunt* and their later, obsessive, engrossed, passionate debate over the reality of what they were seeing is explained by James's "shot," in which the mind attempts to leap—assisted by memories of actual violins, bugles, and letters—from the incomplete information provided by visual experience to the full, tactile information contained in an actual object. It was theorized in the nineteenth century that whenever a viewer receives incoming information, it is placed into preexistent mental slots in a process of recognition called *apperception.* Visual sensation "awakens the mental images which answer to past experiences" and, in turn, the mind "now views the impression through the image."[52] In the case of Harnett's viewers, it might be said that the need to assimilate, classify, and name visual sensation created a momentum that propelled them to fill in missing attributes so completely that they wanted "to play on that violin" and "pull at the envelope." But for the few men who rushed at *After the Hunt,* that momentum was incomplete. Their touching of the picture was an extreme effort to resolve a crisis of inference; to determine, by way of concrete "tangibles," the correct mental slot for what they were experiencing.

James's theory is based on the unsteady foundations of belief and mental predisposition, so the determination of something as real or unreal often hinges on nonintrinsic properties, such as the vividness of experiencing it. Recall Melville's claim that the ideal victim of a con game desires more reality than real life can show. *"Vividness or pungency,"* James proposes, *"is then the vital factor in reality."*[53] Upon close inspection, a trompe l'oeil, such as *The Old Violin,* may not have all the minute details of an actual object, but because of the extraordinarily vivid terms in which Harnett represented objects—in strong raking light, in intimate proximity, with dramatic contrasts in textures, in suspended balance—they acquire such a "sense of realness," as James would put it, that they can challenge actual objects, present or remembered, as authoritative reality.

Vividness is the odd companion of apperception. The stronger the visual impact and the weaker the viewer's ability to reflect on what he is seeing (that is, the more automatic his process of apperception), the more convincing the illusion. The more unreflective the viewer, the more habitual and restricted his response will be to visual sensations. Following these lines of late-nineteenth-century theory, Harnett's illusionism might be said not only to differentiate between levels of perceptual sophistication but also to separate those of inquiring, probing, doubting, unrestricted, reflecting mind from those who receive and interpret visual sensation unreflectingly and habitually. Harnett's hyperillusionistic pictures may traffic in

style, but nineteenth-century responses to them were about class and culture, which was continually being tested by the show of one's powers of cognition and recognition. "City men," one commentator observed in the differing responses to *After the Hunt,* were "enraptured" by the picture, but they seemed to understand that what they were looking at was merely "extraordinary imitation." But "gentlemen from the country, and especially from Chicago, who see it for the first time" declare that "the objects are real objects."[54] "Only children and half-taught people," noted a critic for the *Studio,* "take pleasure in such tricks of the brush."[55]

The identification of representation as representation created a threshold of class and culture because the ability to do so was seen as a sign of discernment, taste, judgment, probity, and cosmopolitanism. Conversely, those who turned the viewing of art into a public spectacle, who sparred with the pictures, who in effect thought of still life as a form of entertainment appropriate to saloons, were considered a threat to the genteel order that held art to be polite, elite, intellectual, moral, and sacred.[56] Such was the rhetoric of highbrow critiques against Harnett and his illusionism. "Mere accuracy and vividness of delineation," wrote the Reverend Frederick Taylor Gates about *The Old Violin,* "is of minor consideration in estimating the true worth of a picture." The painting, he continued, "is simply a trick. The thought in the mind of the artist is simply, 'Only see how I can deceive you.' 'Just see me do it.'" Viewing a Harnett could be considered an amoral experience, for "there is nothing whatever in the picture to please or instruct or elevate you."[57] Clarence Cook, writing for the *New-York Daily Tribune,* made a similar claim, that few "artists of merit" ever stoop "to the sole purpose of imitation." Harnett and his colleagues in illusion were accused of engaging in a demeaning "painting of externals." After all, "this imitative work is not really so difficult," for only "time and industry" are needed, and many "sign-painters" could do the same were they not committed to "their honest calling."[58] Even the nineteenth-century landscape painter George Inness entered the debate, acknowledging that *After the Hunt* might be clever, but that it was nonetheless "a lie" despite its verisimilitude because it was lacking in "truth," which, he felt, ought to have a metaphysical dimension.[59]

The charges of amorality, facileness, speciousness, and dishonesty were indirect ways of sheathing the elite's paranoia over the erosion of their cultural authority.[60] Their reply to the threat of middle-class viewers who craved entertaining art was either to control culture, cultural institutions, and responses to culture, or, echoing Inness's comments on Harnett, to become critics, isolated from the material vulgarities of the world and seeking instead "the truth of things and the inner reality of facts."[61] To the elite, Harnett's crime was democratizing high culture—as well as debasing and displacing it—by diffusing it in unconventional exhibitions and by turning it into a spectacle. That threat had haunted the elite since the cultural revolution sparked by P. T. Barnum, who had created museumlike amusement centers in the antebellum period. After the Civil War, in part following Barnum's lead, there emerged a popular culture eager for spectatorship and sensationalism, obsessed with imitation and illusion, attracted to interplays between true and false, and preferring outward signs to inward quality.[62] It was a middle-class world that was afflicted with what historian William R. Thayer called "epidermism" in an 1894 essay.[63] What its members enjoyed were the simulacra of reality—that which was more entertaining, more vivid, more material, more factual than quotidian life. Facts—and vivid illusions of facts—appealed to them. "Facts please the many," wrote Hiram M. Stanley, an evolutionary psychologist, in the year of Harnett's death; "the crowd seek not truth but sensation in either reality or its transcript."[64] They demanded a new American theater in which acting and sets closely mimicked life. They bought new, cheap, and stunningly mimetic chromolithographs that not only reproduced but also redistributed high culture across class lines. And they reveled in Harnett's extreme illusions of real objects.

The appeal of Harnett's pictures was similar to that of the work of his fictional counterpart Jared Stiles, a still-life painter in Henry B. Fuller's short story "Dr. Gowdy and the Squash" (1901). Jared's extraordinary trompe-l'oeil paintings of squash, each framed by "four neatly mortised lengths of fencing, lichened and silvered by a half-century," were put on display (recalling the setting for *After the Hunt*) in "almost every large house of public entertainment."[65] In an unnamed metropolis of "strange and shifting life," visiting "provincials" encountered a "simple, tangible, familiar, appealing" squash still life, which was displayed next to an actual squash. "'Which is which?' cried the dear people, delightedly."[66] Jared's picture, like Harnett's, glorified doubt. It also captured the viewers' love of sentimental nostalgia as "their eyes filled, their breasts heaved, their gullets gulped, their rustic boyhood was with them poignantly once more."[67] Popular interest in Jared's picture was excited by Barnum-like editorials "that contrasted the sturdy and wholesome truthfulness of his genius with the vain imaginings of so-called idealists."[68] But recalling the critical debate over Harnett's works, Jared came under attack by the Reverend Dr. William Gowdy, "one of

the trustees of the Art Academy," who believed "the regeneration and salvation of the human race came to little more than a mere matter of putting paint upon canvas."[69] Dr. Gowdy, one of the "idealists" who would have identified with late-nineteenth-century academic painting, thought Jared's trompe-l'oeil images were "odious daubs" because of the "discordant mingling of the simulated and the real."[70] Jared's pictures also seemed to do nothing "toward the building up of character."[71] Instead, as Fuller wickedly parodied Harnett's critics, Dr. Gowdy winced at "'this folly, this falsity, this bumptious vulgarity'" of someone who "had never drawn from the antique."[72]

What Harnett—and Jared—had done was not only to erode the distinction between reality and representation but also to enfranchise the middle class as vocal, participatory viewers by, to paraphrase Barnum, giving them what they wanted. But where did Harnett himself stand on issues of class and art? On one hand, he produced art of the highest technical quality that was sincerely admired by an amused middle class that coveted information and showy signs of artistic craftsmanship. When viewing one of his illusionistic pictures, they could put aside the problems of trying to understand the abstract aesthetic principles underlying the highbrow art forms of the Gilded Age. Instead, they could engross themselves, without apology, in the joys of probing the boundaries between reality and illusion, in the stimulating competition between a visual deception and their own powers to determine where and how it was operational. On the other hand, Harnett's ability to convert viewers into performers, if not fools, and to turn art appreciation into a debate that tested visual—and cognitive—sophistication, would indicate an imperial position in which the artist retained power for himself and his pictures. Although Harnett rarely shared his thoughts and never offered anything approaching social analysis, he seems to have benignly worked both sides of the class fence. He had an instinct for what pleased and excited the public; he recognized differences in visual sophistication; he gratified middle-class viewers' needs; and, at the same time, he manipulated, exploited, and profited by their aesthetic susceptibilities. Like Barnum, he understood that "everything depended upon getting people to think, and talk, and become curious and excited over and about the 'rare spectacle.'"[73] Like that master showman, moreover, Harnett seems to have realized the value of visual trickery to a middle class that "appears disposed to be amused even when they are conscious of being deceived."[74]

NOTES

▼

Many individuals contributed to the research and conceptual development of this essay. I wish to thank Donald Weber, Heather McPherson, Teri Edelstein, Richard Wendorf, and Linda Docherty for helping to expand and refine some of the issues I raise. I am also indebted to Rachel Layton, who contributed to my understanding of the confidence game, P. T. Barnum, and the material culture of deceit. Thayer Tolles Mickel was not only indefatigable in her efforts but also eternally pleasant in spite of the outrageous demands placed on her.

1. Clipping from an 1886 Cincinnati newspaper (otherwise unidentified), Blemly scrapbook, Alfred Frankenstein Papers, Archives of American Art, Smithsonian Institution, Washington, D.C., microfilm, roll 1374, frame 281.

2. I have been influenced by Warwick Wadlington's excellent study *The Confidence Game in American Literature* (Princeton and London: Princeton University Press, 1975). His thesis is essentially phenomenological, stressing the activeness of the reader in his negotiations with fiction. I have benefited from the major theoretical works of Erving Goffman, especially *Frame Analysis: An Essay on the Organization of Experience* (Cambridge, Mass.: Harvard University Press, 1974); *Interaction Ritual* (Garden City, N.Y.: Anchor Books, 1967); and *Strategic Interaction* (Philadelphia: University of Pennsylvania Press, 1969), especially the unit "Expression Games: An Analysis of Doubts at Play." Although it is not aimed at American trompe l'oeil, there are many stimulating passages in Norman Bryson, *Looking at the Overlooked: Four Essays on Still Life Painting* (Cambridge, Mass.: Harvard University Press, 1990).

3. In contextualizing Harnett's illusionism, I do not intend to argue for American exceptionalism. There is, after all, a similar illusionistic tradition in European art of this period. My aim here is to study the affective value of his pictures as rituals of perception that were enacted in America.

4. In addition to the citations in the notes below, on the subject of paper money in Harnett's work, see, for example, Walter Benn Michaels, *The Gold Standard and the Logic of Naturalism: American Literature at the Turn of the Century* (Berkeley and Los Angeles: University of California Press, 1987), pp. 160–66; Bruce W. Chambers, *Old Money: American Trompe l'Oeil Images of Currency*, exhib. cat. (New York: Berry-Hill Galleries, 1988), passim; and Edward J. Nygren, "The Almighty Dollar: Money as a Theme in American Painting," *Winterthur Portfolio* 23 (Summer–Autumn 1988), pp. 129–50. On illusionism, see Albert A. Hopkins, ed. and comp., *Magic: Stage Illusions and Scientific Diversions including Trick Photography* (New York: Munn & Co., 1897). The two literary monuments to American life as a public illusion are Thorstein Veblen, *The Theory of the Leisure Class: An Economic Study of Institutions* (New York: B. W. Huesch, 1912); and Henry James, *The American Scene* (New York and London: Harper & Bros., 1907).

5. William James, *Principles of Psychology,* 3 vols. (Cambridge, Mass., and London: Harvard University Press, 1981), 2, p. 924.

6. "A Wonderland," *Cincinnati Enquirer,* September 19, 1886, p. 12.

7. "The Art Gallery," *Cincinnati Commercial Gazette,* September 16, 1886, n.p.

8. "Art's Counterfeiting: Some Notable Examples of Deceiving the Eyes by Pictures," *Star* (New York), December 30, 1885, p. 6.

9. "Aus dem Kunstverein," clipping from the *Handelsblatt,* 1884 (otherwise unidentified), Blemly scrapbook, frame 335, quoted in Alfred Frankenstein, *After the Hunt: William Harnett and Other American Still Life Painters, 1870–1900,* rev. ed. (Berkeley and Los Angeles: University of California Press, 1969), p. 69.

10. "The Art Gallery"; and a clipping from an 1886 Cincinnati newspaper (otherwise unidentified), Blemly scrapbook, frame 282.

11. Quoted in Frankenstein, *After the Hunt,* p. 38. *Shinplaster with Exhibition Label* and *Still Life—*

Five-Dollar Bill were likely the paintings in question.

12. Ibid., p. 80.

13. All quotations are from clippings in the Blemly scrapbook.

14. "Art's Counterfeiting," p. 6.

15. "Theodore Stewart's Collection," clipping from an unidentified and undated newspaper, Blemly scrapbook, frame 328.

16. "A Fine Still-Life Painting," *Springfield Daily Republican,* November 7, 1887, p. 6. The smoke described in this article is no longer visible in the painting (pl. 41), which was damaged, cut down, and restored, probably before 1910.

17. James Sully, *Illusions: A Psychological Study* (New York: D. Appleton & Co., 1882), p. 107.

18. Wadlington discusses this phenomenon at length in *Confidence Game,* pp. 3–36. It is also the thesis of Miles Orvell, *The Real Thing: Imitation and Authenticity in American Culture, 1880–1940* (Chapel Hill and London: University of North Carolina Press, 1989), pp. 33–137. See also Neil Harris, *Humbug: The Art of P. T. Barnum* (Boston and Toronto: Little, Brown & Co., 1973).

19. Horatio Alger, *Struggling Upward and Other Works* (New York: Crown Publishers, 1945), pp. 180–85.

20. See David W. Maurer, *The American Confidence Man* (Springfield, Ill.: Charles C. Thomas, 1970); Gary Lindberg, *The Confidence Man in American Literature* (New York: Oxford University Press, 1982); Karen Halttunen, *Confidence Men and Painted Women: A Study of Middle-Class Culture in America, 1830–1870* (New Haven and London: Yale University Press, 1982); Richard Boyd Hauck, *A Cheerful Nihilism: Confidence and "The Absurd" in American Humorous Fiction* (Bloomington and London: Indiana University Press, 1971); and Susan Kuhlmann, *Knave, Fool, and Genius: The Confidence Man as He Appears in Nineteenth-Century*

American Fiction (Chapel Hill: University of North Carolina Press, 1973).

21. In a different context, Bryson discusses hospitality in antique still lifes (*Looking at the Overlooked,* pp. 23–26). Following Bryson, I will claim that Harnett's still lifes at first ingratiate themselves with viewers in an expanding threshold of access before they close down and cocoon themselves in an obfuscating strategy that differentiates, rather than elides, classes.

22. "Kunst," *New Yorker Staats-Zeitung und Herald,* November 25, 1888, p. 4.

23. Using a strategy similar to Harnett's, the con game ducats requires calling cards be marked, turned upside down, concealed, and then replaced by substitute cards.

24. "Queer Art Illusions: Some of the Many Methods Employed to Produce Them," clipping from an unidentified and undated newspaper, Blemly scrapbook, frame 327.

25. On *bracketing,* the exclusionary habits of a person engrossed, see Goffman, *Frame Analysis,* p. 7.

26. Goffman would say that in this experience, "reality anomically flutters" (ibid., p. 379).

27. See ibid., p. 120, for an extended discussion of this phenomenon.

28. "Queer Art Illusions."

29. Maurer brilliantly discusses this point in *American Confidence Man,* p. 110.

30. Contrary to my interpretation, Frankenstein was adamant about reading the impasto as "light traps" that are "meaningless in any descriptive sense, and cannot be interpreted in any other terms" (*After the Hunt,* p. 40). Parallel to Harnett's impasto was a phenomenon in parlor theatricals of mid-century, in which players would drop out of character to reveal themselves as private persons, thus revealing the play's theatricality (see Halttunen,

Confidence Men, p. 185).

31. See Leon Festinger, *A Theory of Cognitive Dissonance* (Stanford: Stanford University Press, 1957). James discusses this as well, claiming that belief "fills the mind solidly to the exclusion of contradictory ideas" (*Principles,* 2, p. 914).

32. See Goffman, *Frame Analysis,* p. 347. In *Strategic Interaction,* Goffman describes the game of wits that occurs in situations of doubt: "The observer, suspecting that what he might have treated as an unwitting move is actually or possibly an obfuscation or misrepresentation, suspecting that what appears to be ingenuous fact could be shot through and through with a gamesman's manipulation and design, suspecting this, he can attempt to crack, pierce, penetrate, and otherwise get behind the apparent facts in order to uncover the real ones" (pp. 17–18). Illusion theory, which posits the idea that one is seeing what it is that is being represented, is often the subject of debate in art-historical and psychological literature, encompassing the divergent works of scholars E. H. Gombrich, *Art and Illusion: A Study in the Psychology of Pictorial Representation,* 2nd ed. (London: Phaidon Press, 1962); and, in opposition, Richard Wollheim, *Art and Its Objects: An Introduction to Aesthetics,* 2nd ed. (Cambridge, New York, and Melbourne: Cambridge University Press, 1980). For an overview of the debate, see Catherine Wilson, "Illusion and Representation," *British Journal of Aesthetics* 22, no. 3 (Summer 1982), pp. 211–21.

33. "Queer Art Illusions."

34. Goffman discusses "deceptive clues" in *Strategic Interaction,* pp. 31–32.

35. Goffman would label Harnett a "fabricator" because of his "intentional effort . . . to manage activity so that a party of one or more others will be induced to have a false belief about what it is that is going on" (*Frame Analysis,* p. 83).

36. Herman Melville's con man authenticates one of his many identities by the use of a business card (*The Confidence-Man: His Masquerade* [New York: Grove Press, 1949], p. 29). In the con game ducats, calling cards were used because of their claim to authenticity.

37. "Painted Like Real Things: The Man Whose Pictures Are a Wonder and a Puzzle," interview in *New York News,* probably 1889 or 1890, quoted in Frankenstein, *After the Hunt,* p. 55.

38. Arguably, audience response, both anticipated and actual, affected Harnett over his career. His late work was flatter, larger, and more approximate of actual niches, cupboards, and so forth in an ambitious effort to refine his stylistic gestures in an ever greater wager for confidence.

39. Melville, *Confidence-Man,* pp. 215–16.

40. The key readings from James are from *Principles of Psychology.* Crucial to understanding Harnett are the chapters "The Perception of 'Things'" and "The Perception of Reality."

41. James, *Principles,* 2, p. 913.

42. Ibid.

43. Ibid.

44. Ibid., p. 918.

45. Ibid., p. 920.

46. "Art's Counterfeiting," p. 6.

47. James, *Principles,* 2, pp. 723–24. Here, James paraphrases George Berkeley, *An Essay towards a New Theory of Vision,* in *The Works of George Berkeley, D.D.,* ed. Alexander Campbell Fraser, 4 vols. (Oxford: Clarendon, 1871), 1, pp. 57–58.

48. James, *Principles,* 2, p. 745. James was in part indebted to Hermann L. W. von Helmholtz's theory of signs in perception; see his *Treatise on Physiological Optics,* 3 vols. (Leipzig: Voss, 1867; Rochester, N.Y.: Optical Society, 1924–25).

49. James, *Principles,* 2, p. 724.

50. Ibid., p. 725. James cites the work of fellow psychologist James Sully. However, because Sully's work is adumbrated by James in the literature, and because James is the more acute scholar, I will continue to work with him. Sully is cited in "Queer Art Illusions."

51. James, *Principles,* 2, p. 731.

52. Sully, *Illusions,* pp. 27–28.

53. James, *Principles,* 2, p. 930.

54. "Art's Counterfeiting," p. 6.

55. "The Society of American Artists: Ninth Exhibition," *Studio,* n.s. 2, no. 12 (June 1887), p. 217.

56. The best recent writers on this are Orvell, *Real Thing;* and Lawrence W. Levine, *Highbrow/Lowbrow: The Emergence of Cultural Hierarchy in America* (Cambridge, Mass., and London: Harvard University Press, 1988).

57. "The Churches: Pictures at the Exposition Furnish Material for a Sermon," *Minneapolis Tribune,* September 12, 1887, p. 5.

58. [Clarence Cook], "Academy of Design: Fifty-fourth Annual Exhibition," *New-York Daily Tribune,* April 26, 1879, p. 5.

59. Quoted in George Inness, Jr., *Life, Art, and Letters of George Inness* (New York: Century Co., 1917), p. 124.

60. Orvell discusses this concept in *Real Thing,* pp. 33–137.

61. Hiram Stanley, "The Passion for Realism and What Is to Come of It," *Dial* 14 (April 16, 1893), p. 239.

62. Orvell, *Real Thing,* p. xv.

63. Ibid., p. 34; and William R. Thayer, "The New Story-Tellers and the Doom of Realism," in *Realism and Romanticism in Fiction: An Approach to the Novel,* ed. Eugene Current-García and Walton R. Patrick (Chicago: Scott, Foresman & Co., 1962), p. 158.

64. Stanley, "Passion for Realism," p. 239.

65. Henry B. Fuller, "Dr. Gowdy and the Squash," in *Under the Skylights* (New York: D. Appleton & Co., 1901), pp. 343, 346.

66. Ibid., p. 350.

67. Ibid., p. 359.

68. Ibid., p. 356. Jared himself pandered to the press by affecting a rustic dialect for a lowbrow newspaper and an intellectual cadence for a highbrow one.

69. Ibid., pp. 328–29.

70. Ibid., p. 349.

71. Ibid., p. 329.

72. Ibid., p. 362.

73. *Struggles and Triumphs; or, Forty Years' Recollections of P. T. Barnum, Written by Himself* (Buffalo: Courier Co., 1882), p. 76.

74. *Struggles and Triumphs; or, The Life of P. T. Barnum, Written by Himself,* ed. George S. Bryan, 2 vols. (New York and London: Alfred A. Knopf, 1927), 1, p. 129.

PERMANENT OBJECTS
IN A CHANGING WORLD

▾

Harnett's Still Lifes as a Hold on the Past

DAVID M. LUBIN

William Michael Harnett was a portraitist—not of people but of thing, old things. He preferred them that way. As he once explained, "The chief difficulty I have found has not been the grouping of my models, but their choice. To find a subject that paints well is not an easy task. As a rule, new things do not paint well. . . . I want my models to have the mellowing effect of age . . . the rich effect that age and usage gives."[1]

Thus, aside from current newspapers, recently postmarked envelopes, and an occasional calling card, the models Harnett typically chose were remnants of an earlier day: well-thumbed books, seasoned pipes, dented horns, frayed sheet music, rusty horseshoes, an ivory-handled revolver yellowed with age, and other objects that were veterans of considerable use—Turkish rugs, Dutch jars, and German beer mugs that might have been handed down from generation to generation or found fortuitously in an attic. Unlike fruit, flowers, and other perishables, the physical entities Harnett favored were inorganic rather than organic and thus had something of permanence about them. More often than not, they were handmade, maybe even homespun, the antithesis of machine-made, mass-produced, mass-consumed, store-bought commodities. As such, they must have seemed to him and his contemporaries notably premodern. This is not to say that these objects lacked contemporary usefulness or value. Surely books could be read, violins played, mugs drunk from, and artistic bric-a-brac admired. But parallel to their practical, leisure, or status value was their usefulness as emblems of bygone days, reminders of supposedly simpler, less hurried and rapacious times.

In the so-called Gilded Age following the Civil War, when excesses of wealth and ostentation astounded observers across the land, the representation of objects that bespoke a less materialistic and greedy past must have seemed comforting indeed. Hence, it was in this sense, too, and not simply that of painterly technique, that the models Harnett chose to portray conveyed the mellowing—the meliorating—effects of age. In most scholarly assessments, however, Harnett's exuberant mimesis of cherished physical items, whether commonplace or rare, is thought to be of a piece with Gilded Age proclivities toward material accumulation and conspicuous consumption. Generally, his work has been regarded as a painterly ancillary to the era's outsized appetite for collecting and displaying objects old or new. This makes considerable sense, but to abandon analysis at that level is to do an injustice to the complexities of the art and era in question.

Certainly, Harnett's paintings participated in the materialism of their time, but they also subtly resisted it or at least attempted to mediate it by means of their ennobling, quietly inspiring, or even down-home humorous treatment of familiar artifacts that exuded "the mellowing effect of age." This is not to suggest that his art was antimodern or that it failed to take part and pleasure in the era's adoration of accumulation and display, but only that its way of doing so—of reconciling potentially guilty consciences and abundant material success—involved dusting off old objects and bathing them in a reverential light.

Take, for example, Harnett's last work, *Old Models* of 1892 (pl. 49). This atypically large painting serves as a virtual summation of the artist's career. Almost everything about it, not only its title, conveys age. The brass bugle at the top has been knocked about countless times; the ornate cover of the sheet music is tattered from too many rehearsals; the rusty hinge at the upper right barely bridges the yawning gap between two splintered, weathered, nail-holed planks;

Fig. 13. *The Court of Honor, Looking West,*
World's Columbian Exposition, Chicago, 1893.
Photograph. Chicago Historical Society (ICHi-02524)

the thick brown volume on the shelf is torn along the spine; and the Dutch jar appears to have survived this long only by some sort of miracle. The chiaroscuro lighting, with its deep shadows, bright highlights, and golden glow, signifies the faraway days of the Old Masters. While people certainly read books, played music, and drank from quaint drinking vessels during the 1890s, nothing about these activities points to the 1890s themselves as would, for instance, a bicycle wheel or a tennis racquet. Reading, drinking, and music-making are time-honored activities of leisure that, even at the close of the century, possessed a premodern aura because they were reminders of earlier eras.

Harnett painted *Old Models* with the intention of exhibiting it at the World's Columbian Exposition of 1893 in Chicago. This 650-acre celebration of American progress showcased the latest in industrial technology and commercial production and devoted numerous respectful exhibits to the nation's Colonial past. *Old Models* never reached Chicago, however, for Harnett died prior to the opening of the fair. The painting was auctioned as part of his estate.

It is significant, nonetheless, that Harnett devised this work for the exposition, which he may have believed would be the largest forum he would ever attain for his art and the point of view it expressed. Hence the majestic size of the canvas. The title, too, is appropriate, for with it Harnett suggests not simply that the objects portrayed are old studio "models" but that they are also venerable exemplars— that is, "models" for behavior. The painting enjoins

the viewer to admire and follow the old-fashioned way of life, the premodern sensibility, that these long-enduring remnants of the past seem to typify.

How intriguing to imagine this tribute to yesteryear occupying a place in the art pavilion of the fair's "White City," a trompe-l'oeil dreamworld of faux-marble Beaux-Arts edifices erected in lofty homage to genteel good taste (fig. 13). But whereas the academic architecture of the fair recalled Roman and Renaissance ideals, in effect suggesting bureaucratic rationalization and social control as antidotes to what many perceived as the spreading barbarism of the day, *Old Models* prescribes instead a vernacular, plain-speaking, unassuming approach.[2] The simple and good way of life, not the magnificent and majestic, is what Harnett's painting, despite its scale and complexity, "models" for its viewers.

However didactic the "White City" was intended to be, surely Harnett's paintings were neither meant nor regarded as heavy-handed sermons. Their invocations of the past—whether of last night's smoking party (*The Social Club* of 1879, pl. 16) or of old folkways (*Still Life—Violin and Music* of 1888, pl. 43)—were too redolent with feeling to be merely didactic but were nostalgic instead. By devoting such a finely tuned, dramatically lit focus to objects and implied activities associated with a benign past, Harnett invested his paintings—and through them, the past— with a powerful, resonant emotion. In recent years the term *nostalgia* has become discredited, referring to a culturally and politically reactionary frame of mind or to an ersatz emotion artificially stimulated by advertising and the mass media. Previously, however, the word was used to indicate genuine, not manufactured, feelings. In some instances it referred to a terrible, destructive homesickness; coined in the seventeenth century, *nostalgia* was a medical term, a combination of the Greek for "home" and "suffering." More commonly, though, it came to mean warm pleasure derived from thinking about the past mixed with sadness at one's distance from it.[3]

Nostalgia was a hallmark of late-nineteenth-century America. The popular songs of the period (including earlier favorites such as "The Old Folks at Home" and "Home, Sweet Home") frequently alluded to and played upon sentimental longings for the past, as did popular theater, the prints of Currier and Ives, lyric poetry, historical fiction, history painting, and even multivolumed historical treatises. Historian David Lowenthal has observed that prior to the nineteenth century, most people "scarcely differentiated past from present, referring even to remote events, if at all, as though they were then occurring."[4] With all the stupendous changes wreaked upon age-old traditions, a new sensibility arose, one that made the present seem palpably different from the past—for better or for worse. The often-cited formulation of twentieth-century novelist L. P. Hartley, "The past is a foreign country," tells only half the story, for the reverse holds true as well: newcomers to modernity find that it is the present, not the past, that seems distressingly foreign.[5]

"Peter," a tale published in 1892 (the year Harnett painted *Old Models*), concerns the homesick immigrant Sadelack, who cherishes his violin from the old country as though it were his life. Written by Nebraska college student Willa Cather and based on

Fig. 14. William M. Harnett, *The Cincinnati Enquirer,* 1888.
Oil on canvas, 30 x 25 in. The White House Collection, Washington, D.C.

the experiences of the father of a childhood friend, Peter Sadelack's story reappeared years later, even more poignantly, in Cather's well-known novel *My Ántonia* (1918).[6] In both instances, the immigrant farmer, called Shimerda in the novel, is unable to cope with his gnawing loneliness and homesickness. A violin—Harnett's old object par excellence—is the symbol around which this homesickness revolves. Poor refugees to the new land could afford to bring only necessities, so any additional items tended to be of considerable personal significance. Yet when Shimerda's sadness for days gone by grows unbearable, even his beloved violin, with all its happy associations, cannot rouse him. His daughter Ántonia confides in broken English, "My papa sad for the old country. He not look good. He never make music any more. At home he play violin all the time; for weddings and for dance. Here never. . . . Some days he take his violin out of his box and make with his fingers on the strings, like this, but never he makes the music. He don't like this kawn-tree."[7]

Cather's story of a man for whom the true foreign country is not the past but the present has moved readers because it embodies not simply one man's nostalgia but that of an entire generation. Shimerda regards his violin and the memories of community it summons as necessities for survival in an uncongenial environment. He invests this remnant of the past with magical powers, as if it were a talisman, to keep the wolves of despair from his door. If he can no longer bring himself to play his violin, at least he can take it from its box and caress it. But that, finally, is not enough. Shimerda's suicide suggests that emotion-laden objects connected to the past can go only so far in offsetting the pain of irrevocable separation from that which beckons in memory so vividly, so cruelly. Everyday objects are not capable of restoring the past, but they can radiate its aura. And it is precisely such objects with precisely this aura that Harnett was adept at painting.

This ability was probably the reason wealthy Minnesota lumberman Thomas Barlow Walker asked Harnett to produce a still life in commemoration of his recently deceased son (the artist appears to have refused the offer, probably because he was ill at the time). Walker's son, who had met Harnett and admired his work, was a craftsman himself; he had once commissioned "a beautiful Winchester Rifle" and, as a present for his father, made "a very nice tomahawk hunting hatchet."[8] Walker wanted these nostalgic objects re-created as a means of keeping alive the memory of his son and their hunting excursions together (game hunting was commonly seen as a way for fathers and sons to enjoy a fastening of emotional bonds). To the extent that one can recapture through mere personal effects a longed-for past or beloved person who remains transfixed in that past, trompe-

l'oeil painting is an especially potent force: if we can trick the eye, maybe we can also trick time and space and reclaim that prior sense of well-being that evocative objects so powerfully represent.

Shimerda's fiddle, Walker's hunting hatchet—such were the tokens of the past that Harnett portrayed again and again, along with pipes, mugs, sheet music, and horseshoes. Did he himself experience such longings and bittersweet attachments to the objects he repeatedly represented? Probably, though no documents exist to support such a claim. Certainly in his career as an artist he frequently returned to familiar old things. In *Old Models,* the pun in the title refers to the age of the objects depicted as well as to the moral sensibility embodied. There is a more personal pun here, too, for the specific items shown in the painting are props that had appeared previously in other works by Harnett: the Dutch jar, for example, can be seen in *The Cincinnati Enquirer* of 1888 and in *Still Life* of the same year (figs. 14, 74); the violin is featured in *The Old Violin* of 1886 (pl. 37) and reappears in *Old Models.* Even if the artist initially repeated subjects for economic reasons ("I could not afford to hire models as the other students did") and later for more distinctly formal purposes ("As a rule, new things do not paint well"), it seems likely that they grew to have strong personal associations for him—or perhaps they had such associations from the start.[9]

When Harnett sold his first paintings of these studio props, he knew he had found his métier. His viewers were drawn to the work not merely because of the skill with which it recalled familiar, everyday objects, but also because of its ability to summon the past—and not just any past, but the "right" one.

In this context, the "right" past was not necessarily the same as the "real" past, but instead the past as it was preferred. And that past need not be ancient and far away; it could be as recent and close at hand as a meerschaum pipe still smoldering, a German beer mug still cool to the touch. In other words, the close-at-hand items Harnett portrayed were in a sense nostalgic even if they were wholly contemporary, for in a fragmented and stressful world, the pipes, mugs, books, and fiddles bespoke calmer, less hurried times; times that might indeed have been experienced long ago but could just as well have been savored yesterday or today. Objects need not actually have been old to have conveyed a comforting sense of age and permanence; they need only to have appeared enduring and stable in contrast to the unsettling flux of the present.

As already noted, the desire to grab hold of a vanished or vanishing past appears to have been widespread in Harnett's day. Consider the tens of thousands of Americans, whether native-born or immigrant, who, in the decades after the Civil War, abandoned the country for the city, as does the boy in

Fig. 15. Thomas Hovenden, *Breaking Home Ties,* 1890. Oil on canvas, 52⅛ x 72¼ in.
Philadelphia Museum of Art, Given by Ellen Harrison McMichael in memory of C. Emory McMichael

Thomas Hovenden's *Breaking Home Ties* of 1890 (fig. 15), a painting that elicited extraordinarily sympathetic public response when it was exhibited at the Chicago fair. Undertaking forms of labor significantly different from those they had known before and struggling to learn new, unfamiliar urban folkways while unlearning the rural ones by which they had been raised, countless Americans experienced an enormous disruption of custom and dislocation from familiar ground. There was every reason, then, for these multitudes of refugees to modernity, that foreign country, to look yearningly upon the past from which they had become separated.

The need to maintain or revivify memory was thus not merely a private affair dependent upon careful devotion to a personally significant violin, rifle, or beer mug, but was instead a collective problem requiring solutions of a more public nature.[10] What has recently been called "the invention of tradition" dates from this period: national holidays were instituted, public memorials dedicated, family trees traced, and "traditional" ethnic costumes fabricated (for example, Scotch tartans were endowed with a made-up clan significance they never had before).[11] History museums were founded to provide "scientific knowledge" of the social and political past of various nations, while art museums, such as the Metropolitan Museum of Art, established in 1870, served up the past in aesthetic rather than sociological terms.[12] Modern methods of ethnography were developed with the intention not only of transcribing aboriginal customs before the aboriginal peoples became extinct but also of recording ethnic folkways—music, language, legends, dress—before they too were irretrievably forgotten.

This was a time of many marvels connected with mechanical reproduction of sorts. Alexander Graham Bell's telephone, able to reproduce the human voice with amazing fidelity, was introduced to the public at the Philadelphia Centennial Exposition in 1876. Thomas Alva Edison's phonograph, patented in 1877, not only reproduced the voice but also recorded it. George Eastman's dry-plate process, perfected in 1880, soon led to the invention of his popular amateur camera, the Kodak. In each of these instances, what seemed so wonderful was that physical reality could be reproduced in a manner that appeared immediate, free from interference or distortion.

Photography, almost from the start a transcriptive tool for historians and ethnographers, by late in the century became an easy, inexpensive way for tourists to attempt to preserve the present, be it some exotic social group and place or their own friends, families, and homes. One reason photographs seemed so unimpeachable as witnesses was that a mechanical apparatus, a machine, had produced them. Having no mind or emotions, no soul, this machine thereby appeared free of subjectivity: hence the complete "objectivity" of its transcriptions.

Harnett's trompe-l'oeil technique implied a similar degree of objectivity, since it too seemed less the product of the human hand than of a photographic machine. Its glossy, highly finished surfaces, its undetectable brushwork, its offhanded and apparently haphazard method of composition, and its various other suppressions of expressive ("artistic") style all contributed to what theorist Roland Barthes, referring to nineteenth-century French literature, has termed "the reality effect."[13]

Harnett was frequently applauded for his ability not only to reproduce physical reality but also to make it seem as though he had not done so. As an admirer marveled upon viewing *After the Hunt* of 1885 (pl. 34), "The wood *is* wood, the iron is iron, the brass is brass, the leather is leather. . . . We see not the artist nor his method of working. The things themselves only are seen."[14] No matter that the wood really was not wood, the iron not iron, the brass not brass; what counted was that Harnett was able to make his viewers *feel* as though they were seeing the real thing. Paradoxically, he and other trompe-l'oeil artists were praised for both their amazing "truthfulness" to physical reality and, at the same time, their artful sophistication in purveying so-called deceptions—persuasive falsifications of that reality.

Thus, Harnett's paintings invoked the premodern past using techniques associated with the wonders of modernity. Here was a case of having a cake and eating it too. Such was the impulse of the era, as reflected in other areas as well, among them the great world's fairs, which venerated the old while celebrating, and thus legitimizing, the new.[15] To millions of citizens across the land, a symbolic watershed in American history occurred in 1876, the year the mammoth Philadelphia Centennial Exposition glorified both the nation's past and its future. Visitors marveled at the fair's spectacular

Fig. 16. Theodore Russell Davis, "Our Centennial: President Grant and Dom Pedro Starting the Corliss Engine," *Harper's Weekly,* May 27, 1876, p. 421

exhibits of newly developed technological prowess but also at its quieter, museumlike displays of local and regional history.

William Dean Howells, reporting on the fair for *Atlantic Monthly,* was typical in his response in that he extolled both the magnificent, twenty-thousand-horsepower Corliss steam engine that generated electricity for the fair ("an athlete of steel and iron with not a superfluous ounce of metal on it") and an intimate, small-scale, living-history re-creation of domestic labor during the Colonial period (figs. 16, 17). When Howells noticed an elderly Quaker woman emerge from a crowd of visitors to "Ye Olden Time New England Kitchen" in order to demonstrate the way Colonial spinning wheels were actually meant to work, he found the sight "altogether the prettiest thing . . . at the Centennial."[16] However fascinating the complex new technology embodied by the Corliss engine, the older, simpler way of life evinced by this Quaker woman communicated a higher order of good. The new machines were miraculous, but without the human touch and self-effacing authority of the past, what lasting benefit could they truly provide?

Harnett's success with the public derived from the ability of his paintings to bridge that troublesome gap between old and new, agrarian and industrial, human and machine. For all the evident longing conveyed by his obsessive focus on well-worn remnants of the premodern past, the focus itself was achieved with the exceptionally high degree of calibration and impersonality associated with the latest in contemporary devices of mechanical transcription and reproduction.

Take *The Golden Horseshoe* of 1886 (pl. 40), for instance. Horseshoes were by no means obsolete or even old-fashioned in this era preceding the introduction of the horseless carriage. Nonetheless, the horseshoe Harnett depicted is old, worn out, and rusted, retired from duty and hung like a trophy or an amulet against the cracked and splintered planks of the side of a country barn. Even if horseshoes had a current role in modern 1880s urban society, *this* horseshoe was a reminder of rural traditions (upside-down horseshoes are folk symbols of good luck) and a more leisurely pace of life (the shoe, if not the horse that wore it, has been "put to pasture"). Although the objects within the painting signify the old and premodern, Harnett's incredibly precise rendering of them—his virtually microscopic attention to texture, his simulation in oil pigment of oxidized iron, curled paper, a pearl-headed pin, and weather-streaked house paint—is phenomenal, belonging more to the realm of machine than man. True, the artist signed the picture, thus claiming credit for his accomplishment, but by making his name appear carved into wood rather than painted upon canvas, he perpetuated the illusion of this being a "taken" rather than "made" picture (in a sense similar to what we mean when we say that cameras "take" or transcribe views of a preexisting reality rather than "make" or construct them).

Harnett's veneration of long-lived, man-made objects, such as books, violins, mugs, and horseshoes, suggested a former way of life that could usefully endure into the present, just as these objects themselves continued to endure. This concern for enfolding

Fig. 17. *New England Farmer's Home and Modern Kitchen at the Philadelphia Centennial Exposition*, 1876. Photograph, Centennial Photographic Co., Philadelphia. Free Library of Philadelphia

a reliable past into a less reliable present extended beyond the world of art, crossing even into the realm of the economy. In order for Americans to be induced to accelerate patterns of consumption as necessary to justify mass production and distribution, they needed to be convinced not only that buying as a way of life was desirable, but that it was also in line with earlier notions of proper conduct. At this time, age-old injunctions against "throwing away money" were strong indeed. Each act of spending was a morally weighted affair demanding caution and thoughtfulness, a clear-headed sense of responsibility. In the words of founding father Benjamin Franklin, "A penny saved is a penny earned." All the more so did this seem the case as the nation suffered a series of economic depressions during the closing decades of the century.

Given these circumstances, merchants with vision, such as John Wanamaker of Philadelphia and Richard Sears of Chicago, realized that encouraging people to spend was more than a matter of making them want what they saw. They needed to be assured that in consuming, they were still adhering to the traditional Franklinesque virtues of perspicacity, wisdom, and restraint. Wanamaker endlessly proclaimed to his customers the importance of caution and thrift—which, of course, was why they should frequent his establishment, which held such values dear.[17] Just as the Philadelphia Centennial Exposition, of which Wanamaker was an organizer, portrayed industrialism as the compatible outgrowth of old agrarian ways rather than their annulment, the new consumer economy he helped spawn also appealed to tradition for its legitimacy.

All of Wanamaker's sales innovations were thus aimed at assuaging consciences made uneasy by the insistence with which an ethos of spending was replacing that of saving. Inspired by the fair's enormous exhibition halls, which encouraged crowds to ogle items and artifacts gathered from the four corners of the earth, Wanamaker opened his "new kind of store" in an old train depot that had been cleared to make way for two acres of retail space containing

Fig. 18. *R. H. Macy's Department Store Food Counter, Herald Square,* 1902. Photograph.
Museum of the City of New York, The Byron Collection (231)

hundreds of display counters organized in concentric circles radiating from a central core. Such large-scale open display served the dual function of impressing shoppers with the dazzling abundance of goods and of making them feel immune to fraud by allowing them to inspect items closely and at their leisure. Wanamaker's advertising copy, departing from the hard-sell approach associated with bamboozling the public, was written in plain-spoken, everyday language. "No 'catchy headings,' no catches . . . no 'fine writing,'" was how his chief copywriter later described it.[18] In short, shopping at Wanamaker's was not threatening: everything appeared visible, straightforward, truthful. This new style of retailing offered modern, big-city enticements with all the safeguards—and then some—of shopping in traditional, small-town communities.

Harnett's paintings had something in common with the new methods of retailing. In their apparent eschewal of high style, they looked as plain and honest as the new advertising sounded. Not all of his paintings possessed this tone, for some aimed self-consciously at European sophistication, but the "no fine writing" approach is characteristic of popular works such as *The Golden Horseshoe, For Sunday's Dinner* of 1888 (pl. 42), which was actually displayed at Wanamaker's, and *The Faithful Colt* of 1890 (pl. 48). These paintings, like the new retailing, sought to transport old-style agrarian values into a new urban milieu. Moreover, by definition, still-life paintings arranged objects in a manner calculated to please or entice. Their job, in other words, was to put items on display. By doing so in an aesthetically compelling manner, they breathed life into lifeless objects, investing them with magic and wonder—which was, similarly, a goal of the retailer.

Even so, Harnett's still-life arrangements do not resemble late-nineteenth-century merchandise counters and shop windows, as seen in photographs. Inside the emporia, counters are piled high with products stacked in pyramids and towers, the fastidious symmetry indicating the management's laudable attention to organization and detail (fig. 18). The windows are packed with goods from top to bottom and side to side, as if empty space might connote to shoppers an ill-stocked establishment (fig. 19). As L. Frank Baum, inventor of the wonderous land of Oz, advised retailers in his *Art of Decorating Dry Goods Windows and Interiors,* "Many things are to be considered. There are the technicalities to be learned, judgment and good taste to be exercised, color harmony to be secured: and, above all, there must be positive knowledge as to what constitutes an attractive exhibit, and what will arouse in the observer cupidity and a longing to possess the goods you offer for sale."[19]

What a contrast to the wholesaler's world depicted in Harnett's *Job Lot Cheap* of 1878 (pl. 9), where the arrangement of goods seems so casual, even careless.

Fig. 19. *Norman M. Kerr & Co.: Paper Boxes.* Albumen silver print. In Wenderoth, Taylor & Brown, *Gallery of Arts and Manufactures of Philadelphia,* 1871. Library Company of Philadelphia

Worn leather volumes, their forms and textures carefully delineated, jostle one another in precarious stacks on a rude wooden shelf adorned by faded or torn advertising labels—the two that are readable, *Job Lot Cheap* and *Just Publishe[d]*, functioning ironically, for clearly these are not new but old books containing old wisdom that goes, alas, for cheap in a modern era unable to assess wisdom's true worth. The painting was purchased by Byron Nugent, a dry-goods merchant from Saint Louis. Perhaps Nugent admired the work because, even if its subject was musty old objects, it had the look—thanks to Harnett's glossy, invisible brushwork—of an object good as new.

Harnett's paintings were not, after all, old. They did not originate in some agrarian, republican, good old days but were instead products of the urban industrial scene. Painted in Philadelphia, Munich, and New York, exhibited at trade fairs, sold at auctions, and hung in hotel lobbies, offices, department stores, and drinking establishments, they were modern-day commodities, regardless of the precommodity artifacts and eras they so appealingly invoke. For all their apparent veneration of the past, Harnett's paintings seem peculiarly new, what with their shiny, touched-up, high-finish look. The old objects they depict may have movingly implied to viewers a personal history of makers and users who were linked by communal ties or across generations (as Shimerda's violin linked him to Bohemia, or Walker's hatchet connected him to his son). But regardless of the superlative craftsmanship with which Harnett produced his paintings, and regardless of the craftsmanship that is their implied subject, these works originated in and circulated through the impersonal marketplace instead of being anchored to the communal systems they celebrate and to which the artist may or may not have belonged.

The paintings are like commodities in still another manner. Commodities promise to deliver social benefits and improved social relationships for a monetary price. They offer the consumer happiness and well-being for an over-the-counter cost. They purport to provide instant, or relatively instant, satisfactions that in earlier eras most people assumed could be achieved only by means of hard work, if even then. To the extent that Harnett's paintings seemed able—for the price of purchase or admission—to put viewers back in touch with a vanishing past that they were loathe to see disappear, they functioned as commodities. Retrieving the past is never simply a matter of a purchase, even when the item purchased is intended, in all sincerity, as a tribute to that past. The notion that a commodity can make up for lost values and communal relationships may be the greatest illusion of all.

Yet it would be wrong to conclude that Harnett's paintings were meant in bad faith or that, even if well intended, their ultimate effect was to promote commodification rather than resist, or at least soften, its depredations. Here, again, we might look to Harnett's contemporary John Wanamaker, who in old age recalled aspects of his own past with immense nostalgia. "Sitting in my mother's old armchair . . . I seem to lose myself in the flood of memories, and to feel that the arms of the chair have loosed themselves to become my very own mother's arms around me again."[20] Privileged, esteemed, remarkably successful, Wanamaker—unlike Shimerda or Walker—had no obvious reason to invest an ordinary old object with extraordinary powers for recuperating the past. That he did so, that perhaps all of us are inclined to do so, suggests that in modernity the cultural need to retain old value systems is so pressing that no one, regardless of rank, is immune. A century after they were painted, Harnett's trompe-l'oeil still lifes continue to address this need. Whether their meticulous illusions of old objects serve to distance us further from the past or instead genuinely bring us closer to a world that has been lost, there is more to these paintings than meets the eye.

NOTES

▼

1. "Painted Like Real Things: The Man Whose Pictures Are a Wonder and a Puzzle," interview in *New York News,* probably 1889 or 1890, quoted in Alfred Frankenstein, *After the Hunt: William Harnett and Other American Still Life Painters, 1870–1900,* rev. ed. (Berkeley and Los Angeles: University of California Press, 1969), p. 55.

2. On the "White City," see Alan Trachtenberg, *The Incorporation of America: Culture and Society in the Gilded Age* (New York: Hill & Wang, 1982), pp. 208–34.

3. Fred Davis, *Yearning for Yesterday: A Sociology of Nostalgia* (New York: Free Press, 1979), pp. 1–29.

4. David Lowenthal, *The Past Is a Foreign Country* (Cambridge, New York, and Melbourne: Cambridge University Press, 1985), p. xvi.

5. L. P. Hartley, *The Go-Between* (New York: Stein & Day, 1953), p. 3.

6. Willa Cather, "Peter," in *Early Stories of Willa Cather* (New York: Dodd, Mead, 1957), pp. 1–8. "Peter" first appeared in *The Mahogany Tree,* May 21, 1892, and then in the University of Nebraska *Hesperian,* November 24, 1892.

7. Willa Cather, *My Ántonia* (Boston: Houghton Mifflin Co., 1954), p. 89.

8. Walker to Harnett, September 16, 1887, quoted in Frankenstein, *After the Hunt,* p. 86.

9. "Painted Like Real Things," quoted in ibid., pp. 29, 55.

10. See George Lipsitz, *Time Passages: Collective Memory and American Popular Culture* (Minneapolis: University of Minnesota Press, 1990).

11. See Eric Hobsbawm and Terence Ranger, eds., *The Invention of Tradition* (Cambridge and New York: Cambridge University Press, 1983), especially pp. 1–41.

12. See Lawrence W. Levine, *Highbrow/Lowbrow: The Emergence of Cultural Hierarchy in America* (Cambridge, Mass., and London: Harvard University Press, 1988), pp. 146–55.

13. See Roland Barthes, "The Reality Effect," in *The Rustle of Language,* trans. Richard Howard (New York: Hill & Wang, 1986), pp. 141–48.

14. "Queer Art Illusions: Some of the Many Methods Employed to Produce Them," clipping from an unidentified and undated newspaper, Blemly scrapbook, Alfred Frankenstein Papers, Archives of American Art, Smithsonian Institution, Washington, D.C., microfilm, roll 1374, frame 327.

15. As cultural critic Walter Benjamin acidly observed, "World exhibitions are the sites of pilgrimages to the commodity fetish" (*Reflections: Essays, Aphorisms, Autobiographical Writings,* ed. Peter Demetz and trans. Edmund Jephcott [New York and London: Harcourt Brace Jovanovich, 1978], p. 151). See also Neil Harris, "Museums, Merchandising, and Popular Taste: The Struggle for Influence," in *Material Culture and the Study of American Life,* ed. Ian M. G. Quimby (New York: W. W. Norton & Co., 1978), pp. 140–74.

16. William Dean Howells, "A Sennight of the Centennial," *Atlantic Monthly* 38 (July 1876), pp. 92–107.

17. Joseph H. Appel, *The Business Biography of John Wanamaker, Founder and Builder: America's Merchant Pioneer from 1861 to 1922* (New York: MacMillan Co., 1930); and Herbert Adams Gibbons, *John Wanamaker,* 2 vols. (New York and London: Harper & Bros., 1926). See also *Golden Book of the Wanamaker Stores: Jubilee Year, 1861–1911* ([Philadelphia]: John Wanamaker, 1911).

18. John E. Powers in *Printers' Ink,* October 23, 1895, quoted in Stephen Fox, *The Mirror Makers: A History of American Advertising and Its Creators* (New York: William Morrow & Co., 1984), p. 26.

19. L. Frank Baum, *The Art of Decorating Dry Goods Windows and Interiors* (Chicago: Show Window Publishing, 1900), p. 8. See also Stuart Culver, "What Manikins Want: *The Wonderful Wizard of Oz* and *The Art of Decorating Dry Goods Windows,*" *Representations* 21 (Winter 1988), pp. 97–116.

20. Quoted in Appel, *Business Biography,* p. 10.

A Study in Contrasts

The Work of Harnett and La Farge

HENRY ADAMS

The work of William Michael Harnett and John La Farge (1835–1910) could hardly be more different, as a glance at a painting by each of them makes clear.[1] Compare, for example, the most famous still life of each artist, Harnett's *After the Hunt* of 1885 and La Farge's *Wreath* of 1861 (fig. 20, pl. 34). The Harnett is crisply realistic. Its surface is smooth, almost as if it were untouched by human hands, and its subject matter—dead game—evokes masculine pursuits. In contrast, the La Farge is blurred, out of focus. The rich texture of its brushwork plays an important expressive role, and its subject matter—flowers—brings to mind the world of feminine activities and feelings.

Essentially, the works stand at opposite poles of American still-life painting; the artists represent opposite tendencies. Curiously, the significance of these oppositions has never been explored. This essay will examine the general pattern these contrasts form and will work toward a deeper understanding of both artists.[2]

Harnett and La Farge were both still-life painters, were contemporaries, and spent a good part of their lives working in the same city. Moreover, the two stand out as figures of extraordinary significance, both for the quality of their work and for its influence. Harnett carried meticulous realism to a degree unknown before and initiated an entire school of trompe-l'oeil painting. La Farge was the first American to create still life in a painterly mode. In demonstrating the expressive potential of free brushwork, he opened the way for a group of later figures, including Emil Carlsen and William Merritt Chase. In the latter half of the nineteenth century, American still-life painting was divided between artists who worked in a meticulous style and those who favored free brushwork. By comparing and contrasting the work of Harnett and La Farge, we move toward a general understanding of what this stylistic split signified.

Fig. 20. John La Farge, *Agathon to Erosanthe, A Love Wreath,* 1861. Oil on canvas, 22 x 12½ in. Private collection

---

Harnett and La Farge were both Roman Catholics from a class of recent immigrants rather than of old Anglo-Saxon, Protestant stock. Of equal significance, the work of each exhibits a somberness of mood that was new to American still-life painting though characteristic of a general shift of sensibility in American art in the decades following the Civil War. Both explored themes of mutability—Harnett through vanitas compositions of the seventeenth-century Dutch type, and La Farge in his favorite subject, the fading bouquet of flowers, often accompanied by a fallen or falling blossom.

These similarities, however, are of a relatively general nature. On the whole, the most striking thing about these two figures is the degree of difference between them, beginning with their social backgrounds. Harnett's family was extremely poor. As a child, he was obliged to leave school to help support them, first by running errands and selling newspapers. At age seventeen, he was apprenticed to the engraver's trade and turned to painting shortly afterward. Throughout his life, Harnett worked long

hours and lived very modestly. In an interview at the peak of his career, he spoke of his life as if it were a Horatio Alger story in which hard work triumphed over poverty. A central theme of his conversation was the "hard work" that was "necessary for a friendless boy."[3]

In contrast, La Farge's family provided him with both wealth and social connections. His father had built a substantial fortune in shipping, real estate, hotels, and fire insurance; his mother came from an aristocratic family that had fled from France during the Revolution. La Farge was famously extravagant; sometimes he kept taxis waiting while he painted.[4] Once his reputation was established, he sold his work for fabulous sums, but nonetheless he died deeply in debt.[5] His ventures in still-life painting would have been impossible without his inheritance, for he sold almost nothing during the first decade of his career.

The contrast in the backgrounds of the two artists was reflected in their acquaintances. We get a sense of Harnett's social milieu from the people who participated in his funeral: A. A. Ryan, an undertaker; James McCloskey, a house painter; Cornelius Sheehan, a plumber; and William Ignatius Blemly, a silver chaser and designer. La Farge, on the other hand, counted among his friends the social and intellectual elite of America. He was on friendly terms with presidents William McKinley and Theodore Roosevelt, and he belonged to the most exclusive New York clubs.[6] His close friends included John Hay, the secretary of state; Richard Watson Gilder, editor of *Century Magazine*; the novelist Henry James; the sculptor Augustus Saint-Gaudens; and the Japanese writer and art expert Okakura Kakuzo. With some notable exceptions, such as the painter Winslow Homer, there was often a touch of preciousness to La Farge's acquaintances.

This contrast in social milieu was reflected in the life-styles and working habits of the two men. Harnett dressed in a manner that was stiffly formal but far from stylish (fig. 21); one of his friends, the sculptor James Edward Kelly, once commented on the old-fashioned cut of his "funereal Prince Albert."[7] La Farge, on the other hand, was noted for his refinement of dress, which often reflected the latest styles from Paris; he carried himself with the assurance of a true dandy (fig. 22).

Harnett worked in modest studios that were no more than workrooms. Kelly recalled visiting one studio that was "just large enough for an easel, cot, and chair, and had a poor light; squalid surroundings, and the smallest, coolest cook stove in the city."[8] La Farge, in contrast, was a tenant in Richard Morris Hunt's Tenth Street Studio Building, which contained the first studios in America specifically designed to be used by artists. La Farge's atelier was not simply a workplace but an aesthetic sanctuary, an environment markedly different from the world of commerce outside. It was

Fig. 21. *William M. Harnett.* Photograph, Meynen & Co., Philadelphia. Blemly Family Collection

Fig. 22. *John La Farge, Seated in Profile,* ca. 1885.
Photograph. Yale University Art Gallery,
New Haven, Gift of Frances S. Childs
in memory of Henry A. La Farge

filled with prints and portfolios, Oriental paintings and textiles, stuffed peacocks, Polynesian war clubs, and other unusual items of rarity, interest, or beauty.[9]

Harnett produced paintings in a manner reminiscent of a professional craftsman, while La Farge always retained a touch of the amateur and dilettante. Unfortunately, little is recorded of Harnett's working methods, but both his own statements and those of his critics continually stress his hard work. It is tempting to suppose that he learned his work habits during his stint as an engraver and put in an eight- or ten-hour day intently bent over his canvases. We know, for example, that he completed his most ambitious canvas, *After the Hunt,* in a mere three months,[10] which would have been possible only if he had worked long hours each day and been extremely adept at his craft. A visitor

to Harnett's studio recorded that the artist had only one painting on hand at the time,[11] and at his death his estate contained only "five paintings of uncertain value."[12]

La Farge, on the other hand, seems to have alternated between leisurely procrastination and periods of intense activity. When he was caught up in a project, he often lost all sense of time; he occasionally worked on his flower paintings late into the night and early morning, in hope of completing them before the color on the actual petals changed. Unlike Harnett, La Farge worked on several projects simultaneously and accumulated large numbers of tentative studies and sketches. He is recorded to have destroyed fifty thousand drawings in a single year; yet at the time of his death his studio was cluttered with hundreds of paintings, stained-glass windows, and plaster reliefs as well as sixteen large portfolios of drawings and dozens of sketches, many unfinished.[13] La Farge worked on projects fitfully and erratically, often abandoning a work for years or even decades and then returning to it.

Harnett was a steady worker. Nearly 250 of his still-life paintings are extant, an impressive number given that his career lasted only seventeen years. Moreover, the high quality of his craftsmanship seldom slipped. La Farge, on the other hand, often worked quickly but produced a surprisingly small and uneven body of still life. To some extent, of course, the limited number of such paintings reflects his ventures into other avenues of expression, but even in the 1860s, when he concentrated primarily on still-life subjects, he produced a remarkably small number of finished canvases. Only about three dozen of his still-life paintings can now be located, and this includes several unfinished works as well as others that hardly show his artistic skill in a positive light. La Farge's fame as a still-life painter seems to rest almost entirely on the startling originality of four or five of his best pictures.

Both Harnett and La Farge were extremely myopic, but they responded to the condition in opposite ways: Harnett by moving close to the canvas and his subject and rendering microscopic detail; La Farge by standing back from both and re-creating the effect of visual blur.[14] Admirers—and even detractors—of Harnett's work have always marveled at the perfection of his craftsmanship, especially his skill in rendering detail. In 1884, a critic wrote of one of Harnett's works, "There is not a tiny splinter, not a nailhead, nothing that is not depicted to perfection, so that one does not know which to admire more—the artist's gigantic patience or his astonishing powers of observation and imitation."[15] As this suggests, Harnett was admired for his hard work, his perfectionism, and the cleverness of his pictorial illusions. At the same time, his execution was so perfect and unvarying that it seemed machine-like to some nineteenth-century writers. One critic complained that Harnett's paintings were not truly artistic: "Only time and industry are necessary to the indefinite multiplication of them."[16]

Unlike Harnett, La Farge had no interest in detail—"He thinks detail is a bore"[17]—and he often rendered objects out of focus. As we can see in *Wreath*, the edges of shapes are almost never sharp and clean but blend into one another in a variety of complex ways. As with Harnett, La Farge's style has been evaluated both positively and negatively. His fluent brushwork has been viewed both as richly expressive and as careless; as highly individual and as lacking in clear direction or focus. The emotional, intuitive qualities associated with his work, however, clearly stand at the opposite pole from the machinelike qualities associated with Harnett's.

Harnett participated irregularly in the established art exhibitions of his day, and his work was seldom reviewed in the art magazines. On several occasions, he exhibited his paintings in store windows for immediate sale, and he also sent them to industrial expositions. To an unusual degree, Harnett's pictures were purchased for commercial settings, such as hotel lobbies, drugstores, and saloons. The great breakthrough in his career occurred when Theodore Stewart purchased an *After the Hunt* for his popular New York saloon on Warren Street.

La Farge exhibited frequently at artistic societies, both in Boston and New York, but he preferred to show his work in controlled and intimate circumstances, to only one or two people at a time. As Royal Cortissoz noted, "If he wanted to show you a picture in his studio he would make sure of the hour of the day providing just the right light or he would not show it at all."[18] Until 1879, twenty years into his professional career, La Farge could boast that he had never sold a painting from an exhibition. He also scrupulously avoided displaying his work in shop windows or other business settings.

Not surprisingly, both Harnett and La Farge came from the same social class as their patrons. Harnett's clients, while often men of substantial wealth, were mainly figures who had risen, as he had, from rather modest cultural surroundings. They generally did not come from aristocratic families and had not attended Ivy League schools. Their artistic taste tended to be extremely conservative. On the whole, their forte was mechanical ingenuity and hard work.

La Farge's paintings did not appeal to businessmen as much as they did to a more sophisticated audience. He sold his early work slowly and with difficulty, mainly within a limited circle of Boston families that were linked through marriage and social connections. Most of these figures had attended Harvard, and they often had arcane intellectual interests of their own, as was the case, for example, with historian Henry Adams, who published, at his own expense, long books on obscure topics, or William Sturgis Bigelow, who went to Japan to study Buddhism.

Fig. 23. Photograph of William M. Harnett's *Thieves in the Pantry*, 1879.
In Alfred Frankenstein, *After the Hunt: William M. Harnett and Other American Still-Life Painters, 1870–1900*, rev. ed. (Berkeley and Los Angeles: University of California Press, 1969), pl. 33, copyright © 1953, 1969, 1982 Alfred Frankenstein

By the end of his career, Harnett sold his paintings for relatively high prices; nonetheless, those magazines devoted exclusively to artistic matters paid little attention to his work. The press coverage he did receive was in daily newspapers and business journals, and these notices tended to bypass aesthetic considerations and report instead on matters of human interest.

The quantity of writing devoted to La Farge's paintings, while not always favorable in tone, seems out of proportion with their number and importance. Many complex factors contributed to this phenomenon, but the central issue was simply that his pictures are filled with unusual features that made them stand out from the crowd: free brushwork, peculiar and delicate colors, unusual subject matter, and odd, often unbalanced compositional arrangements. Whether critics effusively admired or disliked La Farge's choices, he provided them with issues to discuss.

So far, the contrasts we have noted between Harnett and La Farge are persuasive but not particularly surprising. Not all the differences between them, however, are quite so straightforward. To the Victorians, the distinction between work and leisure was endowed with sexual, moral, and spiritual implications. Men were to spend their time in the workplace earning money, and their identities were defined by activities connected with this role. Women were to rule the home and be concerned with family. Thus, work was associated with men and the business world; leisure, with women and the domestic realm. Things that were strong, hard, and utilitarian were associated with men; things that were delicate, soft, and merely beautiful, with women. The male world was seen as realistic; the female world, as spiritual. The genius of both Harnett and La Farge was to recognize that this key element of social patterning could be expressed metaphorically in the realm of still life with considerable expressive complexity.[19]

As one might expect from his affiliations with the business world, Harnett stands out among American still-life painters for his extraordinary emphasis on man-made objects. He turned to fruit subjects only sporadically during his career; when flowers appear in his compositions, they play a secondary role. Except for some nibbling mice in the lost *Thieves in the Pantry* of 1879 (fig. 23), only dead animals appear in his work, hanging as trophies along with old weapons and other paraphernalia. Thus, they are no longer part of animate nature but have been transformed into a consumable item, something that can be sold or displayed. A contemporary critic complained that Harnett "ought to give wider scope to abilities so genuine and play upon living, breathing subjects."[20]

With the exception of a single early work, in his oil paintings La Farge usually avoided images of food and of glassware, silver, bric-a-brac, and other man-made materials. He was remarkable for his unprec-

Fig. 24. John La Farge, *Flowers on a Window Ledge,* ca. 1862. Oil on canvas, 24 x 20 in. The Corcoran Gallery of Art, Washington, D.C., Museum Purchase, Anna E. Clark Fund

edented interest in plants; moreover, in his depictions of them, he favored flowers over edible fruit or vegetables, thus indicating his interest in nature for its own sake, for its beauty alone, apart from material considerations of cost or usefulness. His work progressed from flowers placed in man-made vessels toward flowers growing naturally, outdoors. While Harnett tended to favor the arena of commerce, La Farge consistently avoided it.

Harnett preferred masculine subject matter. He painted beer steins, pipes, tobacco, guns, dead game, horseshoes, and weathered barn doors—objects that intimate masculine activities. His rack paintings specifically allude to the male business world and contain no references to women.[21] To Victorians, Harnett's paintings of money also suggested the male domain, since handling money and managing financial matters were male prerogatives.

La Farge, on the other hand, stayed away from such emblems of masculinity and concentrated almost exclusively on flowers (figs. 24, 25). In the nineteenth century, flowers were a means by which women asserted their dominion over the home. Between 1830

Fig. 25. John La Farge, *Vase of Flowers,* 1864.
Oil on wood, 18½ x 14 in. Museum of Fine Arts, Boston,
Gift of Louise W. and Marian R. Chase

Those who have praised Harnett have generally concentrated on form, a "masculine" quality; those who have praised La Farge have focused on color, a "feminine" one.

Most nineteenth-century reviewers not only read masculine and feminine traits into the work of Harnett and La Farge but also evaluated these traits in relation to moral and religious qualities. They tended to link Harnett's work with materialism and worldly deception. Thus, the Reverend Frederick Taylor Gates denounced *The Old Violin* of 1886 (pl. 37) as "low and selfish,"[22] while the painter George Inness complained that *After the Hunt* was "a lie."[23]

La Farge's work, on the other hand, was associated with spiritual truth. James Jackson Jarves wrote, "A flower painted by [La Farge] bears the same relation to the real plant that an angel of Fra Angelico does to the actual man. It is an exhibition of its highest possibilities of being rather than of its present material organization."[24] And S. G. W. Benjamin commented that La Farge was "less concerned with the external than with the hidden meaning it has for the soul."[25]

Thus, the work of Harnett and La Farge expressed the cultural values of two distinct nineteenth-century social domains. Harnett's oeuvre might be described as working class, methodical, businesslike, hard-edged, somber in color, masculine, realistic, and worldly; La Farge's, as aristocratic, intuitive, impractical, soft-edged, richly colored, natural, feminine, idealizing, and spiritual. These contrasts form a pattern that is remarkably consistent, whether we apply it to the work of art, the artist, or his patrons. We do not find modes of expression that cross boundaries, that significantly diverge from the general pattern. Harnett's hard-edged realism, for instance, conceivably could have been used to represent feminine subject matter—flowers, for example, or the contents of a woman's sewing basket. Yet, with very few exceptions, both Harnett and his followers rigorously avoided anything feminine and consistently chose subjects with masculine connotations. La Farge's soft-edged style, by the same logic, could have been used to record dead rabbits and six-shooters. Yet, with equal regularity, he avoided such masculine motifs and focused on the world of women. In short, all the contrasts we have pointed out seem to be based on an unconscious infrastructure, not unlike the grammatical rules of a language.

Significantly, once we understand this overall structure of contrasts, our understanding of the work of both artists is enriched, for it enables us to recognize faint or subliminal messages that otherwise would remain hidden. For example, how can our knowledge of this structure of contrasts add to our understanding of Harnett's *After the Hunt* and La Farge's *Wreath*? Let us begin by considering the subject matter and its associations, and then the formal means of expression.

and 1860, dozens of books on the symbolism of flowers, many of them written by women, were published for a female audience. Arranging flowers was an important female occupation, and the artists who specialized in flower paintings were almost invariably female amateurs—Winslow Homer's mother, for example. Among male American artists, La Farge was a leader in concentrating on such subject matter. Rather than seeking to avoid the feminine associations of the genre, he emphasized the aspects that made it seem distinctly feminine: the beauty, softness, and fragility of flowers.

The sexual implications of the subject matter of Harnett and La Farge extend to their manner of execution as well. Harnett's style has often been described as masculine, for it is clear and crisp, and he showed a particular affinity for hard textures. He was fond of cool color harmonies and of the cold sheen of metal. La Farge's style has often been seen as feminine, for it is soft and blurry; he was attracted to soft materials, and his paintings are warm in feeling.

What do the two paintings depict? *After the Hunt* shows dead game, hunting implements, and alpine gear hanging on a weathered barn door, along with a horseshoe (a symbol of good luck) and a large key. *Wreath* shows a single circle of flowers placed on an abutment projecting from a textured stucco wall. Inscribed in red below the wreath is the ancient Greek for "Beautiful Erosanthe," and the painting is signed *Agathon*. The subject alludes to the ancient Greek custom of placing a wreath of flowers against the door of the person one loves as a form of marriage proposal.

The objects in Harnett's painting imply primarily masculine activities, many of them rather violent, such as shooting, stabbing, and drinking, as well as unlocking a door and blowing a horn. Most of these activities commonly appear in language as veiled metaphors for business affairs. In fact, Harnett has provided us with a series of visual puns. Business deals are often described with phrases borrowed from warfare, as, for example, "Let's kill the competition!" For the businessman, a sword comes in handy if he has been "stabbed in the back"; a key is useful in looking for "the key to

Fig. 26. William M. Harnett, *After the Hunt* (detail, pl. 34)

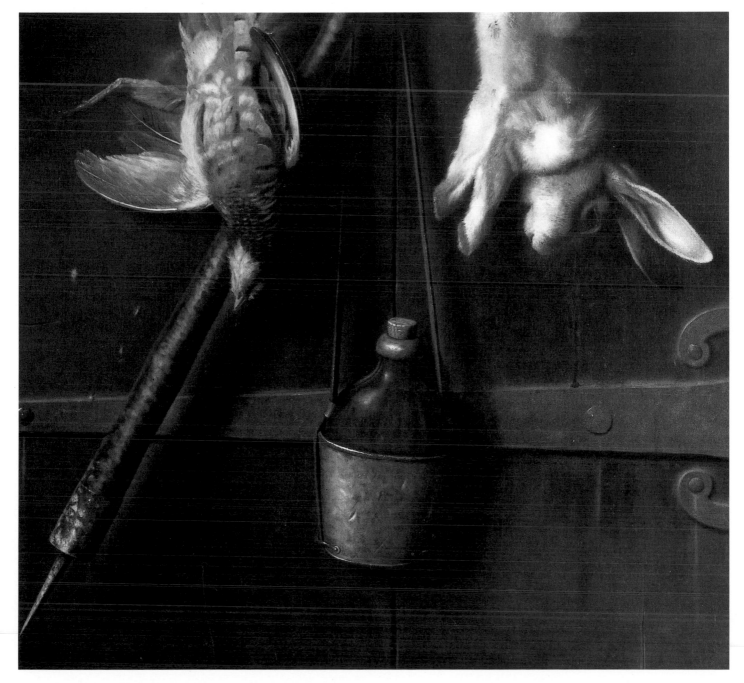

understanding the problem"; a jug is nice to brace his spirits and because being able to hold his liquor provides proof of manhood; an alpenstock will help him in "scaling ever greater heights"; and a horn is necessary because he should be good at "blowing his own horn."[26] In short, in a variety of ways, Harnett's painting suggests a train of associations that lead us toward the competitive business world and its activities.

La Farge's picture brings to mind activities of a very different type. The objects suggest plucking flowers, weaving a wreath, and writing amorous thoughts. The intertwined pattern of the leaves and flowers suggests a pattern of interwoven affections. Perhaps the graffiti provide a hint of social delinquency (reminding us that love, when it is intense, can be a form of madness); but on the whole, these activities are gentle and rather feminine, certainly very different from the murder and mayhem evoked by Harnett. Like Harnett's painting, *Wreath* contains wordplay but of a different import. Perhaps La Farge put the inscription in red to suggest that he was recording a "red-letter day." The name of the beloved, Erosanthe, combines the words *eros,* Greek for "love," and *anthe,* Greek for "flower." Thus, the words *beautiful, love,* and *flower* are blurred together in a kind of distillation of the message of the painting, which speaks of a world from which business affairs have been excluded: the world of love, of women, and of the home.

According to the nineteenth-century viewpoint, logic was an attribute of the male business world; intuition, of the female domestic realm. Thus, in Harnett's painting there is an insistent realism and an emphasis on the structural logic of physical relationships, whereas in La Farge's work there is an emphasis on the overall impression and its emotional influence. Formal elements, such as light and gravity, are consistently employed in a way that articulates these distinctions.

Harnett and La Farge handle light very differently. In *After the Hunt,* the harsh light fully discloses the forms. In contrast, light and dark play over the objects in *Wreath* more irrationally; areas of darkness eat away at forms like acid, or blushes of light from an invisible source suddenly cast them in a spiritual glow. At times, the lighting seems to transcend the laws of physics, since the glow appears to bloom from within the objects. Evidently, the clarity of the light in Harnett's painting serves as a model for mental clarity, since logical thinking is "clear," while the indistinctness of form in La Farge's work serves as a metaphor for the turbulence of emotion and inner feeling. In symbolic terms, Harnett's light plays a factual role and stands for mental control over physical reality. In La Farge's painting, light takes on a spiritual dimension, representing emotion, vitality, and truth, while darkness embodies death.

Harnett and La Farge also handle gravity in different ways. In Harnett's paintings, objects often rest precariously on the edge of a table or hang from a wall, pushing against one another. (The calibration of risk plays a key role in the business world, of course.) Harnett worked out his system of balances so persuasively that few viewers have noted the occasional impossibilities in his paintings, such as the alpenstock in *After the Hunt* that hangs from nothing and simply floats miraculously in the air. Indeed, the complex balance of forces and movements in Harnett's work is analogous to the mechanical forces that we admire in a machine. Harnett's painting style changed little; the chief progression, a gradual shift from small horizontal paintings to much larger vertical ones, served chiefly to emphasize the play of gravity.

Gravity plays a role in La Farge's work as well, but it tends to pull against living objects rather than inanimate ones. We do not find an elaborate play of diagonal forces or mechanical movements, for the physical collisions of daily life do not interest him. For La Farge, objects behave in a vaporous fashion, with a minimum of physical contact, in keeping with his desire to express their *pneumos*—that is to say, their "soul" or "breath." Thus, for La Farge, gravity forms a hierarchy of spiritual values: life and the soul press upward toward the sun; death pulls all things downward. In *Wreath,* gravity is hardly present in the physical sense, for the object floats weightlessly against the wall without visible connection, and its endless rhythm of circulating motion forms a mandala—a shape that, as Carl Jung noted, is often endowed with religious significance and symbolizes harmony, completeness, and union with the divine. Nothing distracts us from looking at the wreath of living flowers, and the center of attention in the painting is not a physical thing but the empty heart of this wreath, which glows with a mysterious luminosity. The painting directs us not toward the physical world but toward the spiritual. In short, Harnett creates a world of physics and fact; La Farge, one of feeling and soul.

Significantly, the general pattern of sexual and economic metaphors that runs through the work of Harnett and La Farge defines not only how their paintings "look"—their subject matter and their formal attributes—but also the process by which they were made and should be experienced. The act of creating these paintings relied on categorically distinct skills, linked with their respective compartments of experience. Harnett's meticulous realism, which shows every object in exactly the same way, presents us with a mechanically repeated operation, like those on which nineteenth-century industry was based. La Farge, on the other hand, painted every sector of his canvases with brushwork of a different rhythm and character, and he presents us with a technique that is intuitive, unpredictable, and calibrated to each nuance of subjective experience.

In examining these very different works, the spectator relies upon qualities from his own experience that are as distinct as the processes that went into making the paintings themselves. Harnett calls upon our logical skills and invites us to appraise his pictures as objects; in a manner similar to a business transaction, we gauge their reality, their age and degree of repair, their adherence to the rules of physics, how expensive they would be to purchase, and the amount of labor the painter put into creating them—that is, the investment that went into making them. La Farge's art, in contrast, calls upon feminine considerations of empathy and emotional sympathy. We are asked, for example, to distinguish a living blossom from a fading one or to appraise how much longer a bouquet will bloom before it fades. We wonder how intense the feelings were that generated the work.

Since art is inherently deceptive, it follows that a painting carries two kinds of metaphors: those that come from viewing the objects in it as real, and those that come from recognizing them as fictitious. On one hand, we can pretend that Harnett was painting actual objects and evaluate these objects in a businesslike fashion. If, on the other hand, we recognize his act of deception, then we are confronted with a somewhat different issue—the difference between true and false. Indeed, early accounts of Harnett's work describe not only the skill of his deception but also the manner in which specific classes of business people responded to it, with particular words of praise for the urban businessman.

The deceptiveness of Harnett's paintings produced an ethical problem not unlike that of trickery in financial dealings. The most frequently discussed episode of his career, his near arrest for counterfeiting currency, raised just this ethical question. The notion that Harnett's deception was not dishonest but was instead a form of "honest counterfeiting" suggests the fine line that could be drawn, and often was drawn, between successful business tactics and actual crime. Indeed, it provides a most intriguing summary of nineteenth-century business ethics.

In La Farge's work, of course, the same duality inherent in representation is played out in a very different fashion. No one would ever confuse La Farge's paintings with reality; their ostentatious brushwork calls attention to their falseness. Yet this falseness, like Harnett's reality, cloaks its opposite, since it serves to represent a deeper emotional and spiritual truth that would not be so apparent if the work had actually deceived us. For example, because we can read La Farge's brushstrokes as gestures that emanate directly from the artist's hand, we can interpret their nuances of emotional expression. La Farge's work thus expresses what many critics have considered the highest form of artistic truth: he was true to himself and the nature of his most intimate feelings.

Today, of course, we no longer immediately recognize some of the cultural cues in Harnett's and La Farge's paintings, which were filled with meaning for their contemporaries. While La Farge was regarded during his lifetime as extraordinarily innovative and modern, to the eye of the 1930s viewer his work began to seem Victorian. Many of the conceptual terms necessary to appreciate his work fully—terms such as *beauty, soul,* and *ideal,* which had definite meanings for his nineteenth-century audience—ceased to be clear or acceptable terms of art criticism after the modern "revolution." Thus, La Farge's work was stripped of much of its metaphysical force and left to stand on considerably more humble formal merits.

By the same token, Harnett's rediscovery and elevation to the rank of a major American artist was largely due to viewers no longer associating his paintings with vulgar businessmen and barroom settings and looking at his compositions afresh, in purely formal terms.[27] To a great extent, our appreciation of the work of Harnett depends not only upon our appreciation of its technical qualities but on our historical distance from the social class and types of settings with which it once was associated.

Notes

▼

1. The chief source of information on Harnett is Alfred Frankenstein, *After the Hunt: William Harnett and Other American Still Life Painters, 1870–1900,* rev. ed. (Berkeley and Los Angeles: University of California Press, 1969). For La Farge, see Kathleen A. Foster, "The Still-Life Paintings of John La Farge," *American Art Journal* 11, no. 3 (Summer 1979), pp. 4–37; and Henry Adams et al., *John La Farge,* exhib. cat., The Carnegie Museum of Art, Pittsburgh, and National Museum of American Art, Washington, D.C. (New York: Abbeville Press, 1987).

2. My approach in this essay was suggested by two works by Claude Lévi-Strauss: *Totemism,* 2nd ed., trans. Rodney Needham (Boston: Beacon Press, 1963); and "The Structural Study of Myth," in *Structural Anthropology,* trans. Claire Jacobson and Brooke Grundfest Schoepf (Garden City, N.Y.: Doubleday & Co., 1967), pp. 202–28.

3. "Painted Like Real Things: The Man Whose Pictures Are a Wonder and a Puzzle," interview in *New York News,* probably 1889 or 1890, quoted in Frankenstein, *After the Hunt,* p. 55.

4. Mabel La Farge, "John La Farge: The Artist," *Commonweal* 22 (May 3, 1935), pp. 7–10.

5. James L. Yarnall, "John La Farge and Henry Adams in the South Seas," *American Art Journal* 20, no. 1 (1988), p. 100.

6. See Patricia O'Toole, *The Five of Hearts: An Intimate Portrait of Henry Adams and His Friends, 1880–1918* (New York: Crown Books, 1990), passim; and John La Farge, S.J., *The Manner Is Ordinary* (New York: Harcourt, Brace & Co., 1954), pp. 6, 7, 58–59.

7. James Edward Kelly, quoted in Frankenstein, *After the Hunt,* p. 38.

8. Ibid.

9. See "Memories of New York's 'Quartier Latin' Centre in Tenth Street Studio," *New York Herald,* March 2, 1913, magazine sect., p. 7; and Mary Sayre Haverstock, "The Tenth Street Studio," *Art in America* 54, no. 5 (September–October 1966), pp. 48–57. For an account of the development of the "artistic" studio, see Celia

Betsky, "In the Artist's Studio," *Portfolio* 4, no. 1 (January–February 1982), pp. 32–39.

10. "Painted Like Real Things," quoted in Frankenstein, *After the Hunt,* p. 55.

11. "Harnett: How George Hulings Lost His Fiddle," *Evening Item* (Philadelphia), June 11, 1895, p. 1.

12. Frankenstein, *After the Hunt,* p. 93.

13. *Catalogue of the Art Property and Other Objects Belonging to the Estate of the Late John La Farge, N.A.,* sale cat., American Art Association, New York, March 29–31, 1911.

14. See Frankenstein, *After the Hunt,* p. 38; Cecilia Waern, *John La Farge: Artist and Writer* (London: Seeley & Co., 1896), p. 16; and Barry Faulkner, *Barry Faulkner: Sketches from an Artist's Life* (Dublin, N.H.: W. L. Bauhan, 1973), pp. 52-53.

15. "Aus dem Kunstverein," clipping from the *Handelsblatt,* 1884 (otherwise unidentified), Blemly scrapbook, Alfred Frankenstein Papers, Archives of American Art, Smithsonian Institution, Washington, D.C., microfilm, roll 1374, frame 335, quoted in Frankenstein, *After the Hunt,* p. 69.

16. [Clarence Cook], "Academy of Design: Fifty-fourth Annual Exhibition," *New-York Daily Tribune,* April 26, 1879, p. 5.

17. [Clarence Cook], "Review of the Thirty-ninth Annual Exhibition of the National Academy of Design," *New-York Daily Tribune,* April 23, 1864, p. 3, quoted in Ruth Katz, "John La Farge as Painter and Critic" (Ph.D. diss., Radcliffe College, 1951), pp. 4–5.

18. Royal Cortissoz, *John La Farge: A Memoir and a Study* (Boston and New York: Houghton Mifflin Co., 1911), pp. 2–3.

19. Humor often provides rich insights into underlying social assumptions, and there is no better introduction to the issue of Victorian male and female stereotypes than Clarence Day, *Life with Father* (New York and London: Alfred A. Knopf, 1935). For a more solemn account of

the role of Victorian women, see "Women's Work: The First Transformation," in Carl N. Degler, *At Odds: Women and the Family in America from the Revolution to the Present* (New York: Oxford University Press, 1980), pp. 362–94.

20. Quoted in Frankenstein, *After the Hunt,* p. 76.

21. The only exception is *The Artist's Letter Rack,* which includes a letter addressed *To the lady of the house* (fig. 10). This was, however, a standard line used by nineteenth-century salesmen to solicit business, and it did not refer to a specific woman.

22. "The Churches: Pictures at the Exposition Furnish Material for a Sermon," *Minneapolis Tribune,* September 12, 1887, p. 5.

23. Quoted in George Inness, Jr., *Life, Art, and Letters of George Inness* (New York: Century Co., 1917), p. 124.

24. J[ames] Jackson Jarves, "Museums of Art, Artists, and Amateurs in America," *Galaxy* 10 (July 1870), p. 54.

25. S. G. W. Benjamin, *Art in America: A Critical and Historical Sketch* (New York: Harper & Bros., 1880), p. 95.

26. These are all rather ancient metaphors, as is confirmed by the entries in *The Oxford English Dictionary* for *stab, key,* and *blow.* In 1599, Shakespeare used the phrase "every word stabs," and a text of 1871 states: "They stab at their neighbor's good name and reputation." The word *key,* in the sense of a "key to understanding," appears in texts of about 1100 and 1200. The word *blow* has the secondary meaning, now archaic, of "to brag" or "to bluster," and the phrase "to blow one's own horn" was described by Anthony Trollope in 1873. The notion of ascent as a form of triumph goes back to St. Augustine and even earlier religious sources and is specifically associated with mountain climbing in Alfred Lord Tennyson's poem "Excelsior."

27. It seems no coincidence that another major American artist rediscovered in the 1930s, George Caleb Bingham, was also associated with barroom settings (see Samuel Isham, *The History of American Painting, with Supplemental Chapters by Royal Cortissoz* [New York: Macmillan Co., 1936], p. 206).

THE PATRONS OF THE ARTIST

Emblems of Commerce and Culture

DOREEN BOLGER

William Michael Harnett left little documentation regarding the owners of his works; their purchases are not recorded consistently in correspondence, diaries, or account books, and they lent their pictures to public exhibitions with relative infrequency. As a result, it has been difficult to establish the identities of his patrons and to determine the dates or circumstances of their acquisitions. Ownership is fairly clear-cut when an individual is listed as a lender to an exhibition, a work is included in an estate sale, or a strong provenance ties a painting to a particular family. Even when an owner's name is known, however, it may not be possible to identify the specific picture owned. In Harnett's 1892 memorial exhibition, the largest gathering of his work in the nineteenth century, lenders were listed separately from the items they lent. In group exhibitions, the titles of Harnett's paintings were often generic (*Still Life* being the most common) or romantic but uninformative (*Mighty Monarchs,* for example). Surprisingly few descriptive reviews of his paintings appeared in newspapers, no less in the established art press, leaving a paucity of documentation about his oeuvre. In the 1940s, when Alfred Frankenstein began his exhaustive research on Harnett, he uncovered information on his patrons but did not systematically document the provenances of the artist's works.

The paintings themselves may be the most illuminating documents, though the clues they offer are by no means easy to decipher. While many of the objects in Harnett's still lifes are familiar studio props that clearly belonged to him, at least some of the books, envelopes, letters, newspapers, and other pieces of paper he included seem to contain fragmentary information about the identities of the original owners of the paintings.[1] In the absence of more concrete evidence,

we cannot be certain whether these still lifes were commissioned or produced in hopes of beguiling a purchaser. Of course, Harnett's references to his patrons become more informative as we know more about their lives. Seemingly meaningless details, such as the inclusion of a newspaper masthead, an envelope, or a printed document, take on significance in this context. If we recall Harnett's biography and reconstruct those of his known patrons, we are left with two seemingly irreconcilable profiles: an immigrant, Irish-Catholic artisan-artist, and patrons who were more often wealthy than middle class and rather uniform in their religious and ethnic backgrounds, both of which were strikingly different from Harnett's. An examination of the shared interests of these patrons may offer some insights into the artist's popularity at the turn of the century.

Never before studied as a group, the artist's patrons have been dismissed as middle-class—even low-brow—businessmen, dry-goods merchants, and hotel and saloon proprietors who were attracted to his work because of the precision with which it imitated reality. In an age when more cosmopolitan patrons seem to have favored academic figure painting with elaborate narrative content, the works of Harnett and his trompe-l'oeil followers were perceived as less "artistic" and elevated. As one critic put it soon after the artist's death, "Phenomenally clever as Mr. Harnett was, he copied only the external form, the body, of his subject."[2] Needless to say, it has been assumed that his patrons and supporters were of similar ilk—less discerning and sophisticated.

The stereotypical description of Harnett's patrons is both simplified and inaccurate. Peter Samuel Dooner (1837–1906), Charles T. Shean (1854–1940), and Theodore Stewart (1838–1887) were the only

Harnett patrons known to have been hotel and saloon proprietors; their notoriety has outweighed their small number. While many of the artist's patrons were businessmen, some of them were also serious collectors of American and European paintings and decorative objects rather than aberrant supporters of just one artist (Harnett) or style (realism). Harnett's works were sought or purchased by some of the leading collectors of American art at the turn of the century—William Barnes Bement (1817–1897), Thomas Benedict Clarke (1848–1931), George Arnold Hearn (1835–1913), George Ingraham Seney (1826–1893), and Thomas Barlow Walker (1840–1928). Even Henry Clay Frick (1849–1919), a prominent American collector of European art, purchased a Harnett, albeit three years after the artist's death.[3] These were all sophisticated men who supported the founding and growth of the museums and art institutions that emerged during this period.

Many of Harnett's other supporters have passed into obscurity since their deaths, but a number of generalizations can be made about these men. In the main, they were his age or older, born before 1850 and deceased about 1900. Only a few served in the Civil War, almost all on the Union side, but most experienced the traumas of the war and Reconstruction and the excesses and abuses of the Gilded Age. They were self-made: they began as store clerks, bookkeepers, and salesmen, and they worked hard to achieve the affluence they enjoyed. In an era when women had begun to exert great influence in decoration and the fine arts, Harnett's patrons—and, indeed, most late-nineteenth-century American art collectors—were still men. While some women must have influenced the choices made by male patrons, only one, Mary R. Kase (about 1827–about 1912), the wife of a Newark, New Jersey, dry-goods merchant and banker, is known to have lent an example of the artist's work to a public exhibition.[4] Most of Harnett's patrons were Protestant; only one, Victor Henry Rothschild (1834–1911), a New York shirt manufacturer, is known to have been Jewish. Relatively few shared Harnett's Catholic background, nor were many Irish.[5] Harnett, who had faced the economic difficulties so often encountered by his fellow countrymen in America, joined the Hibernian Society, which assisted destitute Irish immigrants.[6] His plan to execute a painting of an ivory crucifix (fig. 27) he had purchased in Paris and then present both the painting and the model to Saint Patrick's Cathedral in New York is further evidence of the importance ethnic and religious issues must have held for him.

The nostalgic character of Harnett's still lifes, which so often venerate precious, aged objects imported from the Old World, belies the modernity of many of his patrons. The purchasers of his work were often progressive men who participated in, and even

Fig. 27. *Large Ivory Crucifix,* in *The Wm. Michael Harnett Collection: His Own Reserved Paintings, Models and Studio Furnishings,* sale cat., Stan. V. Henkels at Thos. Birch's Sons, Auctioneers, Philadelphia, February 23–24, 1893, p. 14, no. 110

initiated, the massive social, economic, and technological changes of the age. Bement produced textile machinery in his Philadelphia factory; Henry Bentley (1834–1895), a friend of Thomas Alva Edison's, established telegraph companies in New York and Philadelphia; Pittsburgh industrialist Frick operated coal mines and iron-ore refineries; Joseph Fulton Humphrey (1830 or 1839–1918) was a participant in the expansion of the western railroad; and Seney helped finance the consolidation of the railroad's eastern routes. Many of Harnett's patrons were leaders in the retailing business that was then transforming the face of American life. Byron Nugent (1842–1908), George H. Hulings (1844–1902), and the many dry-goods merchants who purchased Harnett's works joined better-known figures such as John Wanamaker (1838–1922) in the development and promotion of the department store. Druggist Isaac Newton Reed (1846–1891), who displayed Harnett's *Still Life with the Toledo Blade* of 1886 (fig. 100) in his store in Toledo, Ohio, led efforts to restrict the sale of liquor in drugstores and co-founded the Western Wholesale Drug Association, a predecessor of the National Whole Drug Association. In ways small and large, these were men who helped bring the United States into the modern era.

Business was a focal point for Harnett's patrons, and on some level his paintings must have appealed to sensibilities they developed through their work. This is underscored by the number of instances Harnett's paintings are known to have been on view in a business location—a drugstore, department store, or factory office—or at an industrial fair that catered to the interests and needs of the business community.[7] For the dry-goods merchants, who constituted the largest identifiable group among his supporters, Harnett's still lifes must have reflected the growing concern for display in the marketplace—interest in the colors, textures, and shapes of objects that were offered for sale. While Harnett's still-life compositions are far less carefully structured than were contemporary store displays (fig. 18), they include objects—mugs, pipes, books, and bric-a-brac—that were widely available in the department stores of the period. And the highly realistic, even illusionistic, quality of presentation must have enhanced the appeal of Harnett's work even further. His paintings are such convincing, accurate records of the commodities they depict that they served as virtual replacements for them.

Other businessmen also seem to have been drawn to Harnett's work in disproportionately large numbers—newspaper men, bankers, stationers, and brewers. Bentley wrote for the *New-York Daily Tribune* and later became a war correspondent for the *Philadelphia Inquirer.* James Terry Abbe (1849–1907) was president of the company that published the *Springfield Daily Union.* In Philadelphia, Monroe Smith (1852–1906) helped run the type-founding firm MacKellar, Smiths and Jordan. Dooner worked as a pressman for the *Illustrated New Age* and the *Times* for a total of fourteen years, and his counterpart at the *Public Ledger,* Henry A. Rowan (1840–1922), is one of several men whose names are featured in *Mr. Hulings' Rack Picture* of 1888 (pl. 44). Two of Harnett's Massachusetts supporters were involved in the stationery business—Abbe ran an envelope manufacturing plant as well as a newspaper, and art dealer James D. Gill (1849–1937) started out by working for a local paper merchant. These men spent their careers dealing with paper and print, leitmotifs that appear throughout Harnett's pictures. Likewise, the bankers and brokers drawn to the artist—George Henry Moore (1835–1896) of Louisville; Edwin C. Ray (died 1891) of New York; Francis Charles Sessions (1820–1892)

Fig. 28. *Mr. Bement's Dining Room,* in Charles M. Skinner, *Catalogue of Works of Art, with Illustrations and Descriptions; also, Views of the Summer and Winter Homes, etc., of William B. Bement, of Philadelphia, Pa.* (Philadelphia: J. B. Lippincott & Co., 1884)

of Columbus, Ohio; George Seney of Brooklyn; and others—must have readily identified with the stacks of glittering coins and the paper money that appear so regularly in Harnett still-lifes, such as *The Banker's Table* and *Still Life—Writing Table,* both of 1877 (pls. 6, 8). To brewers George Moore and George J. Miller and hoteliers-restaurateurs Dooner, Stewart, and Shean, drinking mugs must have been familiar sights.

For Harnett's patrons, avocation may have been as important as vocation: they demonstrated a considerable interest in the collecting of bric-a-brac and other decorative objects, the items found so often in Harnett's pictures. They may have owned homes like the one described by art critic Earl Shinn: "The art almost insensibly melts and merges into the bric-à-brac and furniture."[8] William Bement crowded the interior of his home (fig. 28) with furniture, textiles, and decorative objects of all kinds; its chronicler saw these and "the paintings, statuettes, vases and unique furniture [combining] to constitute a *tout ensemble.*"[9] William Hazelton Folwell (1840–1900) and Nathan Thomas Folwell (1847–1930), merchants, manufacturers, and perhaps Harnett's most important Philadelphia patrons, owned much of the bric-a-brac the artist depicted in the still-life paintings they commissioned. Frick filled his Pittsburgh home, Clayton, with up-to-the-minute decorations in the fashionable Aesthetic mode and hung Harnett's *Still Life* of 1890 (fig. 29) in its midst. When Walker opened his Minneapolis home to the public, on display were not only paintings but bronzes, ivory carvings, lacquer, glass, and ceramics as

Fig. 29. William M. Harnett, *Still Life,* 1890. Oil on wood, 7½ x 9½ in.
The Helen Clay Frick Foundation, Clayton, Pittsburgh

well. Clarke, best known as a supporter of contemporary American painters, also collected and sold decorative objects.[10] Even in Stewart's renowned New York saloon on Warren Street, Harnett's works were surrounded by objects, including "automatons, costly and queer old clocks, ancient armor."[11]

If some of these men were drawn to Harnett's work by its subject matter, others may have been attracted by its realistic style. George W. Carmer (born 1847), a New York art dealer who handled Harnett's work, later practiced photography. The British painter George Richmond (1809–1896), who purchased a still life (pl. 35) that Harnett exhibited at London's Royal Academy of Arts in 1885, was a draftsman and miniature painter; he must have been particularly fasci-

nated by Harnett's highly finished style. The Folwells may have found Harnett's work appealing for a similar reason: their ancestor Samuel Folwell (1764–1813) was also a miniaturist, and his works remained in their family as treasured heirlooms.

It remains more difficult, perhaps even impossible, to determine the exact chronology of Harnett's interaction with his patrons. The dates of most of his sales are unrecorded, as are the timing and circumstances of his patrons' disposal of their purchases. We can seldom evaluate the role that Harnett's work itself or still-life painting in general played in the evolution of any one patron's taste. Many—Norton Quincy Pope, George Moore, and George Hulings, to name a few—are described as art collectors, but their activities in

Fig. 30. Martin Johnson Heade, *Vase of Mixed Flowers,* ca. 1870.
Oil on canvas, 17¼ x 13¾ in. Museum of Fine Arts, Boston, Bequest of Martha C. Karolik for the
Karolik Collection of American Paintings, 1815–65

Fig. 31. *Earles' Galleries of Paintings
and Looking-Glass Warerooms.* Advertisement.
In Richard Brinsley Sheridan, ed. and comp.,
Club Men of Philadelphia
(Philadelphia: Avril Printing Co., 1894)

and pursuing his art studies at night, Harnett sold, or more likely gave, works to friends, such as William Ignatius Blemly, another silver engraver (fig. 110). Most of the paintings he exhibited were listed "for sale," a hopeful but apparently largely unsatisfied solicitation of support, and this at a time when the asking prices for his works, most often $50, never rose above $150. Harnett, it should be remembered, was beginning his artistic career at an inauspicious moment: the American economy had not recovered from the financial panic of 1873, and he was a homegrown artist competing with more cosmopolitan painters returning from studies abroad. In any event, as the prices of his works rose to the hundreds of dollars in the late 1870s and to the thousands in the late 1880s, Harnett sought a more affluent and ever-widening circle of patrons.

Harnett's return to Philadelphia in 1876 was timely. The Centennial Exposition was on view, heightening the public's awareness of art, particularly of the decorative arts that Harnett would portray in his pictures, and stimulating collectors to purchase paintings. By 1879, James S. Earle and Sons, a Philadelphia firm that sold paintings, engravings, and sculpture alongside looking glasses and frames, was offering his work for sale. A later advertisement (fig. 31) suggests that Earle's proprietors may have recognized the decorative possibilities of Harnett's work; it promises "pictures suitable for the house, physician, merchant; the lawyer, billiard room, stable." *The Smoker's Solace,* an unidentified painting Earle's lent to the Cincinnati Industrial Exposition in 1879, must have been one of the artist's smoking subjects, which would have suited a billiard room, smoking room, or study—essentially any male haunt. Harnett's paintings were evidently so appropriate for specific locations that they fit well into the prevailing Aesthetic mode of interior decoration, which favored different styles for rooms of various purposes. Unfortunately, while a few written accounts and photographs record Harnett's pictures on view in offices and saloons, there is no extant evidence to reveal where or how his work was installed in a domestic scene.[15]

During the early years of his career, and certainly by 1879, Harnett's work had been purchased by two men who were in a position to aggressively promote interest in his work—Dennis Gale (born about 1828), an English "picture dealer" who settled in Philadelphia about 1872, and New Yorker Thomas Clarke, who was increasingly devoting his resources to buying (and reselling) paintings by contemporary American artists.[16] In 1879, Harnett painted two remarkably similar works (fig. 32, pl. 15) with these two gentlemen in mind. Tabletop arrangements of an envelope, letter, folded newspaper, books, ink bottle, and quill pen are featured in each painting, which is personalized by the inscription of the owner's name and address on the

this area have not always been documented. Clarke, who has recently been studied, seems to have begun with a burst of enthusiasm over still life but to have increasingly turned his attention to figural subjects, perhaps tiring of his early purchases.[12] Seney owned several still-life paintings by Frenchmen Antoine Vollon and Blaise Desgoffe.[13] Bement was clearly intrigued by the genre—he owned pictures (figs. 30, 86, 89) by Americans Martin Johnson Heade (1819–1904), Charles Bird King (1785–1862), and Robert Spear Dunning (1829–1905) before acquiring Harnett's masterful *Old Cupboard Door* of 1889 (pl. 45).[14] James Abbe and Charles Shean, both from the Springfield, Massachusetts, area, seem to have favored Harnett's trompe-l'oeil still lifes in particular and also patronized John Haberle (1856–1933), a follower of Harnett's.

While the account of Harnett's patrons is incomplete, the basic outline of his patronage can be surmised. During the eight years he spent in New York, from 1869 to 1876, working as a silver engraver

envelope. The intimate quality of these pictures did not deter their owners from selling them, however—Clarke, within two years.[17] These and a number of Harnett's mug-and-pipe paintings, which include a few simple objects and vary only minimally, are probably works the artist produced for ready sale. Paintings like these, which required mere execution rather than original conception, are far less complicated than the works he undertook for important exhibitions or major patrons.

Between 1876 and 1880, when he had saved enough money to travel abroad, Harnett readily found patrons among the affluent businessmen of Philadelphia. Of the many innovations in his choice of subject matter—mugs and pipes, money, racks, and bric-a-brac—at least a few were conceived in relation to his new patrons. *The Artist's Letter Rack* of 1879 (pl. 17),

the first of two similar compositions showing letters, postcards, and other flat pieces of paper tucked into a tape grid, was likely a commissioned work. It contains references to the Philadelphia firm C. C. Pierson and Sons, which listed its business as "hides," and to other individuals in the same and related businesses.[18] By 1878, Harnett had developed a relationship with the brothers William and Nathan Folwell, the successful owners of Folwell Brothers and Company, a textile and dry-goods firm that had been established thirty years earlier. The Folwells commissioned several works from Harnett and must have helped spread his reputation among the city's dry-goods merchants. *Still Life with Portrait by Raphael* of 1878 (fig. 111), painted for William Folwell, includes his surname on the envelope at the right, slipped discreetly between two books. Folwell is also presumed to have owned

Fig. 32. William M. Harnett, *Still Life with Letter to Dennis Gale,* 1879. Oil on canvas, 11 x 15 in. Private collection, Chevy Chase

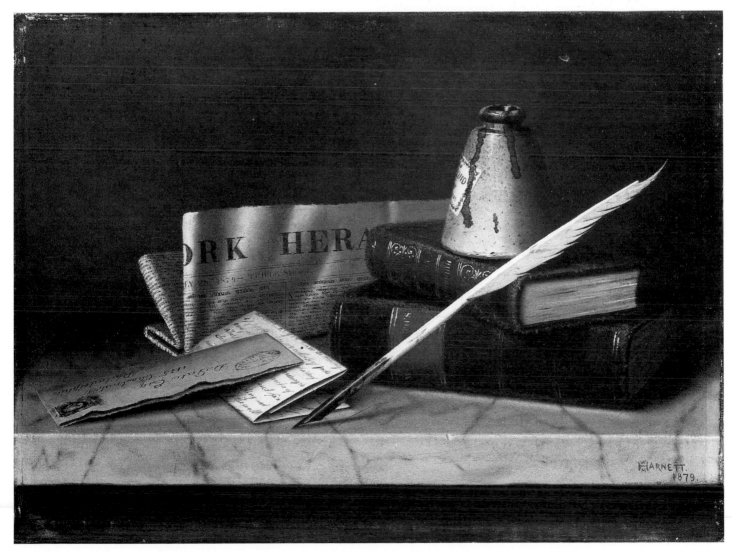

Fig. 33. William M. Harnett, *Still Life for Nathan Folwell,*
1878. Oil on canvas, 26 x 21 in. Private collection

an importer and auctioneer, owned an unidentified
Still Life exhibited at the Pennsylvania Academy of the
Fine Arts in 1879; George Hulings purchased several
works, including his rack picture (pl. 44) and a fruit
study; the proprietors of Strawbridge and Clothier
displayed one of Harnett's works in their counting-
house; and *For Sunday's Dinner* of 1888 (pl. 42) is
probably the hanging game piece the artist described
as "the chicken" when it was shown in a display
window at John Wanamaker and Company in the
winter of 1888.[22]

Dry-goods merchants from as far afield as Saint
Louis, Missouri, and Newark, New Jersey, are known
to have purchased still-life paintings by Harnett. So,
too, did a number of patrons who later left the business
to pursue other careers—among them, Frick, Clarke,
and Sessions. "It is gratifying to the dry goods trade
that so many of his masterpieces should be in the
hands of dry goods merchants of this country," a writer
for the *Dry Goods Economist* observed at the time of
Harnett's death.[23] Some of these men undoubtedly
knew one another. Dry-goods merchants from all
over the region, even the country, must have come
to Philadelphia, then an active wholesale center for
the trade, and these visits occasioned more than
business transactions.[24]

Fig. 34. William M. Harnett, *Still Life with Mug and Pipe,*
1878. Oil on canvas, 12½ x 10 in. Private collection

the items depicted in *Still Life with Bric-a-Brac* of the
same year (fig. 9), since at least half of the fifteen
decorative objects it features remained in the possession of his family after his death.[19] Likewise, *Still Life for
Nathan Folwell,* also of 1878 (fig. 33), seems to depict
objects selected by its one-time owner, as the watch,
the odd statue of a dog, and the pseudo-Greek vase are
not familiar from other works by Harnett.[20] These
paintings, the first in which Harnett lavished such
attention on decorative bric-a-brac, seem to have
originated from the artist's special relationship with
this mercantile family.

The Folwells' enthusiasm for Harnett's work was
taken up by members of their circle. Joseph Haines, Sr.
(1863–1921), began to work for Folwell Brothers in
1879, becoming a partner some fifteen years later, and
in the process he acquired a mug-and-pipe picture
(fig. 34) by the artist. German-born Philip Heebner,
who was working for the Folwell firm by 1878, owned
a Harnett of a basket of grapes or cherries, presumably
an early work such as *A Wooden Basket of Catawba
Grapes* of 1876 (pl. 1).[21] Other dry-goods merchants in
the city followed suit: Lewis Wiener (1847–1893), also

Nevertheless, shared mercantile interests seem an inadequate explanation for such a remarkable concentration of Harnett's patrons in one business. Indeed, the dry-goods enthusiasm for Harnett may have been fostered by the artist's early friend and biographer Edward Taylor Snow (1844–1913).[25] Snow is usually described as a painter or an art dealer and advisor, but he also worked in the dry-goods trade—at Cooper and Conard, John Wanamaker and Company, and Strawbridge and Clothier—for four decades, from about 1855 until his retirement in 1894.[26] Until then, his artistic work seems to have been confined largely to summer vacations, when he made sketching excursions to the Jersey shore.[27] Harnett inscribed a photograph of Byron Nugent's *Job Lot Cheap* of 1878 (pl. 9): *To E. T. Snow, thanks for the idea, Yours Truly, William M. Harnett.*[28] The "idea"—whether it was the choice of subject, composition, or patron—underscores the importance of Snow's role as a promoter of the artist's work.[29] Even the repeated involvement of his employers with Harnett's paintings (Strawbridge and Clothier as an owner and John Wanamaker and Company as an exhibitor) is suggestive. Moreover, as a dry-goods wholesaler, Snow must have been in contact with a nationwide network of dry-goods salesmen, buyers, and merchants, placing him in an ideal position to bring Harnett's work to the attention of businessmen who lived in or visited Philadelphia.

In spite of Harnett's apparent success in Philadelphia, he was anxious to continue his studies and went to London in 1880. After he had been there a few months, he was visited by "an old acquaintance," an unidentified resident of Frankfort, Germany, who had already purchased his work in Philadelphia.[30] The artist later recalled his dilemma:

> He invited me to spend a few months at his home and work exclusively for him. It is needless to say that I accepted the offer.
>
> I stopped in Frankfort for six months and filled all the orders that he gave me until I grew impatient of the work. I wanted to go to Munich and go on with my studies. Every time I had hinted of leaving Frankfort my friend suggested a new order, and it took some time and considerable obstinacy on my part to finally get away.[31]

Harnett seems to have felt constrained, even trapped, by this patron, and these feelings may have made him less willing to undertake still-life paintings "to order" in the future. Once settled in Munich, he seems to have had little difficulty finding buyers for his work. "I sold pictures to American travelers; Germans, Frenchmen and even Englishmen were numbered among the purchasers."[32] Sojourning in Paris, he painted *After the Hunt* (pl. 34) and exhibited it at the prestigious Salon in 1885, the year he also sent a submission to the Royal Academy in London (pl. 35). Successful but homesick, Harnett returned to the States, where, in his absence, his work had been exhibited with increasingly higher price tags.

A few works undertaken soon after his return are pointedly inscribed as being done "to order," and in at least one case we know enough about the models to speculate on the patron's involvement in their selection. *Ease* of 1887 (pl. 41), commissioned a year earlier by James Abbe, reportedly is comprised of "personal or family property," including an envelope, likely the product of Abbe's factory, and the "old account book" that belonged to his partner.[33] According to an 1887 article, the account book had been used by Thomas Noble, a governor of Indiana, and it contained "the record of 'Black Tom's and Sarah's children'—Black Tom having been a slave of Mr. Noble in Kentucky and one of the originals of Mrs.

Fig. 35. John Haberle, *Grandma's Hearthstone*, 1890. Oil on canvas, 96 x 66 in. The Detroit Institute of Arts, Gift of C. W. Churchill in memory of his father

Stowe's 'Uncle Tom.'"[34] Abbe, an ardent Republican, easily could have selected this item for political reasons. Given the personal nature of its contents, it seems incredible that Abbe was willing to part with *Ease* in 1888, the year he sold it to railroad owner Collis Potter Huntington (1821–1900). Abbe's decision may have been prompted by financial considerations: in January 1888, a fire destroyed the factory where *Ease* had been displayed, and Abbe may have been hard-pressed to rebuild his business.[35] Abbe later repeated a similar commission and selection process with the painter John Haberle, whose *Grandma's Hearthstone* of 1890 (fig. 35) shows Abbe family heirlooms arranged around a fireplace.[36] It thus seems probable that Abbe, not Harnett, initiated the selection of models and that his interaction with Harnett, like the Folwells', was atypical.

As Harnett's reputation grew, however, he received at least one more offer for a commission of this kind. The Minneapolis lumber magnate and philanthropist Thomas Walker approached the artist in 1887, shortly after the death of his son Leon, who had been impressed by a visit to Harnett's studio. Walker asked Harnett to create a painting like those in the *After the Hunt* series, using one of the boy's guns and a hunting hatchet he had made as well as other hunting paraphernalia.[37] The work was intended as a memorial to Leon Walker and perhaps as a statement about his father's child-rearing philosophy. The elder Walker emphasized manual training for his sons and, according to one report, "encouraged the boys in all out-of-door amusements, especially hunting, which he has shared with them."[38] In this instance, the patron wanted Harnett to take one of his most successful subjects, already done in four versions, and personalize it for him. Even though he had frequently repeated similar compositions, Harnett was unwilling to fill this commission, perhaps because he was not eager to pursue orders whose contents were dictated by patrons. And this offer did come at the time Harnett was embarking upon his most original and ambitious

works, large-scale arrangements of musical instruments and other decorative objects.

Mr. Hulings' Rack Picture of 1888 (pl. 44), Harnett's second and final rack picture, was executed for dry-goods merchant George Hulings. Harnett may have undertaken this very personal "to order" painting out of friendship or obligation, perhaps specifically to mollify Hulings after selling *The Old Violin* of 1886 (pl. 37), Hulings's commission, to another purchaser.[39] The correspondents cited in the picture were not Hulings's business associates, even though most of their communications are addressed to his business address, but friends who belonged to his congregation at Wharton Street Methodist Episcopal Church and to the same Masonic organizations—Melita Lodge No. 295 and Mary Commandery No. 36. Like Hulings, two of the men, William Macpherson and J. Wesley Bowen, had served in the Civil War, and their letters are paired, one overlapping the other.[40]

From 1886 to 1892, Harnett seems to have enjoyed continuous and remunerative patronage, regularly receiving payment well in the four figures for his work. Stewart paid $4,000 for *After the Hunt* of 1885 (pl. 34); Bement, $5,000 for *The Old Cupboard Door* of 1889 (pl. 45); and even the artist's friend Dooner paid $1,500, for *Just Dessert* of 1891 (pl. 47).[41] The purchase price of *Ease* of 1887 (pl. 41) is not known, but when Abbe sold it in 1888, it reportedly fetched $5,000.[42] Nevertheless, while Harnett's patrons were spending more money on his pictures during the final years of his career, they remained, to the end, the same class of wealthy businessmen that had supported him almost from the start. This mercantile network enabled Harnett, an immigrant and artisan, to find a new and ready market for his paintings among collectors who otherwise might not have sought his work in more conventional ways. This was a practical, businesslike response to the American art market of the 1870s and 1880s, when more people had begun to purchase paintings, but relatively few strong commercial outlets for American works had yet been developed.

NOTES

▼

I am grateful to the Amon Carter Museum for granting me leave to spend the summer of 1990 as an Ailsa Mellon Bruce Fellow at the Center for Advanced Study in the Visual Arts, National Gallery of Art, Washington, D.C., where I researched Harnett and his patrons. Several individuals were indefatigable in their support of my research: Andrew Walker, who mined Philadelphia libraries and archives in pursuit of information on the artist and his circle; Thayer Tolles Mickel, who often interrupted her own work to answer my queries; Milan Hughston, librarian at the Amon Carter Museum, who sought and found the innumerable obscure publications required for this essay; and Sally Monroe and, later, Carolyn LeMaster, both curatorial secretaries at the Amon Carter, who kindly made their many efforts on this project appear effortless. In the process of reconstructing the biographies of Harnett's patrons, I was aided by individuals at the following institutions: Baldwin-Wallace, Berea, Ohio; National Library of Medicine, Bethesda; Fogg Art Museum, Harvard University, Cambridge, Mass.; Pioneers' Museum, Colorado Springs; Columbus Museum of Art, Ohio; Colorado Historical Society and Denver Public Library; Westmoreland Museum of Art, Greensburg, Pa.; Victoria and Albert Museum, London; The Filson Club, Louisville, Kentucky; Drew Theological Seminary Library, Madison, N.J.; The New Jersey Historical Society, Newark; New York Public Library, New York Athletic Club, and Sotheby Parke Bernet, Inc., New York; St. Charles Borromeo Seminary, Overbrook, Pa.; The Civil War Library and Museum, Free Library of Philadelphia, Historical Society of Pennsylvania, Library Company of Philadelphia, The Masonic Museum and Library of Pennsylvania, Pennsylvania Academy of the Fine Arts, Philadelphia Museum of Art, Register of Wills in and for the County of Philadelphia, St. George's M. E. Church, Strawbridge & Clothier, and University of Pennsylvania, Philadelphia; The Frick Art Museum, Pittsburgh; Portland Museum of Art, Maine; Missouri Historical Society and the St. Louis Mercantile Library Association, St. Louis; The Getty Center for the History of Art and Humanities, Santa Monica; Mount Holyoke College Art Museum, South Hadley, Mass.; Connecticut Valley Historical Museum, Springfield, Mass.; Toledo–Lucas County Library, Ohio; Archives of American Art of the Smithsonian Institution and Library of Congress, Washington, D.C.; and Historical Society of Delaware, Wilmington.

Collectors of Harnett's pictures and descendants of his friends and patrons were also helpful: Jean Nugent Geyer, Dr. and Mrs. Walter Goldfarb, Peggy Simpson Johnson, Mrs. Franklin M. Nugent, Joy Peto Smiley, and Peter Strawbridge. This, like other studies of Harnett, is based upon the pioneering work of Alfred Frankenstein. I attended Professor Frankenstein's course on Harnett and his circle at the University of Delaware in 1972.

1. Many of his models are listed and some are illustrated in *The Wm. Michael Harnett Collection. His Own Reserved Paintings, Models and Studio Furnishings,* sale cat., Stan. V. Henkels at Thos. Birch's Sons, Auctioneers, Philadelphia, February 23–24, 1893.

2. Louisa Trumbull Cogswell, "Art in Boston," *Arcadia* 1 (December 1, 1892), p. 306. I am grateful to Jennifer Hardin for bringing this article to my attention.

3. Kahren Jones Hellerstedt et al., *Clayton: The Pittsburgh Home of Henry Clay Frick, Art and Furnishings* (Pittsburgh: Helen Clay Frick Foundation, 1988), p. 70.

4. *First Loan Exhibition,* exhib. cat. (Newark, N.J.: Essex Art Association, 1883), *Still Life,* no. 106. For biographical information on Kase, see U.S., New Jersey, Newark, Second Ward, *Census of 1860: Index,* p. 61, New Jersey Historical Society, Newark.

5. The obvious exceptions were the Irishmen Peter Dooner of Philadelphia and Charles Shean of Springfield, Mass. And several Irishmen, clearly close friends, served as Harnett's pallbearers: Charles and Joseph McCann, A. A. Ryan, and James McCloskey (Alfred Frankenstein, *After the Hunt: William Harnett and Other American Still Life Painters, 1870–1900,* rev. ed. [Berkeley and Los Angeles: University of California Press, 1969], p. 93). They were mechanics and tradesmen, economically a more humble group than Harnett's merchant patrons, and if they owned works by the artist, likely received them as gifts.

6. "Minute Book of the Hibernian Society," September 17, 1890, Historical Society of Pennsylvania, Philadelphia. Dooner proposed Harnett for membership.

7. See Frankenstein, *After the Hunt,* p. 7, "Trade in

Philadelphia," *Dry Goods Economist* 47, no. 2521 (November 12, 1892), p. 38; and "A Fine Still-Life Painting," *Springfield Daily Republican,* November 7, 1887, p. 6.

8. Edward Strahan [Earl Shinn], ed., *The Art Treasures of America Being the Choicest Works of Art in the Public and Private Collections of North America,* 3 vols. (Philadelphia: George Barrie Publisher, 1879), 1, p. 134. Shinn was discussing the lavish home of New Yorker Catharine Lorillard Wolfe.

9. Charles M. Skinner, *Catalogue of Works of Art, with Illustrations and Descriptions; also, Views of the Summer and Winter Homes, etc., of William B. Bement, of Philadelphia, Pa.* (Philadelphia: J. B. Lippincott & Co., 1884), unpaginated.

10. H. Barbara Weinberg, "Thomas B. Clarke: Foremost Patron of American Art from 1872 to 1899," *American Art Journal* 8, no. 1 (May 1976), p. 64.

11. "Theodore Stewart's Collection," clipping from an unidentified and undated newspaper, Blemly scrapbook, Alfred Frankenstein Papers, Archives of American Art, Smithsonian Institution, Washington, D.C., microfilm, roll 1374, frame 328.

12. Weinberg, "Thomas B. Clarke," pp. 69–70.

13. *Catalogue of Mr. George I. Seney's Important Collection of Modern Paintings,* sale cat., American Art Association, New York, February 11–13, 1891, nos. 35, 126, 222.

14. Skinner, *Catalogue of Works of Art;* and Frankenstein, *After the Hunt,* p. 88.

15. At Theodore Stewart's Warren Street saloon, Harnett's paintings were "magnificently draped in crimson velvet, whose rich folds form a beautiful foreground" ([Theodore D. Rich], *Theodore Stewart* [New York: L'Artiste Publishing Co., 1888], p. 19). *Ease* was installed in a room off James Abbe's office, "framed in a dark and unobtrusive, though rich, carved frame, set in red plush and curtained with maroon plush" ("A Fine Still-Life Painting," p. 6).

16. Gale has never been fully documented. He married a Canadian woman and seems to have lived in Canada from approximately 1866 to 1871, before moving to Philadelphia (U.S., Pennsylvania, Philadelphia, *Census of 1880,* vol. 66, enumeration district 216, sheet 18, l. 48).

17. Weinberg, "Thomas B. Clarke," pp. 60, 75.

18. Doreen Bolger Burke, *American Paintings in the Metropolitan Museum of Art,* vol. 3, *A Catalogue of Works by Artists Born between 1846 and 1864,* ed. Kathleen Luhrs (New York: Metropolitan Museum of Art, 1980), pp. 50–52.

19. Frankenstein discovered seven of these objects (fig. 112) in the home of Folwell's daughter May Hoisington and traced an eighth to the Public Library at Columbus, Ga., where it had been presented by her sister Mrs. Thomas Hudson (Frankenstein, *After the Hunt,* p. 46).

20. Ibid., p. 47.

21. Heebner is first listed in Philadelphia directories as Philip A. Hubner. He changed the spelling of his name to Heebner about 1886. His employment by Folwell Bros. is documented (W. H. Folwell, N. T. Folwell, B. J. Lloyd, Jos. Z. Batten, E. R. Fiske, and Ph. A. Hübner, agreement, January 14, 1878, Chambers-Folwell Papers, Historical Society of Pennsylvania). Information about his owner-ship of a Harnett was provided by his daughter (see Ann H. McDonald to Frankenstein, June 28, n.d., Frankenstein Papers, roll 1374, frame 1245).

22. See "Trade in Philadelphia," p. 38; *Illustrated Catalogue of the First Annual Exhibition of the Philadel-phia Society of Artists, held at the Pennsylvania Academy of Fine Arts, Cor. Broad and Cherry Streets, Philadelphia,* exhib. cat. (Philadelphia: Philadelphia Society of Artists, 1879), p. 9, no. 98; and Harnett to William J. Hughes, January 24, 1889, Frankenstein Papers, roll 1375, frame 543, quoted in Frankenstein, *After the Hunt,* p. 90.

23. "Trade in Philadelphia," p. 38.

24. For example, Paul H. Hacke, a Pittsburgh dry-goods merchant who lent a work to Harnett's memorial show in

1892, was listed earlier that year among the visitors to the city's horse show, where he was "surrounded by some of his mercantile friends, his face beaming with enthusiasm" ("Our Philadelphia Letter," *Dry Goods Economist* 47, no. 2498 [June 4, 1892], p. 38).

25. For biographical information on Snow, see "Hermit Artist's Funeral: Edward Taylor Snow Will Be Buried Tomorrow," *Record* (Philadelphia), September 28, 1913, p. 2; and obituaries in *American Art Annual* 11 (1914), p. 398; *New York Times,* September 28, 1913, sect. 4, p. 5; and *American Art News* 12, no. 1 (October 11, 1913), p. 7.

26. See "E. T. Snow, Painter, Dies," *New York Times,* September 28, 1913, sect. 4, p. 5; E. T. Snow, Late Manager of the Wholesale Department of Cooper & Conard's, "John Wanamaker, Wholesale Department, Market, Chestnut and City Hall Square," printed announcement, January 1, 1887, E. Taylor Snow Papers, Historical Society of Pennsylvania; and E. T. Snow, "A Business Man's Forecast," *Dry Goods Economist* 46, no. 2474 (December 19, 1891), p. 39.

27. See "Our Philadelphia Letter," *Dry Goods Economist* 47, no. 2504 (July 16, 1892), p. 41; "Our Philadelphia Letter," *Dry Goods Economist* 47, no. 2507 (August 6, 1892), p. 40; and "Philadelphia Trade," *Dry Goods Economist* 48, no. 2560 (August 10, 1893), p. 39.

28. Frankenstein, *After the Hunt,* p. 47.

29. Snow may even have written "Trade in Philadelphia," an article on Harnett's patrons, for the 1892 *Dry Goods Economist;* he was often mentioned in that periodical and contributed a letter and a signed article to it the previous year ("Unloading Goods" [E. T. Snow, letter to the editor, November 25, 1891], *Dry Goods Economist* 46, no. 2471 [November 28, 1891], p. 20; and Snow, "A Business Man's Forecast," p. 39).

30. Frankenstein found some evidence of this gentleman, who was perhaps Johann Conrad Cronau, as well as of two German families named Badersbach and Moehring that had a connection to Harnett (*After the Hunt,* p. 62).

31. "Painted Like Real Things: The Man Whose Pictures

Are a Wonder and a Puzzle," interview in *New York News,* probably 1889 or 1890, quoted in Frankenstein, *After the Hunt,* p. 55.

32. Ibid.

33. "A Fine Still-Life Painting," p. 6.

34. Ibid.

35. See *Biographical Review: This Volume Contains Biographical Sketches of the Leading Citizens of Hampden County Massachusetts* (Boston: Biographical Review Publishing Co., 1895), p. 55; and "Envelopes by the Million: The Holyoke Envelope Company's New Building," *Paper World* 16, no. 4 (April 1888), pp. 1–2.

36. For a contemporary account of Haberle's ambitious trompe-l'oeil paintings, see "It Fooled the Cat: Realistic Painting by John Haberle, the Artist," *Evening Leader: New Haven,* June 10, 1893, p. 2; and "Haberle's Masterpiece," *Evening Leader: New Haven,* May 15, 1894, p. 3.

37. Walker to Harnett, September 16, 1887, quoted in Frankenstein, *After the Hunt,* p. 86.

38. "Thomas Barlow Walker," in *National Cyclopaedia of American Biography,* 15 vols. (New York: James T. White & Co., 1896), 6, p. 251, quoted in *Sketches of the Life of Honorable T. B. Walker* (Minneapolis, Minn.: Lumberman Publishing Co., 1907), unpaginated.

39. "Harnett: How George Hulings Lost His Fiddle," *Evening Item* (Philadelphia), June 11, 1895, p. 1.

40. Doreen Bolger, "'Cards and Letters from His Friends': *Mr. Hulings' Rack Picture* by William Michael Harnett," *American Art Journal* 22, no. 2 (1990), pp. 4–32.

41. See "Artist Harnett Dead: The Well-Known Still-Life Painter Dies in Hospital," *New York Times,* October 31, 1892, p. 3; and "Art Loses a Master: William M. Harnett, the Painter of 'Still Life,' Dead in New York," *North American* (Philadelphia), November 1, 1892, p. 1.

42. "Artist Harnett Dead," p. 3.

THE ARTIST'S PUBLIC FACE

▼

Lifetime Exhibitions and Critical Reception

WILLIAM H. GERDTS

William Michael Harnett's known paintings number about 250, though additional works continue to appear. The meager size of his output is attributable, in part, to the brevity of his career.[1] Harnett died at forty-four and was continuously ill during his last years, so that his known production was limited to ten paintings between 1889 and his death in 1892. His exhibition record is equally modest: according to available evidence, he showed only eighty-two works, an exceedingly limited display record, even if one assumes that his entries were not always recorded in the accompanying catalogues and often went unmentioned by the press. The exhibited pieces cannot consistently be linked to paintings that are known today: many of his titles are similar; reviews of his work are brief and rare; and while nineteenth-century critics were often descriptive, Harnett repeatedly used the same models and compositions. Harnett is known to have displayed his work in fifteen different American cities, taking advantage of the vast increase in exhibition opportunities after the Civil War offered by local art academies and associations, industrial expositions, and the new public art museums. He also participated in the more established shows sponsored by such art organizations as the National Academy of Design in New York and the Pennsylvania Academy of the Fine Arts in Philadelphia. With the exception of the National Academy, where he exhibited sporadically after 1875, Harnett tended to show his work only once or twice at most venues.[2] After he left for Europe in 1880, he did not contribute his work to annuals at the Pennsylvania Academy or show with the Philadelphia Society of Artists, but he remained a regular contributor at the National Academy of Design. Some of his paintings were on view at commercial galleries, but almost a third were on display at such surprising locations as

the jewelry store Black, Starr and Frost in New York; Wanamaker's department store in Philadelphia; the drugstore of Isaac Newton Reed in Toledo, Ohio; and the saloons of Theodore Stewart in New York.[3] Harnett's paintings were lent most often by the artist himself or by a commercial representative, not by private collectors. Fewer than ten of his pictures were lent to exhibitions by purchasers, so that he rarely benefited from the promotional value of such prestigious loans, which were often calculated to attract more patronage.

Of course, the great intangible here, as with the exhibition activities of many artists, is the lack of information about works that were submitted by Harnett but rejected by exhibition organizers and juries. These pictures may not have been less worthy than those that were accepted and displayed. It is difficult to believe that the artist did not attempt to show more paintings than were ultimately on view. Harnett certainly needed to exhibit and sell his work. Although he eventually developed a modest reputation and may even have enjoyed special financial support from some of his patrons, he was hardly well-off, and he did not supplement his income with teaching, illustration, or the like, as did many of his contemporaries. His prices rose from an initial fifty dollars to seventy-five to a more comfortable range of two hundred to five hundred dollars in the 1880s; a few works brought several thousand dollars late in his life.

The relative infrequency with which Harnett contributed to exhibitions may have resulted in part from the chronic lack of critical reaction to the works he did display. While he was not totally ignored, it is striking how often he was overlooked. Many factors may have exacerbated this situation: competition from well-publicized and well-received paintings

---

Opposite: William M. Harnett, *Emblems of Peace* (detail, pl. 46)

by other artists in the same shows; the relatively small size of the majority of Harnett's pictures; and, in all likelihood, the unfelicitous placement of his entries at a time when exhibition walls were often crowded from floor to ceiling, with the more desirable places "on the line" commonly reserved for works by artists of greater reputation or for works of more commanding presence.

Harnett's choice of subject matter, still life, and his treatment of that theme—particularly his use of a highly illusionistic painting style—may also account for the critical neglect, even condemnation, of his art. During the late nineteenth century, reviews of major exhibitions in newspapers and magazines were often arranged by subject, with figure paintings, portraits, landscapes, marines, and so forth considered together. Still-life paintings usually received short shrift and generally appeared last in reviews; if something had to be cut, the comments on them would have been the first to go. Admittedly, the traditional estimation of still life, which had long occupied the lowest rung of the hierarchical ladder of artistic themes, had been challenged during the nineteenth century, but several factors worked against the acceptance of the particular type of still-life painting espoused by Harnett. About mid-century, the influential English aesthetician John Ruskin had convinced many to recognize the least pretentious of God's creations as more worthy subjects than the generally esteemed historical themes. But Harnett's pipes and tobacco, paper money and coins, and objets de virtu—all man-made or manufactured items that were removed from the natural world—would have had limited appeal even to Ruskinians. Indeed, by the time Harnett was active, the hierarchy of subjects had lost much of its force among artists, critics, and patrons, all of whom showed greater concern for artistic expression than for anecdotal subject matter. Yet many of the more progressive art observers and critics continued to demand an infusion of spiritual, or at least elevated, meaning in works of art, and for some, still life simply seemed an inadequate means for conveying such values.

Harnett also may have been denigrated because of his painting style. Committed as he was to a highly realistic presentation, he was compelled to adopt a meticulously precise technique. Such an aesthetic was much in vogue, especially among painters of still life and intimate genre scenes, when he worked in Munich in the 1880s. Even the radical group of German artists who had gathered there around Wilhelm Leibl turned from the vigorous, slashing brushwork and dramatic facture that characterized their work in the 1870s and in the following decade favored a more precise and controlled aesthetic. They chose Hans Holbein and Dutch masters of the seventeenth century, such as Gerard Terborch, for their models, in place of bolder painters, such as

Fig. 36. John La Farge, *The Last Water Lily*, 1862. Oil on wood, 9⅝ x 7⁷⁄₁₆ in. Private collection. Courtesy of Thomas Colville, Inc., New Haven

Frans Hals and the French Realist Gustave Courbet. Several Americans, including Harnett, followed this trend and were condemned by art critics who derisively designated them as the "Furniture School" upon their return to the United States.[4] Ironically, the Harnetts that eventually drew the attention of the public and critics alike were pictures that embodied his most radical form of deceptive realism—vertical still lifes of hanging objects such as *After the Hunt* of 1885, *The Old Violin* of 1886, and *For Sunday's Dinner* of 1888 (pls. 34, 37, 42). The critical need to recognize and sometimes to argue against the effectiveness of these pictures or to insist upon their inability to attain the status of "high art" related directly to public enthusiasm for them.

What is significant about Harnett's critical triumphs, such as they were, is that they occurred largely outside the conceptual and actual strongholds of "high art." When his work appeared in traditional displays at the Pennsylvania Academy, the Museum of Fine Arts in Boston, the Art Institute of Chicago, the Brooklyn Art Association, and above all, the National Academy, they were often ignored, and if they were noticed, it was usually with disdain. The criticism, often aimed at the absurdity of "imitative" painting, reveals an elitist distinction between the standards of the connoisseur and those of the masses. This division was also drawn along geographic lines. Critics in provincial locations—say Louisville or Cincinnati—extolled his work for precisely the same reasons it was derided in the more established art centers. One might read into this situation a relative lack either of sophistication or aesthetic awareness on the part of local inhabitants and writers, since they were essentially unconcerned with the limitations of transcriptive art or with the appreciation of technical virtuosity. There is some reason to believe that the artist himself chose the more customary, traditional art displays in the East, and that astute dealers such as Dennis Gale and exhibition coordinators such as Edwin Mehner often directed his paintings to industrial fairs and expositions in the provinces, where they drew plaudits. At these venues, band concerts, not orchestral performances, were the musical order of the day, and, likewise, it was Harnett's trompe-l'oeil pictures, not the more subtle flower pieces of such aristocratic artists as John La Farge, that satisfied the crowds. Unfortunately, no information on Harnett's attitudes toward different venues survives, so we cannot determine whether he made conscious distinctions about what types of works he would send to each kind of exhibition. Nevertheless, a survey of the critical reaction to his work illustrates the pattern of responses—from established Eastern centers to provincial localities—and defines the basic aesthetic issues raised by the artist's contemporaries.

At his first major annual, the 1875 spring exhibition of the National Academy, Harnett's entry *Fruit* went unmentioned. His humble edible subject must have been overshadowed by major figure pieces by Winslow Homer and Eastman Johnson, much-praised landscapes by Albert Bierstadt and George Inness, and more progressive works sent from Munich and Paris by young artists such as William Merritt Chase, J. Alden Weir, and Frederick Arthur Bridgman. Those still lifes that did receive notice were more impressive floral subjects, including La Farge's *Last Water Lily* of 1862 (fig. 36), which was extolled for its "high nobility."[5] The works of several female painters, notably Helena de Kay and William Morris Hunt's student Elizabeth Greene, were also singled out for commendation.[6] The situation was virtually the same the following November, when Harnett contributed *Basket of Fruit,* probably *Still Life* of 1875 (fig. 37), to a show at the Brooklyn Art Association.

Fig. 37. William M. Harnett, *Still Life,* 1875. Oil on canvas, 18 x 26¼ in.
Reading Public Museum and Art Gallery, Pa., Gift, Honorable Thomas P. Merritt, 1916

The response was markedly different that year, when Harnett sent *Muscatel Grapes* to the Louisville Industrial Exposition, which attracted submissions from many prominent American painters. Harnett's picture, along with a similar subject by the obscure Amelia N. Henshaw,[7] elicited surprising commendation from a reviewer for the *Courier-Journal:*

> To say that the fruit seems real would hardly convey the perfect impression. The bunches stand out in bold relief from the canvas, and each particular grape projects itself from the other as naturally as though they had really grown from the stem and were hanging ready to be plucked by some dainty hand to please the taste of those fond of the luscious fruit.[8]

What obviously impressed the Louisville critic was not merely the sense of reality conveyed by Harnett's grapes but also the illusion of actual projection of the whole bunch, and each individual component, toward the viewer—the very qualities that would later identify Harnett as the most masterful of America's trompe-l'oeil painters.

This pattern of exclusion or disparagement in eastern art centers versus appreciation at more distant venues was to repeat itself, even after 1877, when Harnett chose new and more individual subjects: first, tabletop pictures of man-made objects, then vertical compositions with suspended objects. His new thematic direction was heralded by a group of five works included in a display arranged by Philadelphia art dealer Dennis Gale at the Twelfth Industrial Exhibition of the San Francisco Mechanics' Institute. Gale's presentation, numbering some 440 paintings by both American and European artists, included a good many still lifes—fruit paintings by the Englishman George Clare, oyster subjects by the Baltimore artist Andrew John Henry Way, and flower pieces by Philadelphian George Cochran Lambdin—all likely for sale.[9] The largest selection of Harnett's work shown during his lifetime, the exhibition featured *Materials for a Quiet Evening; Mynheer's Lunch; Books, Inkstand, Coin, etc.;* a work simply identified as *Pendant* to the last; and *Materials for a Leisure Hour.*[10] These paintings enjoyed a rather positive reception, being acclaimed in the catalogue for "their careful finish and close attention to reality."[11] *Materials for a Quiet Evening* was praised as representing "its title very cosily indeed." The writer catalogued the objects depicted (a newspaper, a glass of beer, a pipe, and some tobacco) and concluded with enthusiasm, "The minutæ [sic] are wonderful."[12]

Back in Philadelphia, the New York pattern was repeated: *A Study Table* and *Fruit*, both exhibited at the 1877 spring annual of the Pennsylvania Academy, went unnoticed by critics. When Harnett showed *Bachelor's Comfort* with the Philadelphia Society of

Fig. 38. John Moran, *Interior of James S. Earle & Sons, 816 Chestnut Street, Philadelphia*. Stereograph. Library Company of Philadelphia

Artists in April 1878, it was described as "a clever but overlabored study of inanimate objects."[13] Later that month, his painting of peaches was included in a group exhibition at James S. Earle and Sons, a commercial gallery (fig. 38), and dismissed passingly as "careful work."[14] Harnett's submission to the 1878 annual at the Pennsylvania Academy, *An Evening's Comfort,* was not only ignored by critics but ridiculed in the burlesque catalogue *L'Académie pour rire,* which noted forty-six works and caricatured all but one of them in drawings (figs. 39, 40).[15] The neglected piece was Harnett's picture, which is represented by a frame surrounding the inscription *L'intérieur de ce cadre se trouve chez tous les marchands de tabac.* Even for the parodist, Harnett's painting did not merit serious consideration.

By the end of the decade, the New York critical establishment finally began to offer a limited assessment of Harnett's place in the contemporary American art world. The three paintings he displayed at the National Academy in 1878—*After a Hard Night's Work, A Bad Counterfeit—Panel,* and *Jakes' Solace*—were relegated to the corridor, an undesirable location that was often reserved for pictures deemed to be of lesser merit, significance, or size, or for works by artists of limited reputation. The most ambitious of the three, *After a Hard Night's Work,* rather expensively priced at six hundred dollars, was condemned as "a hard and metallic still-life," while the others were at least acknowledged as "two wonderful pieces of realism."[16] *A Bad Counterfeit—Panel* earned Harnett an additional one-line kudo for his "great dexterity."[17] The following November, however, his work was completely overlooked at an important exhibition at the Seventh Regiment New Armory Fair, to which he contributed *Bric-a-Brac,* possibly the first public exposure of his depiction of objets de virtu, and a work entitled *Smoker's Companions.*

The display of Harnett's *Social Club* of 1879 (pl. 16) at the spring annual of the National Academy that year inspired the first lengthy critical reactions to the artist's work within the context of other highly realistic paintings. The critics were unanimous in defining the limitations they perceived in his art: it was devoted to *imitation;* it lacked artistic purpose; and it was disappointing even in its technical virtuosity. One writer, most likely Clarence Cook, associated *The Social Club* with works by Seymour Guy, Morston Ream, Daniel Huntington, and Martin Johnson Heade, all representatives of the previous generation of painters then passing out of favor. Heade's still-life entry was described as a "neat carefully painted scientific illustration of certain botanical facts" but very definitely not "a work of art." The writer asked: "Is it not plain that in most of these examples, art has had nothing

to do with their production, that they are only mechanical toys?" His analysis of Harnett's accomplishments was perhaps the first to address seriously the issue of the aesthetic value of the artist's work.

Last year Mr. William M. Harnett had several pictures in the Exhibition of the same general character as this "Social Club" and they attracted the attention that is always given to curiosities, to works in which the skill of the human hand is ostentatiously displayed working in deceptive imitation of Nature. An essay might be written on this subject of imitative art, and it could be shown by a score of examples culled from the old books, from Pliny down to Vasari, that even in the ages we call the best this attempt to deceive the senses has been reckoned one of the legitimate aims of art. But it is equally true that all the greatest artists—even Dürer and Holbein—have known how to keep this imitative skill in its true place, as servant not as master, as a means or adjunct, not as an end, while the very greatest names of all in the list of men of genius never attempted imitation at all; Raphael in the details of some of his matchless portraits . . . coming as near to the dangerous point of excess as is compatible with the true aims of art. Only a very few artists of merit

Figs. 39, 40. *L'Académie pour rire,* 1878. Pennsylvania Academy of the Fine Arts, Philadelphia, Archives

have ever condescended to apply their skill to the sole purpose of imitation, making so-called pictures out of dead objects painted to deceive the eye as far as possible, for there still remains a little dignity of purpose attaching to flower-pieces, fruit-pieces, game-pieces and the like, and great painters, among them Vollon, of our own time, have occasionally wreaked their superfluous strength and sportive leisure on the painting [of] pots and pans so sublimely as almost to make us ashamed of our principles. But we must remember that this is only the play of good painters, never their serious employment. . . . The real fact is that this charge of inferiority is justified by the consideration that this imitative work is not really so difficult as it seems to the layman, and though there are degrees of it, yet when we come down to works like this of Mr. Harnett, it is evident that only time and industry are necessary to the indefinite multiplication of them. There are sign-painters in plenty in this city of ours—and in all great cities today—who have only to be sufficiently discontented with their honest calling to aim at the name of artist, to rival Mr. Harnett, Mr. Guy, Mr. Ream, Mr. Huntington himself in the painting of externals.[18]

Despite critical disapproval, *The Social Club* was purchased at the exhibition.[19]

Just after Harnett left for Europe in 1880, there was a brief hiatus in his exhibition activities. For the next year or so, he did not display at his usual venues, such as the National Academy. He may have left some pictures at commercial galleries in the States while seeking new opportunities for exhibition abroad, particularly during his long stay in Frankfort, but he may simply have been too preoccupied with his changing situation and new experiences to arrange for submissions of any kind.

In 1881, Harnett again began contributing to American exhibitions, more often in New York than at provincial venues.[20] That spring, he displayed *Still Life* at the National Academy and, in what would prove to be his final exhibition at the Pennsylvania Academy, *Materials for a Leisure Hour* and *Still Life (Bank Notes, Coin, etc.).* None of these works seems to have received critical attention. Two, and possibly all three, appear to have been done before his departure for Europe and left behind. It may well be that Harnett was not yet ready to send his European pictures home, even though such trans-Atlantic exhibition arrangements were vital for establishing or maintaining the reputations of expatriate American artists.

Harnett subsequently became a frequent participant at the fall shows instituted by the National Academy in 1882. This new series of exhibitions, never the equal of the spring annuals, was introduced to promote sales; some artists even resubmitted works

shown earlier, and others took up the suggestion that they contribute more moderately sized pictures. Harnett responded with two paintings entitled *Still Life,* one on the miniaturistic scale he began to explore during his European sojourn. The critic for the *New-York Daily Tribune*[21] received *Still Life* with new enthusiasm:

> Mr. Harnett has applied his imitative skill, hitherto exercised on too large a scale, to the production of a miniature piece well worth looking at as a curiosity. Nor is it without merit as a picture, but in artistic treatment shows a decided advance on the artist's part.[22]

While his work was commended, there was also the usual negative reaction to his style; another writer noted the undeveloped "sense of arrangement and color" in still-life paintings by Harnett, William Mason Brown, and Milne Ramsey.[23] In 1884, when Harnett contributed an unidentified *Still Life* to the National Academy's third autumn exhibition, a similar theme was taken up by a writer for the *Studio,* presumably the vituperative but incisive Clarence Cook, the magazine's editor and principal writer. Cook likened Harnett's picture to *The Lost Genius* (fig. 41) by the Munich-trained Henry Alexander:

> Mr. Alexander and Mr. Harnett, although mistaken in their methods, paint for people who . . . take pleasure in seeing a man try to paint things as they are. . . . It is plain that there has been close study of the things represented, and a desire to paint them as they really look. The fault in the two pictures is a want of artistic subordination of the unimportant to the important, and there is, in both, a deficient sense of beauty; each of these artists chooses ugly or uninteresting things to paint, and has not . . . the power to bewitch us into thinking them beautiful. And then, again, beside the want of subordination in the things themselves, there is the want of subordinatio[n] in the pictorial treatment; how much in managing such a subject as these depends on the lighting? And how crude and uninteresting is the way in which the light falls upon the objects in Mr. Harnett's picture.[24]

With obvious ignorance of the years Alexander and Harnett had already spent abroad, the commentator concluded:

> And, yet, with all the shortcomings of execution, and want of taste, that make these pictures so unsatisfactory, so disagreeable, we have no doubt that a month in Holland, or in Paris, with the old Dutch painters of such scenes, would do wonders for both Mr. Alexander and Mr. Harnett. They have developed so far in a vacuum; to have done so much, with no examples and no teaching, is

Fig. 41. Henry Alexander, *The Lost Genius.*
Oil on canvas, 21¾ x 29⅞ in. University Art Museum,
University of California at Berkeley,
Bequest of Hannah N. Haviland (1921.4)

creditable to them, and gives good ground for believing that with enlarged opportunities they might become interesting painters.[25]

Thus, even during the 1880s, New York critics continued to question the artistic validity of Harnett's highly realistic aesthetic.

The foreign exhibition of Harnett's work, which dates from the years he spent abroad, 1880 to 1886, was rather favorably received; European critics often sided with provincial American reviewers and praised Harnett for some of the same reasons he had been condemned in New York and Philadelphia.

Harnett seems to have first developed his most radical form of deceptive realism in Munich, where it appears his pictures were much admired. In 1881, he joined the Kunstverein, a group of artists and patrons who sponsored a series of weekly exhibits of painting and sculpture. Unfortunately, no catalogues of their exhibitions were printed and no records of the participants survive, so it is not possible to determine precisely how often he showed with the group or which works he displayed.[26] The following year, he exhibited *Table with Books, Sheet Music, and Musical Instruments*, most likely *A Study Table* of 1882 (pl. 26).[27] One critic called it "a masterpiece of its type" and found its flute and sheets of music provided "more food for thought than any of your wooden, badly executed human figures."[28] In 1883, *Hunting Gear and Wild Ducks*, almost certainly one of the two first versions of *After the Hunt* (pls. 28, 29), was exhibited and sold to a private collector, but it apparently received no mention in the press, perhaps

because critical attention was focused on a larger, more important exhibition at Munich's Glaspalast.

This 1883 exhibition, arguably the most prestigious in which Harnett would ever participate, featured an exceptional group of almost three hundred paintings, graphics, and stained-glass works by such distinguished American artists as Thomas Eakins, Winslow Homer, George Inness, and William Merritt Chase. A few Americans then residing in Munich—including David Neal, Carl von Marr, Toby Rosenthal, and principally J. Frank Currier—also contributed to the show. Harnett's entry, entitled simply *Still Life,* was prescribed as a model for the Austrian figure painter Anton Romako, whose "sketches" one writer found lacking in "formal composition."[29] A fellow American, most likely either Otto Henry Bacher or Sion Longley Wenban, confirmed the German enthusiasm for Harnett's work in a letter sent to their home city, Cleveland: "Harnett, a Philadelphian who couldn't get into the school two years ago, has a large still life which the Germans think a masterpiece; it is very fine, wonderfully deceptive, and reminds one of the old German masters."[30]

In 1884, when Harnett displayed the third version of *After the Hunt* (pl. 33), with the Kunstverein, German reviewers finally turned to some of the issues that had been plaguing New York critics, including Cook. One writer called Harnett "a modern Parrhasios," one of the greatest painters of ancient Greece, and claimed that his work was capable of completely deceiving his audience.

> One would think it is possible to remove the hat, the hunting horn, the flintlock, the sword, the powder horn and the game bag from their nails and with them equip one's self for the hunt. One could become a veritable Nimrod with these hunting utensils which project so plastically from the old door that serves as background. There is not a tiny splinter, not a nailhead, nothing that is not depicted to perfection, so that one does not know which to admire more—the artist's gigantic patience or his astonishing powers of observation and imitation. But the pendantry shown in the rendering also dominates the composition. For us this is . . . far too painstaking in its orderliness, so that its painterly effect is impaired. . . . Harnett's still life is surrounded by an astonished, admiring crowd, and we do not wish to be last to voice our wonder at this eminent "work of art."[31]

Late in 1884, Harnett traveled to Paris, where he had been once before, and the following spring he exhibited the fourth and largest version of *After the Hunt* (pl. 34) at the Salon. Displayed as *Trophée de Chasse* and dated 1885, the picture was completed, if not totally painted, in Paris. The artist's most majestic painting, it was warmly greeted by critic Louis Enault, who was willing to "swear that all this is done with the free hand," diverting any accusations of technical manipulation. "I would not be just if I refused to recognize the dexterity of hand of which Mr. Harnett has given a high degree of proof in this decorative panel," wrote Enault. "I have rarely seen a relief more powerful."[32] Around this time, Harnett was showing, and perhaps living, in London, for when he lent *Still Life* of 1885 (pl. 35) to the exhibition of the Royal Academy, he gave that city as his place of residence. Described as an "'outsider'" by a reviewer for the *Times* of London, Harnett was praised for creating "one of the most miraculous representations of books, a flute, some sheets of music, and a brass lamp that we have ever seen."[33] Whereas Harnett's Paris Salon entry was returned to the artist at the close of the exhibition, this still life was sold to the popular British portrait painter George Richmond. The year 1885, then, marked Harnett's greatest success in the international art arena.

Upon his return to the States in 1886, Harnett settled in New York, where several of his works—the fourth *After the Hunt, Music, Ten-Dollar Bill, The Sideboard* (also called *Fruit Scene*), and *Still Life—Five-Dollar Bill*—were soon put on permanent display in rather unconventional venues—two New York saloons run by Theodore Stewart, who had commissioned all these paintings save the first. The clientele of the bars represented a very different segment of society, one perhaps more favorably disposed to works of illusionism than the audience that attended exhibitions at the National Academy of Design. In barrooms, deceptively realistic still lifes and female nudes were favored subjects, both aimed at a predominantly male audience, though women were occasion-

ally in attendance.[34] Stewart's paintings quickly elicited a wealth of favorable commentaries in the New York press. Admittedly, many of these notices were published upon the initial appearance of the pictures, which soon became popular fixtures rather than centerpieces of an ongoing aesthetic commentary.[35] *After the Hunt,* called one of the "counterfeits of today," was draped with a crimson velvet curtain, which concealed gas jets that lit the picture.[36] According to this account, men "stand before this picture for fifteen minutes at a time," with "city men. . . enraptured" and "gentlemen from the country" maintaining "that nobody can take them in and that the objects are real objects hung up with an intent to deceive people."[37] In this commentary, at any rate, the tables had been turned, and the urban and provincial roles of Harnett's viewers reversed, with the latter becoming the skeptics. Another writer praised *After the Hunt* as one of "the most remarkable illusions ever produced by the brush of an artist."

> Indeed, the management of light, shade and harmony of color in these works has reached a point of perfection which amounts to complete illusion. The spectator may place himself at any point of observation, remote or near, and he will find it difficult, if not impossible, to convince himself that he is not looking at real objects. . . . By dint of long study of the picture he at length admits that it is "*all painting,*" but the illusion even then persists, and he at last turns away, generally with the exclamation, "Marvellous! The most remarkable thing I ever saw!"

For this critic, Harnett's work succeeded because, "The wood *is* wood, the iron is iron, the brass is brass, the leather is leather." He concluded that the technique of Harnett's paintings was "simply perfect" because "the illusions produced by them are so powerful."[38] However, George Inness, a leading American landscape painter, considered *After the Hunt* "a lie." Most likely speaking of this picture, he asserted, "'Imitation is worthless. Photography does it much better than you or I could. . . . Now, in art, true art, we are not seeking to deceive.'"[39]

Reaction to Harnett's contributions to exhibitions often continued the same patterns established before his years abroad. *Still Life* (private collection), shown at the 1886 spring annual of the National Academy, seems to have been ignored, while *The Old Violin* of 1886 (pl. 37), one of three works on view at the Thirteenth Cincinnati Industrial Exposition that year, drew more attention than Harnett was ever again to enjoy as the result of an exhibition during his lifetime. *The Old Violin* was a late arrival at the show, but it immediately caused a "furore" and "a crowd of bewildered gazers [was] continually about it."[40] "A policeman stands by it constantly, lest people reach

Fig. 42. John Haberle, *Imitation,* 1887. Oil on canvas, 10 x 14 in. Courtesy of Berry-Hill Galleries, New York

over and attempt to see if the newspaper clipping is genuine by tearing it off. They want to pull at the envelope as well," noted one account.[41] The picture was on display at the Second Minneapolis Industrial Exposition the following year, this time offered for sale at $3,300. "It is not a work of high art," concluded one newspaper writer, "and yet it is exceedingly interesting."[42] President and Mrs. Grover Cleveland admired the painting when they and their party visited the exposition.[43] However, the Reverend Frederick Taylor Gates, minister of the Baptist Central Church in Minneapolis, questioned its moral propriety and aesthetic significance. "The picture conveys no worthy thought or emotion. It is simply a trick," suggested Gates, whose sermon was directed to those considering purchasing works of art for the home.[44]

By 1888, it was clear that the paintings by Harnett that most intrigued the general public and elicited the most critical attention were his vertical still lifes of hanging objects, perhaps because their format enhanced the element of deception. It is surprising that the artist did not display more of these works during the last years of his life. Of course, they may have been submitted for exhibition and refused due to their lack of conformity to the notions of "high art"; or, perhaps Harnett preferred not to have his reputation entirely aligned with an especially imitative and deceptive art form. When the artist exhibited *For Sunday's Dinner* of 1888 (pl. 42), a vertical composition featuring a plucked chicken, at the autumn exhibition of the National Academy in 1888, for example, a writer for the *New Yorker Staats-Zeitung und Herald* called it "Vexir," or teasing, art and likened it to *After the Hunt,* then on view in New York at one of Stewart's saloons. "If, however, a savvy cat, while prowling over neighborhood roofs, would mistake this chicken to be the real thing is highly questionable."[45] A writer for the *New York Herald* offered an encomium of sorts: "W. M. Harnett has never painted a better piece of still life than his plucked fowl, 'For Sunday's Dinner.'"[46] The general public seemed equally enthusiastic about this witty rendition of what was traditionally a very *in*artistic subject treated in an *un*artistic manner. The illustrator Walt McDougall later recalled that when his brother recommended that he see Harnett's "nude" while it was on view at the National Academy, "I took the trouble, as I was rather doubtful of Harnett's rendition of nude flesh, only to find that the picture was that of a dressed turkey hanging from a kitchen door!"[47] Meanwhile, *Recreation,* the second work displayed by Harnett at this National Academy exhibition and probably not a vertical composition, generally seems to have been ignored by critics and visitors alike.

Harnett maintained his exhibition activity nationwide but seemingly receiving even less critical attention. In Philadelphia, one of his new pipe-and-newspaper pictures was on view at James S. Earle

and Sons, and *For Sunday's Dinner,* which had been purchased from the National Academy exhibition, appeared in the window of Wanamaker's department store. Joseph Fulton Humphrey lent his Harnett, *Still Life,* to a benefit show in Colorado Springs, where the weekly newspaper focused its attention on the local art community and described the picture as merely "a realistic portrayal of a pipe, a newspaper, etc."[48] The artist also sent *Suspended* to the first annual of the Art Institute of Chicago; the painting which was offered for sale at two hundred dollars, elicited no critical comment.[49]

During the late 1880s, another variable was added to the critical appraisal of Harnett. Having spawned a group of followers and imitators working within the aesthetics of trompe l'oeil, Harnett was now being overlooked in favor of his disciples. In the 1888 Chicago exhibition, *Reproduction* of about 1886 (fig. 5) by John Haberle (1856–1933) caused a sensation not unlike the earlier response given to Harnett's *Old Violin.* Writers hailed Haberle's "imitation" as "capital" and related the reactions of amazed viewers.

> One observer, disgusted that so much work should be wasted for results so insignificant, said to a trustee standing by: "I should think you would not have consented to putting those things in there. It was bad enough to paint a dollar bill." Even a second examination failed to convince her that they were not apart from the painting. But everything under the glass is brushwork.

This critic eventually dismissed *Reproduction,* and perhaps Harnett's *Suspended* as well, with the damning comment, "It is a pity they waste time and ability upon such worthlessness [*sic*]."[50] The same condescending attitude is evident in a notice about Haberle's *Imitation* of 1887 (fig. 42), exhibited at the National Academy the previous fall. "Of course no Academy exhibition would be complete without a presentation of the humorous side of art, any more than a circus could get on without a clown. It is Mr. Haberle who wears the cap and bells this time," commented a writer for *Art Review.*[51]

Both Haberle and Harnett were included in the 1889 fall annual at the National Academy—with *Editorial Board* and *Still Life,* respectively. Harnett garnered little notice for his contribution. *Art Amateur* acknowledged his name in a mention of the still lifes on display, and a reviewer for the *New York Times* noted the "more vulgar deceptiveness" of Harnett's *Still Life* in comparison to the entries of fruit, vegetables, and other still-life subjects.[52]

During the last few years of Harnett's life, his painting and exhibition activities were severely curtailed, perhaps because of deteriorating health. His known works done in 1890 number only five, and he does not seem to have submitted entries to any of the

Fig. 43. "Gill's Art Store," *Progressive Springfield* 2, no. 1 (June 1891), p. 2

annual exhibitions, not even that of the National Academy. But *Emblems of Peace* and *The Faithful Colt,* both of 1890 (pls. 46, 48), appeared in the showrooms of the New York jewelry firm of Black, Starr and Frost. Harnett was thus showing what were probably his two most important pictures of that year, in contrasting formats. Although they were on view outside the mainstream of art exhibitions and critics, they were favorably received by a writer for the *Epoch:*

> Both paintings are executed with that painstaking care so characteristic of Harnett. . . . Everything is delineated with truth in the minutest detail. This realistic fidelity in the representation of such familiar objects appeals to very many; and these pictures are sure to be much admired by the numerous visitors to their present quarters.[53]

Only four known pictures date from 1891, and Harnett submitted only two works to exhibitions that year. *A Bachelor's Friend,* shown at the spring annual of the National Academy, went unnoticed.[54] *Emblems of Peace* was dispatched to an exhibition at James D. Gill's Art Galleries in Springfield, Massachusetts, where

Harnett had shown *Still Life* in 1889 (fig. 43). Gill had first organized his group exhibitions in 1878, and by 1891 they were so highly regarded and commercially successful that several writers caustically suggested that the National Academy open its annual in Springfield rather than New York.[55] *Emblems of Peace* went unnoticed in the press but sold for the asking price of two thousand dollars; indeed, it was by far the most expensive work on exhibition.[56]

It is remarkable that the criticism of Harnett's work focused so often upon technique rather than content. There was precious little commentary on the elaborate formal structuring of his paintings, no attempt to discern any message or motivation within his thematic choices, and no cognizance of the innovations he had effected in the wide range of still-life subjects he addressed. Harnett expanded the boundaries and changed the rules of still-life painting in America, but contemporary commentators refused to acknowledge his achievements. This recognition was not to come until the twentieth century, when scholars and collectors alike approached Harnett's work with a new and more sympathetic set of expectations.

NOTES

1. It should be noted that Harnett's output compares favorably with that of other painters who adopted a similar meticulous aesthetic, such as his contemporaries John Haberle and Jefferson David Chalfant, also still-life specialists.

2. Harnett skipped the National Academy's spring annual in 1880 and after 1882 more often chose the somewhat less significant fall exhibition.

3. Alfred Frankenstein, *After the Hunt: William Harnett and Other American Still Life Painters, 1870–1900,* rev. ed. (Berkeley and Los Angeles: University of California Press, 1969), pp. 91, 90, 7, 38, 78–82.

4. The term was used in reference to the work of Harnett's Munich-trained colleagues Louis Moeller and Charles Ulrich ("Art Notes and News," *Art Interchange* 14 [May 7, 1885], p. 121).

5. "The Academy of Design," *Scribner's Monthly* 10 (June 1875), p. 252.

6. [Clarence Cook], "Fine Arts: National Academy of Design—Fiftieth Annual Exhibition," *New-York Daily Tribune,* April 26, 1875, p. 7; and "The Arts," *Appletons' Journal* 13 (May 8, 1875), p. 600.

7. Henshaw was from Elizabeth City, N. J. The wife of real-estate developer John C. Henshaw, she exhibited still-life paintings and an occasional landscape between 1865 and 1885. Her listing disappears from city directories after 1889. I am grateful to Roman Sawycky, head of the Art and Music Department of the Free Public Library of Elizabeth, for his assistance.

8. "At the Exposition," *Louisville Courier-Journal,* September 14, 1875, n.p.

9. "Pavilion Pastimes," *San Francisco Sunday Chronicle,* August 26, 1877, p. 8.

10. *Mynheer's Lunch* is probably one of the many mug-and-pipe pictures painted by Harnett in 1877; a picture with the same title but dated 1879 was sold at Sotheby's, New York, on October 25, 1973. The others may well be known tabletop and smoking still lifes. A painting entitled *Materials for a Leisure Hour* is presently in the Thyssen-Bornemisza Collection, but the date 1879 is on the masthead of the newspaper depicted in it and it is also inscribed with that date. None of the works in the San Francisco exhibition can be identified as *Still Life with Letter to Dennis Gale* of 1879 (fig. 32).

11. *Catalogue of Art Department of the Twelfth Industrial Exhibition, Held under the Auspices of the Mechanics' Institute* (San Francisco, 1877), p. 7.

12. "The Eastern Art Collection," *San Francisco News Letter and California Advertiser,* September 1, 1877, p. 5. I am much indebted to my good friend and colleague Alfred Harrison for bringing the reviews of the exhibition in this publication to my attention.

13. "The Fine Arts: The Artists' Reception," *Evening Telegraph* (Philadelphia), April 2, 1878, p. 8.

14. "Original Paintings: A Sale by Messrs. James S. Earle & Sons," *North American* (Philadelphia), April 27, 1878, p. 1.

15. *49ᵐᵉ Exposition des Beaux Arts, Philadelphie, 1878: L'Académie pour rire.* Copy in the archives of the Pennsylvania Academy of the Fine Arts, Philadelphia. Cheryl Leibold, archivist at the academy, has suggested that J. McLure Hamilton may have been the author and illustrator of this publication.

16. "Fine Arts," *New York Mail,* April 1, 1878, p. 4.

17. "The Academy Exhibition," *New York Times,* April 21, 1878, p. 6 (reprinted in "Art: Philadelphia's Contribution to the New York Academy Exhibition," *North American* [Philadelphia], April 22, 1878, p. 1).

18. [Clarence Cook], "Academy of Design: Fifty-fourth Annual Exhibition," *New-York Daily Tribune,* April 26, 1879, p. 5. Also see the discussion of this critique in Frankenstein, *After the Hunt,* pp. 50–51; and Frankenstein, "Harnett: One Century," *Art News* 47, no. 5 (September 1948), pp. 17, 52.

19. "National Academy of Design: Close of the Annual Exhibition," *New York Times,* June 1, 1879, p. 2.

20. *Consolation,* one of the few works by Harnett known to have been on display in the Midwest during his years abroad, was at least noticed at the eleventh annual Chicago Inter-State Industrial Exposition, in September 1883. It was lent by Norton Quincy Pope, who concentrated on contemporary paintings by such European masters as Horace Vernet, Jean-Louis-Ernest Meissonier, and Jehan Georges Vibert and displayed only three American pictures among the thirty he lent to the show. *Consolation* was praised for "tell[ing] the story with sufficient directness" ("Art and Artists," *Chicago Tribune,* September 16, 1883, p. 10).

21. Although Clarence Cook had written for the *Tribune* earlier, this piece was probably by someone else, since Cook had a falling out with the paper's editor, Whitelaw Reid, in 1880.

22. "Fine Arts: National Academy of Design, Special Autumn Exhibition," *New-York Daily Tribune,* October 21, 1882, p. 5.

23. "Art Notes," *Art Journal* 8 (November 1882), p. 350.

24. Clarence Cook[?], "The National Academy of Design: The Autumn Exhibition," *Studio,* n.s. [1], no. 7 (November 8, 1884), p. 81.

25. Ibid.

26. Only occasional reviews, mainly those in the Blemly scrapbook (Alfred Frankenstein Papers, Archives of American Art, Smithsonian Institution, Washington, D.C., microfilm) document Harnett's involvement in Kunstverein exhibitions.

27. Assuming that Harnett would have shown his latest productions with this artists' group, of his known works the picture of 1882 that best conforms to this descriptive title is *A Study Table.* My suggestion endorses that made previously by Chad Mandeles in his essay on the painting in Paul D. Schweizer, ed., *Masterworks of American Art*

from the Munson-Williams-Proctor Institute (New York: Harry N. Abrams, 1989), p. 223, no. 36, n. 1.

28. "Neues aus dem Kunstverein," clipping from the *Münchner Neueste Nachrichten und Münchner Anzeiger,* August 1882 (otherwise unidentified), Blemly scrapbook, frame 335, quoted in Frankenstein, *After the Hunt,* p. 62, n. 34.

29. "Theater, Kunst und Wissenschaft," *Münchner Neueste Nachrichten und Münchner Anzeiger,* July 6, 1883, n.p. I am grateful to Beate Hirsch, intern at the Metropolitan Museum of Art, for locating this and other Munich reviews.

30. "An Interesting Letter," *Sketch Book* 1, no. 7 (July 1883), pp. 76–77.

31. "Aus dem Kunstverein," clipping from the *Handelsblatt,* 1884 (otherwise unidentified), Blemly scrapbook, frame 335, quoted in Frankenstein, *After the Hunt,* p. 69. Frankenstein states that the clipping came from the Munich *Handelsblatt,* but Mrs. Hirsch has ascertained that no newspaper by that name was published in Munich, though there was one in Berlin.

32. Louis Enault, *Paris-Salon, 1885,* 2 vols. (Paris: E. Bernard & Cie, 1885), 2, p. 8.

33. "Royal Academy: Third Notice," *Times* (London), May 25, 1885, p. 4.

34. For a brief, lively treatment of saloons with suggestions about some of the art that might have been found in such establishments, see Gerald Carson, "The Saloon," *American Heritage* 14, no. 3 (April 1963), pp. 24–31, 103–7.

35. Since Harnett returned to the United States in 1886, and Stewart died on August 11, 1887, all Stewart's commissions except *After the Hunt* were almost surely painted in 1886 or early 1887 at the latest (see Wm. I. Blemly, "Honor to Whom Honor Is Due," *World* [New York], August 14, 1887, p. 5).

36. "Art's Counterfeiting: Some Notable Examples of Deceiving the Eyes by Pictures," *Star* (New York), December 30, 1885, p. 6.

37. Ibid.

38. "Queer Art Illusions: Some of the Many Methods Employed to Produce Them," clipping from an unidentified and undated newspaper, Blemly scrapbook, frame 327.

39. Quoted in George Inness, Jr., *Life, Art, and Letters of George Inness* (New York: Century Co., 1917), p. 124.

40. This quotation from an 1886 Cincinnati newspaper (otherwise unidentified) appeared in a brochure that was issued in conjunction with the publication of a chromolithograph of *The Old Violin* by the F. Tuchfarber Co. of Cincinnati in 1887 and is contained in the Blemly scrapbook, frame 281.

41. Ibid. Similar accounts appeared in "A Wonderland," *Cincinnati Enquirer,* September 19, 1886, p. 12; "The Art Gallery," *Cincinnati Commercial Gazette,* September 16, 1886; and in the F. Tuchfarber Co. brochure.

42. "Auspiciously Opened," *St. Paul and Minneapolis Pioneer Press,* September 1, 1887, p. 8.

43. "At the Exposition Building," *St. Paul and Minneapolis Pioneer Press,* October 12, 1887, p. 2.

44. "The Churches: Pictures at the Exposition Furnish Material for a Sermon," *Minneapolis Tribune,* September 12, 1887, p. 5. As Mrs. Hirsch has pointed out, Gates was instrumental in raising funds for the University of Chicago, particularly the contribution of John D. Rockefeller. He later became a guiding force in many of Rockefeller's enterprises and helped develop the policies that led to the establishment of the Rockefeller Foundation.

45. "Kunst," *New Yorker Staats-Zeitung und Herald,* November 25, 1888, p. 4, translated by Beate Hirsch.

46. "In the Domain of Art: A Last Glance around the Autumn Academy Display," *New York Herald,* December 9, 1888, p. 19.

47. Walt McDougall, *This Is the Life!* (New York: Alfred A. Knopf, 1926), p. 92.

48. "Loan Exhibition," *Weekly Gazette: Colorado Springs,* October 20, 1888, p. 3.

49. The title suggests a vertical rendition of a hanging object, Harnett's most popular still-life form, but the low price would indicate a small picture, perhaps one of the two versions of his *Meerschaum Pipe* (pl. 39 and Allen Memorial Art Museum, Oberlin College, Ohio). As suggested by the comparative criticism, however, Harnett may have contributed one of his money pictures. One writer, after discussing Haberle's *Reproduction,* also on view in the exhibition, observed, "Up-stairs there is a $10 bill painted by another equally accurate and painstaking man" ("Art Institute Pictures," *Chicago Tribune,* June 3, 1888, p. 26).

50. Ibid.

51. "Exhibitions of the Month, in New York: II. National Academy of Design," *Art Review* 2, no. 4 (December 1887), p. 87.

52. "Paintings at the Academy," *New York Times,* November 26, 1889, p. 5.

53. Frank Linstow White, "Art Notes," *Epoch* 8 (December 12, 1890), p. 300.

54. This may be the similarly titled *A Bachelor's Friends* (Kennedy Galleries, Inc., New York), which is dated 1891.

55. "A Notable Art Center," *Progressive Springfield* 2, no. 1 (June 1891), p. 5.

56. Confirmation of the sale and price can be found in "Mr. Gill's Annual Sale," *Collector* 2, no. 14 (May 15, 1891), p. 164.

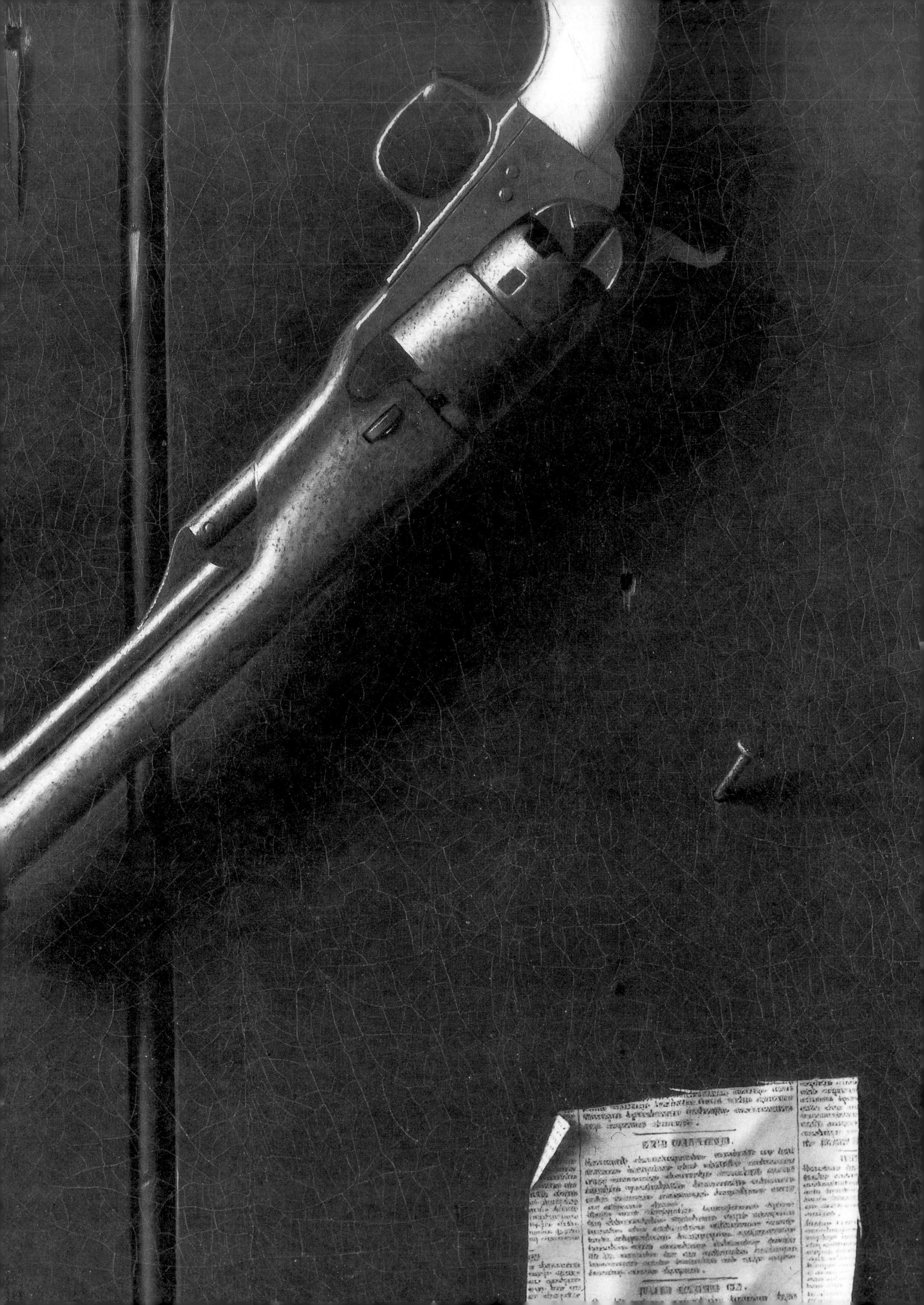

Harnett Enters Art History

ELIZABETH JOHNS

When William Michael Harnett died in 1892, newspapers hailed him as a master. The *New York Times* lamented the loss of "one of the best known still-life painters in the country"; the *World* noted the "many evidences of his genius" that were in New York collections; the *Boston Evening Transcript* described him as a "famous still-life painter"; and in his native Philadelphia, the *Evening Bulletin* mourned the death of "one of the greatest painters of 'still life' in this country."[1] Within the decade, however, Harnett was to fall into obscurity. Collectors turned to European styles, especially Impressionism, that featured figure painting and landscape. As time passed, the burgeoning varieties of modernism in the 1910s and 1920s put "native" American traditions at an even greater psychological distance.

In 1935, however, Harnett began to be rescued from oblivion. The people who participated in this process of rediscovery, documentation, and interpretation provide a vivid example of how the status of a dead artist—often one long dead—is shaped and reshaped by a complex network of agents. Included are the dealers who prolong or revive interest in the artist's work; the collectors who buy it; the reviewers who find it of potential interest to their readers; the art historians who look to trends in their field and to their own interests; the museum curators who ponder acquisitions and exhibition possibilities; and the conservators. In addition, there are the institutions that take part in securing the artist's reputation: museums; colleges and universities; funding organizations that subsidize scholarship; and publishing operations. Finally, there are also the workings of the art and auction markets as well as various trends in the mass media.

Following Harnett's death, the exhibition of his paintings in late 1892 and the sale of his studio effects in Philadelphia in 1893 brought good publicity and high prices for most of his works because the artist died at the peak of his career.[2] Despite his popularity among certain patrons, however, his detailed illusionism ran counter to the dominant taste for a soft, poetic style that informed the American art market until the 1920s.

Harnett's "rediscovery" began in the spring of 1935, when *The Faithful Colt* of 1890 (pl. 48), a rather startling juxtaposition of a gun against a worn green door, painted with striking illusionistic effect, came on the art market. At the time, Surrealist paintings and Cubist montages by Pablo Picasso, Fernand Léger, Salvador Dali, Pierre Roy, and Kurt Schwitters were being bought by private collectors and museums, and exhibitions were being mounted to interpret the principles of abstraction. Moreover, the collecting of American folk art and crafts had reached a virtual frenzy, with dealers scouring the countryside in New England and the Middle Atlantic states for "primitive" paintings, carved figures, and weathervanes that somehow exemplified a pure American past. Edith Gregor Halpert, a New York gallery owner who specialized in American art, was thoroughly engaged in these projects (fig. 44). Defining herself as a sponsor of American and contemporary painting, Halpert had two specialties: the current "immaculates" and "romantics" (later called the Precisionists and Magic Realists), especially Charles Sheeler and Ben Shahn, and American folk art of the eighteenth and nineteenth centuries, which she actively sought from a diverse group of regional dealers and in turn offered to collectors such as Abby Aldrich Rockefeller.

An alert "scout" offered Harnett's *Faithful Colt* to Halpert in April 1935.[3] The day after purchasing it, she wrote to A. Everett Austin, Jr., director of the Wadsworth Atheneum, Hartford, Connecticut, and offered him

---

Fig. 44. Charles Sheeler, *Edith Gregor Halpert*.
Photograph. Downtown Gallery Papers, Archives of
American Art, Smithsonian Institution, Washington, D.C.

the picture. Surely it was this unusual painting, as opposed to other, more prosaic images that Harnett had created, that gave the revival such energy. Austin had a strong interest in Surrealism and in images that suggested it; earlier in the decade, Halpert had offered him Raphaelle Peale's *Venus Rising from the Sea—A Deception* (also called *After the Bath*) of 1822 (fig. 3), an image that combined a look of mystery and a nineteenth-century American provenance, but he had lost the painting to the William Rockhill Nelson Gallery of Art and Mary Atkins Museum of Fine Arts in Kansas City, Missouri. Halpert urged Austin to avoid another disappointment: "This is the most extraordinary canvas we have located in all these years, aside from the Peale, with which it can be favorably compared. *The Faithful Colt* can well be hung next to a Pierre Roy" (fig. 45).[4] When Austin expressed interest but did not make an offer, she wrote again, this time with the information that Alfred H. Barr, Jr., director of the Museum of Modern Art, New York, who was putting together the exhibition *Fantastic Art, Dada, Surrealism,* had been "tremendously impressed" with the painting on a visit to her gallery.[5]

By June, Austin had bought *The Faithful Colt* for the Atheneum (at a judiciously reduced price), making it the first Harnett to be purchased for a public collection.[6] Almost immediately, the painting was in demand for exhibitions, as it focused attention on the American visual past, on still life in general, and on paintings that were forerunners of modern trends. The College Art Association, for instance, which was encouraging interest in American art, included the work in *Thirty Paintings of Early America* in 1935.[7] Three years later, the Atheneum showed it in *The Painters of Still Life,* an exhibition that explored still life from past to present. And later in 1938, Barr selected *The Faithful Colt* as one of 228 paintings that provided the French with a glimpse of American artistic

achievement in the exhibition *Trois siècles d'art aux Etats-Unis,* held at the Musée du Jeu de Paume in Paris in May and July.[8] Grouping Harnett's painting with Peale's *Venus Rising from the Sea* and a still life by an unknown folk artist, Barr argued for a specifically American tradition that was also distinctly "modern." So persuasive was the Harnett as a "forerunner" of Surrealism that in March and April 1939, the Institute of Modern Art in Boston included it in the exhibition *The Sources of Modern Painting*. And Harnett was such a powerful practitioner of a distinctly American style that in 1943 the Museum of Modern Art included the recently rediscovered *Music and Good Luck* (now called *Still Life—Violin and Music*) of 1888 (pl. 43) in *American Realists and Magic Realists,* a show chosen by Dorothy C. Miller to demonstrate that *"sharp focus and precise representation"* are "a widespread but not yet generally recognized trend in contemporary American art."[9]

At her Downtown Gallery, Halpert acted on her conviction—certainly borne out by her sale of *The Faithful Colt*—that Harnett was a painter of interest and importance. From 1935 to 1939, she quietly amassed a storeroom of Harnett's paintings. Having acquired thirteen works she attributed to the artist, Halpert organized the exhibition *"Nature-Vivre" by William M. Harnett* in 1939.[10] To those works that she had on hand, she wisely added *The Faithful Colt, Emblems of Peace* of 1890 (pl. 46), and a chromolithograph after *The Old Violin* of 1886 that was lent by the Whitney Museum of American Art, New York.[11] Halpert wrote a brief essay in which she first distinguished the motivation of Harnett's original buyers from that of the current collectors:

> While his recognition in the nineteenth century may have been due to his "artistic composition" and his reputation as "the most realistic painter of his age", our present interest in Harnett is based on more contemporary considerations. We marvel at the fact that he anticipated a style practiced today by the vanguard in France and in this country. His color is brilliant, the painting flawless, and the composition organized in abstract pattern.

She moved on to insert Harnett into an art-historical framework that began in the seventeenth century. "But it is Harnett's combination of meticulous realism with an arbitrary juxtaposition of unrelated objects that may be said to provide a link between Dutch art of the seventeenth century and sur-realism of the twentieth." Finally, she placed Harnett in a specifically American visual past: "The contemporary school of imaginative realism is enriched by another American ancestor presented in this exhibition."[12]

This interpretive framework was absorbed and transmitted to readers of newspapers and journals by enthusiastic reviewers of Halpert's exhibition.

Fig. 45. Pierre Roy, *Daylight Saving Time,*
1929. Oil on canvas, 21½ x 15 in.
The Museum of Modern Art, New York,
Gift of Mrs. Ray Slater Murphy

National art magazines also took notice, and their celebration of "the most recent resurrection in the art field" was typical of the delight that journalists would take in the unfolding drama over the next few years.[13] Distinguished collectors such as Nelson Rockefeller, Barr, and A. Conger Goodyear, most of whom were also involved in collecting modern art, bought Harnetts almost as quickly as they were exhibited, as did museum directors.[14]

Having piqued substantial publicity about Harnett, Halpert put *"Nature-Vivre"* on the road.[15] She used her extensive network of dealers and her friendships with museum directors and curators to arrange for the exhibition to appear in cities carefully selected to take advantage of local collectors who were beginning to come into prominence. In each location, the paintings on display varied slightly, as new works came in and sales flourished. Due to the publicity generated by the traveling exhibition, paintings ascribed to Harnett began to appear on the market with increasing frequency over the next several years. By 1947, approximately one hundred works attributed to the artist had entered private and public collections.[16]

With the rejuvenation of spirit that followed the end of World War II, the art world moved into high gear. Although Harnett's work was now of interest to a committed group of collectors, not much was known about him in wider circles, and the totality of his work was as yet unclear. What was needed was an art historian to write a biographical study and catalogue. In 1946, Alfred Frankenstein, a critic of art and music for the *San Francisco Chronicle* who had given Harnett's works appreciative recognition in 1940, stepped forward to claim the task (fig. 46).[17] He secured the enthusiastic endorsement of Halpert, who stood to benefit both materially and in prestige from the project, and he received the blessing of Barr, who had expressed an interest in Harnett's works (and had bought several for himself) and whose leadership in interpreting Surrealism and abstraction was fundamental to the growing appreciation of the artist.[18] Halpert permitted Frankenstein to photocopy all the notebooks and photographs she had compiled on Harnett over the eleven-year period since she had bought *The Faithful Colt.* The two began an extensive correspondence about the ongoing project, and Frankenstein kept in frequent touch with Barr as well.

The project grew in complexity, and in April 1947 Frankenstein received a Guggenheim Fellowship, through the encouragement primarily, it seems, of Barr.[19] The fellowship meant that the journalist could take a leave from his responsibilities at the *Chronicle* and spend the next year examining records and paintings in the East. Buoyed by such prestigious institutional support, Frankenstein thereafter referred to the project as being under the sponsorship of the Guggenheim Foundation and gave correspondents its address as his point of contact in New York.[20] He announced his own award in the *Chronicle* in May in the article "The Full Story behind a Guggenheim Award and an Artist Named Harnett."[21] *Art Digest* publicized the fellowship with the promise that the "respected art and music critic" was "well qualified for the necessary sleuthing."[22]

In the summer of 1947, shortly after Frankenstein had taken up his work for the fellowship year in earnest, he began to suspect that some of the paintings signed "Harnett" were actually by another artist. Halpert herself mentioned the occasional signed Harnetts she had been offered that were obviously forgeries because they were so clumsy. What worried Frankenstein was another phenomenon: two groups of still-life models, two painting styles, and at least two signature conventions seemed to separate the Harnett paintings into two distinct groups. He paid particular attention to details on two paintings attributed to Harnett that included dates after Harnett's death. His confusion finally began to clear when he visited the Island Heights, New Jersey, studio of John Frederick Peto (1854–1907), an admirer of Harnett's who had

Fig. 46. *Portrait of Alfred Frankenstein.* Photograph. Alfred Frankenstein Papers, Archives of American Art, Smithsonian Institution, Washington, D.C.

used a remarkably similar approach to still-life painting. On July 21, 1947, Frankenstein wrote Barr asking advice "concerning the incredible and somewhat frightening discoveries" he had made there.[23] In Peto's studio, maintained by his daughter, Mrs. George Smiley, Frankenstein had discovered paintings signed by Peto that were executed in a "soft" tonality then associated with Harnett, as well as many of the models featured in those works. Moreover, in talking with Mrs. Smiley, Frankenstein had learned biographical details about Peto that irrefutably connected him to pictures that were attributed to Harnett—most notably *Old Scraps* (now called *Old Time Letter Rack*) of 1894 (fig. 47), then owned by Rockefeller. In a report Frankenstein compiled after his visit, he concluded that "a considerable number of Petos have, through forged signatures, been attributed to W. M. Harnett."[24]

Frankenstein took on the demeanor of a detective. At the time, the art world was agog with a major problem in the history of connoisseurship that had a direct bearing on Frankenstein's and Halpert's enterprises: forgery. Hans van Meegeren, a contemporary Dutch painter, was being unmasked as the forgerer of recently rediscovered "lost Vermeers," shocking experts who had been completely duped. Forgery

fundamentally threatened the connoisseurship, collecting, and interpreting of art, and the potentially sensational topic appeared frequently in art journals. Previous certainties about the reliability of the trained eye were now seriously compromised.

In this charged atmosphere, Frankenstein enlisted science—X rays, ultraviolet and infrared analysis, and the removal of overpaint—to sort out the real Harnetts. Barr arranged for Sheldon Keck, conservator at the Brooklyn Museum, to X-ray Rockefeller's *Old Scraps* and Pittsburgh collector Edgar Kaufmann's *Career's End.*[25] By October 21, 1947, Keck had established through the removal of overpaint that the authentic signature on *Old Scraps* was "without any doubt" that of Peto.[26] In the meantime, Frankenstein had arranged for *Old Souvenirs,* which belonged to the Phillips Memorial Gallery, Washington, D.C., to be X-rayed and then cleaned at the National Gallery of Art; it proved to be by Peto as well.[27]

More work followed, as the group committed to the project of separating Harnetts from Petos now included the director of museum collections of the Museum of Modern Art, prestigious private collectors, Frankenstein, and, by implication, the director and trustees of the Guggenheim Foundation. Halpert, however, was not included. Chafing to release material, Frankenstein wrote Barr that he wished "we could break the Peto story right now . . . but it wouldn't be fair to Edith Halpert or the Guggenheim Foundation."[28] Frankenstein's correspondence and articles conveyed his conviction that establishing Harnett's body of work was a mission against such forces of darkness as unscrupulous dealers, collectors without visual sensitivity, and forgers. He contracted with *Life* magazine to write an exposé.[29] In a subtle but unequivocal shift, Halpert became his enemy; certainly from her point of view, he became hers.

In mid-December, when Halpert accidentally learned of these proceedings, the tension among all the parties concerned reached a virtual breaking point.[30] Frankenstein revealed that he had tested Halpert's complicity in the forged signatures and that she had almost implicated herself. "[My] experiment of floating a Peto through the ordinary channels of the trade has proved . . . that the forging of Petos as Harnetts, in this case by means of an inscription on the back, is still going on."[31] He hired a handwriting expert to distinguish authentic Harnett signatures from those on some of the paintings sold by Halpert.[32]

Frankenstein's investigative enthusiasm and his plan to display that enthusiasm in *Life* began to alarm others, and on March 5, in the office of the Guggenheim Foundation, a substantial cast of participants gathered to evaluate the implications of Frankenstein's work: Frankenstein, Halpert, Barr, Henri Marceau of the Philadelphia Museum (he had accompanied Frankenstein to Peto's studio), art historians Lloyd Goodrich and Millard Meiss, conservators Keck and David Rosen, attorneys for both Halpert and Frankenstein, and the president of the Guggenheim Foundation, Henry Allen Moe.[33] Although no official minutes of the meeting survive, subsequent letters and documents suggest that several things were accomplished: Halpert felt she was vindicated;[34] Frankenstein felt he now had the authority to insist on scientific examination of all Halpert's pictures and of those she had sold;[35] and Barr demanded not only that Frankenstein delay publication until further laboratory work was carried out but that he publish the findings in a scholarly manner (to be achieved with the help of Goodrich) in the *Art Bulletin,* the official publication of the College Art Association, and not in *Life.*[36]

The paths of Halpert and Frankenstein diverged further. In January, the dealer had begun writing letters to clients who had purchased Harnetts from her, warning of the potential change in attribution and asking that the works be X-rayed or bought back.[37] Resistant to many of Frankenstein's reattributions and reluctant to interrupt the success she was having selling Harnetts, she mounted a centennial exhibition of the artist's work in April and May 1948, in which she displayed yet more Harnetts that had come to light (including some paintings that would later be reattributed to Peto).

Frankenstein began validation of his work by publishing within an art-historical, rather than a journalistic, framework. After toning down some of the sensationalism, he published "Harnett, True and False" in the *Art Bulletin* in March 1949.[38] Setting forth his mastery of stylistic and iconographic analysis, he concluded with a list of nineteen paintings in major private collections and museums that were attributed to Harnett but were actually Petos.[39]

Published in 1953 by the University of California Press, *After the Hunt: William Harnett and Other American Still Life Painters, 1870–1900* was Frankenstein's major contribution to the study of Harnett and American still life and to American art history. In its organization and choice of vocabulary, however, the book belongs more to the genre of investigative reportage than to an academic discipline. *After the Hunt* was the title Harnett gave to a series of four paintings; as Frankenstein's name for his reconstruction of Harnett's achievement, the phrase emphasizes the author's investigative work and calls up associations of a hunter boasting about his prowess after a kill. Frankenstein opened the book with a chapter called "The Problem and Its Solution" and laid out his results by beginning with Harnett and then devoting the rest of the study to the artists he distinguished as "not Harnett." He ranked them in descending order according to their importance: after Harnett comes Peto and then John Haberle; next, in "The Second Circle," are still-life painters such as Jefferson David Chalfant and

Fig. 47. John F. Peto, *Old Time Letter Rack,* 1894. Oil on canvas, 30 x 25 in. Manoogian Collection

Richard La Barre Goodwin; and in "The Third Circle" are Henry Alexander and Joseph Decker, among others. Frankenstein's narrative flow is akin to that of an unfolding mystery novel, especially in such digressions as, "The hunt for hitherto unknown Harnetts had to be dropped entirely for a time because of startling and unexpected developments."[40]

Despite art-historical conventions and Barr's objections from early in the project, Frankenstein deliberately used the term *forgery* in an idiosyncratic manner: "Here, and throughout this book, unless otherwise specified, the word 'forgery' is used in a special sense, to imply paintings innocently and legitimately created by contemporaries of Harnett to which false Harnett signatures have been added by persons unknown. Ordinarily the word is used in art criticism to signify works made by one artist in the style of another with deliberate intent to deceive the purchaser. Harnett forgeries of this type are rare."[41] Frankenstein apparently retained his use of the term because he was reluctant to drop such a strong link to the concerns about forgeries in the art world at large and the dramatic power that the word gave his own role in the detection.[42] "Going back over the *Nature-Vivre* catalogue," Frankenstein wrote, putting his acuity at the center of the history, "I saw that seven of the fourteen works which that show had contained were Peto forgeries."[43] In addition to his insistence on the term *forgery,* Frankenstein's other word choices also convey the sense of conspiracy that had become integral to his project: "Confused standards for Harnett's style had been implanted in the minds of the art world from the very beginning . . . the Peto forgeries had attracted an immense amount of notice and were in some of the country's most important public and private collections."[44]

Despite or perhaps because of its unusual nature, Frankenstein's *After the Hunt* was reviewed enthusiastically. Halpert wrote a notice for *Art Digest* that combined an outwardly gracious thank you for a "much anticipated book [that] is welcome, indeed" with the self-preserving observation that the author unfortunately tended to move "from esthetic considerations to detection," which led to "occasional errors in fact or attribution."[45] Barr sent Frankenstein a congratulatory note that revealed one of the greatest ironies of the detection project: many of the first buyers of Harnetts preferred the softer style and warm tonality of the works that were ultimately attributed to Peto. Having a sensibility for modern painting that favored the painterly and fluid surface rather than the hard-edged, Barr had earlier chastised Frankenstein for describing Harnetts as "hard" in style, suggesting they were admirable, and Petos as "soft," implying they were somewhat careless.[46] Upon the publication of the book, Barr made his aesthetic preferences absolutely clear, a position that could hardly have pleased Frankenstein: "My only objection to a book which I am sure is a masterly job of research is your captioning. A number of first-rate Petos are attributed to Harnett with no indication that they are actually by Peto. I realize that we disagree about the relative importance of these two men but since in my mind your book is chiefly important for its reconstitution of Peto, I must object."[47]

Frankenstein continued to keep track of the Harnetts that came on the market following publication of *After the Hunt.* When the University of California Press published a second edition of the book, in 1969, Frankenstein simply provided a new preface, an occasional footnote to update blatantly superseded commentary in the first edition, and an enlarged critical catalogue of Harnetts. The preface shows him to have been incorrigible in his use of *forgery:* barely into his text, he begins a major section with the phrase "The Harnett forgery department."[48] Just how much the first edition had helped bring Harnett to public attention is clear in the figures Frankenstein cited in a magazine article timed to advertise the publication of the second edition: "The first edition of *After the Hunt* accounted for 102 extant paintings by Harnett, three full-dress drawings (as opposed to little sketches, dozens of which survive) and 21 lost paintings known through photographs; 69 forgeries or misattributed pictures were also listed. The second edition, which the University of California

Press will publish in October, lists 151 extant paintings, five full-dress drawings, one piece of sculpture and 17 paintings which have survived only in photographs; the tally of forged or misattributed pictures has grown by ten."[49]

Intriguing as his story is, seen through the eyes of Frankenstein, Harnett did not assume integral significance as an American artist until more traditional art-historical practices began to ascribe importance to still life itself and to American still life in particular. Another factor was fundamental as well: historians needed to demonstrate that the history of American art was coherent and worthy of attention.

A mutually reinforcing series of monographs, museum exhibitions, gallery shows, and survey texts were produced that asserted the attractiveness as well as the art-historical significance of still life, both American and international. The exhibitions of still life in galleries and museums in the late 1930s and early 1940s formed a prelude to this movement, and more extensive undertakings followed the war, assisted by and assisting a revived wave of collecting. Wolfgang Born argued in *Still-Life Painting in America* (1947), the first monograph devoted to American still life, that the genre was important because it revealed the particular stylistic idiom of objectivity and magic hermeticism that seemed to be an indigenous American approach to painting.[50] In 1956, the Milwaukee Art Institute and the Cincinnati Art Museum mounted *Still Life Painting since 1470,* and American still-life exhibitions included the Corcoran Gallery of Art's *American Still Life Painting from the Paul Magriel Collection* in 1957; the Newark Museum's *Nature's Bounty and Man's Delight: American Nineteenth-Century Still Life Painting* in 1958; the American Federation of Arts' traveling exhibition *A Century of American Still-Life Painting, 1813–1913* in 1966 and 1967; and Coe Kerr Gallery's *150 Years of American Still-Life Painting* in 1970.[51] Monographs about still life integrated such paintings into the larger flow of art history. In 1959, Charles Sterling analyzed the history of European still-life painting in his highly respected *Still Life Painting from Antiquity to the Present Time;* and in 1971, William H. Gerdts and Russell Burke published *American Still-Life Painting,* a major text that continued the work of ordering the achievements of late-nineteenth-century painters that Frankenstein had begun in 1959. Museums began to mount one-man exhibitions on still-life artists other than Harnett who had come to be appreciated for having a distinctive, and perhaps even preferable, appeal. The first artist to be so distinguished was Peto, when Smith College, the Brooklyn Museum, and the California Palace of the Legion of Honor hosted an exhibition on the artist in 1950, shortly after it was revealed that Smith's "Harnett" was actually a very fine Peto.[52] About a decade later, John Haberle received a one-man show.[53] By the time Gerdts organized the exhibition *Painters of the Humble Truth*, in 1981, the number of works by Harnett and his followers had grown substantially.

Within the sphere of still-life painting, curators planned exhibitions that focused on illusionism. Once still life, which had always been ranked at the bottom of aesthetic achievements, had been restored to respectability, illusionistic still life, which had always been viewed as mere "trickery," could be advanced as worthy of notice. An early exhibition of illusionistic painting was *American Still-Life: Peale to Peto* held in 1953 at the Lawrence Art Museum, Williams College, Williamstown, Massachusetts, but the most influential shows were mounted in the 1960s, many of them with Frankenstein as a contributor: La Jolla Museum of Art and Santa Barbara Museum of Art, *The Reminiscent Object: Paintings by William Michael Harnett, John Frederick Peto and John Haberle*, 1965; Landau-Alan Gallery, New York, *Illusionism in American Art*, 1968; *The Reality of Appearance: The Trompe l'Oeil Tradition in American Painting*, 1970;[54] and *Reality and Deception*, an exhibition held at the University of Southern California in 1974 that included eighty-eight examples of both European and American illusionistic painting from the seventeenth through the nineteenth century. Because still-life painting had only recently been deemed legitimate and of art-historical interest, the number of private lenders to many of these exhibitions was almost as great as that of institutions.

While still life was being given a place of respectability in the history of art, historians were constructing a tradition that viewed the genre as integral to American artistic achievement. Harnett's work had no place in turn-of-the-century texts that ambitiously put forward a European-oriented standard for current American painting and chose its "ancestors" accordingly. For instance, Charles Caffin's popular *American Masters of Painting* (1902) does not even allude to still life, let alone Harnett. His contemporary masters were such painterly artists as George Inness, John La Farge, James McNeill Whistler, and Alexander Wyant, and his "Old Master" was Gilbert Stuart.[55] Once Harnett had come to national attention, however, still life, and Harnett in particular, began to rate at least a mention. Oliver W. Larkin, in *Art and Life in America* (1949), devoted one paragraph to Harnett and illustrated *Old Models* of 1892 (pl. 49). Larkin made clear, however, that Harnett's realism was not "expressive" like that of the best artists of the late nineteenth century, such as William Morris Hunt, George Fuller, and Albert Pinkham Ryder, but that neither was it quite so literal a realism as Harnett's benighted buyers had assumed.[56] Three years after Frankenstein's *After the Hunt* appeared, E. P. Richardson's *Painting in America: The Story of 450 Years* (1956) gave much more importance to Harnett as well as to still-life painting in general.

Characterizing artists of the late nineteenth century as impelled by three different kinds of values, he placed Harnett along with Winslow Homer and Thomas Eakins as "objective realists" or "independents," in contrast to "cosmopolitans" like John Singer Sargent, Mary Cassatt, and Whistler, who were attracted to Europe and European styles, and "idealists" like La Farge and Ryder, who painted to an inner drummer.[57]

The most influential assertion of Harnett's place in the history of American art was that of Barbara Novak in her *American Painting of the Nineteenth Century* (1969). She placed Harnett solidly in the stream of an indigenous American tradition that she called "conceptual realism." Stressing the clarity of Harnett's imagery—its stillness, its integrity of idea—and the absence of personal brushstroke, she wrote, "Much American art of the late eighteenth century and of the nineteenth century can in fact be seen as still life, whether a portrait by Copley or a landscape by Lane."[58] She identified Harnett not as an "independent," as had Richardson, but as an embodiment of a unique American tradition that included artists as diverse as William Sidney Mount and Eakins. And thus, Harnett's realism came to be seen as central to American art. This interpretation informed the Metropolitan Museum of Art's *Nineteenth-Century America: Paintings and Sculpture* of 1970, which constructed a history of still life that emphasized a tradition of precise, detailed realism. (The show did not include still lifes by La Farge or William Merritt Chase, for instance.)[59] In recent survey texts used by students of American art history, Harnett is fundamental to the thesis that Americans had a strong attachment to realism, whether psychological or social.[60]

The exhibition of Harnett that has occasioned this publication brings into play virtually all the factors that contributed to the establishment of the artist's reputation. Both still life and American art are now of widespread interest, and Harnett is solidly in the canon of American masters: he produced a number of paintings of quality, variety, and interest; he was the leading exponent of a "school" of American still-life painting in the late nineteenth century; and realism is a major phenomenon in the history of American painting in general. Moreover, this realism has strong relationships to contemporary culture, especially to trends in painting and photography, and appeals to the broad public that museums are eager to attract. Perhaps of greatest significance as far as the book is concerned is that this opportunity to interpret such an exhibition comes at a time when scholars with a wide range of points of view are contributing to the field of American art history. The catalogue conveys this diversity. The story about an artist is always a story about art history and even about art historians themselves, who stand within that story, seeking to find a pattern in its workings.

NOTES

I want to thank Diane Tepfer, whose dissertation on Halpert and discussion with me about the implications of this project were invaluable (see Diane Tepfer, "Edith Gregor Halpert and the Downtown Gallery Downtown, 1926–1940: A Study in American Art Patronage" [Ph.D. diss., University of Michigan, 1989]).

1. "Artist Harnett Dead: The Well-Known Still-Life Painter Dies in Hospital," *New York Times,* October 31, 1892, p. 3; "Paintings Left by Artist Harnett," *World* (New York), November 1, 1892, p. 10; "Recent Deaths: A Famous Still-Life Painter," *Boston Evening Transcript,* November 1, 1892; and "William M. Harnett Dead: Demise of a Well-Known Painter of 'Still Life' Subjects," *Evening Bulletin* (Philadelphia), October 31, 1892, p. 6.

2. These were the last displays for almost fifty years: *Paintings of the Late W. M. Harnett on Exhibition,* exhib. cat. (Philadelphia: Earle's Galleries, 1892); and *The Wm. Michael Harnett Collection: His Own Reserved Paintings, Models and Studio Furnishings,* sale cat., Stan. V. Henkels at Thos. Birch's Sons, Auctioneers, Philadelphia, February 23–24, 1893. Only fourteen of the thirty-eight paintings exhibited at Earle's were for sale.

3. The scout is identified in Halpert's records as Ernest Weiss, who apparently worked for another dealer but recognized *The Faithful Colt* as pertinent to Halpert's interests (see Downtown Gallery Papers, Archives of American Art, Smithsonian Institution, Washington, D.C., box 104).

4. Halpert to Austin, April 13, 1935, Wadsworth Atheneum, Hartford, Conn., curatorial files. Peale's *Venus Rising from the Sea* had been exhibited in 1931 in the show of folk art that Halpert titled *American Ancestors;* she was to allude to Harnett, too, as an "American ancestor" (*"Nature-Vivre" by William M. Harnett,* exhib. cat. [New York: Downtown Gallery, 1939], unpaginated). Elizabeth Kornhauser, curator at the Wadsworth Atheneum, generously shared her research on Austin, Halpert, and Harnett, to be analyzed in detail in her forthcoming *American Paintings before 1945 in the Wadsworth Atheneum.*

5. Halpert to Austin, June 12, 1935, Wadsworth Atheneum, curatorial files. Halpert told Austin that she was contemplating an exhibition in which she combined "a group of paintings in the folk art tradition . . . with modern French pictures. We have many examples by unknown artists which definitely resemble work by Picasso, Matisse, Van Gogh, Chagall, Cezanne [*sic*], Rousseau, etc. . . . Every French artist whose attention I have called to the matter agrees with me that the character is very much related." The Museum of Modern Art's *Fantastic Art, Dada, Surrealism* (December 7, 1936– January 17, 1937) followed its seminal 1936 *Cubism and Abstract Art.* The catalogue for the Surrealism show illustrated such international artists as Pierre Roy as well as American artists whose work resembled Surrealism, including Arthur B. Dove, Georgia O'Keeffe, Pennsylvania German fraktur painters, and children. Barr was also a student of American art—with Holger Cahill he edited *Art in America: A Complete Survey* (New York: Reynal & Hitchcock, 1935).

6. The revolver in the painting is a .44-caliber model 1860 army revolver manufactured in Hartford by gunsmith Samuel Colt, and it has been claimed that Austin's interest in the painting was to pay tribute to the "Colt Manufacturing Company's long affiliation with the city" (Carol Troyen, "William Michael Harnett, *The Faithful Colt,* 1890," in Theodore E. Stebbins, Jr., et al., *A New World: Masterpieces of American Painting, 1760– 1910,* exhib. cat. [Boston: Museum of Fine Arts, 1983], pp. 285–86). Elizabeth Kornhauser, however, believes that the picture's attractiveness was based on its relationship to particular Surrealistic images exhibited earlier at the Atheneum (see *American Paintings before 1945 in the Wadsworth Atheneum*).

7. The exhibition ran at the Springfield Museum of Fine Arts, Mass., from September 28 to October 17, 1935, before traveling to the Hood Museum of Art, Dartmouth

College, Hanover, N.H.; Lyman Allyn Museum, New London, Conn.; and The Currier Gallery of Art, Manchester, N.H. From May to June 1936, the painting was at the Smith College Museum of Art, Northampton, Mass.

8. *The Painters of Still Life* ran from January 25 to February 15, 1938. The catalogue, *The Painters of Still Life* (Hartford, Conn.: Wadsworth Atheneum, 1938), featured a foreword by Austin and Henry-Russell Hitchcock, Jr. *The Faithful Colt* was then shown at the Julien Levy Gallery in New York in the exhibition *Old and New "Trompe-l'Oeil"* (March 8–April 3, 1938). After its showing in Paris, there followed *Early American Genre and Still-Life Paintings* at Victor D. Spark, New York, May 5–June 5, 1941; and Spark's *American Still-Life Paintings, 1820–1920,* May 11–June 30, 1946. For a complete bibliography of exhibition catalogues, see William H. Gerdts, *Painters of the Humble Truth: Masterpieces of American Still Life, 1801–1939,* exhib. cat., Philbrook Art Center, Tulsa, Okla. (Columbia, Mo., and London: University of Missouri Press, 1981), pp. 273–77.

9. Dorothy C. Miller and Alfred H. Barr, Jr., eds., *American Realists and Magic Realists,* exhib. cat. (New York: Museum of Modern Art, 1943), p. 5.

10. The show was on view from April 18 to May 6, 1939. Two paintings came in after the catalogue was printed, as Halpert noted in a letter to Austin, April 15, 1939, Wadsworth Atheneum, curatorial files.

11. *Emblems of Peace* was given by Charles T. and Emilie Shean to the Springfield Museum of Fine Arts in March 1938 and published in "'Emblems of Peace' by William M. Harnett," *Springfield Museum of Fine Arts Bulletin* 4, no. 9 (June 1938), unpaginated. *The Old Violin* is the only Harnett after which a print was made.

12. *"Nature-Vivre."*

13. See, for example, "Harnett Resurrected from the Shadows," *Art Digest* 13, no. 15 (May 1, 1939) p. 7.

14. The museums that bought Harnetts included the Smith College Museum of Art, Northampton, Mass.; Phillips Memorial Gallery, Washington, D.C.; The Detroit Institute of Arts; Museum of Fine Arts, Boston; and The Metropolitan Museum of Art, New York. It was ultimately determined that all of these works were not by Harnett.

15. The show was seen at the Detroit Society of Arts and Crafts, November 21–December 12, 1939; The Arts Club of Chicago, March 5–23, 1940; M. H. de Young Memorial Museum, San Francisco, April 15–May 16, 1940; William Rockhill Nelson Gallery of Art and Mary Atkins Museum of Fine Arts, Kansas City, Mo., July 1–31, 1940; Portland Museum, Oregon, August 18–September 15, 1940; University of Nebraska Art Galleries, Lincoln, 1941; and Carnegie Institute, Pittsburgh, 1941.

16. Halpert's gallery records contain several lists of the owners of these works, evidence of her pride in placing Harnetts in major collections both public and private (see Downtown Gallery Papers).

17. Frankenstein broached the possibility of writing a study to Barr on August 7, 1946 (letter in Alfred H. Barr, Jr., Papers, owned by the Museum of Modern Art, microfilmed by the Archives of American Art, roll 2173, frame 827). Frankenstein's 1940 review was headlined "Around the Art Galleries: The Strange Case of True Art and the Counterfeit Money," *San Francisco Chronicle,* April 21, 1940, "This World" sect., p. 28.

18. Barr to Frankenstein, July 12, 1946 (Barr Papers, frame 826). Barr writes about having previously attempted to persuade other scholars to write a book on the artist.

19. Frankenstein to Halpert, August 27, 1946 (Downtown Gallery Papers, box 101).

20. See, for instance, Frankenstein to Halpert, July 13, 1947: "I can always be reached at the Guggenheim

Foundation office, 551 Fifth Avenue" (Alfred Frankenstein Papers, Archives of American Art, box 9).

21. Alfred Frankenstein, "Art and Music: The Full Story behind a Guggenheim Award and an Artist Named Harnett," *San Francisco Chronicle,* May 4, 1947, "This World" sect., pp. 24, 26.

22. "Frankenstein Gets Guggenheim," *Art Digest* 21, no. 15 (May 1, 1947), p. 10.

23. Frankenstein to Barr, July 21, 1947 (Frankenstein Papers, box 9).

24. "Report from Island Heights," July 20, 1947 (ibid.). In his informal report, Frankenstein assessed the following pictures as actually by Peto: *Old Souvenirs* (The Metropolitan Museum of Art, New York), then owned by O. B. Jennings; *Old Reminiscences,* owned by the Phillips Memorial Gallery; three pictures owned by Barr (*The Marked Passage, Old Friends,* and *Box of Books*), and eleven others.

25. Barr to Frankenstein, September 18, 1947 (Barr Papers, frame 810).

26. Barr to Frankenstein, October 21, 1947 (ibid., frame 797).

27. Frankenstein and Barr carried out these examinations without telling Halpert. See Frankenstein to Elmira Bier, assistant to the director of the Phillips Memorial Gallery, October 12, 1947, in which he warns, "I have not said anything to Mrs. Halpert about this as yet and I shall not for some time to come" (Downtown Gallery Papers, box 104). After finding out about the secret investigations, Halpert secured copies of the correspondence from the Phillips Memorial Gallery on January 12, 1948 (Bier to Halpert, January 12, 1948, ibid.).

28. Frankenstein to Barr, October 24, 1947 (Barr Papers, frame 794).

29. This agreement was revealed after the fact; see Barr to Frankenstein, December 29, 1947 (ibid., frame 787); see also Barr to Frankenstein, June 8, 1948 (ibid., frame 751).

30. Halpert indicated that she found out about the suspicions through her doctor on December 17 and demanded a meeting with Frankenstein. This is implied by a letter from Frankenstein to Halpert, December 20, 1947, and made clear in an undated document that is apparently a report of the meeting on March 5 (Downtown Gallery Papers, box 104).

31. Frankenstein to Halpert, January 2, 1948 (ibid.). Some six months after the fact, Frankenstein wrote Halpert of the deception that he had practiced in July 1947, when his suspicions had first been aroused. He had taken an unsigned Peto from Island Heights, placed a mark on the back for later identification, and sold it to Halpert's Philadelphia runner through an agent. When Frankenstein saw the picture at the Downtown Gallery in December, it had an inscription on the back citing Harnett's authorship.

32. See Albert D. Osborn, "Examiner of Questioned Documents," to Frankenstein, February 24, 1948, conveying the results of the handwriting examination (Frankenstein Papers, box 9).

33. Barr to Frankenstein, January 5, 1948 (Barr Papers, frame 779).

34. See Moe to Halpert, May 3, 1948, explaining that the meeting was so complex that all records proved inadequate (Downtown Gallery Papers, box 104). Halpert's reactions are contained in an unsigned, detailed analysis (ibid.); they are also clear in some of her correspondence, such as her letter to Francis Taylor, director of the Metropolitan Museum of Art, March 6, 1948 (ibid.).

35. Frankenstein to Halpert, March 9, 1948 (ibid.).

36. Frankenstein to Barr, June 8, 1948 (Barr Papers, frame 751). An article by Olive Bragazzi, Barr's secretary when Frankenstein was working on Harnett, finds Frankenstein less than aboveboard in his Harnett project. The article elicited a rejoinder from John I. H. Baur, then director emeritus of the Whitney Museum of American Art, that defended Frankenstein and found Halpert culpable (Olive Bragazzi, "The Story behind the Rediscovery of William Harnett and John Peto by Edith Halpert and Alfred Frankenstein," *American Art Journal* 16, no. 2 [Spring 1984], pp. 51–65; and "Letters: John I. H. Baur and Olive Bragazzi," *American Art Journal* 17, no. 1 [Winter 1985], p. 93).

37. She seems to have begun writing these letters as early as January 10, 1948, soon after learning about Frankenstein's investigations. Virtually no one accepted her offer to repurchase, replying that they liked the paintings anyway. For an offer to repurchase, see Halpert to Barr, February 4, 1948 (Downtown Gallery Papers, box 104). An example of Halpert's determination to have the pictures authenticated with technical examination is her letter to Smith College requesting permission to X-ray *Discarded Treasures,* February 7, 1948 (ibid.). Collector Robert H. Tannahill, in a letter to Halpert of February 13, 1948, wrote, "As far as I am concerned it makes no difference who painted the three charming pictures I bought from you" (ibid.).

38. Alfred Frankenstein, "Harnett, True and False," *Art Bulletin* 31 (March 1949), pp. 38–56. Immediately following Frankenstein's article is Lloyd Goodrich, "Notes: Harnett and Peto, A Note on Style," pp. 57–58.

39. Frankenstein, "Harnett, True and False," p. 46. This list includes three paintings owned by Barr (*The Marked Passage, Old Friends,* and *Box of Books*); Rockefeller's *Old Books; Old Scraps,* which had been bought from *"Nature-Vivre"* and donated to the Museum of Modern Art; *The Old Cremona,* owned by the Metropolitan Museum of Art; and *Old Reminiscences,* owned by the Phillips Memorial Gallery.Ultimately, everyone con-

cerned with the case agreed that the false signatures had been added long before the 1930s, perhaps in the first few years after Harnett's death, and certainly not by Peto.

40. Alfred Frankenstein, *After the Hunt: William Harnett and Other American Still Life Painters, 1870–1900* (Berkeley and Los Angeles: University of California Press, 1953), p. 7.

41. Ibid., p. 16, n. 10.

42. Barr to Frankenstein, September 6, 1948, admonishing him that the paintings are Petos with "forged Harnett signatures" (Barr Papers, frame 745).

43. *After the Hunt,* p. 16.

44. Ibid.

45. Edith Gregor Halpert, "The Harnett Tradition," *Art Digest* 28, no. 1 (October 1, 1953), p. 23. A typical review was Joseph Henry Jackson, "Solving the Mystery of the Artist with Two Styles—Hard and Soft," *San Francisco Chronicle,* September 13, 1953, "This World" sect., pp. 14, 16. Art historian James Thomas Flexner also reviewed the book ("Uncommon Commonplace," *New York Times,* September 13, 1953, sect. 7, p. 7).

46. Barr to Frankenstein, September 6, 1948 (Barr Papers, frame 745).

47. Barr to Frankenstein, September 23, 1953 (Frankenstein Papers, box 9).

48. Alfred Frankenstein, *After the Hunt: William Harnett and Other American Still Life Painters, 1870–1900,* rev. ed. (Berkeley and Los Angeles: University of California Press, 1969), p. x.

49. Alfred Frankenstein, "The American Nineteenth Century, Part 2: Saloon Salons," *Art News* 67, no. 5 (September 1968), p. 45.

50. Wolfgang Born, *Still-Life Painting in America* (New York: Oxford University Press, 1947), passim.

51. Philip R. Adams and Edward H. Dwight, *Still Life Painting since 1470,* exhib. cat. (Milwaukee: Milwaukee Art Institute; Cincinnati: Cincinnati Art Museum, 1956). *American Still Life Painting from the Paul Magriel Collection,* foreword by John I. H. Baur, exhib. cat. (Washington, D.C.: Corcoran Gallery of Art, 1957). William H. Gerdts, *Nature's Bounty and Man's Delight: American Nineteenth-Century Still Life Painting,* exhib. cat. (Newark, N.J.: Newark Museum, 1958). William H. Gerdts, *A Century of American Still-Life Painting, 1813–1913,* exhib. cat. (New York: American Federation of Arts, 1966). William H. Gerdts, *150 Years of American Still-Life Painting,* exhib. cat. (New York: Coe Kerr Gallery, 1970). Two other exhibitions at dealers' rooms included *Magic of Flowers in Painting,* Wildenstein Gallery, New York, April 13–May 21, 1954; and *Inaugural Exhibition of American Still Life Paintings,* M. Knoedler & Co., New York, October, 1954.

52. Alfred Frankenstein, *John F. Peto,* exhib. cat. (Brooklyn: Brooklyn Museum and Brooklyn Institute of Arts and Sciences, 1950).

53. *Haberle,* foreword by Alfred Frankenstein, exhib. cat. (New Britain, Conn.: New Britain Museum of American Art, 1962).

54. *The Reality of Appearance* was exhibited at the National Gallery of Art, Washington, D.C.; Whitney Museum of American Art, New York; University Art Museum, Berkeley; California Palace of the Legion of Honor, San Francisco; The Detroit Institute of Arts. Advertised as the "first major museum exhibition of American *trompe l'oeil* painting" (p. 5), it placed Harnett at the apogee of this tradition by featuring 106 paintings by twenty-nine artists, of which 37 were by Harnett and 16 by Peto, including several works that still bore forged Harnett signatures (Alfred Frankenstein, *The Reality of*

Appearance: The Trompe l'Oeil Tradition in American Painting, exhib. cat. [(Greenwich, Conn.): New York Graphic Society, 1970], pp. 3–5, 156). Of the shows listed here, Frankenstein did not contribute to the Landau-Alan exhibit.

55. Charles H. Caffin, *American Masters of Painting* (New York: Doubleday, Page & Co., 1902).

56. Oliver W. Larkin, *Art and Life in America* (New York: Rinehart & Co., 1949), p. 265.

57. E. P. Richardson, *Painting in America: The Story of 450 Years* (New York: Thomas Y. Crowell Co., 1956).

58. Barbara Novak, *American Painting of the Nineteenth Century: Realism, Idealism, and the American Experience* (New York, Washington, and London: Praeger Publishers, 1969), p. 221.

59. The still lifes in the exhibition were Charles Bird King's *Poor Artist's Cupboard* of about 1815 (fig. 86); Raphaelle Peale's *Dish of Blackberries* of about 1816 (private collection) and his *Venus Rising from the Sea— A Deception* of 1822 (fig. 3); James Peale's *Balsam Apple and Vegetables* of the 1820s (The Metropolitan Museum of Art, New York); John F. Francis's *Still Life with Wine Bottles and Basket of Fruit* of 1857 (fig. 91); Harnett's *Artist's Letter Rack* of 1879 and his *After the Hunt* of 1883 (pls. 17, 29); Peto's *Poor Man's Store* of 1885 (Museum of Fine Arts, Boston); and Haberle's *Bachelor's Drawer* of 1890–94 (The Metropolitan Museum of Art, New York).

60. See, for example, John Wilmerding, *American Art* (Harmondsworth, England: Penguin Books, 1976); and Matthew Baigell, *A Concise History of American Painting and Sculpture* (New York and Toronto: Harper & Row, 1984). Recent texts, as indicated in the Bibliography, have taken Harnett's realism for granted and examined the cultural implications of his iconography.

Pl. 18. William M. Harnett, *Still Life with Three Castles Tobacco,* 1880. Oil on canvas, 11 x 15³⁄₁₆ in.
The Brooklyn Museum, Dick S. Ramsey Fund (41.221)

Pl. 19. William M. Harnett, *Philadelphia Public Ledger, March 2, 1880,* 1880. Oil on canvas, 10 x 14 in.
Westmoreland Museum of Art, Greensburg, Pa., Anonymous Donor, by Exchange

Pl. 20. William M. Harnett, *Cigar Box, Pitcher, and "New York Herald,"* 1880. Oil on canvas, 9½ x 7¾ in.
Courtesy of Berry-Hill Galleries, New York

Pl. 21. William M. Harnett, *New York Herald, July 11, 1880,* 1880. Oil on canvas, 5⅜ x 7⅛ in.
Mr. and Mrs. Garett Albert

Pl. 22. William M. Harnett, *Still Life with Fruit and Vase,* 1881. Oil on wood, 5⅜ x 7⅜ in.
Private collection

Pl. 23. William M. Harnett, *Still Life with "Le Figaro,"* 1882. Oil on canvas, 9½ x 12 in. Private collection

Pl. 24. William M. Harnett, *Munich Still Life,* 1882. Oil on canvas, 24⅝ x 30⅟₁₆ in.
Dallas Museum of Art, Dallas Art Association Purchase

Pl. 25. William M. Harnett, *Plucked Clean,* 1882. Oil on canvas, 34⅛ x 20¼ in.
The Corcoran Gallery of Art, Washington, D.C., Museum Purchase, William A. Clark Fund

Pl. 26. William M. Harnett, *A Study Table,* 1882. Oil on canvas, 39⅞ x 51⅜ in.
Munson-Williams-Proctor Institute Museum of Art, Utica, N.Y.

Pl. 27. William M. Harnett, *Still Life with Bust of Dante,* 1883. Oil on wood, 10¼ x 13¾ in.
High Museum of Art, Atlanta, Gift of Mr. and Mrs. James M. Dyer and Mr. and Mrs. Truman Bragg
in Memory of Mrs. Mary Newcomb Bull and Robert Scott Newcomb (64.27)

Pl. 28. William M. Harnett, *After the Hunt,* 1883. Oil on canvas, 52½ x 34 in.
Courtesy of Kennedy Galleries, Inc., New York

Pl. 29. William M. Harnett, *After the Hunt*, 1883. Oil on canvas, 52½ x 36 in.
Columbus Museum of Art, Ohio, Bequest of Francis C. Sessions, 1919 (19.1)

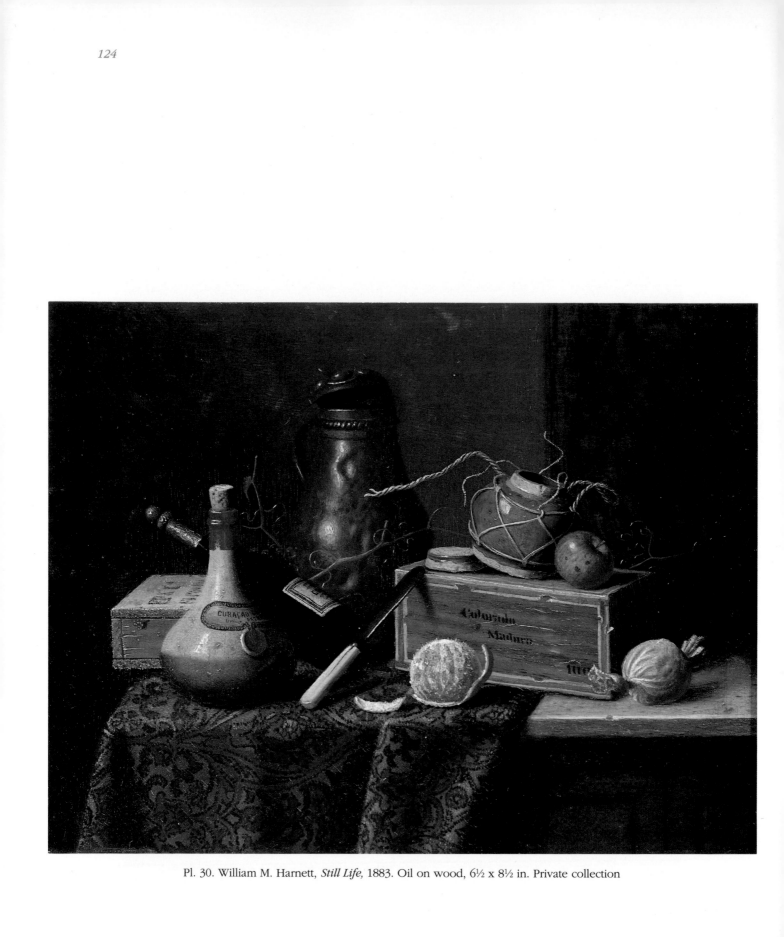

Pl. 30. William M. Harnett, *Still Life,* 1883. Oil on wood, 6½ x 8½ in. Private collection

Pl. 31. William M. Harnett, *Munich Still Life,* 1884. Oil on wood, 14⅝ x 11¾ in.
The Newark Museum, N.J., Purchase 1958, Mrs. Felix Fuld Bequest Fund

Pl. 32. William M. Harnett, *Still Life*, 1884. Oil on wood, 9¹⁵⁄₁₆ x 12⅛ in.
Flint Institute of Arts, Mich., Gift of Mr. and Mrs. William L. Richards through the Viola E. Bray Charitable Trust (63.8)

Pl. 33. William M. Harnett, *After the Hunt,* 1884. Oil on canvas, 55 x 40 in.
The Butler Institute of American Art, Youngstown, Ohio

ELEMENTS
OF
ARTISTIC
DEVELOPMENT

BURIN TO BRUSH

Harnett as an Artisan

PAUL RAYMOND PROVOST

Scholars have always seen a relationship between William Michael Harnett's tight, linear painting style and his early experience as a silver engraver, and their descriptions of his work often reflect this association. Alfred Frankenstein labeled the artist's style "hard" and his handling of paint "extremely meticulous and detailed," and conservator Sheldon Keck noted, "Harnett's lines, highlights, and edges are very sharp and definite."[1] Lloyd Goodrich eloquently summarized the artist's style as having "a sense of design, a clarity of vision."[2] In addition to its impact on his style, Harnett's work as a silver engraver influenced his working method and technique and encouraged his interest in decorative objects as subjects for his paintings. As a result, Harnett the still-life painter was remarkably similar to Harnett the silver engraver.

A few extant documents allow us to reconstruct the artist's early career. Harnett recalled—albeit broadly—that he began to practice engraving in Philadelphia in 1865, when he was seventeen years old.[3] He first worked on steel, copper, and wood and eventually became an accomplished engraver of silver flatware.[4] After moving to New York in 1869, he was employed by a couple of large jewelry and silver manufacturers, including Tiffany and Company, where he engraved monograms on flatware.[5] At one of these firms, Wood and Hughes (fig. 48), Harnett shared a workbench with the engraver William Ignatius Blemly, who became a lifelong friend.[6] Harnett presented Blemly and his family with modest gifts of engraved pieces of sterling, and it is through these objects that we have come to know Harnett the craftsman.

Harnett continued to work as a silver engraver until 1875, when his still lifes began to sell and his financial success as painter seemed more certain. His friend and early biographer Edward Taylor Snow claimed that Harnett was forced out of the silver

industry by technological advances. Painting, however, was no doubt more attractive to Harnett than engraving monograms on flatware, which must have seemed rather tedious and wearisome in comparison.

By mid-century, the craft tradition of silversmithing had evolved into a modern industry. Industrialization and the introduction of electroplating in the 1840s changed the working process and permitted the adoption of factorylike production methods. Silver engravers did not generally create original patterns but worked from detailed drawings prepared by more highly trained designers. Harnett probably was employed in a production-line arrangement, but the

Fig. 48. Interior of a silver-engraving shop believed to be Wood & Hughes. *Left to right:* unknown, Cornelius Sheehan, William A. and William I. Blemly. Photograph. Blemly Family Collection

Opposite: William M. Harnett, *The Artist's Letter Rack* (detail, pl. 17)

Fig. 49. William M. Harnett, *Iris,* ca. 1870. Pencil, India ink, and wash on paper, 8¾ x 6¾ in. Collection of Susan and Herbert Adler

The crisp edges of the form also suggest that this may have been intended as a design for silver.

Harnett also made less fully realized drawings of silver patterns in an early sketchbook (fig. 50). He drew these freehand or laid out the principal components of the design with a compass and then added embellishments. Whether working from pattern books or his own imagination, Harnett recorded a variety of design motifs with precision, using strong contour lines and delicate hatching; some designs include fine lines that terminate in patterns of dots and dashes. These drawings fill the pages of the sketchbook and underscore the artist's fascination with line and its expressive potential. Some designs recall sensual Rococo forms as they swirl across the sheet, whereas others are more exotic and originate in patterns from the Near and Far East. Many of these designs are essentially ovoid and may have been used on flatware handles. Both the variety of the patterns and their exacting clarity would become the hallmark of Harnett's mature work as a painter.

The engraving style on the napkin rings that Harnett presented to Blemly and his wife (fig. 51) matches the drawing style seen in the sketchbook. Harnett used analogous techniques to produce a pleasant, decorative surface on an otherwise plain silver cylinder. By varying the character of the line, either by gently wiggling the burin or altering the depth of the cut, Harnett produced a lively, animated surface. A silver matchbox that Harnett inscribed for Blemly (fig. 52) bears a small still life painted in brown on white enamel that is reminiscent of his *After the Hunt*

final stages of silver manufacture were completed by hand, and objects with engraved or chased designs required substantial skill with the burin on the part of the craftsman. Harnett also may have taken part in other stages of production, such as repoussée work and chasing, which involved striking the object with punches or hammers to create a design in relief.

There is no evidence that Harnett participated in the design process, but he may have had aspirations in that direction. In 1870, he enrolled in classes at the Cooper Union for the Advancement of Science and Art, which offered practical training to artists, artisans, and designers. One of Harnett's drawings from this period, *Iris* (fig. 49), resembles the type of design often used in the silver trade. A single flower projects from an undefined space in an elegantly simplified composition that suggests an Oriental source of inspiration. The area surrounding the single flower is easily read as the flat, unadorned surface of a silver object.

Fig. 50. William M. Harnett, sketchbook, early 1870s. Pencil on paper. Alfred Frankenstein Papers, Archives of American Art, Smithsonian Institution, Washington, D.C.

Fig. 51. William M. Harnett, *Napkin Ring*. Silver, ca. 1½ x 2 in.
Inscribed: *MJB*. Blemly Family Collection

Fig. 52. William M. Harnett, *Matchbox*. Silver with white enamel and brown paint, 2½ x 1½ in.
Inscribed on verso: *From/W. M. Harnett/to/W. I. Blemly/1886*; on recto: *New York*. Blemly Family Collection

compositions. This gift is symbolic, in a very real sense, of the connection in Harnett's oeuvre between the painting of still life and the engraving of silver objects. Although Harnett gave up silver engraving professionally in 1875, the matchbox proves that he continued to work in this medium on an informal basis.

Harnett's paintings from the 1870s reveal his development from an accomplished engraver to a successful still-life painter. These works also show how he adopted the aesthetic sensibility of the silver designer, particularly in the use of a carefully controlled line. Some of Harnett's early paintings include images of engraved and printed materials that lent themselves to the decorative mode of drawing in which he was already proficient. *The Artist's Letter Rack* of 1879 (pl. 17), for example, shows envelopes, cards, and other printed material held in delicate compositional balance by taut pieces of vivid pink tape. The circular drawing at the left was seemingly made with a compass, a tool already familiar to Harnett from the silver trade. Other elements, such as the column of figures, were painted with short, straight brushstrokes, creating the illusion that they were actually scored into the "wooden" support as the writer pressed down on his pencil. The wisps of blue-gray pigment next to the black lines give the numbers the metallic aspect of graphite. These details reveal an essentially linear treatment of form in which Harnett used paint additively to draw on canvas in much the same way he had used the burin subtractively to create patterns on silver.

Other aspects of *The Artist's Letter Rack* also recall Harnett's training as a silver engraver. The stippling he utilized to represent the black-and-green pattern of the ten-cent bill glued to the board is not unlike a technique used in engraving silver. Harnett chose a sharp instrument, most likely a pin or an etching needle, to scratch lines into the painted surface of the bill. Under close scrutiny, this cross-hatching resembles a practice used by engravers to suggest three-dimensional form. Perhaps less confident with a brush than a burin, the artist quite naturally transferred the devices he had used in metalworking to his new medium.

The manner in which Harnett chose his models and composed his pictures also owes a debt to his experience in the silver trade. Harnett the engraver was familiar with aesthetic conventions that encouraged modifying and juxtaposing decorative motifs from a variety of periods and cultures. The artists who designed silver patterns were not concerned with the accurate replication of historic styles; instead, they reinterpreted sources, infusing them with an overriding decorative sensibility. Harnett's involvement with silver-making and his first years as a painter coincided with the emergence in America of the Aesthetic movement, which fostered unrestrained eclecticism. A passage from an 1868 article on silver illustrates the contemporary vocabulary applied to the design process:

> All beauty is akin. . . . It is interesting to walk about the warerooms and see how the whole realm of beauty has been despoiled for the decoration of human life. Every pretty leaf, tendril, bud, blossom; every arch, groin, and pinnacle; every pleasing bird, animal, and fish; every hideous monster and reptile; all that ancient art, tradition, and literature have of elegant, grotesque, or curious, . . . here you behold it, in brilliant silver and burnished gold.[7]

The silver objects Harnett engraved were thus conceived and designed in this aesthetic spirit. Decorative motifs were selected, combined, and modified to harmonize with the shape of an object. While individual elements were repeated from other designs, they assumed new meaning each time they were recombined and reinterpreted.

This practice of selection and modification was at the heart of Harnett's method of composing still-life paintings in the late 1870s and the 1880s. His compositions depict objects drawn from diverse periods and cultures, often rearranged and varied slightly from painting to painting. Much of his success in still life was due to his repetition and variation of certain themes. In choosing a motif, modifying it, and then giving it a new context in other paintings, Harnett made use of working practices he had learned as an engraver.

Harnett was a participant in the artistic and decorative innovations of his age. His illusionistic still-life paintings, conceived in the eclectic spirit of the time, employ synthetic arrangements of objects and forms from many periods, cultures, and styles. These paintings were executed with the precision and detail characteristic of the work of a craftsman, his use of brush and pigment inspired by his experience with burin and metal. Harnett continued as he had begun, an artist whose greatest creative accomplishments have their origins in his work as an artisan.

NOTES

1. Alfred Frankenstein, "Harnett, True and False," *Art Bulletin* 31 (March 1949), p. 39; and Sheldon Keck, quoted in Frankenstein, "Harnett, True and False," p. 49.

2. Lloyd Goodrich, "Notes: Harnett and Peto, A Note on Style," *Art Bulletin* 31 (March 1949), p. 58.

3. "Painted Like Real Things: The Man Whose Pictures Are a Wonder and a Puzzle," interview in *New York News,* probably 1889 or 1890, quoted in Alfred Frankenstein, *After the Hunt: William Harnett and Other American Still Life Painters, 1870–1900,* rev. ed. (Berkeley and Los Angeles: University of California Press, 1969), p. 29.

4. *The Wm. Michael Harnett Collection: His Own Reserved Paintings, Models and Studio Furnishings,* sale cat., Stan. V. Henkels at Thos. Birch's Sons, Auctioneers, Philadelphia, February 23–24, 1893, p. 3.

5. Frankenstein, *After the Hunt,* p. 33.

6. Alfred Frankenstein Papers, Archives of American Art, Smithsonian Institution, Washington, D.C., microfilm, roll 1374, frame 110. Frankenstein's papers contain mention of a sterling butter knife dated 1869 and engraved with a "B" that bears the mark of Tiffany & Co.; according to Frankenstein, the knife was monogrammed by Harnett and given to Blemly.

7. James Parton, "Silver and Silver Plate," *Harper's New Monthly Magazine* 37 (September 1868), p. 443.

THE ARTIST AND
AMERICAN ART ACADEMIES

MARIA CHAMBERLIN-HELLMAN

William Michael Harnett pursued an academic education with great vigor and determination, studying in three different institutions in two American cities for at least eight terms over a twelve-year period. In the late 1860s and early 1870s, while he was a practicing silver engraver, art academies provided him with the means to become a painter. The classes he attended at Philadelphia's Pennsylvania Academy of the Fine Arts and at the Cooper Union for the Advancement of Science and Art and the National Academy of Design in New York helped him move, as he put it, "wholly into painting" in the mid-1870s.[1] One can argue that it was due primarily to his classes, many of which were taken at night and all of which were available at little or no expense, that Harnett was able to make the critical transition from artisan to artist.

We may not think of Harnett as an academic artist, but his experiences and connections within the academies were quite significant for his work. His exposure to the art of the past, his familiarity with the methods and work of other students, teachers, and practicing artists, and much of his knowledge of the art exhibited in Philadelphia and New York during these years came from his contact with American art schools. Harnett later acknowledged this when he was asked to comment on his path to success. Hoping the story of his education might inspire others, he told an interviewer, "Perhaps what I may say will be of some encouragement to young men who are situated as I was, and possibly my experience may prove to them that money and friends are not wholly necessary in beginning a career as an artist."[2] What was "wholly necessary" for the aspiring artist, however, was the art academy.

Harnett was working as an engraver of silver and other materials when he sought his first formal training by entering the antique class at the Pennsylvania Academy in January 1866.[3] Obliged to support his widowed mother and his siblings, he worked during the day and drew from casts of antique sculpture in the evening. Once issued an admission ticket for antique study, an academy student could attend the drawing sessions as frequently and for as long as he wished. Following European practice, students with some experience drew from plaster casts of parts of statues (noses, hands, and heads, for example), eventually graduating to work on entire figures. After extended antique study, a pupil could advance to the life class by presenting a suitably accomplished drawing of a cast of a complete figure to the professional artists in charge of the curriculum.[4] In the post–Civil War period, the antique and life classes at the Pennsylvania Academy were overseen by the Committee on Instruction, a group of board members who were particularly interested in art education.[5] Professional artists who frequented the academy also offered advice to the beginning students. Instruction, however, was far from consistent.

As a consequence of this loose arrangement, the academy's directors occasionally received requests for greater commitment to the educational mission of the institution. In February 1868, eleven female and thirty male students, including Harnett, sent a plea for "a suitable instructor" to the Committee on Instruction. The students suggested Joseph John, an obscure genre and landscape painter who had been curator at the academy since 1863,[6] believing he had "manifested great interest in [their] progress."[7] While artists were frequently hired to fill this position, the curator usually functioned more as a monitor, doorkeeper, and janitor than as a teacher. John, however, had lectured on artistic anatomy and offered some organized instruction to Harnett and his fellow students.[8] Harnett would also have received critiques of his cast drawings from members of the Committee on Instruction, among them John Sartain, an artist who took great interest in the Pennsylvania Academy schools over a period of many years.

From their 1868 petition, it is obvious the academy pupils felt something more substantial in the way of teaching was called for, and, at this time, so did the Committee on Instruction and the Board of Directors. They decided to hire Christian Schussele, an Alsatian who had settled in Philadelphia in 1848 and become an active member of the artistic community.[9] Schussele produced genre and history paintings, making good use of his own training at the Ecole des Beaux-Arts in Paris. Since he assumed leadership of the revitalized Pennsylvania Academy in September 1868, it is possible Harnett studied with him briefly.

Three years after starting at the Pennsylvania Academy, Harnett found work as an engraver in New York, where he intended "to study in the National Academy of Design and take advantage of the free art school in the Cooper Institute."[10] The Cooper Union attracted Harnett first; he is recorded as a "subscriber" there during the school year 1870–71.[11] The school had been established in 1859 to provide education in science and art to working-class people. Its free schools of art offered courses in the fine, decorative, and industrial arts to women and men in day and evening sessions. Harnett's specific course of study was not recorded, though he probably spent one term drawing from antique casts, a major element of the school's curriculum. If so, he would have joined about fifty other young men in this endeavor under the tutelage of one Robert Lennox. Harnett did not enroll for the next school term, perhaps because Cooper Union students who did not wish to become art teachers, engravers, or draftsmen were often sent to other New York schools where they could receive more advanced training for professional artists.

One such school, where Harnett studied between 1872 and 1876, was the National Academy of Design, which had been founded in 1825.[12] The National Academy's Antique School attracted practicing painters, engravers, lithographers, and sign painters as well as true beginners. Everyone drew from casts at the school, while many also took private lessons from established artists. After mid-century, the National Academy schools suffered from a number of financial, enrollment, and instructional difficulties. These problems reached a critical point in the 1860s, when the bulk of the institution's resources and energies were devoted to the construction of a new building, completed in 1865. The new National Academy, an elaborate Venetian palazzo, was designed with exhibition space rather than classroom facilities in mind; the school was relegated to a "crypt" below street level.[13]

Disagreements over the instructional program, which relied on volunteer teachers, divided the academicians into rival factions. The liberal group wanted the academy to expand its schools and hire one or

Fig. 53. F. Lathrop, *Antique Class, National Academy of Design: L. E. Wilmarth, Teacher.* Wood engraving. In William C. Brownell, "The Art-Schools of New York," *Scribner's Monthly* 16 (October 1878), p. 765

more competent instructors and to mortgage the new building to do so. The conservative group thought the students were being offered free instruction by artists of renown and should be well satisfied with the school. After much controversy and aborted discussions about merging with the art schools of the Cooper Union, the National Academy eventually borrowed money to support its own educational programs and hired a salaried professor, Lemuel E. Wilmarth, in January 1870.[14]

Wilmarth, who continued teaching at the National Academy for nearly twenty years, had extensive experience in art academies in the United States and abroad. After training as a watchmaker and studying at the Pennsylvania Academy, he enrolled at the Royal Academy in Munich under Wilhelm Kaulbach and then at the Ecole des Beaux-Arts in Paris under Jean-Léon Gérôme along with other Americans, including Thomas Eakins.[15] Wilmarth's initial years as an artisan, his early training at the Pennsylvania Academy, and his subsequent studies in Europe parallel Harnett's own experiences, though Harnett never actually enrolled in a European academy.

The National Academy's antique classes (fig. 53), almost all of which were taught by Wilmarth, counted Harnett as a member during the school terms of 1872–73, 1873–74, 1874–75, and 1875–76; he was also a member of the life class during the 1874–75 term.[16]

The National Academy registers for antique and life study for this period record the names of all the students in two annual lists but do not indicate if, for example, two students were in the same class. Among the male students of the antique during Harnett's tenure were Albert Pinkham Ryder, George de Forest Brush, Abbott Thayer, and Thomas P. Anshutz. Also enrolled were Joseph Decker, a German emigré who specialized in still life, and Louis Moeller, a genre painter who included still-life elements in his work. Both Decker and Moeller subsequently studied in Munich and produced paintings that have intriguing stylistic parallels to Harnett's. In the women's antique classes of these years were still-life painters Maria Oakey Dewing, Helena de Kay, and Virginia Granberry.

From all available evidence, Harnett, who was described by a fellow evening pupil as "tall, lean, solemn, Celtic and wise," seems to have been a fairly typical National Academy student of the 1870s.[17] Most of the other students were roughly his age, in their mid-to-late twenties, though older and younger pupils were also in attendance. Many of those who took evening classes pursued remunerative jobs during the day; as an observer commented, "The best work is done by the night life-class perhaps, the majority being men who have some employment in the day-time, more or less remotely connected with aesthetics,—engraving of various sorts, for example."[18]

Since Harnett had studied from the antique for several years by the time he enrolled at the National Academy, he advanced to work from the more complex casts with some rapidity. Among those he drew in 1873 were the *Borghese Warrior* (fig. 54), which lunges diagonally across a large sheet, casting dramatic shadows against a murky background, and the *Venus de Milo* (fig. 55), in which the figure stands demurely against a light ground, her body and drapery carefully shaded to indicate volume and different textures. These figures are the type of work that would have been reviewed by a council of academicians to decide when a pupil would advance to life study.

Less typical is a pencil and charcoal of the same year, *A Sprig of Plums* (fig. 56), a firm rendering of a decorative relief, a type of cast found in academic collections. Here, forms from nature have been presented as elements of a finished shading exercise in solid geometry. Similar exercises were advocated by American drawing manuals, which counseled students to draw "ovals of various proportions . . . in

every direction, to acquire facility in executing a form that is the element of so many beautiful objects."[19] The controlled linear elements and palpable surface tension of *A Sprig of Plums* are perhaps attributable to Harnett's experience as a silver engraver.

During the 1874–75 school term, eight years after he had commenced academic study, Harnett began to paint in oil. While drawing had long been the medium of choice at most academies for both antique and life study, National Academy students deemed sufficiently advanced to move into life class could also attempt painting. As a critic noted, "Mr. Wilmarth, so far from objecting to painting, encourages it if a student is not too manifestly a beginner to attempt it and if he [has] a liking to do so."[20]

While the lack of actual instruction in painting for all but advanced pupils would strike the modern art student as odd, it was common academic practice through most of the nineteenth century. Students were generally expected to acquire practical skills in painting outside the academy, usually in the studio of a practicing artist. Harnett described his own disheartening attempt to learn to paint in a private studio:

Fig. 54. William M. Harnett, *Borghese Warrior,* 1873. Charcoal and white chalk on pink laid paper, 39½ x 34 in. Pennsylvania Academy of the Fine Arts, Philadelphia, Presented by Mr. and Mrs. David J. Grossman

Fig. 55. William M. Harnett, *Venus de Milo,* 1873.
Charcoal on brown wove paper, 27⁵⁄₁₆ x 18 in.
Yale University Art Gallery, New Haven,
John Hill Morgan, B.A. 1893 Fund

I ventured to take a course of lessons from Thomas Jensen, who was at that time a famous painter of portraits. I paid him in advance and intended to finish the course, but I couldn't do it. He didn't exactly say that I never would learn to paint, but he didn't offer me any encouragement. After I had studied with him ten days, I asked him how a certain fault of mine should be corrected. I shall never forget his answer.

"Young man," he said, "the whole secret of painting lies in putting right color in the right place."

The next day I went back to my old way of study.[21]

As a result of his brief apprenticeship, Harnett dedicated himself with renewed vigor to his classes. "I devoted more than half my days and evenings to my art studies, only working at my trade enough to supply me with money for clothes, food, shelter, paints and canvas. Consequently I had no money to spare."[22]

Harnett executed a number of oils in 1874. Two of them, a head of Minerva and a Cupid, were paintings of plaster casts probably executed in the National Academy's antique galleries.[23] Also from 1874 are a small finished painting and oil studies of fruit, glass objects, a meerschaum pipe, a pottery jar, and a rutabaga, which document Harnett's early interest in still-life subjects. *Study of a Pipe and Other Objects* of September 1874 (fig. 57) shows isolated studies of tabletop items—a pipe, a glass tumbler, and a small white pot as well as a rather flat-looking apple and a rutabaga—in which the fledgling painter attempted to work out rudimentary problems in the rendering of three-dimensional objects, complete with shadows and light reflections.

Fig. 56. William M. Harnett, *A Sprig of Plums,* 1873.
Graphite and charcoal on gray paper, 13¼ x 9 in.
National Gallery of Art, Washington, D.C.,
Collection of Mr. and Mrs. Paul Mellon

Fig. 57. William M. Harnett, *Study of a Pipe and Other Objects,* 1874. Oil on canvas, 11⅞ x 8⅝ in. The Fine Arts Museums of San Francisco, Gift of J. Benbow Bullock (1981.67)

For his National Academy students, Wilmarth believed in the value of both drawing and painting still-life subjects. As he explained:

> If I were going to take charge of a class of beginners, I would first put them through a course of study from still life and casts, no matter how brief. Then they would learn to observe light and shade, form, rotundity, relations of tint, and master difficulties which must be mastered.[24]

Wilmarth himself executed numerous still lifes, exhibiting paintings of grapes and peaches as well as genre scenes.

During the 1870s, the painting of still life started to enter the American academic curriculum. The drawing of such subjects had a long history in the art schools, especially those for women. Later in the decade, a still-life painting class for women was taught at the Cooper Union by R. Swain Gifford,[25] and a drapery class instituted by Schussele at the Pennsylvania Academy included the painting of "various objects of still life."[26] As early as 1856, the Pennsylvania Academy directors had started to form a "Cabinet of Materials of Costume, of Ceramic Wares, of Ornamented Metals, and of Arms and Armor" for the use of the students.[27] Painting courses dedicated specifically to still life were further institutionalized at other American art schools in the last decades of the century, fostering a greater interest in the subject among artists.

In September 1874, Harnett painted his first finished still life known today. *Paint Tube and Grapes* (fig. 58) features an unusual collection of studio

Fig. 59. *Thomas Eakins,* ca. 1879. Photograph. The Metropolitan Museum of Art, New York, Gift of Charles Bregler, 1961

objects—a small cluster of smooth, dark grapes; a lettered wooden cigar box; and a slender, creased tube of oil color—and gives us a preview of Harnett's lifelong interest in the meaningful juxtaposition of selected natural and man-made objects of contrasting colors, shapes, and textures presented in a limited space. Two different styles of lettering—the stencil on the box and the printed label on the tube—foretell the artist-engraver's fascination with the painted word and the interplay between images of lettered forms and their content.

Harnett enrolled briefly in life classes at the National Academy during the 1874–75 term, but none of his life studies is known. He undoubtedly drew from the nude with fellow academy students, but perhaps realizing that his interests lay in inanimate rather than living models, he returned to antique study during the following term. His decision may have resulted in part from disturbing events at the institution, including the lack of a paid instructor during the 1875–76 term.[28] Under Wilmarth, the National Academy schools had flourished until serious financial concerns obliged the academicians to consider charging fees for the classes. While Harnett continued his studies at the troubled academy, Wilmarth and many of his advanced pupils left to set up the Art Students League, which was organized to allow

Fig. 58. William M. Harnett, *Paint Tube and Grapes,* 1874. Oil on canvas, 4¾ x 4⅞ in. Collection of The Chase Manhattan Bank, N.A.

artists to determine their own courses and conditions of study.[29]

Harnett, already working and exhibiting as a professional artist, moved back to Philadelphia in 1876 and reentered the Pennsylvania Academy, an institution significantly different from the one he had left eight years earlier. In the interim, the old academy on Chestnut Street had been closed, classes had been suspended, and a new academy had been built on Broad Street. This Victorian Gothic structure designed by Frank Furness to accommodate classrooms as well as galleries, opened in 1876 in the midst of the Philadelphia centennial celebrations. The school attracted quite a number of practicing artists and students that year. Some of Harnett's former classmates from the old Pennsylvania Academy who were now professional artists—Catherine Drinker, for example—reenrolled at this time. The Centennial Exposition also attracted some new students to Philadelphia and then to the academy, among them Robert Frederick Blum and Kenyon Cox.

Antique and life classes resumed in September 1876 under the direction of Schussele, and soon Eakins (fig. 59) was acting as his assistant and substitute in the evening classes. Most of Eakins's students from the Philadelphia Sketch Club, where he had taught earlier in the decade, had registered for life study at the academy as practicing artists or advanced pupils. Among them were the sculptor Alexander Milne Calder and Thomas Anshutz, Harnett's former National Academy classmate.

Harnett was admitted to the life class (figs. 60, 61) slightly after Anshutz, at the beginning of the fall term of 1876.[30] Harnett probably submitted a work from his National Academy days for review. He is also listed as having a life-class ticket and studying in the antique class (a common practice) in February and March 1877.[31] Although his name does not appear again in school documents, Harnett may have continued his studies at the academy after this time, and he maintained professional ties with the institution for many years.

In 1876, the Pennsylvania Academy's official position on the drawing versus painting issue was similar to that of other schools.[32] Even though Schussele continued to advocate a thorough "apprenticeship in drawing with the point or stump" and insisted on a "long preliminary study of the antique," many advanced students chose to work with the brush, a course strongly advocated by Eakins when he assumed more authority at the school (fig. 62).[33] Eakins felt that students could advance in their work by painting available models, both living and still life. A number of his pupils followed his advice to paint eggs, oranges, colored cloth, and paper to further their understanding of form, space, and light.[34] Schussele, as professor of drawing and painting, and the Committee on Instruc-

Fig. 60. *Register for the Life Class,* 1876–77. Pennsylvania Academy of the Fine Arts, Philadelphia, Archives

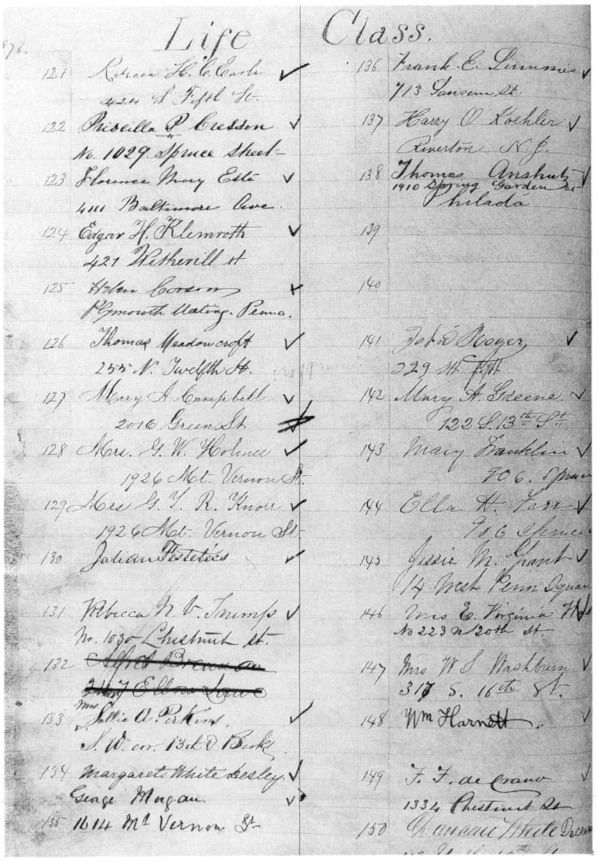

Fig. 61. Walter M. Davis, *The Male Life Class.* Wood engraving. In William C. Brownell, "The Art-Schools of Philadelphia," *Scribner's Monthly* 18 (September 1879), p. 737

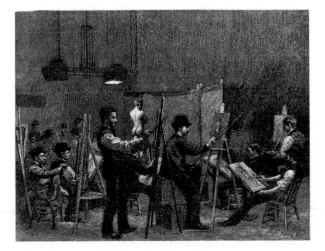

Fig. 62. Thomas Eakins, *An Eakins Drawing Class at the Pennsylvania Academy of the Fine Arts*, ca. 1878. Photograph. Philadelphia Museum of Art, Gift of George Barker

tion oversaw the efforts of the other instructors: Joseph A. Bailly, a sculptor who taught clay modeling; J. H. Kirby, an artist who lectured on perspective; and William Williams Keen, M.D., who directed the study of artistic anatomy, a subject that became one of the outstanding features of the revitalized Pennsylvania Academy (fig. 63).[35] During the 1876–77 school term, Harnett would have worked with Schussele, Eakins, and Keen. He may have participated in the drapery class, in which both antique and life pupils studied from "grouped objects of art; various objects of still life and also from the draped Mannikin."[36] It was also in 1877 that Harnett probably met fellow student John Frederick Peto (1854–1907). The two remained friends for some time, sharing their affinity for certain still-life motifs yet rendering them in distinctive styles.[37]

When Harnett reenrolled at the academy in 1876, he was a professional artist with a growing list of exhibited and sold paintings to his credit. Between 1876 and 1880, when he left Philadelphia for Europe, his works were consistently accepted for the important annuals at the National Academy and the Pennsylvania Academy as well as at other places. The exhibition of his work at these particular institutions was another aspect of his professional association with the schools.

Harnett was almost thirty years old when he left the Pennsylvania Academy, the first and last of the American academies with which he had been associated since the age of about eighteen. The Cooper Union, the National Academy, and the Pennsylvania Academy gave Harnett the training considered necessary for a professional artist in the late nineteenth

century. At these recognized schools, he was exposed to the art of the past in the form of casts of famous works of sculpture and reproductions of European paintings and to the art of the present through works shown in the museums and annual exhibitions of the institutions. Harnett became familiar with the teaching methods of European-trained artists, both American and foreign. He also got to know some of the practicing artists who frequented the academies and gave advice to earnest pupils. Harnett came into contact with an intriguing variety of art students, some of whom, like himself, were intent on graduating from craftsmen to fine artists. Frequent academy exhibitions gave him the opportunity to show his paintings to a wide audience.

American art academies provided Harnett with the education and academic credentials that allowed him to become a painter. The academies, where personal and professional relationships were formed, were essential to Harnett's life as an artist. Harnett himself perceived the institutions as such, since he took care to include references to all three schools in his account of his career. Secure in the belief that patient dedication led to success, Harnett proffered this advice to others contemplating a similar quest:

> In this sketch of my life, with its struggles and its victories, I have given you a fair idea of the hard work that is necessary for a friendless boy to undergo before he becomes recognized. Art is not an easy mistress and those who win her favors must work patiently and strive persistently.[38]

Persistence, patience, and three American art academies helped transform an unknown, youthful engraver into a recognized, mature artist.

Fig. 63. Thomas P. Anshutz, *The Dissecting Room.* Wood engraving. In William C. Brownell, "The Art-Schools of Philadelphia," *Scribner's Monthly* 18 (September 1879), p. 747

NOTES

▼

For their patient assistance in the preparation of this essay, I would like to thank Thayer Tolles Mickel and archivists Cheryl Leibold of the Pennsylvania Academy of the Fine Arts, Ulla Voulk of the Cooper Union for the Advancement of Science and Art, and Thérèse Diamand-Rosinsky of the National Academy of Design.

1. "Painted Like Real Things: The Man Whose Pictures Are a Wonder and a Puzzle," interview in *New York News,* probably 1889 or 1890, quoted in Alfred Frankenstein, *After the Hunt: William Harnett and Other American Still Life Painters, 1870–1900,* rev. ed. (Berkeley and Los Angeles: University of California Press, 1969), p. 29. A number of errors appear in this interview.

2. Ibid.

3. "Register for the Antique Class," January 24, 1866 (ticket no. 480), Pennsylvania Academy of the Fine Arts, Philadelphia, Archives. In "Painted Like Real Things" (quoted in Frankenstein, *After the Hunt,* p. 29), Harnett erroneously states that he entered the academy in 1867 at age nineteen.

4. For an analysis of the methodology and a survey of the programs at the Pennsylvania Academy as well as at other American art schools of the time, see Doreen Bolger, "The Education of the American Artist," in *In This Academy: The Pennsylvania Academy of the Fine Arts, 1805–1976,* exhib. cat. (Philadelphia: Pennsylvania Academy of the Fine Arts, 1976), pp. 51–74; and Ronald J. Onorato, "The Pennsylvania Academy of the Fine Arts and the Development of an Academic Curriculum in the Nineteenth Century" (Ph.D. diss., Brown University, 1977), pp. 71–103. See also Joshua C. Taylor, "The Academic Tradition," in Lois Marie Fink and Joshua C. Taylor, *Academy: The Academic Tradition in American Art,* exhib. cat., National Collection of Fine Arts, Smithsonian Institution, Washington, D.C. (Washington, D.C.: Smithsonian Institution Press, 1975), pp. 11–28.

5. For a history of the Pennsylvania Academy, see Frank H. Goodyear, Jr., "A History of the Pennsylvania Academy of the Fine Arts, 1805–1976," in *In This Academy,* pp. 12–49.

6. Joseph John first applied for the position of curator in July 1863; he exhibited a variety of works, mostly genre paintings, in annual exhibitions of the academy in the late 1850s, the 1860s, and the early 1870s.

7. "Petition to the Committee on Instruction from Richard N. Brooke et al.," [February 1868], Pennsylvania Academy of the Fine Arts, Archives. This previously unpublished document (located by Cheryl Leibold) is referred to in "Minutes of the Committee on Instruction," February 10, 1868, ibid.

8. Most of Harnett's fellow students (those who registered for antique study shortly before or after he did, and fellow petitioners of 1868) have remained obscure figures. Among the exceptions: William Henry Lippincott, who later studied with Léon Bonnat in Paris and became a teacher at the National Academy; Catherine (Kate) Drinker (Janvier), who was a member of the first ladies' life class, in 1869, and became the first woman to teach (perspective) at the academy, in 1878; and Ida Waugh, daughter of painters Mary Eliza Young and Samuel Bell Waugh, a member of the ladies' life class of 1869 who exhibited paintings and sculpture at the academy and elsewhere during her long career.

9. On Schussele (or Schuessele), see the Reverend George H. Johnston, *A Sermon Memorial to Christian Schussele, for Eleven Years Professor of Drawing and Painting in the Pennsylvania Academy of the Fine Arts, Philadelphia* (Philadelphia: Collins, 1879); and Ronald J. Onorato, "The Context of the Pennsylvania Academy: Thomas Eakins' Assistantship to Christian Schuessele," *Arts Magazine* 53, no. 9 (May 1979), pp. 121–29.

10. "Painted Like Real Things," quoted in Frankenstein, *After the Hunt,* p. 29. Harnett erroneously states that he found work two years later.

11. *Twelfth Annual Report of the Cooper Union for the Advancement of Science and Art . . . May 31, 1871* (New York: Cooper Union for the Advancement of Science and Art, 1871), p. 23. For a contemporary account of the school, see William C. Brownell, "The Art-Schools of New York," *Scribner's Monthly* 16 (October 1878), pp. 761–81.

12. On the history of the National Academy of Design schools in the nineteenth century, see Fink and Taylor, *Academy,* pp. 29–37, 50–67.

13. Brownell, "Art-Schools of New York," pp. 768–69.

14. On Wilmarth and his teaching, see ibid., pp. 766–70, 779–81; "Talks with Artists [Lemuel Wilmarth]: I.—The Life Class," *Art Amateur* 16 (January 1887), pp. 30–31; "Talks with Artists [Lemuel Wilmarth]: II.—The Life Class and the Teacher," *Art Amateur* 16 (March 1887), p. 78; Fink and Taylor, *Academy,* pp. 52–63; and Bolger, "Education of the American Artist," pp. 59, 62.

15. See H. Barbara Weinberg, *The American Pupils of Jean-Léon Gérôme* (Fort Worth: Amon Carter Museum, 1984).

16. "Register of the Schools of the National Academy of Design: The Antique School and The Life School," 1872–73, 1873–74, 1874–75, and 1875–76, National Academy of Design, New York, Archives.

17. James Edward Kelly, quoted in Frankenstein, *After the Hunt,* p. 38.

18. Brownell, "Art-Schools of New York," p. 770.

19. Rembrandt Peale, *Graphics: A Manual of Drawing and Writing, for the Use of Schools and Families* (New York: J. P. Peaslee, 1835), p. 25. On these manuals and their impact, see Peter C. Marzio, *The Art Crusade: An Analysis of American Drawing Manuals, 1820–1860* (Washington, D.C.: Smithsonian Institution Press, 1976).

20. Brownell, "Art-Schools of New York," p. 769. A separate painting class for advanced students to study from both nude and draped models and from still life had been approved by the National Academy in 1870 as part of the upgrading of the schools; there is no indication, however, that it met until 1873. During Harnett's years at the academy, only one list was kept of students in a "painting school" taught by Thomas LeClear; Harnett was not among the twenty-three students listed as participants in the class instituted on January 13, 1873 ("Register of the Schools of the National Academy of Design," 1872–73).

21. "Painted Like Real Things," quoted in Frankenstein, *After the Hunt,* p. 29.

22. Ibid.

23. These works are unlocated today; Frankenstein was shown photographs of them before 1953 (see ibid., p. 37).

24. "Talks with Artists: II," p. 78.

25. Brownell, "Art-Schools of New York," p. 771.

26. Christian Schussele, "Views upon the Organization of the School," n.d. [ca. June 1877], p. [6], Pennsylvania Academy of the Fine Arts, Archives.

27. "Committee on Instruction Minutes," 1856, ibid.

28. On the National Academy crisis, see Fink and Taylor, *Academy,* pp. 53–58. The 1875–76 term started in the late fall with three volunteer instructors—portrait and genre painters John G. Brown, Thomas W. Wood, and Seymour Guy—overseeing antique study for a diminished group of students and irregular classes in life study for even fewer. Harnett undoubtedly came into contact with these artists during his last year at the school.

29. On the founding and subsequent history of the Art Students League, see Marchal E. Landgren, *Years of Art: The Story of the Art Students League of New York* (New York: Robert M. McBride & Co., 1940).

30. "Register for the Life Class," 1876 (ticket no. 148), Pennsylvania Academy of the Fine Arts, Archives.

31. "Student Attendance Register," March–April 1877; and "Student Address Book," 1877, ibid.

32. For a detailed analysis of the Pennsylvania Academy schools at this time, see Maria Chamberlin-Hellman, "Thomas Eakins as a Teacher" (Ph.D. diss., Columbia University, 1981), pp. 126–308.

33. William C. Brownell, "The Art Schools of Philadelphia," *Scribner's Monthly* 18 (September 1879), p. 740.

Eakins was considered radical for his views on this course of study.

34. On Eakins's still-life classes at the Pennsylvania Academy and the use of still-life elements in Eakins's work, see Chamberlin-Hellman, "Thomas Eakins," pp. 276–72.

35. On Bailly, a French emigré sculptor, see *Philadelphia: Three Centuries of American Art,* exhib. cat. (Philadelphia: Philadelphia Museum of Art, 1976), pp. 383–84. Kirby, professor of perspective, was paid to deliver lectures at the academy. Both instructors stopped teaching there in spring 1878. On Keen, a distinguished surgeon, anatomist, and writer who conducted the Philadelphia School of Anatomy from 1866 to 1875 and was professor of artistic anatomy at the academy from 1876 to 1890, see *The Art of Philadelphia Medicine,* exhib. cat. (Philadelphia: Philadelphia Museum of Art, 1965), p. 63.

36. Schussele, "Views upon the Organization of the School." It should be noted that anatomical study at the National Academy was rudimentary during Harnett's years there. In 1872, Wilmarth was directed to have his students draw a skeleton to scale for their anatomy study (see "Minutes," May 9, 1872, National Academy of Design, cited in Bolger, "Education of the American Artist," p. 59). Harnett demonstrated his contemporary interest in anatomy by portraying a human skull in his *Mortality and Immortality* of 1876 (pl. 3). Seen within the context of anatomical study, this memento mori is a clever still-life application of an element of academic education.

37. On Harnett and Peto at the Pennsylvania Academy, see John Wilmerding, *Important Information Inside: The Art of John F. Peto and the Idea of Still-Life Painting in Nineteenth-Century America,* exhib. cat., National Gallery of Art, Washington, D.C. (New York: Harper & Row, 1983), pp. 57–68, 98, n. 2. For a discussion of academy documents concerning Harnett and Peto (who studied there from 1877 to 1879), see Chamberlin-Hellman, "Thomas Eakins," pp. 178, n. 163; 179, n. 165.

38. "Painted Like Real Things," quoted in Frankenstein, *After the Hunt,* p. 55.

NOTES OF CHANGE

▼

Harnett's Paintings of the Late 1870s

JOHN WILMERDING

The double meanings of the title of this essay perfectly suit the nature of William Michael Harnett's style in the last years of the 1870s, prior to his departure for Europe in 1880. *Notes* refers both to the notations, or narrative facts, of the artist's work and to the controversies over bank notes and coinage during the period; *change* suggests the handling of money as well as the pervasive sense of transition in America at the time of the nation's centennial. During his early maturity, Harnett established a pattern of working in clusters of subjects, which he would amplify and develop over the rest of his career. But, more important, at this time he created a new still-life imagery for himself and for American art. By examining the core group of his paintings from 1877 to 1880, we may glimpse his special process of testing variations, of pictorial inquiry and decision making. These pictures are an index not only of his artistic thought and style but also of many larger currents in American culture during the last third of the nineteenth century.

Following his early academic study in Philadelphia and New York and his work as a silver engraver, Harnett returned to Philadelphia in 1876 and to further classes at the Pennsylvania Academy of the Fine Arts. The experience and technical expertise he had gained in those two preeminent urban centers of commerce, plus the stimulating forces of the Philadelphia artistic tradition from the Peales to Thomas Eakins, now brought Harnett to the threshold of his first significant original works. With almost no precedents in American art, *The Banker's Table* of 1877 (pl. 6) is startling in its level of quality and choice of subject matter. Decisively shifting from the imagery of Raphaelle Peale's fruit compositions, John F. Francis's dessert tables, and Severin Roesen's flower bouquets, Harnett, virtually alone, introduced an imagery for a post-Darwinian

world, a turbulent America in the strains of Reconstruction, industrial growth, and political and financial corruption. Nature's bounty was now exchanged for material possessions and wealth. Contemplation of the expansive landscape yielded to concentration on the private corners of the desk and study. Harnett's taste celebrated not the senses of the palate but the inclinations toward leisure and business.

A summary inventory of the items included in his compositions of the late 1870s offers a revealing indication of what the artist selected as significant from the world about him. Old books, letters, quill pens, ink bottles, wax sticks and seals, candles, letter cases, and sheets of paper speak of familiar routines; coins and greenbacks, letter racks and business cards, of personal commerce; tobacco canisters, pipes, matches, and newspapers, of domestic pleasures; table knives, mugs or stone jars, and biscuits, of mealtime occupations; and flutes and sheets of music, of quiet relaxation.

As a backdrop, the decade saw the establishment of several businesses serving the popular needs of a rapidly expanding population. A and P (Great Atlantic and Pacific Tea Company), soon to become the nation's largest grocery-store chain, was formed in 1870; Montgomery Ward, the first mail-order house, began operations in Chicago two years later; and at the end of the decade, F. W. Woolworth opened the first successful five-and-ten.

But issues of banking institutions and practices, financial systems and abuses, dominated the affairs of this period. In 1871, Boss Tweed was indicted in New York for fraud and tax favors. Ulysses S. Grant was elected president the following year, and his administration was marked by stock scandals and corruption investigations, including the tax conspiracy of the so-

---

Opposite: William M. Harnett, *The Banker's Table* (detail, pl. 6)

called Whiskey Ring in 1875 and the impeachment a year later of the secretary of war, William Worth Belknap, for taking bribes. Early in the decade, Congress passed the Coinage Act, making gold the standard and eliminating silver currency; further legislation soon followed, allowing the resumption of coinage payments, and in 1878 Congress forced the Treasury to purchase large quantities of silver bullion for coins. At the same time, arguments over farm debts and inflated currency led to the organization of the Greenback party in Indiana, later known nationally as the Greenback-Labor party. By the end of the decade, the face value of greenbacks was declared equivalent to that of gold. In fact and fancy, money seemed to be on everyone's mind. Mark Twain and Charles Dudley Warner's novel *The Gilded Age* (1873) gave its name to these years of greed, consumption, and money making.[1] Against such a backdrop, it is no wonder the observant Harnett began in 1877 to fill his foregrounds with single five-dollar bills, gold and silver coins, and rolls of greenbacks, in still lifes with titles such as *American Exchange, The Banker's Table,* and *The Broker's Table* (private collection).

The Philadelphia to which Harnett returned after his training in New York was itself conspicuously involved in unfolding financial activities, for it was the failure of the New York branch of a Philadelphia firm, Jay Cooke and Company, that precipitated the Panic of 1873, the fall of the New York Stock Exchange, and a six-year depression. Growth and failure seemed to go hand in hand: even though the Franklin Savings Fund collapsed at this time, the number of Philadelphia's banks doubled during the decade following the Civil War. In this expansionist environment, John Wanamaker, "the city's fastest rising merchant prince,"[2] presided over comparable growth in his new retail business. Established in 1861, his department store had become a major operation by 1876, when it moved into the remodeled freight building of the Pennsylvania Railroad on Market Street, its new Grand Depot store.[3]

On most accounts, the mid-1870s would have been a stimulating time for an artist in Philadelphia. In

Fig. 64. William M. Harnett, *American Exchange,* 1878. Oil on canvas, 8 x 12 in. The Detroit Institute of Arts, Gift of Robert H. Tannahill

the two years prior to the centennial celebration, many of the city's civic and cultural institutions were built, refurbished, or expanded. Projects included the building of the massive City Hall at Market and Broad streets, restoration of Independence Hall as a museum and memorial, expansion of Fairmount Park, opening of the city zoo and Horticultural Hall, and construction of the bold Pennsylvania Academy of the Fine Arts building, designed by Frank Furness and opened in 1876. In addition, there were several smaller arts organizations that contributed to the cultural liveliness of the area—most notably, the Philadelphia Sketch Club, the School of Design for Women, the Fairmount Park Art Association, and the Social Art Club.[4] Fairman Rogers assembled an eminent art collection of his own on Rittenhouse Square, and Haseltine Galleries on Chestnut Street was among the leading art dealers of the city, noted for showing Eakins's *Gross Clinic* of 1875 (Medical College of Thomas Jefferson University, Philadelphia).

No doubt dominating the city's consciousness at the time of Harnett's return was the great Philadelphia Centennial Exposition, which had been in preparation for two years and opened on May 10, 1876, reputedly to the largest crowd "ever assembled on the North American continent."[5] On opening day, some two hundred thousand people visited over two hundred buildings on 450 acres set aside in Fairmount Park. Among the multitude of international displays of industrial developments were new inventions. The most celebrated of these was the giant Corliss steam engine in Machinery Hall (fig. 16), but of comparable interest were Alexander Graham Bell's new telephone, the latest telegraph, electric arc lights, air brakes, and various tools. On display in the art building were hundreds of academic paintings and sculptures, both European and American, said to total "two and a half miles of art exhibits."[6] At such a moment, would not any young aspiring artist on the verge of maturity respond to the attendant issues of artistic achievement and change?

Deliberate or accidental changes were occurring in the country at large. In October 1871, the great fire of Chicago razed much of the city, and precipitated in its rebuilding were the beginnings of modernist American architecture. A year later, fire devastated Boston, and in its wake the young Henry Hobson Richardson designed Trinity Church, his first neo-Romanesque masterpiece. The early 1870s also saw important changes in American landscape painting. While older Hudson River School artists John Frederick Kensett, Albert Bierstadt, and George Inness were creating some of their major late works, a new severe realism was appearing in the first great images of Winslow Homer and Eakins. Whereas fire had physically shaped the country's vision of renewal, the centennial period more broadly engendered feelings of nostalgia and

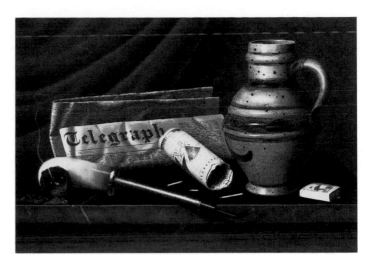

Fig. 65. William M. Harnett, *Still Life with Telegraph,* 1880. Oil on canvas, 14⅛ x 20 in. The Denver Art Museum

pride in the paradox of America's stability and youth. Whether in the form of the Corliss engine, Chicago's new construction methods, or the challenging theories of Charles Darwin (whose *Descent of Man and Selection in Relation to Sex* appeared in 1871), change has been described as "the modern's defining characteristic."[7]

When we return to *The Banker's Table,* we can see how truly it depicts both small change, as the phrase goes, and change more profound. This picture and its companions of the next few years—*Music and Literature, American Exchange, Memento Mori*— *"To This Favour," Secretary's Table, Philadelphia Public Ledger, March 2, 1880,* and *Still Life with Telegraph*—also need to be considered in the light of the presence of Thomas Eakins (1844–1916) as an artist and a teacher in Philadelphia during the 1870s. Eakins himself returned to the city at the beginning of the decade, after training in Paris and travel in Spain, having mastered his teacher Jean-Léon Gérôme's techniques of precise draftsmanship and polished brushwork. In both his interior domestic scenes and sunlit rowing pictures of the early 1870s, Eakins was most concerned with an exacting process of integrating all compositional elements. At mid-decade, he began work on his monumental *Gross Clinic* for submission to the Centennial Exposition. Its rejection by John Sartain and the selection committee and the subsequent storm of criticism over its perceived brutal realism are now well known. Five of Eakins's other entries were selected, however, including the shadowy but meticulously executed *Professor Benjamin Howard Rand* of 1874 (Medical College of Thomas Jefferson University, Philadelphia) and *The Chess*

Fig. 66. Thomas Eakins, *The Chess Players*, 1876.
Oil on wood, 11¾ x 16¾ in. The Metropolitan Museum
of Art, New York, Gift of the Artist, 1881

Players of 1876 (fig. 66). The controversy over *The Gross Clinic* surely would have been familiar to any artist associated with Philadelphia, let alone with the Pennsylvania Academy. But the other works Eakins exhibited, though nominally portraits, are even more striking for their genre and still-life elements. In viewing their clarity of detail and execution, their underlying sense of planar and geometric form, and the elegant qualities of surface and texture, one cannot help sensing their potential relevance to the still lifes Harnett completed in Philadelphia in the late 1870s. Even more convincing than Eakins's orderly designs and style of painting is his conscious attention to critical still-life details: the exquisite array of scientific instruments, papers, and textiles across the foreground of the Rand portrait; and the delicate table and glassware at the left of *The Chess Players,* echoing the fragile elderly men concentrating on their chess pieces at center. In addition, furniture and other decorative elements play a distinctive role in several of Eakins's paintings from 1877; for example, the lavish pile of the model's clothes in the center foreground of *William Rush Carving His Allegorical Figure of the Schuylkill River* (fig. 70), and the Colonial-revival chair in *Seventy Years Ago* (The Art Museum, Princeton University) and table in *Young Girl Meditating* (The Metropolitan Museum of Art, New York). Eakins not only treated these accessories with the attention given to still-life objects, but he also calculated with great care their placement within the composition.

Equal to the examples of Eakins's art that might have influenced Harnett was the force of his actual presence. Eakins was only four years older than Harnett, and when the latter enrolled at the Pennsyl-

vania Academy upon its reopening in 1876, the two men (at ages thirty-two and twenty-eight) must have felt as much like colleagues as teacher and student. Eakins had been involved in planning the new teaching spaces and was a volunteer instructor of the men's evening life class under the aged Christian Schussele. In 1876, Harnett was issued a ticket to the life class, and the following year he attended the antique class as well, in February and March.[8] Eakins asserted his fresh views on instruction using live models and set about redesigning the curriculum. Upon Schussele's death in 1879, the Committee on Instruction put Eakins in charge of all the classes and appointed him professor of drawing and painting. Even while Harnett was enrolled in Eakins's classes, the latter may have been contemplating the teaching of still life, for in 1883 he wrote to the Board of Directors that he was "very anxious to have a still life painting class where color and tone experiments may be made. . . . The knowledge obtained from the study of strong colors is of very great importance."[9]

Eakins urged the study of simple forms to capture "color, modeling, texture, and translucency." "Paint an egg, as it teaches you to paint well." "Take an egg or an orange, a piece of black cloth, and a piece of white paper, and try to get the light and color." "Take a lump of sugar, a piece of chalk, and get the texture." "These simple studies make strong painters." Aside from essential shapes, he also recommended that one "always think of the third dimension." "The more planes you have to work by, the solider will be your work. One or two planes is little better than an outline."[10] While the subject matter of Harnett's still lifes of this period may have been inspired by the commercial and financial environment, it appears equally indebted to Eakins's methodology for assembling clearly defined volumes in legible spaces.

In *The Banker's Table*, content and form gracefully fuse, playing off items of relaxation and business in formal groupings both casual and orderly. This work and Harnett's other money pictures of the late 1870s allude to the offices of businessmen and presumably appealed to their patronage.[11] The partially seen letters and envelopes addressed to specific individuals even suggest a form of surrogate portraiture, just as in their evocation of daily affairs and social discourse the various accumulations of library objects might be said to represent a sort of inanimate genre painting. Harnett's *Banker's Table* and his illusionistic *Still Life—Five-Dollar Bill,* also of 1877 (fig. 68), are apparently among the first still-life money pictures in the history of American art. Of course, Harnett may have been familiar with the pictures of books and papers on shelves painted at the beginning of the nineteenth century by Charles Bird King[12] as well as with the previously cited tabletop still lifes of food, fruit, and flowers by the Peales, Francis, and Roesen that were well known in Philadelphia. But for all their relevance, these works only confirm the novelty of Harnett's visual dialogue between paper and coins.

There are both gold and silver coins in *The Banker's Table*. Numbers and letters are engraved, printed, or penned by hand or machine on almost every item: inkwell label, envelope and stamp, book binding, coins, and bills. Like an arrow, the quill pen cuts across the center of the composition, an agent of communication and information, pointing from contemplation to action, from leisure to commerce. The stack of coins and folded paper bills hint of banking transactions and accumulated wealth. Harnett reinforced these simple references to human conduct through his repeated formal rhythms of circles, planes, and arcs. Perhaps noticeable first are the circular echoes in planar form of the postmark, single coins, and open mouth of the ink bottle versus the cylindrical volumes of the full bottle and column of coins. Equally orchestrated are the hard and soft rectangular planes, beginning with the marble tabletop on which are piled the paper letter, bills, and leather books. The eye notes the more subtle arcs of gentle curves and foreshortened circles in the bill folds, book spines, and resting pen, and even in the spiraling pile from envelope to bottle. Within this chamber music of shapes, one finally notes Harnett's playful variations of paper types—ink label, book pages, envelope, greenbacks, and coin wrapper—all only partially visible, whether covered, closed, turned away, torn, or folded. We are not certain of the bill types; they are worn, circulated, and generic. About 1889, the artist recalled, "I always group my figures, so as to try and make an artistic composition. I endeavor to make the composition tell a story. . . . To find a subject that paints well is not an easy task. As a rule, new things do not paint well. . . . I want my models to have the mellowing effect of age."[13] In this work and in the unassuming painted companions to follow, Harnett presented objects from contemporary experience that had been subjected to use and wear, thereby linking the past to the present. He created a still life that joined the private to the public; a meditation on order, process, and social structure.

The Banker's Table was one of several similarly composed still lifes that Harnett painted between 1877 and 1880. Indeed, the versions seem so intimately related as to suggest a conscious effort to pursue a particular arrangement through its possible permutations. For example, there followed *American Exchange* of 1878 (fig. 64), with its ink bottle, roll of bills, and folded letter; *Secretary's Table* of 1879 (pl. 13), with yet other letter-writing paraphernalia; and *Still Life with Letter to Thomas B. Clarke*, also of 1879 (pl. 15), with its marble tabletop, envelope, and folded newspaper. These subjects are about intellectual, as well as business, exchanges. Besides the circulation of currency, they speak of the transmission of what was current. The letters, books, and newspapers all communicate information, old or new, and reflect the Victorian habit of writing letters as well as the broadening literacy of the population. In this regard, it is worth noting that in 1873 the government issued the first penny postcards and provided free mail delivery in all cities with a population over twenty thousand. Whether intentionally or not, Harnett was observing the status and sociology of learning in America in these emblematic vignettes.

Directly paralleling this first group is a second, composed around a newspaper, a pipe and burnt matches, and the cylindrical form of either a tobacco canister, stoneware jar, or mug. This series begins in 1877 with *Still Life* (pl. 5), followed in 1880 by works such as *Still Life with Telegraph* and *Philadelphia Public Ledger, March 2, 1880* (fig. 65, pl. 19). Falling into a third category of variations are paintings such as *Music and Literature* of 1878 and *Memento Mori—"To This Favour"* of 1879 (pls. 10, 12), which display amplifications in compositional complexity and anecdotal subject matter, respectively. In *Music and Literature*, Harnett took his basic piles of objects, a larger pyramidal grouping to the left and a smaller one to the right, and created a complicated and intricate play of rhythmic geometric forms, using not only many more books but adding sheet music and instruments as well. In *Memento Mori*, he repeated a vanitas subject he had first tried three years before in *Mortality and Immortality* (pl. 3). The inclusion of a skull along with the candle and hourglass represents Harnett at his most prosaic and conventional in this direct borrowing from seventeenth-century Dutch still lifes that he could have seen in New York or Philadelphia in his student years. Although *Memento Mori* is a more sophisticated and finely executed picture than the stiffer, earlier *Mortality and Immortality*, its message about the passage of life seems obvious in comparison to the evocative contemporaneity of the money and newspaper still lifes. In these images of the late 1870s, it is as if Harnett were attempting new pictorial formulas and then testing them against past conventions or enlarging upon his own focused arrangements with a singular and more ambitious effort like *Music and Literature*. In fact, the process of tangential elaboration upon both subject and design established in these works was to be a pattern of creativity Harnett would follow for most of his career. By such means, he was consistently able to be both methodical and inventive, traditional as well as original.

With these paintings, Harnett created a distinctive and coherent body of work that comments upon the corruptions of the flesh and spirit with the balanced eye of a journalist and the private meditations of a personal correspondent. There are illuminating parallels in the compact and private poems of Emily Dickinson (1830–1886), written about the same time. A reclusive New Englander who traveled little and published almost nothing during her lifetime, Dickinson composed her poems as memoranda to herself or as letters to others. Like Harnett, she shaped her art with refined concentration and shadowy closure, employing repeated rhythms of nearly rhyming words, economy of form, and concern for the transience of life. Writing from the late 1860s to the early 1880s, Dickinson also celebrated the intimate and private in both idea and scale. Her reductive verse is as framed as the painter's tabletop spaces. Both enjoyed the contemplative stance and the juxtaposition of pure forms: "Best Witchcraft is Geometry / To the magician's mind— / His ordinary acts are feats / To thinking of mankind."[14]

While Dickinson more frequently turned to the natural and spiritual worlds, several of her subjects relate to Harnett's: "The Only News I know / Is Bulletins all Day / From Immortality." Words and books provided solace and stimulated the imagination, as in these opening stanzas of two poems: "There is no Frigate like a Book / To take us Lands away / Nor any Coursers like a Page / Of prancing Poetry—" and "Unto my Books—so good to turn— / Far ends of tired Days— /. . . I thank these Kinsmen of the Shelf—." By similar means, she elevated the commonplace and immediate into something distilled and timeless. Both artists sought to find or impose order in a transient world: "Crumbling is not an instant's Act / A fundamental pause / Dilapidation's processes / Are organized Decays."[15] Just as Harnett constructed his compositions with the clear planes and volumes of his objects, so Dickinson employed her words as literal and metaphoric building blocks to perfect the structure of a poem:

> The Props assist the House
> Until the House is built
> And then the Props withdraw
> And adequate, erect,
> The House support itself
> And cease to recollect
> The Auger and the Carpenter—
> Just such a retrospect
> Hath the perfected Life—
> A past of Plank and Nail
> and slowness—then the Scaffolds drop
> Affirming it a Soul.[16]

Fig. 67. Winslow Homer, *The Cotton Pickers,* 1876. Oil on canvas, 24 1/16 x 38 1/8 in. Los Angeles County Museum of Art, acquisition made possible through museum trustees: Robert O. Anderson, R. Stanton Avery, B. Gerald Cantor, Edward W. Carter, Justin Dart, Charles E. Ducommun, Mrs. Daniel Frost, Julian Ganz, Jr., Dr. Armand Hammer, Harry Lenart, Dr. Franklin D. Murphy, Mrs. Joan Palevsky, Richard E. Sherwood, Maynard J. Toll, and Hal B. Wallis

If history and genre paintings may be said to be analogous to prose, then still lifes are comparable to poems. As worldly as are Harnett's subjects and as cerebral as are Dickinson's, both painter and poet created art forms of metaphoric power and formal purity.

Given the apparent internal logic and methodical development of Harnett's paintings from 1877 to 1880, we need to account for three unusual works of this period that stand out for their differences in style or subject. The first is *Attention, Company!* of 1878 (pl. 11), striking as a sympathetic depiction of a black youth and a rare Harnett figural or portrait image. Although the newspaper hat and the presence of various printed and lettered signs tie this to Harnett's library still lifes of the same time, and the stiffly centralized placement of the boy suggests the sensibility of a figural still life, the unnerving emotional directness and relative shallowness of the composition are new for the artist.

On one level, such an image is not surprising in the period after the Civil War, with its many racial issues left unresolved. Indeed, just as the 1870s began, the Fifteenth Amendment to the Constitution was ratified, giving black males the right to vote; in 1875, Congress passed the first Civil Rights Act, allowing blacks equal access to public places and to juries. Two years later, Reconstruction formally ended, less than successfully, as federal troops withdrew from the South. Yet, except for this general background, Harnett's picture is not a particular social or political reference to any explicit event or situation. While one can decipher the fragments of words inscribed on the wooden boards and tattered posters (such as *Ledg[er]*, *Not[ice]*, and *Gr[and] Excu[rsion]*), they stop short of narrative content. Although the youth's paper hat, solemn face, and mop or broom by his side allude to a military posture, the image never takes on the moral or anecdotal character of a genre or history painting. The boy stands as motionless and fixed as a still-life object in a shallow illusionistic space. Despite his academic training at the National Academy of Design and the Cooper Union for the Advancement of Science and Art in New York and at the Pennsylvania Academy in Philadelphia, it appears Harnett never felt comfortable rendering the human form.

Harnett was most likely aware of, and perhaps inspired by, recent images of blacks in American art, whether stereotypical or serious. The numerous rural farm hands painted between the 1830s and 1860s by William Sidney Mount and James Goodwyn Clonney come to mind. Even more relevant for Harnett in New York in the late 1860s and early 1870s were the dignified black subjects undertaken by Eastman Johnson and Winslow Homer.[17] During and after the war, Homer was well known for his illustrations of blacks published in *Harper's Weekly*. These progressed steadily

from superficial and caricatured types to rather powerful and sympathetically presented figures. Blacks appear in Homer's Civil War oils, such as *Inviting a Shot before Petersburg* (also called *Defiance: Inviting a Shot before Petersburg*) of 1864 (The Detroit Institute of Arts) and *Army Teamsters* of 1866 (private collection), but of even greater immediacy are his paintings of the mid-1870s, some of which were executed or exhibited in New York at the National Academy. Most notable are *Uncle Ned at Home* of 1875 (private collection), followed in 1876 by *A Visit from the Old Mistress* (National Museum of American Art, Washington, D.C.), *The Cotton Pickers* (fig. 67), and *The Watermelon Boys* (Cooper-Hewitt, National Museum of Design, Smithsonian Institution, New York). *A Visit* was exhibited at the National Academy in 1875, the year Harnett submitted a work for the first time. The stilled postures and pensive faces in *The Watermelon Boys* seem especially reminiscent of the figure in *Attention, Company!*, executed two years later. If Homer's paintings of blacks inspired Harnett in New York, he returned to Philadelphia to find Eakins also at work on similar subjects. *Pushing for Rail* of 1874 (The Metropolitan Museum of Art, New York) and *Will Schuster and Blackman Going Shooting* of 1876 (Yale University Art Gallery, New Haven) are more outdoor genre scenes, but *Whistling Plover* of 1874 (The Brooklyn Museum) and *Negro Boy Dancing* of 1878 (The Metropolitan Museum of Art, New York) show the isolated concentration on a figure that would have appealed to Harnett.

The other Harnett pictures that stand apart from his sequential patterns of the late 1870s are *Job Lot Cheap* of 1878 and *The Artist's Letter Rack* of 1879 (pls. 9, 17). Both share a somewhat lighter palette and depict a similar blond wood and probably owe their character to Harnett's slightly younger colleague John Frederick Peto (1854–1907). Born and raised in Philadelphia, Peto began sketching as a boy; in 1877, a year behind Harnett, he entered the Pennsylvania Academy, where he remained, also studying under Eakins, through 1879.[18] Peto and Harnett soon became friends and genial competitors, undertaking common subjects and compositions over the next couple of decades. But even from Peto's first dated works of about 1878, he practiced a looser style with greater attention to expressive textures and colors. His pictures display a sense of the melancholy decay and deterioration of objects, which only deepened as he grew older. Although he took up the same still-life models as Harnett—newspapers, pipes, and mugs, along with piles of old books—from the start, Peto's style was personal and subjective (despite the long history of confusion between their works after their lifetimes).[19] *Job Lot Cheap,* with its more scripted signature and compressed clutter of bent and angled books, looks more like a Peto than a Harnett, having little of the clear

Fig. 68. William M. Harnett, *Still Life—Five-Dollar Bill,* 1877. Oil on canvas, 8⅛ x 12 in.
Philadelphia Museum of Art, Alex Simpson, Jr., Collection

geometries and calculated arrangement of the latter's familiar still lifes of this period. Yet we know the circumstances of its undertaking and its entire provenance, which confirm its tie to Harnett.[20] On one hand, its atypicality can best be explained as an example of the painter pushing the formulas of his serial compositions to a new extreme; on the other, as a response to the more romantic and dense compositions of his friend. It is interesting to note that both artists were taking up the subject of books and their implied relationship to contemporary habits of collecting, learning, and libraries just as the celebrated philanthropist Andrew Carnegie was beginning the establishment of more than two thousand libraries throughout America and the English-speaking world.

The Artist's Letter Rack is almost an isolated image in Harnett's career, with the exception of one major reprise, *Mr. Hulings' Rack Picture* of almost a decade later (pl. 44). As an illusionistic exercise, *The Artist's Letter Rack* had little precedent in Harnett's work to date, save the shallow vertical orientation of *Attention, Company!* and of *Still Life—Five-Dollar Bill.* Its ultimate source was the inherited conventions of Dutch Baroque examples, but it seems most immediately linked to a favorite picture type of Peto's, begun at virtually the same time. Since Harnett was interested in the ephemera of daily correspondence and in the balanced formal play of lines, planes, and rectangles, a rack with letters, envelopes, and paper currency certainly fit his artistic temperament. But the extreme two-dimensionality of the design was more a challenge of technical dexterity, a tangential digression at this juncture, than the sustained exploration of the format then being initiated by Peto. The latter's *Office Board for Smith Bros. Coal Co.* (fig. 69), dated June 1879, employs a similar pink tape, torn label, and dangling loop of string. *The Artist's Letter Rack* includes a card bearing a postmark of August 26, suggesting the two friends were working simultaneously, if not side by side, on their pictures.[21] While Harnett immediately returned to painting tabletop compositions, Peto continued working in the two-dimensional format, with *Rack Picture with Telegraph, Letter, and Postcards* of November 1880 (private collection), *The Rack* of 1880 (University Art Collections, Arizona State University, Tempe), *Office Board for Christian Faser* of 1881 (private collection), *Old Souvenirs,* begun in 1881 and

reworked in 1900 (The Metropolitan Museum of Art, New York), *Rack Picture for William Malcolm Bunn* of 1882 (National Museum of American Art, Washington, D.C.), and *Office Board* of April 1885 (The Metropolitan Museum of Art, New York).[22] After a lapse of nearly a decade, Peto again took up a sequence of rack pictures that are even more moody

Fig. 69. John F. Peto, *Office Board for Smith Bros. Coal Co.,* 1879. Oil on canvas, 28 x 24 in. Addison Gallery of American Art, Phillips Academy, Andover, Mass. (1956.13)

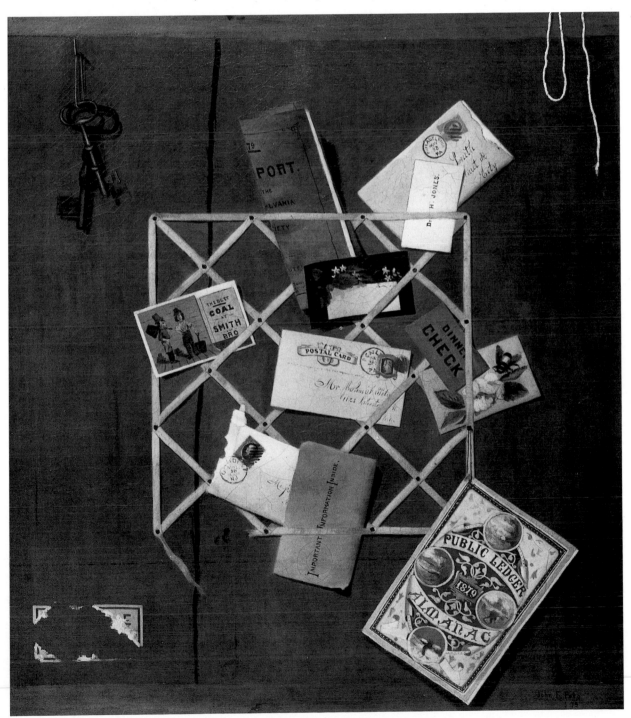

and abstracted. In contrast, Harnett returned to the subject only once, with *Mr. Hulings' Rack Picture*, almost as if to upstage his rival with a dazzling tour de force of illusionism.

Whatever the association between the two painters at this moment, Harnett seemed to conclude the first stage of his artistic development with a process of experimentation and consolidation. Some artistic need for challenge or change now prompted him to go abroad. During this period, a number of American artists felt a similar impulse of transition or disjunction. A fellow Philadelphian, Mary Cassatt, moved in 1873 to Paris, where she remained for much of her career. In his mid-forties, Winslow Homer decided to leave New England in 1881 for a two-year stay at Tynemouth, England—a major break and turning point in his development.[23] The key intellectual of this generation, Henry Adams, returned from his youthful travels and study abroad to assume a teaching position at Harvard University in the early 1870s. Upon accepting a second five-year appointment, he wrote, "I am going on to thirty-eight years old, the yawning gulf of middle age . . . grumbling has become my favorite occupation. I have ceased to grow rapidly either in public esteem or in mental development."[24] Following the contested presidential election of Rutherford B. Hayes, Adams moved to Washington, D.C., in late 1877, obsessed with questions about currency, political fraud, and the economic upheavals that were taking place at the end of the decade. He left again, for London and Europe, and when he returned the new decade was to be disrupted by the assassination of President Garfield in 1881. Meanwhile, in Philadelphia, Eakins was experiencing growing criticism over the forthrightness of both his paintings and his teaching methods, which led to his dismissal from the Pennsylvania Academy later in the 1880s.

For these and others, it appeared a time of unease, challenge, and ambition, precipitated in part by the march of age, in part by the answers and questions of artistic accomplishment. Early in 1880, Harnett left Philadelphia for London, Frankfort, Munich, and Paris. His pattern and process of creativity continued from his habits of the late 1870s: clusters of sequential works, close variations, simplified as well as more complicated resolutions of a particular subject, and the occasional major punctuation of a tangential format or spatial arrangement. The methods he shaped for himself between 1877 and 1880 persisted throughout his career, which at every subsequent step brought forth richer, more refined, and self-confident works of art.

NOTES

1. For a concordance of this factual information, see Laurence Urdang, ed., *The Timetables of American History* (New York: Simon & Schuster, 1981), pp. 228–41. See also Bruce W. Chambers, *Old Money: American Trompe l'Oeil Images of Currency,* exhib. cat. (New York: Berry-Hill Galleries, 1988), pp. 13–21.

2. Russell F. Weigley, ed., *Philadelphia: A 300-Year History* (New York and London: W. W. Norton & Co., 1982), pp. 432, 444.

3. Ibid., p. 444.

4. Ibid., pp. 426, 448–50.

5. Ibid., p. 466.

6. Ibid., pp. 459, 466–69.

7. Ross Miller, *American Apocalypse: The Great Fire and the Myth of Chicago* (Chicago and London: University of Chicago Press, 1990), p. 30.

8. "Register for the Life Class," 1876 (ticket no. 148); and "Student Attendance Register," March–April 1877, Pennsylvania Academy of the Fine Arts, Archives. See also Lloyd Goodrich, *Thomas Eakins,* 2 vols. (Cambridge, Mass., and London: Harvard University Press, 1982), 1, p. 169.

9. Goodrich, *Eakins,* 1, p. 182.

10. Ibid., pp. 182, 185.

11. See Chambers, *Old Money,* p. 18.

12. See Alfred Frankenstein, *After the Hunt: William Harnett and Other American Still Life Painters, 1870–1900,* rev. ed. (Berkeley and Los Angeles: University of California Press, 1969), p. 88; and William H. Gerdts, *Painters of the Humble Truth: Masterpieces of American Still Life, 1801–1939,* exhib. cat., Philbrook Art Center, Tulsa, Okla. (Columbia, Mo., and London: University of Missouri Press, 1981), pp. 157–58.

13. "Painted Like Real Things: The Man Whose Pictures Are a Wonder and a Puzzle," interview in *New York News,* probably 1889 or 1890, quoted in Frankenstein, *After the Hunt,* p. 55.

14. *Final Harvest: Emily Dickinson's Poems,* [ed.] Thomas H. Johnson (Boston and Toronto: Little, Brown & Co., 1961), p. 253.

15. Ibid., pp. 206, 267, 153, 230.

16. Ibid., pp. 251–52.

17. See Peter H. Wood and Karen C. C. Dalton, *Winslow Homer's Images of Blacks: The Civil War and Reconstruction Years,* exhib. cat., Menil Collection, Houston (Austin: University of Texas Press, 1988); and Guy C. McElroy, *Facing History: The Black Image in American Art, 1710–1940,* exhib. cat., Corcoran Gallery of Art, Washington, D.C. (San Francisco: Bedford Arts Publishers, 1990).

18. See John Wilmerding, *Important Information Inside: The Art of John F. Peto and the Idea of Still-Life Painting in Nineteenth-Century America,* exhib. cat., National Gallery of Art, Washington, D.C. (New York: Harper & Row, 1983), pp. 67, 98–99.

19. See Frankenstein, *After the Hunt,* pp. 3–24; and Wilmerding, *Important Information,* pp. 11–34.

20. See Frankenstein, *After the Hunt,* pp. 45–48; and Wilmerding, *Important Information,* pp. 126–30.

21. Perhaps emulating Peto, Harnett changed the tape in his *Artist's Letter Rack* from blue to pink (see Jennifer Milam, "The Artist's Working Methods," p. 170).

22. See Doreen Bolger Burke, *American Paintings in the Metropolitan Museum of Art,* vol. 3, *A Catalogue of Works by Artists Born between 1846 and 1864,* ed. Kathleen Luhrs (New York: Metropolitan Museum of Art, 1980), pp. 50–53; and Wilmerding, *Important Information,* pp. 206–20.

23. See John Wilmerding, "Winslow Homer in the 1870s," in John Wilmerding and Linda Ayers, *Winslow Homer in the 1870s: Selections from the Valentine-Pulsifer Collection,* exhib. cat. (Princeton: Art Museum, Princeton University, 1990), pp. 13–17.

24. Quoted in Ernest Samuels, *Henry Adams* (Cambridge, Mass., and London: Harvard University Press, 1989), p. 107.

COMMON OBJECTS OF EVERYDAY LIFE

ROXANA ROBINSON

An editorial in *Appletons' Journal* in 1870 pronounced the hope that "the common . . . and ugly objects of our every-day life, in time, shall be replaced by objects and forms that will give pleasure, soften manners, and counteract the now unmitigated exercise and influence of mere industrialism."[1] The idea that certain objects might exert this beneficial effect, merely by their presence, was part of the prevailing view of art as a moral force that provided spiritual uplift through an idealized and sometimes sentimentalized vision of the world. William Michael Harnett was very much an artist of his time, and his work reflects contemporary attitudes. He grew up poor, Irish, and Catholic in Protestant, patrician Philadelphia, and as an outsider struggling for acceptance by the establishment, he tended toward conventional behavior. His work had wide commercial appeal, and he supported himself by its sale.

It is particularly in his ambitious tabletop still lifes that Harnett demonstrated a commitment to the prevailing cultural ethos. Formally as well as thematically, these paintings celebrate culture and civilization; they represent an idealized world of the intellect and the soul through the portrayal of great books, music, and works of art. Objets d'art were widely collected during this period, and Harnett himself prized his cherished assortment of carved wood and ivory, hand-wrought metals, antique goblets, books, weapons, instruments, and Turkey carpets—the glories of past cultures, all of which he used as models.

Despite the views of the establishment, however, commitment to the culture of the ideal was not unanimous. Since mid-century, the tide of realism had been rising in Europe, where writers and artists were rejecting the historic, heroic, and sacred in favor of the mundane. In America, too, there were mavericks at work. Exhibition lists from the 1880s show a predominance of sentimental and idealistic themes, but there are intimations of change. Realism was providing a strong undercurrent to the mainstream of idealism.

Winslow Homer, many of whose early oils depict the leisure hours of the urban upper middle class, left the States in 1881 seeking a sterner vision of life among English fishermen. Upon his return two years later, his compositions were simpler and stronger, and thereafter he drew his images from the austere realities of provincial life. Philadelphian Thomas Eakins, whose work was known firsthand by Harnett, had steadily pursued an objective, particular, and realistic muse, exploring the laws of optics and physics to determine the precise nature of visual perception. His approach to subject matter was antiheroic; in *William Rush Carving His Allegorical Figure of the Schuylkill River* of 1877 (fig. 70), Eakins deliberately flouted the notion of the ideal by recording the specific reality behind the allegory. His paintings present a calm and objective vision that accurately renders a spatial and temporal world while presenting an underlying emotional reality that is subtle, complex, and disturbing—the antithesis of the ruling cheap and easy sentimentality.

Harnett, who was well aware of emerging anti-idealistic trends, possessed a healthy interest in conventional success that did not preclude an irreverent sense of humor and a streak of pragmatic populism. These liberating qualities gave him license to flout the solemn admonitions of *Appletons'* and to examine iconoclastic subjects. Departing from the list of approved objects, he chose instead things that were ordinary, contemporary, or American: paper money, newspapers, dead chickens, cast-off horseshoes, cheap pipes, and old-fashioned guns. With authority and assurance, he used all of these as models in a curious series of single hanging objects painted between 1882 and 1890.

In these, some of his most radical works, Harnett challenged the culture of the ideal. The "common" and

Fig. 70. Thomas Eakins, *William Rush Carving His Allegorical Figure of the Schuykill River,*
1877. Oil on canvas, 20⅛ x 26⅛ in. Philadelphia Museum of Art,
Gift of Mrs. Thomas Eakins and Miss Mary Adeline Williams

"ugly" objects he portrayed would neither soften manners nor counteract industrialism, but they were rendered with a degree of elegance and precision that would. Such technical brilliance applied to "ugly" objects was shocking. Conceptually, too, Harnett's were troubling works that, in effect, questioned the very premise of nineteenth-century aesthetics: if a painting neither achieved noble sentiment nor provided spiritual uplift, how could it be art?

Some of Harnett's earliest ventures in trompe l'oeil were pranks. Anecdotal accounts tell of him painting a dollar bill "pasted" to a dues notice and a stamp on a letter that went through the mail unchallenged.[2] Even after his decision, in 1875, to become a full-time artist, his iconoclastic attitude persisted, despite *Appletons'* sober counsel.

Between 1877 and 1879, Harnett painted images of paper money "pasted" to a wooden wall. In his choice of subject, filthy lucre itself, Harnett deliberately poked fun at a solemn contemporary warning against

"the strongholds of . . . materialism" and flatly refuted the notion of the moral responsibility of art.[3] Despite their subject, these works do not celebrate wealth. The banknotes are of small denominations, and some are, in fact, worthless—a double fraud. Physically these paintings are modest, and conceptually they are cheerfully iconoclastic. One of them hung in a saloon, and others may have been commissioned by friends, as was probably the case with *The Artist's Letter Rack* of 1879 (pl. 17), a "portrait" of commercial ephemera. These works seem to have been viewed as tricks— prestidigitation, not art—and Harnett's astonishing mastery of form and space do impart a magical air. The money paintings are antithetical to the prevailing solemn mood in American art, and their size, scarcity, and provenance suggest that the artist intended them as private asides as much as public declamations.

In Munich, Harnett painted a trompe-l'oeil picture that conveyed quite a different message. *Plucked Clean* of 1882 (pl. 25), a vivid, life-size image of a dead chicken hanging against a rough wooden wall, was intended to be neither humorous nor radical. It was, instead, an artistic statement that affirmed Harnett's intellectual and aesthetic alliance with a European tradition and signaled his involvement with a specifically German sensibility. In its meticulous examination of the physical reality of a lowly object, *Plucked Clean* strongly reflects the influence of the Leibl-Kreis. This circle of artists, a powerful presence in Munich during the 1870s, still exerted a considerable effect upon the artistic community during Harnett's stay there, from 1881 to 1885. *Still Life with Hen* of 1881 (fig. 137) by Nikolaus Gysis, a well-known Munich artist closely associated with the Leibl-Kreis, seems to be a direct predecessor of Harnett's picture.

The spectacularly unidealized subject of *Plucked Clean* marks a departure from the usual American treatment of still life. American paintings had typically shown food fully prepared on the dining-room table among linens, porcelain, and silver. *Plucked Clean* lies within the European tradition of kitchen still lifes, in which food is presented in a raw, natural state: dead fowl, rabbits, fruit, and vegetables lie in pleasing disarray on fire-blackened stone. Harnett's straightforward approach to death is also European; American paintings of the period either treat the subject with deep sentimentality or avoid it altogether. Harnett's abstract and emotionless approach marks his further departure from American attitudes.

From 1883 to 1885, Harnett continued to use the single hanging object and the trompe-l'oeil format to explore the theme of hunting, producing two paintings of hanging ducks, a hanging rabbit, and four versions of *After the Hunt.* Harnett, whose background was poor and urban, was probably first introduced to hunting while in Munich, and his experience with the sport was probably entirely secondhand. Hunting was a favorite pastime of the Leibl Kreis and the subject of some of their most famous paintings. As a theme in German art, hunting predates the work of this group, however, and hunting gear appears in genre scenes throughout the nineteenth century, as seen in Moritz von Schwind's *Visit* of about 1855 (fig. 133).

Harnett's trompe-l'oeil *Trophy of the Hunt* of the same year (pl. 36) is his most sensuous work, a brilliant counterpoise of the intellectual and the voluptuous. The dead rabbit is devoid of pathos, its form balanced by the shapes of the man-made metal door hinges and iron handle. The silky richness of the exquisitely rendered fur is countered by the rough surface of the wood, the severity of the composition, and the mood of absolute detachment.

Harnett's hanging still lifes tend toward a static and immobile perfection. The objects are suspended firmly and absolutely by visible strings and sturdy nails; their weight and solidity fix them immutably in place. To infuse a sense of motion and liveliness into these works, Harnett introduced secondary elements that are flimsy, mobile, and weightless: loose pages, puffs of feathers, and, most frequently, peeling scraps of newspaper. These ancillary objects serve not only as a contrast between the fixed and the mobile but as diversionary tactics, drawing the eye away from the central deception to a smaller and apparently simpler one. An early example of this technique occurs in *Shinplaster with Exhibition Label* of 1879 (fig. 7), in which a label appears pasted to the front of the canvas. The trompe-l'oeil newspaper clippings in these pictures are small, scrappy, and grimy, with carelessly scissored edges. These are private mementos that look real and readable but are neither. The presence of these enigmatic clippings is a recurring reminder of the ambiguous presence of the artist and of information withheld.

Harnett returned to America in 1886 and executed an unusual number of works of single suspended objects that reflect an exuberance consonant with his recent successes in Paris and London. In contrast to his pre-European trompe-l'oeil paintings, modest in size and intention, these pictures reveal a new boldness and self-confidence. Moreover, they demonstrate an aesthetic progression from the artist's alliance with previous traditions to a more radical and solitary stance.

The Old Violin of 1886 (pl. 37) suggests this transition. The size of the work, its frontality, and the shallow format are strongly reminiscent of the artist's German trompe-l'oeil images, but the subject reveals a cultural assimilation: now an ideal object has been placed against a commonplace background. In the complexity of its composition, the painting also functions as a formal link between Harnett's pictures of isolated subjects and the more complicated works of hanging objects that both precede and follow it.

The violin, with its pattern of discolored varnish and scattering of rosin beneath the strings, was probably modeled on the eighteenth-century Cremona, signed and dated *Joseph Guarnerius, 1724,* that is described in Thomas Birch's sale catalogue of Harnett's effects. According to this catalogue, Harnett bought the instrument "at a great cost from a celebrated collection in Paris."[4] It was a trophy, a measure of his financial, personal, and professional triumph. The letter in the picture, which is addressed to Harnett in New York and postmarked in Paris on April 27, 1886, suggests the painting is an announcement of the artist's return; certainly it operates as a celebration of his European venture.

In 1886, Harnett also produced two horseshoe paintings: *Colossal Luck* and *The Golden Horseshoe* (fig. 71, pl. 40). The horseshoe had appeared earlier in Harnett's work: one presides benignly over *After the Hunt* of 1885 (pl. 34) like a good luck charm. The

Fig. 71. William M. Harnett, *Colossal Luck,* 1886. Oil on canvas, 26½ x 22½ in. Private collection

Birch catalogue mentions five lots of "London horse-shoes,"[5] and, indeed, Harnett used more than one as a model: the broad shoe of a dray horse in *Colossal Luck*[6] is larger than the one in *The Golden Horseshoe,* while that in *After the Hunt* is narrow and elegant, for a thoroughbred hoof. Both expensive and crucial to

the animal's soundness, horseshoes were treated care-fully, and a thrown shoe would be retrieved. A lost shoe was rare and meant good luck for the finder. The horseshoe was a popular symbol of good luck (fig. 72) and an emblem of good fortune in pre-Christian European folk tradition. In pagan times,

Fig. 72. Brainerd & Armstrong trade card. Library Company of Philadelphia

the blacksmith had special powers, and a horseshoe nailed on a barn wall protected the inmates from the depredations of the Devil.[7] The image of the horseshoe was common in both America and Germany in Harnett's day. Whether or not he took the symbolism seriously, the artist seems to have kept the horseshoes he acquired in London, transporting the heavy objects from country to country and bringing them back to America, perhaps as personal charms.

Luck itself is specifically associated with Ireland—"the luck of the Irish"—and *Colossal Luck* may hint at Harnett's cultural heritage. Executed during the months following his greatest aesthetic triumphs in Paris and London, the picture might also allude to Harnett's success. The work, however, seems to function on another level as well. Alfred Frankenstein, examining the painting in the late 1940s, recorded finding an old newspaper clipping fixed to the back of the canvas. Much of the text was gone, but the story clearly concerned a prizefight. The text, in Frankenstein's brisk scrawl, reads:

> ...second bout: Wal...
> ...drew with Tom...
> ...ocker slugfest. T...
> ...Roy [Boy?] Ennis ove...
> ...bout. Joh...[8]

John L. Sullivan, the "Boston Strong-Boy," heavyweight champion during 1886, was once awarded a huge horseshoe of flowers—but four years earlier, in Boston.[9] Sullivan had three matches in 1886, and there were prizefights in other classes that year as well, but nothing seems to make sense of the newspaper scrap.[10] This clipping, like those Harnett painted, divulges only a tantalizing hint, and the connection between luck, the prizefight, and the painting remains a mystery.

The Golden Horseshoe is less difficult to decipher: it is a visual pun. The discrepancy between title and subject is evident at once, for the shoe is not gold but rusted iron. An artist who could paint the difference between ivory and bone would hardly have confused gold with base metal, and the title clearly refers to something other than the image. Frankenstein believed that the small polished globe beneath the inner rim of the horseshoe was not another nail but a pearl stickpin that would have been worn with a man's silk evening scarf.[11] Similar silvery globes appear in other Harnett paintings—*The Meerschaum Pipe,* for instance (pl. 39). But here, a pearl stickpin is particularly appropriate, for "the golden horseshoe" was a well-known phrase in Harnett's time, and it had nothing to do with dray horses.

In 1883, while Harnett was in Europe, the Metropolitan Opera opened a magnificent new building in New York. The expensive and exclusive parterre boxes were set in a graceful semicircle, gilded and hung with gold curtains.[12] The shape, décor, and social implications earned this setting the name "The Golden

Horseshoe." Indeed, on the opera's opening night, in 1886, the society column in the *New York Herald* was entitled "Round the Horseshoe."[13]

The title *The Golden Horseshoe* suggests an elegant evening scene of well-dressed connoisseurs in a glittering setting. In the painting, we find instead a visual jest: a homely farrier's product beams forth rustily from a battered wooden door. This form of humor, the double-entendre, was characteristic of the period, and Harnett used it himself in *The Social Club* and *Just Dessert*. This sort of innocent trickery depended on a gullible public that expected a title to establish a work's emotional content, an assumption lampooned by Mark Twain in *Life on the Mississippi* (1883): "In Rome, people with fine sympathetic natures stand up and weep in front of the celebrated 'Beatrice Cenci the Day before her Execution.' It shows what a label can do. If they did not know the picture, they would inspect it unmoved, and say, 'Young girl with hay fever; young girl with her head in a bag.'"[14]

Harnett's smoking pictures also challenged the culture of the ideal. In 1886, he produced two similar paintings of simple meerschaum pipes, one distinguished by the inclusion of an enigmatic newspaper clipping (pl. 39). Clay meerschaum pipes were particularly popular during the period, and people amassed huge collections of the simplest and cheapest ones as well as of the most intricately carved and valuable.[15] The pipe, like money, represented everyday life. Smoking was considered a slightly reprehensible habit, and pipes were thought to be socially inferior to cigars. The pipe suggested a man at ease in the masculine world, perhaps in a saloon, which was an important social institution of the period. Fittingly, a number of Harnett's trompe-l'oeil paintings—among them, one of money and one of a pipe—hung in the New York saloons of Theodore Stewart.

In 1888, Harnett executed three trompe-l'oeil paintings of subjects he had previously pursued. In *For Sunday's Dinner* (pl. 42), a close variant of *Plucked Clean,* he corrected the earlier misplacement of the eye of the bird and placed the chicken against a door instead of a wall. This placement allowed him to include ornate iron hinges and a skewed keyhole. The artist sent *For Sunday's Dinner* to the National

Academy of Design, with the stiff price of one thousand dollars. Response was positive, and the work was quickly purchased by a dealer and exhibited later that winter in Philadelphia.

Harnett's paintings of everyday objects reach an apotheosis in *The Faithful Colt* of 1890 (pl. 48), first called *An Old-Fashioned Colt.* This austere and elegant work shows Harnett at his best: engaged, meditative, and unpretentious. The composition is a masterpiece of simplicity in which a revolver hangs upside down above a cryptic scrap of newspaper against the delicate craquelure of a painted wall. The subject is a common .44-caliber model 1860 army revolver, manufactured by Samuel Colt and widely used during the Civil War and afterward on the frontier.[16] Harnett did not fight in the Civil War or travel West, and while he did collect antique weapons, the Colt would not have qualified as such, being merely outdated, or "old-fashioned."

With *The Faithful Colt,* Harnett produced a powerful challenge to nineteenth-century notions of idealism. Like money and pipes, the revolver was part of a profoundly masculine and mundane world, one of hard facts, coarse talk, business, and death. It was a world far removed from notions of antiquity, sentiment, and the ideal. The painting asserts that an ordinary industrial item is the aesthetic equivalent of a rare antique. Harnett's earlier trompe-l'oeil paintings made similar assertions about common objects, but *The Faithful Colt* is one of the first American paintings to confer iconic stature on a mass-produced object.

In *The Faithful Colt,* Harnett's philosophical exploration becomes most profound and complex. A gun is the antithesis of the veneration of the ideal: whereas a polished objet d'art represents the life of the mind, a gun represents death. And this particular gun represents not only death but, by virtue of its machine-made nature, the very essence of "mere industrialism" that so threatened the culture of the ideal. In this painting, Harnett examined crucial contemporary issues, raising questions regarding the nature of art and subject matter, of idealism and industry. His quiet and exquisite posing of these questions reveals not only the changing nature of American art but his own discreet and significant contribution to those changes as well.

NOTES

▾

I would like to thank Doreen Bolger and John Wilmerding for their valuable assistance in the planning of this essay and Thayer Tolles Mickel for her very generous assistance regarding archival information and for her general helpfulness.

1. Eugene Benson, "Museums of Art as a Means of Instruction," *Appletons' Journal* 3 (January 15, 1870), p. 80.

2. E. Taylor Snow, "William Michael Harnett, A Philadelphia Catholic Artist," *American Catholic Historical Researches* 10 (April 1893), p. 76. The first incident took place in the 1870s; no date can be found for the second (Alfred Frankenstein, interview with Mary St. Clair Mulholland, Alfred Frankenstein Papers, Archives of American Art, Smithsonian Institution, Washington, D.C., microfilm, roll 1374, frame 951).

3. S. G. W. Benjamin, "Fifty Years of American Art, 1828–1878: III," *Harper's New Monthly Magazine* 59 (October 1879), p. 688, quoted in John A. Kouwenhoven, *Made in America: The Arts in Modern Civilization* (Garden City, N.Y.: Doubleday & Co., 1948), p. 112.

4. Harnett owned two old violins. He used both instruments as models, though the Birch catalogue is tantalizingly vague about this. The Cremona was used in "several of his pictures, including his last painting"; the other was used in "'Old Cupboard Door,' 'Artist's Table,' 'Music,' and other noted pictures" (*The Wm. Michael Harnett Collection: His Own Reserved Paintings, Models and Studio Furnishings*, sale cat., Stan. V. Henkels at Thos. Birch's Sons, Auctioneers, Philadelphia, February 23–24, 1893, p. 10, nos. 55½, 57).

5. Ibid., p. 17, nos. 169–74.

6. Ibid., p. 8, no. 34.

7. Bruce W. Chambers, "The Golden Horseshoe," in *American Paintings V: 1988* (New York: Berry-Hill Galleries, 1988), p. 179.

8. Frankenstein Papers, roll 1375, frame 404.

9. Michael T. Isenberg, *John L. Sullivan and His America* (Urbana and Chicago: University of Illinois Press, 1988), p. 117.

10. I consulted the *New York Times, New York Herald,* and *New-York Daily Tribune* for 1886.

11. Frederick D. Hill, director of Berry-Hill Galleries, New York, interview with author, October 11, 1990.

12. Frank Merkling et al., *The Golden Horseshoe: The Life and Times of the Metropolitan Opera House* (New York: Viking Press, 1965).

13. "Round the Horseshoe," *New York Herald,* January 5, 1886, p. xx.

14. Mark Twain, *Life on the Mississippi* (Boston: James R. Osgood & Co., 1883), p. 448.

15. "Meerschaum Pipes: How They Are Carved, Colored and Some Well-Known Collectors of Them," *New York Herald,* January 5, 1890, p. 20.

16. See Carol Troyen, "William Michael Harnett, *The Faithful Colt,* 1890," in Theodore E. Stebbins, Jr., et al., *A New World: Masterpieces of American Painting, 1760–1910,* exhib. cat. (Boston: Museum of Fine Arts, 1983), p. 286.

THE ARTIST'S WORKING METHODS

JENNIFER MILAM

Viewers have always appreciated the paintings of William Michael Harnett for their precise illusionistic effects, yet surviving documentation has yielded relatively little information about the artist's working procedures. Most contemporary articles focus on the surface qualities and visual trickery of his paintings rather than on the artistic methods that produced those results. The only known specific reference to Harnett's working methods comes from his friend Edward Taylor Snow, who claimed the artist "would make a finished lead-pencil drawing, with minute details" prior to executing a painting.[1] Were these drawings independent works on paper that are now lost, or were they executed on the painting support itself?[2] With the help of recent scientific innovations in the study of art objects, it is now possible to investigate far more of the entire creative process by viewing what lies beneath the final, visible surface.

In the technique of infrared reflectography,[3] a vidicon camera is placed before the work, and the painting is illuminated with two equidistant infrared lamps on dimmers. The light passes through the overlying paint layers, is absorbed by any area that contains carbon black, and is reflected by the white ground. The resulting image, called a *reflectogram,* appears on a high-resolution television monitor. The picture is documented by taking a sequence of overlapping camera shots from the monitor. These prints are then pasted together to form a photomontage of any existing underdrawing in its entirety. All carbon-containing materials within the intermediate and surface paint layers absorb the infrared rays and do not allow them to pass through, thus appearing black. Through the use of this technique, it is possible to draw several conclusions regarding the way Harnett approached the painting process.

While the consideration of Harnett's painting style has played an important role in issues of attribution during the past fifty years, modern scholars have not yet fully considered his working methods.[4] The artist's microscopic vision and meticulous handling have been accepted without close examination of his works themselves. It has been assumed that he planned and executed his compositions decisively, without making any changes.[5] This simply is not the case. In several works it is now possible to view, even with the naked eye, adjustments that have begun to show through the final paint layer. In *Still Life—Violin and Music* of 1888 (pl. 43), a slightly wider plan for the scroll of the violin and the initial placement of the matchbox to the right side of the canvas are now visible. Pentimenti are also evident in *Mr. Hulings' Rack Picture* of the same year (pl. 44) under the typescript and outline of Harnett's business card, both of which were larger in the initial layers.

The extreme refinement of Harnett's execution leads one to expect that he used preliminary drawings in planning spatial relationships and choosing a system of light and shade. Such studies would have allowed him to determine the composition before approaching the prepared support and would have served as a reference while he applied the paint. However, very few known independent drawings on paper can be related to specific paintings; most are merely quick notations or records rather than part of an ongoing creative process.[6] Harnett's rare oil sketches, all from early in his career, isolate individual objects for general study rather than form preparatory compositional arrangements, thus eliminating the possibility that the artist constructed his paintings using them.[7] Most of his surviving still-life drawings seem to be quick studies or investigations in the grouping of models, not necessarily for paintings.[8] They do not display any active interest in light effects, perspective, or the detailed appearance of forms. Experimentation in these areas was confined instead to the paint layers.

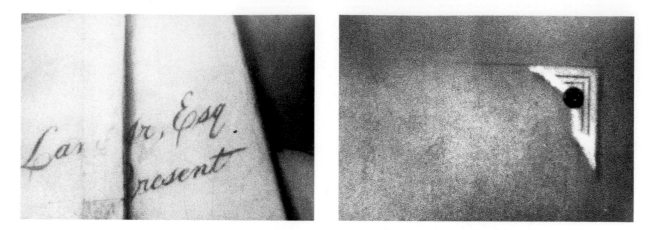

Fig. 73. Infrared reflectograms of William M. Harnett's *Artist's Letter Rack* (pl. 17)

Intermediary steps, from fleeting ideas to formal compositions, cannot be explained by these drawings.

Harnett's own comments late in his career disclose that he manipulated the true forms of his models, which were "only suggestions" of their appearance in paint[9]—the Delft jar with a pewter top, for example, that appears in several works.[10] The artist consistently changed the size and shape of the object, at times even removing the handle and lid to convert it into a vase.[11] Harnett seems to have determined the final, painted form in his mind rather than by working directly from the model, which suggests that some type of preparatory drawing played a part.

From available information, it appears Harnett did not rely on the use of underdrawing when planning his early paintings. Three works from the first period of his activity were examined with infrared reflectography: *The Banker's Table* and *Attention, Company!*, both of 1878 (pls. 6, 11), and *The Artist's Letter Rack* of 1879 (pl. 17). Only the last painting discloses even a minimal use of underdrawing on the prepared canvas. Rough mapping lines can be seen through the rack ribbons and in the area of the torn label (fig. 73). Harnett squared-off the corners of the piece of paper as if it were actually intact, yet the entire rectangular shape was not delineated. His concern was with the achievement of correct spatial relationships between the corners of the objects, not with the basic planning of the composition. In *Attention, Company!* he used scored lines rather than underdrawing to delineate the boy's figure and costume. The green-black background actually covers the entire canvas. Harnett impressed his design into this dark base layer with a blunt tool, possibly the end of his brush, then painted all of the forms on top of it. These indentations, particularly visible around the boy's jacket, guided the artist as he continued to paint.

Despite the meticulous application of details, Harnett's technique in his early works was not completely rigid. Although changes are often difficult to see with the naked eye, X radiographs and stereomicroscopic examinations indicate the locations of revisions. Remains of bright blue paint, for example, are visible around the edges of the pink ribbon in *The Artist's Letter Rack*. The ribbon was originally blue, but Harnett repainted it pink. X radiographs of this work also reveal variations in the thickness of the paint. Harnett adjusted the sizes of the envelopes and cards as he searched for overall harmony. Microscopic examination of *Attention, Company!* discloses minor, carefully concealed alterations of contours and forms, indicating an evolving creative process. One such change is below the elbow of the left sleeve. The darker edges around the left shoulder and cheek reveal that the green-black background extended underneath these forms but was scraped away to accommodate the colors of the upper layers. Nevertheless, the changes in these works were not dramatic and occurred only in the final stages of production, which suggests Harnett approached each canvas already having carefully planned the entire composition. His technical achievements are so fine and controlled that it seems impossible that he worked spontaneously, without any preparatory studies. The early paintings must have been made with the help of independent drawings, such as those described by Snow, which are now lost.

Technical examination of two later works, from 1888, uncovered a significantly different method of production. In *Still Life* and *Still Life—Violin and Music* (fig. 74, pl. 43), Harnett laid out his compositions directly on the blank support.[12] The underdrawing in *Still Life—Violin and Music* is limited to the rendering of the outlines of forms and their placement in the composition (fig. 76). In the subsequent paint layers, Harnett made slight adjustments to the objects by moving them to the right and diminishing their size and shape. He also planned the basic format of

Fig. 74. William M. Harnett, *Still Life,* 1888. Oil on canvas, 14 x 17⅛ in. The Metropolitan Museum of Art, New York, Bequest of Susan Vanderpool Clark, 1967

Fig. 75. Infrared reflectograms of William M. Harnett's *Still Life* (fig. 74)

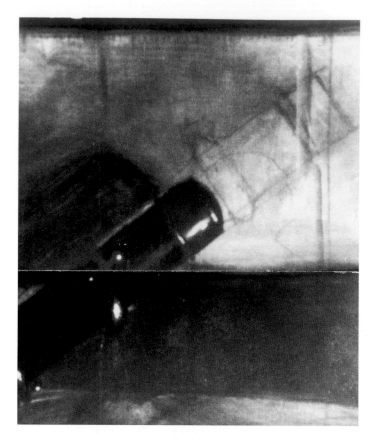

Fig. 76. Infrared reflectogram of William M. Harnett's
Still Life—Violin and Music (pl. 43)

a rounded stein at the right behind the newspaper. The contour lines are tentative, particularly at the top. A second drawing for the mug protrudes from the simple object that was his final choice. Diagonal perspective lines determine the relationship between the mug and the corner of the table, and curving lines serve to place the table's edge. In this work, the artist used underdrawing to plan the entire compositional structure and arrangement of forms. He followed a similar process in *La Flûte Enchantée,* drawing the composition directly on the panel and planning the forms as he went (fig. 79). Harnett first ruled lines for the table across the entire panel and then drew in the objects. Some of these forms, such as the cigar box on the right, were excluded in the final paint layers. The artist may have reworked his familiar tabletop pictures in an effort to concentrate on the issues of space and positioning. Particularly confident in the successful execution of these favorite subjects, he began to heighten the compositional complexities, using underdrawing to guide his brush. Indeed, the late works manifest an additional degree of assurance in the handling of line and paint.[13]

Although Harnett appears to have altered his working methods considerably over time (that is, he increasingly used underdrawing), the additive nature of his painting process remained constant. Beginning with the background, he built up his compositions by painting complete objects, one on top of the other. The lines for the ribbons in *The Artist's Letter Rack,* for example, extend through all the other objects (fig. 73). Harnett painted the envelopes, including their complete inscriptions, and then painted the rack on top of

Still Life before approaching the canvas, making compositional adjustments as he painted. He reduced the bulbous jar to a shape that is less obtrusive and more in harmony with the shapes of the other objects (fig. 75). The painted candlestick leans farther to the right, increasing the sense of instability. Furthermore, by lengthening the candle and excluding the additional sheets of music on the left, Harnett emphasized the clean sweep of the angle that sends the eye to the center of the painting. The composition as it exists in the underdrawing is expansive and stable. Harnett contracted the forms as he painted to create a complex balance between the precarious positioning of objects and the stable appearance of the whole.

Among the works examined, *La Flûte Enchantée* of 1887 and *New York News* of 1888 (figs. 143, 77) exhibit the strongest evidence of working underdrawings. This type of tabletop composition recurs throughout Harnett's career. Curiously, the many changes between underdrawing and paint layers indicate that he was unsure of the final compositional design of each work and explored ideas directly on the support. The underdrawing in *New York News* shows how Harnett sought the final shape of the mug that anchors the composition (fig. 78). He originally drew

Fig. 77. William M. Harnett, *New York News,*
1888. Oil on wood, 5½ x 7½ in.
The Metropolitan Museum of Art, New York,
Gift of Mr. and Mrs. William McKim, 1973

them. The letters that are hidden under the final painted ribbon can be seen in an infrared reflectogram. *Attention, Company!* and *The Banker's Table* also show evidence of an additive painting procedure. Under the microscope, it is possible to see the different layers of covered objects through cracks in the paint.

Harnett's perfection of his working methods is evident in *Mr. Hulings' Rack Picture* (pl. 44), painted toward the end of his life.[14] While he still preferred to build compositions in an additive manner, he must have learned that colors would often show through in areas where they were not desired. In the early paintings, this forced him to work in thicker paint layers and to scrape away paint in problematic zones. To avoid such measures, *Mr. Hulings' Rack Picture* went through four stages of design. Harnett first drew the composition. He then added dark paint as a woodlike background, reserving space for objects or using an oil resin to preserve areas of drawing.[15] In the third stage, he painted in the ribbons, cards, and envelopes, making initial changes to their shapes. His final decisions regarding the form and position of

objects required some scraping away of old paint and the adding of new; however, the overall application of paint layers was now more efficient.

To make definitive statements regarding Harnett's working methods, a larger group of paintings will need to be studied scientifically. At this stage of investigation, however, it is possible to formulate several generalizations that may guide further research. The precision and surface quality of the paintings, as well as the mental transformation of the forms of the models, imply that Harnett needed some sort of drawing to assist in planning his compositions. Although no detailed preliminary drawings on paper have survived, he must have depended on this type of study for his early paintings, as no evidence of complex underdrawings has been found. Furthermore, he did not spontaneously work out the early compositions on the canvas, even though there are some indications of changes. The paintings are too carefully structured and methodical to refute a preparatory stage. In the late works, however, Harnett laid his designs for compositions directly on the support.

Fig. 78. Infrared reflectogram of William M. Harnett's *New York News* (fig. 77)

He then applied paint in the most economical manner, reserving areas for objects to minimize paint loss as he refined his forms. In general, the changes he made between underdrawings and surface layers heighten the complexities of perspective and the interrelationships of objects. The artist left these formal issues to be resolved in the final stages of production, when he felt most technically confident.

Fig. 79. Infrared reflectogram of William M. Harnett's *La Flûte Enchantée* (fig. 143)

NOTES

Unless otherwise noted, scientific examination was completed in the Department of Paintings Conservation at the Metropolitan Museum of Art. The infrared reflectography was conducted under the guidance of Maryan W. Ainsworth, Research Fellow; Jeffrey Jennings, Art History Intern; and Teresa Russo, Research Associate. Conservator Dorothy Mahon conducted the X radiography and offered her expertise in examining the paintings with the author under the stereomicroscope. Paintings Conservation intern Larry Keith, Mr. Jennings, and Dr. Ainsworth were also indispensable in this capacity.

1. *The Wm. Michael Harnett Collection: His Own Reserved Paintings, Models and Studio Furnishings,* sale cat., Stan. V. Henkels at Thos. Birch's Sons, Auctioneers, Philadelphia, February 23–24, 1893, p. 4.

2. After Harnett's death, some of his drawings were retained by Ella Harnett, his sister; some were given to a Miss Enright, his fiancée; and the rest were sold at auction (see Alfred Frankenstein, *After the Hunt: William Harnett and Other American Still Life Painters, 1870–1900,* rev. ed. [Berkeley and Los Angeles: University of California Press, 1969], p. 93). The whereabouts of most of these drawings is unknown.

3. For a complete description of the process, see Johan Rudolph Justus van Asperen de Boer, *Infrared Reflectography: A Contribution to the Examination of Earlier European Paintings* (Amsterdam: Central Research Laboratory for Objects of Art and Science, 1970). Eight of Harnett's paintings were examined with infrared reflectography for this essay.

4. Regarding fakes, forgeries, and paintings wrongly attributed to Harnett, see Frankenstein, *After the Hunt,* pp. ix–xvi; and Frankenstein, "Harnett, True and False," *Art Bulletin* 31 (March 1949), pp. 38–56.

5. See Frankenstein, "Harnett, True and False," p. 48; and Lloyd Goodrich, "Notes: Harnett and Peto, A Note on Style," *Art Bulletin* 31 (March 1949), pp. 57–58.

6. See Alfred Frankenstein, "New Harnett Discoveries," *Magazine of Art* 44, no. 2 (February 1951), pp. 62–63. Some of these drawings are now in the Alfred Frankenstein Papers, Archives of American Art, Smithsonian Institution, Washington, D.C., microfilm, roll 2813, frames 1007–32. See also *Important American and European Paintings,* sale cat., Butterfield's, San Francisco, September 22, 1983, nos. 2105–18, 2120; and *American Drawings and Watercolors of the Nineteenth and Twentieth Centuries,* sale cat., Christie's East, New York, January 24, 1990, no. 77A.

7. The oil sketches, all still lifes from 1874, exhibit a fairly naive handling. Apparently, Harnett gave up this type of study, as no others seem to have been made. Examples are reproduced in Frankenstein, *After the Hunt,* pl. 25;

and Frankenstein, "New Harnett Discoveries," p. 64. The most well-known of these sketches is *Study of a Pipe and Other Objects* (fig. 57).

8. One drawing that has a more clearly defined relationship with a painting is a sketch inscribed *the old cupboard* (Butterfield's, sale cat., September 22, 1983, no. 2114; and Frankenstein, *After the Hunt,* pl. 80). This sketch may have served as a source of ideas, if only marginally, for *The Old Cupboard Door* of 1889 and for *Old Models* of 1892 (pls. 45, 49). The representation of alternative ledges in the drawing suggests Harnett was exploring possible compositions.

9. "Painted Like Real Things: The Man Whose Pictures Are a Wonder and a Puzzle," interview in *New York News,* probably 1889 or 1890, quoted in Frankenstein, *After the Hunt,* p. 55.

10. Compare the jars in *Still Life with Violin* of 1885 (private collection), *The Cincinnati Enquirer* of 1888 (fig. 14), and *Old Models.*

11. See Frankenstein, *After the Hunt,* p. 179. The design on the vases in *Music* of 1886 (pl. 38) and *Still Life* of 1887 (Mr. and Mrs. Meyer P. Potamkin) is identical to that on the jar mentioned earlier. The jar is listed as "Antique Pitcher" in *Wm. Michael Harnett Collection,* p. 11, no. 71.

12. The underdrawings exhibit a style and medium (without pigment analysis, it is characteristic of pencil) consistent with those of his drawings on paper. Several independent drawings depict groups of objects with quick, summary contour strokes, set within a rectangular boundary.

13. This development was noted by several authors, including Frankenstein, *After the Hunt,* p. 92; William H. Gerdts and Russell Burke, *American Still-Life Painting* (New York, Washington, and London: Praeger Publishers, 1971), pp. 142–43; and M. L. d'Otrange Mastai, *Illusion in Art: Trompe l'Oeil, A History of Pictorial Illusionism* (New York: Abaris Books, 1975), p. 293.

14. *Mr. Hulings' Rack Picture* was examined with infrared reflectography at the Los Angeles County Museum of Art. I am grateful to Julian Ganz, Jr., and John Wilmerding for their help in arranging this opportunity. Joseph Fronek, Virginia Tasmussen, and Pieter Meyers of the museum's conservation department offered much-appreciated assistance with the technical process as well as valuable observations and suggestions.

15. A pure oil or oil resin used as a base layer for the objects is easily noted around the scroll of the violin in *Still Life—Violin and Music.* The same type of oil base was also seen around the edges of objects in *La Flûte Enchantée* and *New York News.*

HARNETT AND PHOTOGRAPHY

DOUGLAS R. NICKEL

Upon the death of William Michael Harnett in 1892, a writer observed that "he copied in oil with the accuracy of a camera, and some of his paintings have attained wide celebrity by reason of their astonishing fidelity to their models."[1] Indeed, such a comparison was almost inevitable, for Harnett painted at a time when the medium of photography was considered the ne plus ultra of realism, the touchstone of representational exactitude. Harnett's popularity rested in part upon a painting style that might be loosely described as "photographic"; his imperceptible brushwork and seemingly equal regard for every detail and surface made his works appear more the creation of a machine than of the human hand. It has long been assumed that Harnett used photographs directly as an aid, but his alliance with the camera goes even deeper than this. The significance of Harnett's forthright appropriation of photographic sources for his *After the Hunt* series can be understood only in the context of contemporary aesthetic tenets—theories that made the faithful transcription of material objects into paint a central issue of art criticism. These theories could propose trompe l'oeil as a suitable goal for pictorial representation and, to this end, take photography as their paradigm.

Harnett began his career when the propriety of excessive graphic detail, which once would have elicited official and critical disapproval, was a topic of considerable import to artists. In 1770, Sir Joshua Reynolds counseled his Royal Academy of Arts students that "the whole beauty and grandeur of the art consists . . . in being able to get above all singular forms, local customs, particularities, and details of every kind."[2] Neoclassical art theory maintained that nature offered us only imperfect manifestations of ideal forms, and that it was the artist's function to discover and present the Platonic essence that lay behind any chosen subject. Ideal beauty was arrived at by a process of selection and generalization and by the omission of extraneous information; the artist was not to suppress *all* detail in his work, of course—only that which was accidental or peculiar to his model. In 1759, when Samuel Johnson bid that "the business of a poet . . . is to examine, not the individual, but the species; to remark general properties and large appearances: he does not number the streaks of the tulip, or describe the different shades in the verdure of the forest," he did so with the faith that those properties were fixed, timeless, and God-given.[3] For the Neoclassicist, undue particularity in a work of art could only distract from the universals it aspired to portray.

In the early nineteenth century, picturesque theory contended that one might regard selected parts of nature for their visual felicities alone, thus shifting the Neoclassical emphasis from the subject and its related ideal to the perceiver and his experience. Romantic critics likewise stressed affect over essence, while still adhering to a Neoclassical belief in universals. For them, the best way for an artist to arrive at essential truths was *through* particularity; the Romantic did not consider nature a defective copy of the ideal but a participant in it, simply waiting for a sensitive, responsive beholder. William Blake's world in a grain of sand and heaven in a wild flower epitomized the belief that nature, when properly considered, revealed its creator. Every detail of it, therefore, held potential significance.

The most ardent and influential spokesman for the Romantic model of art was John Ruskin, who denounced the idealizing tendencies fostered by Reynolds. "It is just as impossible to generalize granite and slate as it is to generalize a man and a cow," he wrote in 1844.[4] Ruskin believed that God was immanent in nature; the landscape painter honored the almighty by recording His works with all possible accuracy. But in the mid-nineteenth century, the very concept of nature was changing: it now carried with it the burden of the discoveries and methods of the natural sciences. Ruskin advocated scientific precision in the rendering of natural facts—and demonstrated it in his own drawings (fig. 80)—but to him accuracy was only a means to an end, and that end was ultimately moral.

In the United States, any theory linking morality with nature (which America had in abundance) was bound to find a receptive audience. The Transcendentalists had already argued the case for pantheism, and artists Thomas Cole and Asher B. Durand introduced such ideas into the practice of painting. Books by Ruskin were accordingly venerated here, and American devotees founded their own Ruskinian journals (*The Crayon,* and later *The New Path*) to spread his teachings.[5]

In the United States and Britain, however, Ruskin's ideas were taken up only selectively. Especially misunderstood were his injunctions about the use of pictorial detail. Despite Ruskin's characterization of artistic imitation as "Mirror's work, not Man's,"[6] the Pre-Raphaelites took his call for truth to nature as a mandate for an exacting realism, one distinguished by an obsessive attention to detail, an overload of sensory information. At mid-century, as scientific discoveries seemed to undermine religion, morality, and the political order, the world was increasingly perceived as a mass of disparate facts, of particulars, rather than as a rational system. In the field of poetry there arose a corresponding aesthetic of particularity. Tennyson, for instance, imbued his "Maud" with detail so minute it becomes hallucinatory, detached from symbolic reference, and irrelevant to the ostensible narrative.[7] The Pre-Raphaelites also resolved to be scientific in their creative approach: they gathered their information from a direct observation of nature and filled their canvases from edge to edge with exhaustive visual fact. Truth, it seemed, would henceforth be calculated quantitatively, measured out detail by painstaking detail.

Central to the ascent of realism was the emergence of photography. At the very moment of its introduction in 1839, the medium was seen to carry dangerous implications for the Romantic model of art, for here was a picture-making process—truly a product of science—that would record nature exactly, indiscriminately, and automatically. Whether or not a subject had moral significance was irrelevant to the camera: it made pictures unselectively, without regard for higher meanings.

The idea of photography became central to those artists educated in its shadow. Realist painters soon endeavored to paint as if they were cameras. William Holman Hunt ensured the authenticity of his *Scape Goat* of 1854–55 (Merseyside County Council, Lady Lever Art Gallery, Port Sunlight) by transporting a live

Fig. 80. John Ruskin, *Study of Kingfisher, with Dominant Reference to Colour,* ca. 1870. Watercolor and pencil on paper, 10³⁄₁₆ x 8⁹⁄₁₆ in. Ashmolean Museum, Oxford

goat to the shores of the Dead Sea, and John Everett Millais searched London for a genuine carpenter to pose as Joseph in *Christ in the House of His Parents* of 1850 (Tate Gallery, London). The near-photographic studies of unembellished natural fact by Ruskin and his English followers found their counterparts among the Pre-Raphaelites active in America, in the work of painters such as Thomas Farrer and John William Hill (fig. 81). Those critical of the realist project derided any such servile procedures, whether the medium chosen was paint or poetry. They invoked a comparison with photography scornfully. Reviewing *Leaves of Grass,* for example, *The Crayon* charged:

> According to Whitman's theory, the greatest poet is he who performs the office of camera to the world, merely reflecting what he sees—art is merely reproduction.[8]

But "merely reflecting" what is seen was a condition to which some artists positively aspired in the decades of declining Romantic influence.

Harnett, who began his career as a painter in the wake of the realist controversy, formulated a style that combined rigorous attention to surface detail with a

Fig. 81. John William Hill, *Dead Blue Jay,*
ca. 1865. Watercolor on paper, 5¼ x 12 in.
The New-York Historical Society

marked avoidance of traditional moralizing or narrative programs of content. The artist's assertion that his works "tell a story,"[9] and his occasional excursions into obvious symbolism notwithstanding, Harnett's art was perceived as one of appearances, not of deeper meanings—a fact not lost upon his critics. His gravitation toward a kind of still life in which objects reside existentially,[10] without real iconographic or narrative purpose, may be seen as his solution to the problem of painting in an age that was abandoning its faith in the redemptive potential of art. Materiality was Harnett's subject, and particularity was the means he developed to convey that subject. His style of painting—eminently optical, often illusionistic—suited a market that had come to value aspect more than substance and that wanted its pictures comfortably exoteric.

Harnett established his interests and dominant style before his departure for Europe in 1880, but by 1878 he had become dissatisfied and wanted to strike out in other directions.[11] After several months in England, and perhaps a stop in Paris, he traveled to Frankfort, where he painted several commissioned pieces, and then arrived in Munich in late 1881. After Paris, Munich was then the most important art center in Europe, and Harnett remained there four years, showing his work in the local Kunstverein exhibitions and perhaps taking private instruction. Under the influence of new creative stimuli, he began to introduce novel elements, such as armor, draperies, ornate carpets, and lobsters, into his still lifes. He also explored new pictorial sources for his compositions, drawing upon both local traditions and popular art. Whether out of artistic emulation or to please his clientele, Harnett now made works closer in spirit to the traditional European still-life painting he found around him. It was a formative period for him, one that he later came to view as a turning point in his career.[12]

In 1883, when Harnett undertook the first two versions of *After the Hunt* (pls. 28, 29), he was aware of the Bavarian and Alsatian traditions of game and hunting pieces, but it was to a photographic source that he turned—to the large still-life compositions made and sold by the Alsatian photographer Adolphe Braun. The firm of Braun et Cie, located in Dornach, was the largest manufacturer of art reproductions in the world, and its products were widely advertised and exhibited. Braun had begun his career as a textile designer but turned to photography about 1853 as a means of securing source material for his printed motifs. His involvement with reproductive photography grew, and in 1855 he won a gold medal at the Exposition Universelle for his decorative flower compositions. He formed a company to market views of Alsace and Switzerland, and in 1866 he expanded into art reproductions, eventually making inventories of collections in Basel, Dresden, Vienna, Venice, Florence, Rome, and Paris. With his steam-powered presses, Braun produced fifteen hundred prints a day, which he distributed to middle-class art lovers throughout Europe and the United States. He strove to make his reproductions veritable facsimiles, and the results were considered "so exact that under glass they have already fooled people."[13]

The photographic game pieces that Braun began creating in 1867 are exceptional in his oeuvre, for they were large, expensive, and clearly not meant to serve the informational purposes of his other works (figs. 82, 83). He executed no more than eight of these and seems to have intended them to be used as wall decorations. They were designated "game trophies, hunting subjects" in the Braun company catalogue and described as "suitable for decorating a dining room."[14] Indeed, these game pieces represented a photographic version of those chromolithographed reproductions of hunting subjects (similarly described as "Dining-Room Pictures") that were popular at the time in America (fig. 92).[15] For the bourgeois home owner, Braun's works furnished an economical alternative to genuine oil paintings, one that brought the transcriptive properties of the camera to a subject already steeped in artistic tradition.

The allure of such photographs for someone with Harnett's interests can be imagined, and his indebtedness to them seems undeniable. Although hunting pictures were ubiquitous in Northern Europe, it is the recurrence of a limited set of motifs—game bag, circular horn, dead rabbit and duck, diagonally slung rifle, nails—that links Harnett's and Braun's series and distinguishes them from others of the type. Both Harnett and Braun favored directional, raking light to enhance the volume of their subjects; each increased the customary scale of his work to accommodate his theme. Harnett's estate sale included many of the items employed as models in the *After the Hunt*

Fig. 82. Adolphe Braun, *Pheasant and Grouse*. Carbon print.
The Metropolitan Museum of Art, New York, The David Hunter McAlpin Fund, 1947

Fig. 83. Adolphe Braun, *Hare and Ducks*. Carbon print.
The Metropolitan Museum of Art, New York, The David Hunter McAlpin Fund, 1947

Fig. 84. Untitled, French, probably 1870s.
Tissue stereograph, albumen silver print.
Private collection

a multitude of stereo subjects (fig. 84) issued by companies like Braun's, and Harnett's familiarity with them is probable.

If photography was seen at mid-century as the standard of pictorial realism, the introduction of stereo photography raised that standard considerably. Stereo cards were cheap, plentiful, and easily distributed. Their appeal was universal, and every respectable household had a collection. The stereo photograph contributed to a growing popular taste for purely optical art; its remarkable simulation of reality guaranteed nothing more than a retinal experience of its subjects, so its subjects aspired to nothing more than visual interest. Oliver Wendell Holmes noted:

> The stereoscopic views of the arches of Constantine and of Titus give not only every letter of the old inscriptions, but render the grain of the stone itself. On the pediment of the Pantheon may be read, not only the words traced by Agrippa, but a rough inscription above it, scratched or hacked into the stone by some wanton hand during an insurrectionary tumult.
>
> This distinctness of the lesser details of a building or a landscape often gives us incidental truths which interest us more than the central object of the picture.[19]

What Holmes described is a wholesale inversion of traditional assumptions about art: intention was now secondary to irrelevant detail. The more accidental such details become, "the more trivial they are in themselves, the more they take hold of the imagination."[20] The popularity of the stereograph helped promote an aesthetic of ocularity, one in which the sensation of viewing tended to displace concern for conspicuous meaning.

Like the stereograph, trompe-l'oeil painting aimed to be experiential, to report "incidental truths" primarily for the interest of their visual appearance. Harnett's use of photographs as aids is hardly suprising, but his decision to work in a genre that was conceptually aligned with and indebted to such popular art forms as photography and lithography raises questions about what he envisioned as his audience. His approach to still life is characterized by a general absence of semantic depth and an emphasis on the act of sheer perception. Such an approach had wide appeal, for it presupposed nothing but normal human vision. In the period after 1865, when the art world could not form a consensus about the social function of art, one option, as demonstrated by the widespread popularity of photography, was simply to be optical. Harnett, in choosing to be similarly perceptual, showed himself to be very much an artist of his time.

series,[16] so it is clear he did not paint directly from Braun's photographs, though they must have prompted his selection of elements and his compositional strategies. Moreover, Braun's works were generally acclaimed for their acute sharpness and faithful rendering of texture. "The detail is peculiarly wonderful," wrote one critic, "so true to nature that one is forced to exclaim, Can photography be so real?"[17] Given his own concern for detail, texture, and illusionistic rendering, Harnett might have seen Braun's pictures as a technical challenge, a standard to be matched or even surpassed.

With their large scale, centralized compositions, and strictly limited depth, Braun's trophy pictures represent an approximation of trompe-l'oeil painting that was rare in nineteenth-century photography.[18] Braun's gesture was carried over into a more prevalent form of photographic illusionism, however. The stereograph, at the height of its popularity between 1860 and 1890, offered a delightfully convincing illusion of three-dimensionality, and during this period the Braun firm was a leading European manufacturer of stereo views. Game pieces comprised but one of

NOTES

I would like to thank Martin Gasser and Jacqueline Jacqué, curator at the Musée de l'Impression sur Etoffes, Mulhouse, France.

1. "Artist Harnett Dead: The Well-Known Still-Life Painter Dies in Hospital," *New York Times,* October 31, 1892, p. 3.

2. Sir Joshua Reynolds, *Discourses on Art,* ed. Robert R. Wark (San Marino, Calif.: Huntington Library, 1959), p. 44.

3. Samuel Johnson, "The History of Rasselas, Prince of Abissinia," in *Rasselas, Poems, and Selected Prose,* ed. Bertrand H. Bronson (New York: Holt, Rinehart & Winston, 1971), p. 628.

4. *The Works of John Ruskin,* ed. E. T. Cook and Alexander Wedderburn, 39 vols. (London: George Allen; New York: Longmans, Green & Co., 1903–12), 3, p. 34.

5. Roger B. Stein, *John Ruskin and Aesthetic Thought in America, 1840–1900* (Cambridge, Mass.: Harvard University Press, 1967), p. 38. See also Linda S. Ferber and William H. Gerdts, *The New Path: Ruskin and the American Pre-Raphaelites,* exhib. cat. (Brooklyn: Brooklyn Museum, 1985).

6. *Works of John Ruskin,* 14, p. 237.

7. Carol T. Christ, *The Finer Optic: The Aesthetic of Particularity in Victorian Poetry* (New Haven and London: Yale University Press, 1975), pp. 26–29.

8. "Studies among the Leaves: Leaves of Grass" *Crayon* 3 (January 1856), p. 32, quoted in Stein, *John Ruskin,* p. 114.

9. "Painted Like Real Things: The Man Whose Pictures Are a Wonder and a Puzzle," interview in *New York News,* probably 1889 or 1890, quoted in Alfred Frankenstein, *After the Hunt: William Harnett and Other American Still Life Painters, 1870–1900,* rev. ed. (Los Angeles and Berkeley: University of California Press, 1969), p. 55.

10. Barbara Novak, *American Painting of the Nineteenth Century: Realism, Idealism, and the American Experience,* 2nd ed. (New York: Harper & Row, 1979), p. 221.

11. Indicative of this urge are such unusual and ambitious works as *Attention, Company!* of 1878 and *The Artist's Letter Rack* of 1879 (pls. 11, 17).

12. See "Painted Like Real Things."

13. Thiébault Sisson, "La Photographie artistique et les travaux de la maison Braun," *Revue alsacienne* 9 (1885–86), p. 258, quoted in Naomi Rosenblum, "Adolphe Braun: A Nineteenth-Century Career in Photography," *History of Photography* 3 (October 1979), p. 365. See also Naomi Rosenblum, "Adolphe Braun, Revisited," *Image* 32, no. 1 (June 1989), pp. 1–7.

14. Pierre Tyl, "Adolphe Braun: photographe mulhausien, 1812–1877" (master's thesis, Université de Strasbourg, 1982), p. 83. The Braun catalogue lists the 1887 price as fifty francs.

15. Katharine Morrison McClinton, *The Chromolithographs of Louis Prang* (New York: Clarkson N. Potter, 1973), p. 180.

16. See *The Wm. Michael Harnett Collection: His Own Reserved Paintings, Models and Studio Furnishings,* sale cat., Stan. V. Henkels at Thos. Birch's Sons, Auctioneers, Philadelphia, February 23–24, 1893, p. 21. Two lots of photographs (nos. 257–301)—forty-five in all—were included in Harnett's estate, but because the sale catalogue fails to describe them specifically, none can be identified as by Braun.

17. [Edward L. Wilson], "Braun's Carbon Photographs," *Philadelphia Photographer* 4 (December 1867), p. 401, quoted in Eugenia P. Janis, "Photography," in *The Second Empire, 1852–1870: Art in France under Napoleon III,* exhib. cat. (Philadelphia: Philadelphia Museum of Art, 1978), p. 407. Braun's hunting compositions were printed using the carbon process, a photographic printmaking technique that produces a physical relief when held to raking light. The process contributed to the tactile qualities apparent in his work.

18. One could look to the game pieces of British photographers William Lake Price and Dr. Hugh Welch Diamond for precedents, but their still-life compositions lack the scale and textural interest of Braun's prints.

19. Oliver Wendell Holmes, "The Stereoscope and the Stereograph," *Atlantic Monthly* 3 (June 1859), p. 745.

20. Ibid.

THE LATE YEARS

JENNIFER HARDIN

At the height of his career, at age forty, Harnett was diagnosed as having kidney disease, a condition that must have affected his performance as a painter.[1] Within three years, the illness proved fatal. Earlier, Harnett had been hospitalized for rheumatoid arthritis, probably in 1886, but the first sign of a more serious disorder appeared in late 1888.[2] On December 11 of that year, suspecting his rheumatism had worsened, the artist admitted himself to Saint Francis Hospital in Manhattan. On January 24, 1889, he wrote to a friend: "The very day I received your letter I was taken with my old complaint and have been in the Hospital since."[3] He was not discharged until February 22 and was readmitted from March 9 to 16. Upon his admission in March, the hospital staff recorded a more alarming diagnosis: "Acute Uremia, Subacute art.[hritic] rheumatism, and Acute Nephritis."[4] Harnett's disease seems to have been intensifying, perhaps even approaching a critical phase. Acute nephritis (or, more accurately, acute diffuse glomerulonephritis) causes inflammation of the kidneys and may eventually lead to kidney failure, or uremia. Uremia stems from the kidneys' inability to clean the body's toxic waste efficiently and can produce a host of complications: nausea, vomiting, hypertension, anemia, mental impairment, and strokes.[5]

Harnett spent the summer of 1889 abroad in the health spas of Germany.[6] By July he was recovering in Carlsbad, Baedeker's "celebrated watering-place," where he hoped to relieve his pain and renew his strength.[7] During a brief stay at Wiesbaden, he wrote with discouragement to his friend Edward Taylor Snow: "I have not got over my lameness yet."[8] Harnett did recover but only temporarily. By late 1889 his condition had degenerated, and he entered New York Hospital on December 5. Despite another therapeutic excursion, to Hot Springs, Arkansas, in the fall of 1892,

Harnett passed away on October 29. His final medical record states:

> Patient was treated here about 3 years ago for kidney trouble his friends say. Has had rheumatism all summer. This morning did not feel well, vomited and had headache. Suddenly he became unconscious. Was brought in by ambulance in coma. Physical Exam. Account of patient's condition . . . is unsatisfactory.

It also describes him as "anaemic" and "poorly nourished."[9] Harnett's nephritis appears to have produced hypertension, which led to a fatal stroke.

According to Harnett family lore, the artist had become engaged to be married during the last year of his life. Alfred Frankenstein consequently believed Harnett could not have been conscious of the severity of his illness and thus discounted any psychobiographical interpretation of the late works.[10] But Harnett's condition was often painful, and he actively sought to alleviate his suffering by traveling to domestic and European spas. Clearly, ill health *was* a determining factor in his last years, and it should not be dismissed in any interpretation of his final paintings.

The death of Harnett's mother, Honora, in September 1891 might have augmented any depression resulting from his illness.[11] The artist's father had died while Harnett was young, leaving Honora to raise her children alone. Harnett financially supported his widowed mother most of his life. (Indeed, despite enormous popularity during the 1880s and the sale of some high-priced paintings, the artist had little in the way of assets at the time of his death.)[12] The passing of his only living parent must have been a crushing blow.

Alfred Trumble, who had met Harnett while both were students at the National Academy of Design in New York, was a witness to the effects of Harnett's

---

Opposite: William M. Harnett, *The Old Cupboard Door* (detail, pl. 45)

illness. In 1893, after chancing upon the late *Professor's Old Friends* and *Old Models* at Knoedler's, in New York (fig. 124, pl. 49), Trumble recorded what he termed the "pathetic romance" of Harnett's career. In Trumble's eyes, Harnett was reduced to "an old man already," though the artist could not have been more than forty when they renewed their friendship.[13]

Uremia, caused by nephritis, affected more than the artist's physical appearance, as evidenced by the declining number of works he produced and exhibited following the diagnosis. Until 1889, Harnett's output matched the demand for his work. While he completed at least ten paintings in 1888, his entire production for the following year consisted of a single picture, *The Old Cupboard Door.*[14] In the last four years of his life he produced only ten paintings, which include his preferred still-life subjects: the fruit piece, the "bachelor's" still life, the elaborate tabletop, and trompe-l'oeil images of both a single suspended object and more complex arrangements. A concomitant

decline in exhibition activity followed his decrease in productivity. Harnett showed his paintings at only four locations in 1888. He also exhibited at four different venues in 1889, but the works shown that year, such as *Colossal Luck* of 1886 (fig. 71), were probably all done earlier. Harnett showed at only one location in 1890, and this "exhibition" was the thoroughly unofficial display that December of *Emblems of Peace* and *The Faithful Colt* in the window of Black, Starr and Frost, a New York jewelry store.[15] In 1891, the artist participated in only two exhibitions, one of which was the spring annual at the National Academy. This drastic reduction in activity coincided with the onset of his fatal illness.

Subtle stylistic shifts also occurred during this period. Many of Harnett's tabletop still lifes that were "painted to order" include dark, indeterminate backgrounds executed in a perfunctory manner.[16] Compare the backgrounds of *Music and Literature* of 1878 (pl. 10) and *Materials for a Leisure Hour* of 1879

Fig. 85. William M. Harnett, *With the "Staats-Zeitung,"* 1890. Oil on canvas, 14⅛ x 20¼ in.
The Saint Louis Art Museum, Museum Purchase

(Thyssen-Bornemisza Collection) with those of *With the "Staats-Zeitung"* and *Emblems of Peace,* both of 1890 (fig. 85, pl. 46). The rich, luminous settings in the earlier works, achieved by a layering of paint, have been replaced by darker backgrounds in which the brushwork is more visible. In late works such as *My Gems* of 1888 (fig. 126) and *Emblems of Peace,* wooden paneling enshrouds the objects. In more complex tabletop pictures from his last four years, Harnett eliminated the exotic carpets and richly colored draperies that appear in *A Study Table* of 1882 and *Music* of 1886 (pls. 26, 38). Perhaps the execution of such detailed, textural objects would have taxed his diminishing strength and powers of concentration. Some of the late pictures are, in a sense, simplified.

Just Dessert (pl. 47), one of three extant works from 1891 and the only fruit piece among them, provides an excellent example of a sparse tabletop still life. The painting depicts specific objects rendered with equal care, yet it is not as elaborately chaotic as earlier scenes of a meal's end, such as *Still Life* of 1883 (pl. 30). Even though the bottle of maraschino liqueur in *Just Dessert* is tilted, there is a sense of restraint and control in the composition. The background is somber, akin to that of *Emblems of Peace* and *With the "Staats-Zeitung."* Forms upon the table emerge from this obscure setting. All of the objects, with the exception of the branch of bay laurel, represent common desserts in late-nineteenth-century America.[17] They await preparation at the end of the meal, implied by the copper measuring vessel. The purpose of the bay laurel, which sweeps over the composition, is unclear—perhaps it is a visual pun upon obtaining one's "just desserts." The bay branch is not shaped into a wreath, however, the usual iconography for victory, so it may well refer to the medicinal benefits of the plant.[18]

Owing to his ill health, Harnett seems to have reserved his energy for more important paintings—the trompe-l'oeil works. Apart from *After the Hunt* of 1885 (pl. 34), *The Old Cupboard Door* of 1889 (pl. 45) is the largest work in his oeuvre, and one of the most ambitious in the complexity of its composition. Objects and background are given equal attention, successfully producing the desired illusionistic effect. The wealth of detail is even more impressive, considering the painting was completed just after Harnett's release from his second hospital stay.

The Old Cupboard Door was purchased, perhaps even commissioned, by William Barnes Bement, a prominent Philadelphia industrialist.[19] He reportedly paid five thousand dollars for the painting, a staggering sum at the time.[20] Harnett's relationship to this patron has meaningful implications, for Bement already owned Charles Bird King's *Poor Artist's Cupboard* of about 1815 (fig. 86). King's meticulous trompe-l'oeil technique and vanitas symbolism no doubt would have spoken to Harnett.[21] The smooth surface, attention to detail, vertical organization, and subject matter of the King picture are recalled in *The Old Cupboard Door.* Yet Harnett took the conceit one step further by creating a tabletop still life on the shelf and combining it with suspended objects.[22] King's canvas conveys a personal message. A frugal meal, the bankruptcy notice, and books with such titles as *Advantages of Poverty* emphatically declare his cynicism regarding the plight of the artist in American society.[23] There is every reason to believe Harnett was familiar with King's work, and its message might have been in his mind if, and when, Bement commissioned *The Old Cupboard Door.*[24]

Objects in *The Old Cupboard Door* include traditional vanitas symbols such as a snuffed-out candle and books whose covers hang by a thread. Harnett had painted vanitas motifs since the late 1870s, but this is the first painting that incorporates trompe-l'oeil devices into an overtly vanitas iconographic program. The tambourine and statuette of Bacchus refer to revelry and therefore to the transience of earthly pleasures. This allusion is undercut, however, by the dying rose, whose leaves have begun to wither and fall. The picture strikes a somber note, augmented by the sheet music for "La Dernière Rose d'été," a traditional tune with lyrics by Thomas Moore. In the final stanza, the poet compares himself to the solitude and waning beauty of the season's last rose:

> So soon may *I* follow,
> When friendships decay,
> And from Love's shining circle
> The gems drop away.
> When true hearts lie wither'd,
> And fond ones are flown,
> Oh! who would inhabit
> This bleak world alone?[25]

Moore's highly popular lyrics set to a traditional Irish folk tune are desperately melancholic. The deep gash in the door and the rusty, broken hinge, as well as the sheet music from Bellini's *Norma* and volumes of *Don Quixote* and Shakespeare's *Tragedies,* further enhance the plaintive atmosphere.[26]

A second trompe l'oeil from this late period is equally grim. *The Faithful Colt* of 1890 (pl. 48), exhibition companion of *Emblems of Peace,* contains similar gashes in the painted wood background, and the revolver is an antiquated model from the Civil War era. A reviewer described the handle of the gun as "discolored and cracked with age."[27] The instrument itself possesses a dual nature: it can be employed for protection or destruction.

Harnett's last finished work, *Old Models* of 1892 (pl. 49), intended for display at the World's Columbian Exposition of 1893, probably would have caused as much of a stir among the public as *The Old Violin* (pl. 37) had in Cincinnati in 1886 or as *After the Hunt*

Fig. 86. Charles Bird King, *The Poor Artist's Cupboard,* ca. 1815. Oil on canvas, 29¾ x 27¾ in.
The Corcoran Gallery of Art, Washington, D.C., Museum Purchase

continued to in one of Theodore Stewart's saloons in New York. As does *The Old Cupboard Door,* the picture demonstrates Harnett's compulsion about control and detail, and in a more opaque fashion, it is equally pensive. Whether or not the nostalgic title was chosen by Harnett, these are indeed *his* old models. Nearly all of the props were included in his estate sale in February 1893.[28] Ten elements are contained within a composition that again combines the tabletop support and suspended objects. When first encountering *Old Models,* one is struck by its control, harmony, balance, and technical prowess. By excluding the exotic accoutrements of earlier paintings, Harnett called attention to each model and emphasized the major ones—the battered brass horn, the violin, and the earthenware jar—in a solid triangular arrangement.

Upon closer scrutiny, however, this stability and sense of order are contradicted. Even though the scroll of the violin is tremulously balanced against an almost invisible nail, the instrument conveys the illusion of being held up by its own power, ready at any moment to fall from the shallow space of the shelf rather than rest on the door frame. Moreover, the single sheet of music on the ledge is again Moore's "Dernière Rose d'été"—at once a reference to Harnett's earlier works, his Irish ancestry, and his diminishing ability to create. The lyrics would have held additional significance for him because of his mother's recent death. Even the horn, an object he rarely depicted, is old and battered, enhancing the time-worn nature of the scene. Also adding an oppressive aura to *Old Models* and perhaps alluding to the artist's illness are Shakespeare's *Tragedies* and Homer's *Odyssey,* which recounts Odysseus's trials during his seemingly endless voyage home to Ithaca. The volume that leans against the other two may correspond to a seventeenth-century medical guide that was included in the sale catalogue of Harnett's estate: *Bruelis Gualtri. Medicinae Theorica et Empirica . . . Lugduni, 1647.*[29] The *Odyssey* may hint at the troubles the artist encountered during the last years of his life, and he might have included the title of Walter Bruel's do-it-yourself medical reference for curing various diseases because illness was very much at the heart of his own problems.

Despite pain and limited mobility, Harnett was able to achieve brilliant illusionistic effects within these three complex trompe-l'oeil paintings and to compose a sensitive tabletop study such as *Just Dessert.* Still life is a genre in which an artist must choose which objects to include and which to discard. During his entire career, Harnett seemed to favor used-up, dilapidated items, a tendency that appears to have intensified as his career progressed. His last works are about things worn and spent and perhaps, by extension, about his life. One could term these large, late productions private vanitas meditations, in contrast to an earlier work such as *Mortality and Immortality* of 1876 (pl. 3) that has a clearly defined precedent in seventeenth-century Dutch art. The onset of Harnett's illness lends a psychological element to our understanding of *The Old Cupboard Door* and *Old Models*—it is not without reason that one modern writer called him a "necromantic."[30] The late paintings are not only about loss and death, however. They often suggest dualities that are common to the human experience: the comforts of home and the travails of long journeys, love and loneliness, life and death. By infusing his still lifes with references to his past career and with objects related to his state of ill health, Harnett created paintings that are metaphors for his waning powers.

NOTES

▼

I would like to thank Doreen Bolger and Thayer Tolles Mickel for their kind help and infinite patience in preparing this essay. I also wish to express my gratitude to Professor John Wilmerding, whose seminar in American still-life painting inspired this paper, and to Laura A. Coyle, Paul Raymond Provost, Douglas R. Nickel, and Jennifer Milam, my colleagues at Princeton who generously offered their advice and criticism.

1. On Harnett's late period in general, see Alfred Frankenstein, *After the Hunt: William Harnett and Other American Still Life Painters, 1870–1900,* rev. ed. (Berkeley and Los Angeles: University of California Press, 1969), pp. 90–93.

2. George Hulings stated that after finishing *The Old Violin* in 1886, Harnett entered the hospital for "a severe attack of inflammatory rheumatism" ("Harnett: How George Hulings Lost His Fiddle," *Evening Item* [Philadelphia], June 11, 1895, p. 1).

3. The "old complaint" is probably a reference to rheumatism. Harnett to W. J. Hughes, January 24, 1889, Alfred Frankenstein Papers, Archives of American Art, Smithsonian Institution, Washington, D.C., microfilm, roll 1375, frame 543, quoted in Frankenstein, *After the Hunt,* p. 90.

4. Sister Maria, superior, St. Francis Hospital, New York, to Frankenstein, October 27, 1949, Frankenstein Papers, roll 1375, frame 520.

5. See Sidney I. Landau, ed., *International Dictionary of Medicine and Biology,* 3 vols. (New York: John Wiley & Sons, 1986), 3, p. 3070; and Douglas M. Considine, ed., *Van Nostrand's Scientific Encyclopedia,* 6th ed. (New York: Van Nostrand Reinhold, 1983), pp. 1708–15. An odd twist is that acute nephritis is one aspect of Bright's disease, the illness that eventually consumed John Frederick Peto (see John Wilmerding, *Important Information Inside: The Art of John F. Peto and the Idea of Still-Life Painting in Nineteenth-Century America,* exhib. cat., National Gallery of Art, Washington, D.C. [New York: Harper & Row, 1983], p. 25). Bright's disease, described by Richard Bright in 1827, was eventually found to be three separate disorders, one of which is glomerulonephritis.

6. According to his friend Edward Taylor Snow, in 1889 Harnett "was putting the finishing touches to Bement's

picture [*The Old Cupboard Door*] . . . and remarked that as soon as he delivered the painting he was going to Carlsbad to try and regain his health and would not paint another picture for a year" (quoted in Frankenstein, *After the Hunt,* p. 90).

7. Karl Baedeker, *Southern Germany and Austria* (Leipzig: Karl Baedeker, 1891), p. 305.

8. Harnett to Snow, September 5, 1889, Frankenstein Papers, roll 1375, frame 544.

9. See Frankenstein Papers, roll 1374, frame 913; and Adele A. Lerner, archivist at New York Hospital–Cornell Medical Center, to Thayer Tolles Mickel, October 18, 1989.

10. Frankenstein, *After the Hunt,* pp. 83, 90–93. To his credit, Frankenstein may have been resisting the strong currents of psychoanalytic and Freudian interpretations of art in the 1940s. Art historian Wolfgang Born hinted at psychobiographical interpretations of several Harnett paintings. His belief that the artist's ill health and bachelorhood affected his work is problematic, for it predates Frankenstein's discovery of the Harnett forgeries. One work Born subjected to such an interpretation turned out to be by Peto—it contains a photograph of Helen Peto, his daughter. Born misconstrued this photo as a reference to a long-lost love of Harnett's (see Wolfgang Born, "William M. Harnett: Bachelor Artist," *Magazine of Art* 39 [October 1946], pp. 248–54).

11. Honora ("Hannah") Harnett was buried on September 14, 1891 (Frankenstein Papers, roll 1374, frame 913).

12. The estate consisted of finished and unfinished works and about $400 in cash (U.S., Pennsylvania, Philadelphia, 1892, probate material, administration no. 1474, account book no. 173, p. 308). My thanks to Andrew Walker for sharing this information.

13. [Alfred Trumble], "The Awakening of the Giant," *Collector* 4 (October 1, 1893), p. 294. Trumble edited and owned *The Collector,* a journal devoted to art, antiques, and book collecting.

14. Frankenstein, *After the Hunt,* pp. 178–80.

15. Frank Linstow White, "Art Notes," *Epoch* 8 (December 12, 1890), p. 300. In 1892, Harnett evidently showed one

work, *Old Models,* but the newspaper reference is not specific (see "Harnett's Body Here!" *Times* [Philadelphia], November 1, 1892, p. 1). One can, however, corroborate this account with a more descriptive review (see Louisa Trumbull Cogswell, "Art in Boston," *Arcadia* 1 [December 1, 1892], pp. 305–6).

16. The phrase "painted to order" is found on the reverse of some of Harnett's paintings—*Still Life* of 1888, for example (see Frankenstein, *After the Hunt,* p. 179, no. 110).

17. Susan Williams, *Savory Suppers and Fashionable Feasts: Dining in Victorian America* (New York: Pantheon Books in association with the Strong Museum, Rochester, N.Y., 1985), pp. 122–26, 170–73.

18. Native Americans and American settlers used bay for treating rheumatism (see John K. Crellin and Jane Philpott, *Herbal Medicine Past and Present,* vol. 1, *Trying to Give Ease* [Durham, N.C., and London: Duke University Press, 1990], pp. 143–45). In James Hall, *Dictionary of Subjects and Symbols,* rev. ed. (New York: Harper & Row, 1979), p. 190, the bay laurel is equated with preventing illness. Victory over death in vanitas paintings is symbolized by a skull crowned with laurels. For this latter iconography and its depictions, see Alberto Veca, *Vanitas: il simbolismo del tempo* (Bergamo: Galleria Lorenzelli, 1981), pp. 173, 208. Examples by Jan Davidsz. de Heem, Evert Collier, Simon Renard de St.-André, and Lorenzo Lotto are reproduced on pp. 85, 110, 127, 129.

19. See Frankenstein, *After the Hunt,* pp. 87–88; and Doreen Bolger, "Patrons of the Artist: Emblems of Commerce and Culture," pp. 24, 28. Frankenstein states that *The Old Cupboard Door* was "produced for Bement"; and Chad Mandeles ("William Michael Harnett's *The Old Cupboard Door* and the Tradition of *Vanitas,*" *American Art Journal* 18, no. 3 [1986], p. 56) believes the work was commissioned.

20. See "Artist Harnett Dead: The Well-Known Still-Life Painter Dies in Hospital," *New York Times,* October 31, 1892, p. 3.

21. On Harnett's work and symbolism, see Mandeles, "Harnett's *Old Cupboard Door,*" pp. 51–62; and Barbara S. Groseclose, "Vanity and the Artist: Some Still-Life Paintings by William Michael Harnett," *American Art Journal* 19, no. 1 (1987), pp. 51–59.

22. This type of still life has one contemporary American precedent, Peto's *Poor Man's Store* of 1885 (Museum of Fine Arts, Boston). Peto, however, did not fully exploit the ledge as Harnett did by including an array of objects on it. Earlier European precedents for this type of trompe l'oeil exist. Cornelis and Franciscus Gysbrechts, seventeenth-century Dutch painters who excelled in deception, depicted objects on shelves and in cupboards. Cornelis was quite prolific, and some of his works are so similar in conception to Harnett's that it raises the question whether Harnett knew these paintings firsthand, while in Europe, or perhaps from prints, once back in the United States.

23. See Andrew J. Cosentino, *The Paintings of Charles Bird King (1785–1862),* exhib. cat., National Collection of Fine Arts, Smithsonian Institution, Washington, D.C. (Washington, D.C.: Smithsonian Institution Press, 1977), p. 28. More recently, Carrie Rebora has noted that a related King, *Vanity of the Artist's Dream* of 1830 (Fogg Art Museum, Harvard University, Cambridge, Mass.), contains similar commentary: text within the painting documents the indifference to Benjamin West's portrait by Sir Thomas Lawrence at its spring 1823 exhibition in Philadelphia. A "Cats Skin" shown there earned more money than West's portrait (Carrie Rebora, "Sir Thomas Lawrence's *Benjamin West* for the American Academy of the Fine Arts," *American Art Journal* 21, no. 3 [Summer 1989], p. 38).

24. Objects not included in other Harnett paintings (tambourine, statuette, seashell, and copy of *Don Quixote*) might support the notion that Bement commissioned *The Old Cupboard Door.* Yet these articles were all listed in the sale catalogue of Harnett's estate (*The Wm. Michael Harnett Collection: His Own Reserved Paintings, Models and Studio Furnishings,* sale cat., Stan. V. Henkels at Thos. Birch's Sons, Auctioneers, Philadelphia, February 23–24, 1893, p. 10, no. 59; p. 12, no. 83; p. 16, no. 136; p. 24, no. 393). It is plausible that Bement ordered the work and that Harnett made a selection for him.

25. John Francis Waller, *The Poetical Works of Thomas Moore with the Life of the Author* (New York: P. F. Collier, 1880), p. 46.

26. Mandeles discusses the implications of Bellini's tragic opera and the self-delusions of *Don Quixote* ("Harnett's *Old Cupboard Door,*" pp. 53, 56). While Harnett probably

did not read the exact book shown in the painting (for it
is written in Spanish), he may have read an English
version or at least have been familiar with the story.

27. White, "Art Notes," p. 300. Identification of the
revolver is from Carol Troyen, "William Michael Harnett,
The Faithful Colt, 1890," in Theodore E. Stebbins, Jr.,
et al., *A New World: Masterpieces of American Painting,
1760–1910,* exhib. cat. (Boston: Museum of Fine Arts,
1983), p. 285.

28. *Wm. Michael Harnett Collection.*

29. Ibid., p. 24, no. 402. Frankenstein claims Harnett was
"fascinated by books, but he has no interest in their
literary implications. Any book will do . . . what the book
may signify as a work of poetry or prose does not
concern him in the least." Yet he accepts symbolic
meaning in Harnett's music, which "provides us with
unintended clues to his tastes and activities in this art"
(*After the Hunt,* pp. 40–41). On the other hand, Frankenstein has no qualms about interpreting Peto's paintings
biographically: "It does not take a Freudian psychologist
to perceive that Peto's concern with used-up, discarded,
and rejected things parallels his own life" (ibid., p. 107).
One could hardly imagine Harnett plodding through
Medicinae Theorica et Empirica. While the dates on
the actual and painted books do not correspond, the
legible portion of the lettering on the binding, *BRVELIS/
PASCHAL,* does. Here, as in other instances, Harnett
altered the date or title of his original model. A 1639
London edition of Walter Bruel's book—first published in
1579 in Antwerp—is on microfilm (Watson Library,
University of Kansas, Lawrence, roll MiU F60-136). The
classics—Homer, Dante, and especially Shakespeare—
are more plausible reading material. Shakespeare's work
was a frequent model in Harnett's library still lifes
beginning in the late 1870s. For the enormous popularity
of Shakespeare in nineteenth-century America, see Gary
Taylor, *Reinventing Shakespeare: A Cultural History, from
the Restoration to the Present* (New York: Weidenfeld &
Nicolson, 1989), pp. 196–204. Taylor points out that in
the post–Civil War era, Shakespearean plays comprised
between one-fifth and one-quarter of the performances
in this country and were commonly used for recitation
in schools.

30. Edouard Roditi, "William Harnett: American Necromantic," *View* 5, no. 4 (November 1945), pp. 9, 19–20.

Pl. 34. William M. Harnett, *After the Hunt*, 1885. Oil on canvas, 71½ x 48½ in.
The Fine Arts Museums of San Francisco, Mildred Anna Williams Collection

Pl. 35. William M. Harnett, *Still Life*, 1885. Oil on wood, 13¾ x 10⅝ in.
The Armand Hammer Museum of Art and Cultural Center, Los Angeles, The Armand Hammer Collection

Pl. 36. William M. Harnett, *Trophy of the Hunt,* 1885. Oil on canvas, 42⁷⁄₁₆ x 21¹³⁄₁₆ in.
The Carnegie Museum of Art, Pittsburgh, Purchase, 1941 (41.5)

Pl. 37. William M. Harnett, *The Old Violin*, 1886. Oil on canvas, 38 x 24 in. James H. Maroney, Jr.

Pl. 38. William M. Harnett, *Music,* 1886. Oil on canvas, 46¼ x 38½ in.
Manoogian Collection

Pl. 39. William M. Harnett, *The Meerschaum Pipe,* 1886. Oil on canvas, 17⅛ x 12⅛ in.
The Fine Arts Museums of San Francisco, Gift of Mr. and Mrs. John D. Rockefeller 3rd

Pl. 40. William M. Harnett, *The Golden Horseshoe*, 1886. Oil on canvas, 16 x 14 in.
Courtesy of Berry-Hill Galleries, New York

Pl. 41. William M. Harnett, *Ease,* 1887. Oil on canvas, 48 x 52¾ in. Amon Carter Museum, Fort Worth

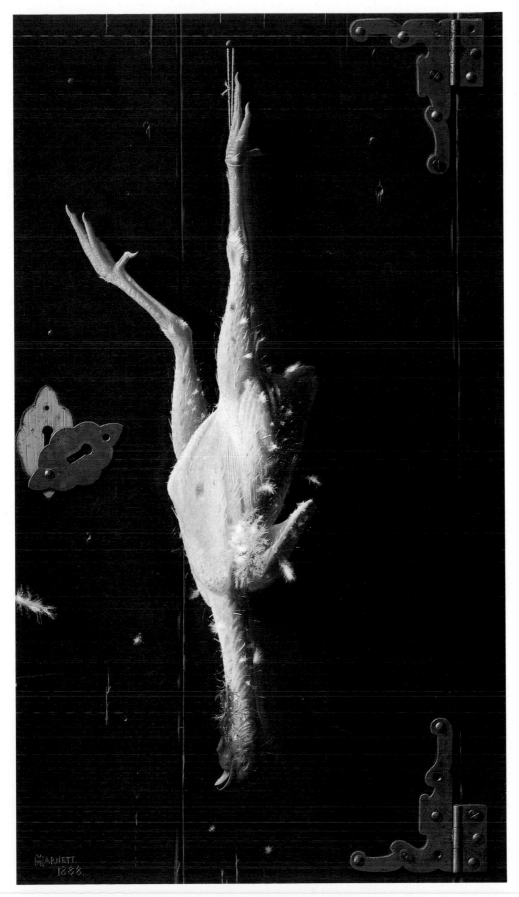

Pl. 42. William M. Harnett, *For Sunday's Dinner*, 1888. Oil on canvas, 37⅛ x 21⅛ in.
The Art Institute of Chicago, Wilson L. Mead Fund (1958.296)

Pl. 43. William M. Harnett, *Still Life—Violin and Music* (*Music and Good Luck*), 1888. Oil on canvas, 40 x 30 in. The Metropolitan Museum of Art, New York, Wolfe Fund, Catharine Lorillard Wolfe Collection, 1963

Pl. 44. William M. Harnett, *Mr. Hulings' Rack Picture*, 1888. Oil on canvas, 30 x 25 in.
Jo Ann and Julian Ganz, Jr.

Pl. 45. William M. Harnett, *The Old Cupboard Door*, 1889. Oil on canvas, 61⅝ x 41 in.
City Art Galleries, Sheffield, England

Pl. 46. William M. Harnett, *Emblems of Peace,* 1890. Oil on canvas, 27½ x 33¾ in.
Museum of Fine Arts, Springfield, Mass., Gift of Charles T. and Emilie Shean

Pl. 47. William M. Harnett, *Just Dessert,* 1891. Oil on canvas, 22¼ x 26¾ in.
The Art Institute of Chicago, Friends of American Art (1942.50)

Pl. 48. William M. Harnett, *The Faithful Colt,* 1890. Oil on canvas, 22½ x 18½ in.
Wadsworth Atheneum, Hartford, Conn., The Ella Gallup Sumner and Mary Catlin Sumner Collection

Pl. 49. William M. Harnett, *Old Models*, 1892. Oil on canvas, 54 x 28 in.
Museum of Fine Arts, Boston, The Hayden Collection

THE
MAJOR
THEMES

PERMANENT PERISHABLES

The Artist's Fruit Paintings

THAYER TOLLES MICKEL

By 1875, when William Michael Harnett turned from silver engraving to painting, fruit still lifes were familiar to Americans, often gracing the walls of their dining rooms, both in domestic interiors and public spaces such as hotels and bars. Fruit appears in Harnett's work in some thirty paintings done throughout his career; he specialized in the subject from 1875 to 1877, his student years in Philadelphia and New York, and from 1881 to 1884, while in Germany.[1] These works clearly demonstrate the artist's debt to European and American sources—formally, aesthetically, and symbolically—and how he assimilated their devices into his own work. As still-life painter Andrew John Henry Way observed, "Each artist impresses on his work more or less of his own individuality however much he may have admired and studied the works of another."[2] Harnett's fruit paintings are distinctive in content and meaning, and they remained important for the artist even after he had progressed to more innovative subjects and compositions. Harnett's fruit subjects reveal a great kinship with his better-known bric-a-brac compositions, and regardless of their humble nature, they poignantly reflect his often-acknowledged goals: to create an artistic composition and to tell a story.

Initially, the young artist may have been motivated to try his hand at fruit painting chiefly for economic reasons. When Harnett abandoned silver engraving and its steady income, he would have looked for established subject matter that was both commercially successful and easy to produce. Finding a plentiful supply of models was as simple as walking to a local fruit market. Apples, grapes, oranges, and pears—all subjects commonly depicted in fruit paintings—were popular in America by then and readily accessible in major urban centers.[3] One of Harnett's friends, the sculptor James Edward Kelly, suggested that fruit had a practical, ancillary purpose: "Harnett said that he differed from most artists, for after painting them, he could eat his models."[4]

Harnett's early training at the Pennsylvania Academy of the Fine Arts, and indeed his youthful years in Philadelphia, familiarized him with the American still-life tradition and its European precedents. This exposure accounts for both the choice of subjects and formal elements in his earliest works, such as *A Wooden Basket of Catawba Grapes* of 1876 (pl. 1). The still lifes of the early-nineteenth-century Americans James and Raphaelle Peale and of their mid-century successors John F. Francis, Severin Roesen, and George Henry Hall attest to the lineage of fruit painting in America. In addition, the influence of Dutch, Flemish, German, and other Continental artists should not be underestimated, as novel compositional and stylistic devices found in works by the seventeenth-century artists Abraham van Beyeren, Jan Davidsz. de Heem, Willem Kalf, and Adriaen Coorte were handed down to successive generations of painters.

While we can only surmise which paintings Harnett actually saw, he surely would have studied fruit still lifes in museums and private collections in Philadelphia and New York—most notably at the Pennsylvania Academy, the New-York Historical Society, and, in particular, the Metropolitan Museum of Art, where accomplished works such as de Heem's *Still Life* (fig. 87) were on display.[5] Regular exhibitions at these institutions as well as at the National Academy of Design, and special displays such as the Philadelphia Centennial Exposition of 1876, also provided Harnett with opportunities to see recently completed canvases from America and abroad. Also accessible in these

Fig. 87. Jan Davidsz. de Heem, *Still Life*. Oil on wood, 9⅞ x 7½ in. The Metropolitan Museum of Art, New York, Purchase, 1871

picture, *Fruit* of 1875, was priced at the rather modest sum of seventy-five dollars at the annual of the National Academy that year.[10] In two similar compositions from this period, *Still Life,* also of 1875 (fig. 37), and *A Wooden Basket of Catawba Grapes,* Harnett adapted formal and compositional devices popularized by the Peales, such as the darkened background, strong and highly focused lighting, pyramidal massing of forms, and intimacy of portrayal, yet his abundant arrangements of fruit recall the more immediate mid-century American tradition of bounty. Harnett was certainly not moved by a spirit of truth to nature, though he must have been impressed by the fecundity depicted in a work such as Robert Spear Dunning's *Apples (Autumn's Bounty)* of 1869 (fig. 89), then in the Bement collection.[11] *Apples* and Harnett's works share a masterful combination of plentitude and specificity of detail. Eschewing Dunning's outdoor setting, Harnett moved his compositions onto the tabletop and, by doing so, devised an innovative synthesis of early- and mid-nineteenth-century conventions. Harnett's fruit is restricted, organized, and confined within and around the wooden baskets, revealing an aura of controlled abundance apart from a natural setting.

Even after he developed his more typical mug-and-pipe compositions in 1877, Harnett continued to pursue fruit themes with *Peaches and Flies* of that year (fig. 90).[12] Such simplified yet charming compositions first became popular in America during the Peale era and were rendered by succeeding generations.[13] Harnett may have been inspired to turn to peaches as a subject after the reopening of the Pennsylvania

cities were fine examples in private collections, such as that of Philadelphian William Barnes Bement, who "freely opened [his] gallery to the public."[6]

Harnett also may have been influenced by the fruit paintings of his contemporaries. Lemuel Wilmarth, one of Harnett's teachers at the National Academy, demonstrated a genuine interest in fruit pictures, often exhibiting them throughout his career. Wilmarth initiated still-life classes at the National Academy in 1877, and though Harnett had returned to Philadelphia by then, we may assume Wilmarth had fostered an interest in the genre among his students.[7] In addition, Harnett met the prominent Pittsburgh artist George Hetzel,[8] whose fruit and game subjects, such as *Still Life with Grapes and Peaches* of 1866 (fig. 88), reflect the training he received in Düsseldorf. Hetzel's paintings, with their tight brushwork and concentrated lighting, must have appealed to Harnett.[9]

Harnett focused on fruit subjects during his first years as a painter; of his ten known works from 1875 and 1876, eight depict this theme. He continued to show only fruit pieces until 1877. His first exhibited

Fig. 88. George Hetzel, *Still Life with Grapes and Peaches,* 1866. Oil on canvas, 14½ x 20 in. Westmoreland Museum of Art, Greensburg, Pa., Gift of the Women's Committee (81.32)

Fig. 89. Robert Spear Dunning, *Apples*
(*Autumn's Bounty*), 1869. Oil on canvas, 19⅝ x 25⅜ in.
Manoogian Collection

Academy in 1876, when Raphaelle Peale's *Fox Grapes and Peaches* of 1815 (Pennsylvania Academy of the Fine Arts) was taken out of storage and put on view in the new building.[14] Harnett, then enrolled in classes at the academy, no doubt was familiar with the style and subject matter of the Peale painting.

In 1876, just before he departed from edibles to inanimate objects, Harnett made great compositional and thematic strides. In *Still Life with Ginger Jar* of that year (pl. 2), the artist introduced a number of man-made elements into a fruit composition. The book and ivory-handled knife thrusting into the picture plane, the sweep of red drapery, and the lowered viewpoint suggest Harnett was studying the works of the Old Masters and assimilating their formal devices. The painting also recalls the mid-century American luncheon piece, best exemplified by the work of Francis (fig. 91), in its depiction of vertical items alternating rhythmically with fruit that has been placed with

Fig. 90. William M. Harnett, *Peaches and Flies,* 1877. Oil on canvas, 6 x 8 in.
Courtesy of Kennedy Galleries, Inc., New York

Fig. 91. John F. Francis, *Still Life with Wine Bottles and Basket of Fruit,* 1857.
Oil on canvas, 25 x 30 in. Museum of Fine Arts, Boston,
Gift of Maxim Karolik for the Karolik Collection of American Paintings, 1815–65

seeming casualness. Although both paintings represent moments of presentation rather than consumption, *Still Life with Ginger Jar* depicts far more humble subjects than does Francis's *Still Life with Wine Bottles and Basket of Fruit.* Harnett's objects are commonplace and worn, and the only exotic touches are the patterned vase and the coconut and pineapple, which were still luxury fruits to Americans of the 1870s.

Harnett also might have been aware of the luncheon still life through pictures by nineteenth-century artists such as Morston C. and Carducius Plantagenet Ream and lithographs after similar works by other artists. The chromolithographs of L. Prang and Company (fig. 92) and of Currier and Ives were widely available in art supply shops and found their way

into many American homes. Even though we cannot directly measure the influence of these decorative prints on Harnett, his paintings were similar in purpose, offering pleasing compositions suitable for decorating the dining room.[15]

Harnett, who stated, "I endeavor to make the composition tell a story,"[16] may have used fruit to imply meaning, in the manner of the seventeenth-century masters who instilled their models, even everyday objects, with symbolism. Dutch and Flemish paintings, readily accessible to Harnett, abounded with reminders, warnings, and allegories, some more comprehensible to the nineteenth-century viewer than others. Whether or not Harnett consciously painted in this iconographic tradition, his exposure to European

Fig. 92. *Dining-Room Pictures,* in *L. Prang & Co., Illustrated Catalogue*
(Boston: L. Prang & Co., 1876), p. 38. Chicago Historical Society

Fig. 93. William M. Harnett, *Still Life with Wine Glass,* 1876. Oil on canvas, 10 x 14 in.
Courtesy of Allison Gallery, New York

models and his Catholic background must have acquainted him with various symbolic programs, and some of these established motifs found expression in his work as early as 1876.[17]

Still Life with Wine Glass of that year (fig. 93), a seemingly simple tabletop composition, can be interpreted as having spiritual associations, particularly references to Christ's Passion. Good and evil are juxtaposed: the apples may be objects of temptation alluding to the Fall of Man, while the grapes and wine may refer to Christ's sacrifice and the Eucharist. Even the hard shells of the almonds may be a reminder of the wooden crucifix. Overall, the message may be read as one of hope and redemption. Similarly, motifs in *Peaches and Flies* may be seen as overt vanitas references. The flies may symbolize the inevitability of death, and the water, an evaporative element, may suggest transience.

About 1877, Harnett completed a series of tabletop paintings that combine fruit with elaborate, decorative objets d'art. In *The Chinese Vase* (Brady Galleries, Inc., South Burlington, Vt.) and *Still Life for William Ignatius Blemly* (fig. 110) a dominant vertical object is placed beside low-lying horizontal ones—a format that was extremely popular in the 1870s. These works demonstrate Harnett's career-long tendency to explore a particular compositional arrangement repeatedly within a group of related pictures, simply substituting objects from a stock of motifs. Having established variations on the overall theme of horizontal and vertical items portrayed at close range, Harnett applied this formula to the depiction of other subjects. In *Still Life for William Ignatius Blemly,* for instance, he depicted a mug and pipe arranged almost exactly like the vase and fruit in *The Chinese Vase,* with a corresponding placement of vertical and horizontal elements. His practice of repeating and varying formats, no matter how different the models, may have enabled him to make the seemingly abrupt shift in 1877 from fruit paintings to images of man-made objects.

Until he departed for Europe in 1880, Harnett filled his canvases with well-worn books, glistening coins, spotted inkwells, and tantalizingly illegible correspondence. The seeming facility and intuitive skill with which he produced these works distracted him from his early, and admittedly more labored, depictions of mundane fruit. In Europe, however, he saw firsthand the still-life masterpieces at the Royal Academy of Arts in London, the Louvre in Paris, and, most important, the Alte Pinakothek in Munich and was perhaps inspired to return to painting and exhibiting fruit pieces. In Germany, when he once again took up the subject, however, he reduced its role substantially; no longer the overall focus of the composition, fruit was one of several items featured. *Still Life* (*Frankfurter Zeitung*) of 1881 (IBM Corporation Collection, Armonk, N.Y.) is the first work in which he rendered fruit as a minor variable within a group of disparate elements.

The inclusion of the wine bottle, tapestry, and repoussé bronze plate suggests a modest version of the elaborate bric-a-brac compositions of then-celebrated French artist Blaise Desgoffe.

Still Life with Fruit and Vase of 1881 (pl. 22), with its prominent display of glistening grapes, shows the influence of mid-century Düsseldorf masters Johann Peter Hasenclever and Johann Wilhelm Preyer, the latter an accomplished technician and leading still-life artist of the nineteenth-century German school.[18] Certainly Harnett was aware of their work before he went to Europe, since he could have seen Preyer's fruit paintings exhibited at the Pennsylvania Academy in 1865 and 1868.[19] Also, an infiltration of the Düsseldorf style is evident in the work of German immigrants working in America, notably Roesen (fig. 94), as well as in the work of German-trained artists, such as Hetzel. The German school was heavily dependent on Dutch and Flemish formal conventions and worked in a tightly rendered style, which Harnett assimilated in *Still Life with Fruit and Vase.* The motifs of the winding grape tendrils and marble tabletop in

Fig. 94. Severin Roesen, *Still Life,* 1854–55. Oil on canvas, 30 x 40 in.
Pennsylvania Academy of the Fine Arts, Philadelphia, Gift of William C. Williamson,
by exchange, and Henry S. McNeil and the Henry D. Gilpin Fund

Harnett's picture are also characteristic of Düsseldorf still-life paintings. Harnett's interest in the play of varied light on surfaces is evident in the virtuoso handling of the grapes. The treatment of grapes and other spherical shapes, long considered an indication of technical prowess, provided Harnett with an opportunity to experiment with light, medium, and dark tones.[20] Raised touches of impasto add to the sparkling surface of the fruit.

The gemlike appearance of *Still Life with Fruit and Vase* and *Still Life (Frankfurter Zeitung)* is enhanced by their miniaturism—the representation of objects on a smaller-than-life-size scale, so that any essence of illusionism is lost. This tendency toward reduction in Harnett's work began shortly before he traveled to Europe, especially in pipe-and-newspaper works such as *New York Herald, July 11, 1880* (pl. 21). With few exceptions, all of his fruit compositions of the early 1880s are diminutive, generally smaller than eight by ten inches. This noticeable change in scale has been ascribed to the influence of the French artist Jean-Louis-Ernest Meissonier, whose miniaturistic figure paintings commanded high prices during the second half of the nineteenth century.[21] Yet Harnett also must have been affected by current-day practice in and around Munich. Many German-trained artists studying in the city, including Americans Louis Moeller and Charles F. Ulrich, were experimenting with small-scale genre compositions modeled after those of seventeenth-century Dutch and Flemish genre painters.[22] Although Harnett did not investigate figural subject matter, his tight brushwork and restricted palette were characteristic of the general movement toward minutiae.

During his career, Harnett's paintings featuring or including fruit progressed conceptually from simple to relatively complex schemes. As fruit ceased to be the central focus of his compositions, it took on a new role, filling and balancing spaces. Undoubtedly inspired by such grand-scale *pronkstilleven* (banquet pieces) as Abraham van Beyeren's *Large Still Life with Lobster* (fig. 95) at the Alte Pinakothek, in 1882 Harnett completed a series of lobster paintings that investigate the rearrangement of a consistent repertoire of objects, including a lobster, a newspaper, and a Dutch jar. In contrast to van Beyeren's canvas, with its pervading sense of horror vacui, Harnett's works appear rather sparse and underdecorated. Conspicuous consumption often found its way into the works of van Beyeren and other seventeenth-century painters, such as Willem Claesz. Heda and Willem Kalf. The mere presence of luxury items in their still lifes serves as a reminder to viewers to enjoy these commodities in moderation. In contrast to the van Beyeren, *Still Life with "Le Figaro"* of 1882 (pl. 23) depicts toned-down, commonplace goods, generally apples ("the most abundant, and most easily obtainable"),[23] scattered

Fig. 95. Abraham van Beyeren, *Large Still Life with Lobster.* Oil on canvas, 49½ x 41⅜ in. Bayerisches Staatsgemäldesammlungen, Munich

among humble bric-a-brac elements. The splintered wooden box containing figs, rumpled newspaper, and bruised apples contrasts sharply with van Beyeren's costly silver plate and ornate nautilus-shell cup. While in his early paintings Harnett most likely gave meaning to individual fruits, such as the apples and grapes in *Still Life with Wine Glass,* similar symbolism is not evident in *Still Life with "Le Figaro."* Rather, Harnett's primary concern was the precise depiction of various objects and textures as well as the skillful arrangement of forms. Although the bruised apples are suggestive of the passage of time, the emphasis is on the physical rendering of their state of overripeness.

Still Life of 1883 and *Still Life* of 1884 (pls. 30, 32) demonstrate Harnett's devotion to an almost scientific observation of nature. These paintings do not emphasize any one element in particular; instead, the fruit seems randomly scattered—a lone grape here, an orange peel there, and the omnipresent apple. Instead of emphasizing luxury goods, Harnett chose to celebrate the pleasures of humble objects.

After his return from Europe, Harnett depicted fruit subjects only intermittently, but the theme remained popular with at least some of his patrons.

Harnett painted *The Sideboard* (*Fruit Scene*) for Theodore Stewart's saloon at 8 Warren Street before 1887 and completed a study of fruit for George H. Hulings at an undetermined date.[24] *Just Dessert* of 1891 (pl. 47), commissioned by Peter Samuel Dooner, is the summation of Harnett's exploration of fruit painting and the antithesis of his miniaturistic works of the early 1880s.[25] As with several of the artist's other ambitious late works, among them *The Old Cupboard Door* of 1889 and *Emblems of Peace* of 1890 (pls. 45, 46), both form and content may be read as personal statements. No longer can we attribute composition or symbolic resonances to the influences of other masters or schools. Rather, *Just Dessert* is a monumental elaboration of Harnett's earlier and more complex tabletop compositions.

More than a masterful "dining-room" picture, *Just Dessert,* by virtue of its title, suggests an element of reward. In 1890, Harnett was proposed for membership in the Hibernian Society, a Philadelphia organization whose efforts centered on relief activities for Irish immigrants. The group promoted their cause through festive banquets held at Dooner's inn, where, not coincidentally, *Just Dessert* was hung.[26] Thus, the painting may have served as a literal reminder for the artist and his friends, many of whom were immigrants, that they were finally receiving their "just desserts." This interpretation is further supported by Harnett's inclusion of a laurel branch, a traditional acknowledgment of valor and good deeds. Included among Harnett's humble studio models are extravagant goods, a halved coconut and maraschino liqueur, rewards more readily available in public eating establishments than in the home.[27]

Harnett turned to fruit painting at two seminal points in his career, both immediately preceding periods of innovation with other subjects. The early, most humble fruit scenes, completed during his student years, were followed by a shift in 1877 to an expanded thematic repertoire, including the inventive tabletop compositions of man-made objects. During his flirtation with fruit themes while in Europe in the early 1880s, Harnett turned to dead game and other vertical hanging subjects, ensuring his reputation with works such as *After the Hunt* of 1885 and *The Old Violin* of 1886 (pls. 34, 37).

Considered as a group, Harnett's fruit paintings played a critical role in the development of his oeuvre. The early works established him as a professional artist and served as a bridge to more varied and original subjects. Experimentation with the fruit theme helped him address compositional issues and formal challenges in works that reveal the vast compendium of European and American sources from which he drew. Harnett's return to fruit paintings throughout his career attests to the significance the theme had for him, and these images concisely demonstrate how he matured conceptually and artistically.

NOTES

I would like to thank Doreen Bolger for her generous assistance in shaping this essay. Marc Simpson and Maria Chamberlin-Hellman also contributed insightful advice for which I am grateful.

1. This essay will not discuss Harnett's student depictions of fruit, such as *A Sprig of Plums* (fig. 56), which are covered in Maria Chamberlin-Hellman, "The Artist and American Art Academies," pp. 137–47.

2. A. J. H. Way, "Fruit-Painting in Oils," *Art Amateur* 16 (December 1886), p. 10.

3. See Richard J. Hooker, *Food and Drink in America: A History* (Indianapolis and New York: Bobbs Merrill Co., 1981), pp. 232–34.

4. James Edward Kelly, quoted in Alfred Frankenstein, *After the Hunt: William Harnett and Other American Still Life Painters, 1870–1900*, rev. ed. (Berkeley and Los Angeles: University of California Press, 1969), p. 38.

5. See "Catalogue of the Permanent Collection Belonging to the Academy," in *Catalogue of the Forty-seventh Annual Exhibition of the Pennsylvania Academy of the Fine Arts, 1876*, exhib. cat. (Philadelphia: Pennsylvania Academy of the Fine Arts, 1876); *Catalogue of the Museum and Gallery of Art of the New-York Historical Society* (New York: New-York Historical Society, 1877); and *Catalogue of Pictures of Old Masters* (New York: Metropolitan Museum of Art, 1880). By 1880, the predominant focus of the Metropolitan's collection was Dutch and Flemish paintings. Of 184 works, 146 were from these schools. I thank Laura A. Coyle for bringing these statistics to my attention.

6. Charles M. Skinner, *Catalogue of Works of Art, with Illustrations and Descriptions; also, Views of the Summer and Winter Homes, etc., of William B. Bement, of Philadelphia, Pa.* (Philadelphia: J. B. Lippincott & Co., 1884), unpaginated.

7. For Wilmarth's influence on Harnett, see Chamberlin-Hellman, "Artist and American Art Academies," pp. 138–39, 142–43.

8. During the late 1870s, both Harnett and Hetzel visited the home of artist Henry Lea Tatnall in Wilmington, Del. (see "Recollections of Henry Lea Tatnall [1829–1885] by His Son Henry Lea Tatnall, Jr.," Henry Lea Tatnall Papers, Historical Society of Delaware, Wilmington, pp. 12–13).

9. For additional biographical information on Hetzel, see Paul A. Chew, ed., *Southwestern Pennsylvania Painters, 1800–1945*, exhib. cat. (Greensburg, Pa.: Westmoreland County Museum of Art, 1981), pp. 51–52; and Paul A. Chew, ed., *Penn's Promise: Still Life Painting in Pennsylvania, 1795–1930*, exhib. cat. (Greensburg, Pa.: Westmoreland Museum of Art, 1988), p. 98.

10. *Catalogue of the Fiftieth Annual Exhibition of the National Academy of Design, 1875*, exhib. cat. (New York: National Academy of Design, 1875), p. 14.

11. See Skinner, *Catalogue of Works of Art*, in which the painting is listed as *Apples and Straw Hat*. The motif of an overturned vessel with fruit spilling out of it was extremely common at the time, due in large part to the widespread distribution of chromolithographs. William Mason Brown's *A Basket of Peaches Upset* was reproduced and marketed in lithograph form, as were Virginia Granberry's *Cherries in a Basket* and *Strawberries in a Basket* (see William H. Gerdts and Russell Burke, *American Still-Life Painting* [New York, Washington, and London: Praeger Publishers, 1971], pp. 68–69).

12. There are two other similar versions of this painting, both from 1877 and both in private collections: *After Lunch II* and *After Lunch III*. *After Lunch II* is identical in size and composition, though it has no flies or drops of water; *After Lunch III* includes grapes.

13. For instance, two versions of Raphaelle Peale's *Still Life with Peach* of about 1816 (both San Diego Museum of Art) and Margaretta Peale's *Still Life with Peaches* (see *American Paintings, Drawings, and*

Sculpture, Sotheby's Arcade Auctions, New York, February 1, 1990, no. 14).

14. "Catalogue of the Permanent Collection Belonging to the Academy," p. 25. This painting, listed as no. 479, was located in the Cope Gallery.

15. During the Harnett "revival" of the 1930s and 1940s, the original painting completed by Carducius Plantagenet Ream for the lithograph *Dessert IV* was attributed to Harnett (see Katharine Morrison McClinton, *The Chromolithographs of Louis Prang* [New York: Clarkson S. Potter, 1973], pp. 180, 183, 184; and Frankenstein, *After the Hunt,* pp. 8, 152).

16. "Painted Like Real Things: The Man Whose Pictures Are a Wonder and a Puzzle," interview in *New York News,* probably 1889 or 1890, quoted in Frankenstein, *After the Hunt,* p. 55.

17. The artist's rendering of *Mortality and Immortality* of 1876 (pl. 3) signals his obvious knowledge of traditional symbolism. The vanitas theme is overtly indicated by the skull, hourglass, and snuffed-out candle.

18. See William H. Gerdts, "On the Tabletop: Europe and America," *Art in America* 60, no. 5 (September–October 1972), p. 65.

19. See Peter Hastings Falk, ed., *The Annual Exhibition Record of the Pennsylvania Academy of the Fine Arts, 1807–1870* (reprint ed., Madison, Conn.: Sound View Press, 1988), p. 175. In 1865, Preyer's *Still Life* was exhibited (no. 533); and in 1868, his *Fruit* (no. 187), *Cherries and Nuts* (no. 230), and *Fruit Drawing* (no. 316) were shown.

20. See Andrea Gasten, "Theodorus Smits, Still-Life with a Crab and Grapes," in E. de Jongh, *Still-Life in the Age of Rembrandt,* exhib. cat. (Auckland, N.Z.: Auckland City Art Gallery, 1982), pp. 109–11. The illusionistic rendering of grapes as a sign of competency finds its roots in the classical tale of birds pecking at Zeuxis's painted grapes.

This legend, which commonly appeared in seventeenth-century writings, such as Roger de Piles's *Cours de peinture par principes,* led to the development of lighting studies of grapes and other spherical objects. Denis Diderot, in his *Pensées détachées sur la peinture,* wrote: "One can reduce all the magic of chiaroscuro to a bunch of grapes; it's a beautiful idea and can be simplified. The most vast scene is nothing but a single grape of the bunch" (quoted in Gasten, "Theodorus Smits," p. 111).

21. Frankenstein, *After the Hunt,* p. 59.

22. Michael Quick, "Munich and American Realism," in Michael Quick, Eberhard Ruhner, and Richard V. West, *Munich and American Realism in the Nineteenth Century,* exhib. cat. (Sacramento: E. B. Crocker Art Gallery, 1978), pp. 28, 33–34.

23. A. J. H. Way, "Fruit-Painting in Oils: II. Treatment of Pineapples, Oranges, Lemons, Bananas, and Apples," *Art Amateur* 16 (January 1887), p. 32.

24. See "Theodore Stewart," clipping from an unidentified and undated newspaper, Alfred Frankenstein Papers, Archives of American Art, Smithsonian Institution, Washington, D.C., microfilm, roll 1377, frame 88; and "Trade in Philadelphia," *Dry Goods Economist* 47, no. 2521 (November 12, 1892), p. 38.

25. On Dooner, see Doreen Bolger, "The Patrons of the Artist: Emblems of Commerce and Culture" (pp. 73–75, 82). I am indebted to the author for sharing her illuminating thoughts on *Just Dessert* with me.

26. John H. Campbell and Daniel J. Dougherty, *History of the Society of the Friendly Sons of St. Patrick for the Relief of Emigrants from Ireland of Philadelphia* (Philadelphia: Friendly Sons of St. Patrick, 1952), p. 32.

27. *The Wm. Michael Harnett Collection: His Own Reserved Paintings, Models and Studio Furnishings,* sale cat., Stan. V. Henkels at Thos. Birch's Sons, Auctioneers, Philadelphia, February 23–24, 1893, p. 22, no. 319.

"THE BEST INDEX OF AMERICAN LIFE"

Newspapers in the Artist's Work

LAURA A. COYLE

Over the course of his career William Michael Harnett masterfully painted reams of dangled, folded, propped, and clipped newspapers. His brilliant exploits with newsprint as a formal device, however, have diverted attention from the intriguing study of what newspapers meant to the artist and his audience. Harnett strove "to make the composition tell a story," while insisting that, "as a rule, new things do not paint well."[1] Yet he regularly depicted newspapers, the newest objects of all, which suggests he painted them for their narrative potential rather than their visual appeal.

Harnett included newspapers in his paintings in two ways. From the beginning of his career until 1890, he painted folded newspapers in tabletop still lifes such as *Still Life with Letter to Thomas B. Clarke* of 1879, *Still Life with Three Castles Tobacco* of 1880, and *Emblems of Peace* of 1890 (pls. 15, 18, 46). The story-telling power of the papers is great, especially when part of the banner and date is revealed. Harnett also painted clippings as if they were pasted onto a flat surface parallel to the picture plane, a device he used a few times early in his career, as in *The Artist's Letter Rack* of 1879 (pl. 17), and more often toward the end, as in *The Faithful Colt* of 1890 (pl. 48). These illegible clippings teased and intrigued his viewers but retained their narrative potential nevertheless.

Earlier American artists had painted newspapers, particularly in genre paintings. William Sidney Mount and Richard Caton Woodville were adept at using them in their pictures to deliver unequivocal political messages (fig. 96).[2] Harnett's use of newspapers marks a significant departure that reflects changes in the papers themselves since Mount's and Woodville's day. Into mid-century, newspapers were primarily devoted to articles about partisan politics, war, and finance; by

the time Harnett painted them, papers covered the whole range of American society and did so more impartially.

Although newspapers played a significant role in the lives of most Americans, they were particularly important for Harnett, who claimed his first job was newsboy for the local paper.[3] Whether or not it was

Fig. 96. Richard Caton Woodville, *Politics in an Oyster House,* 1848. Oil on canvas, 16 x 13 in. Walters Art Gallery, Baltimore

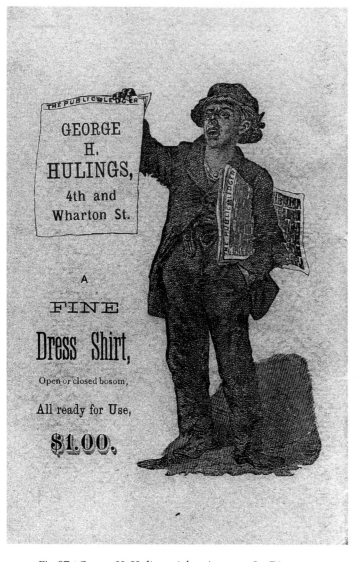

Fig 97. *George H. Hulings.* Advertisement. In *Directory of the Philadelphia Annual Conference of the Methodist Episcopal Church* (Philadelphia: William H. Pile's Sons, 1887), back cover. Historic St. George's United Methodist Church, Philadelphia

we know about his life and work, aside from his paintings and drawings themselves, has been gleaned from newspapers.

Harnett's paintings of newspapers naturally appealed to reporters. Since he worked outside avant-garde art circles, he generally was treated much more kindly by the dailies than by the specialized art press. Not only did reporters appreciate, understandably, newspapers as a subject, but they also had great admiration for Harnett's veristic style, probably because of their appetite for facts.[10] Harnett's paintings do indeed present a convincing depiction of the real world. The successful businessmen who made up a large portion of Harnett's patrons were also less likely to read about culture, and particularly art, in art periodicals than in the newspapers they read every day. They seem to have shared the newspaper writers' affection for convincing assemblages of everyday objects; and if the positive reviews Harnett received did not actually mold the taste of his patrons, presumably they reinforced their materialistic inclinations. An advertisment for the firm of George Hulings, who commissioned the artist's second rack picture (pl. 44), underscores the vital position the papers held in the lives of these men.

Harnett's contemporaries would have immediately associated these paintings with the roles the newspapers occupied in all aspects of daily life. The artist was active during an era of rapid and often difficult change—a time that embraced nostalgia but also acknowledged, and often commended, progress.[11] Harnett's newspaper still lifes may have appealed to his followers on a psychological level because of the way they balance the old (objects softened by the "mellowing effect of age")[12] and the new (the daily newspaper, symbol of contemporary American life). Harnett's incredible fool-the-eye style made this harmony seem real,[13] attracting viewers who were both nostalgic and progressive—potentially a very wide audience during the Gilded Age.

This blending of tradition and modernity may be what Harnett's patrons, particularly the wealthy businessmen, responded to in his still lifes. Although they, like most Americans, wished to uphold the traditional values of honesty, competition, generosity, and fair play, as a group they had called those values into question. One could profit heavily if old-fashioned ethics were sacrificed to the new realities of the market; enormous fortunes were amassed during this period, often through unfair and uncompetitive methods. Successful entrepreneurs may have professed their support for traditional values, but they often must have found it difficult to reconcile words with deeds. With the paintings they purchased from Harnett, however, they could acquire the illusion of accord between the old and the new and take comfort in a convincing but wholly imaginary world.

true, his statement implied that he counted himself among the heroes of the late nineteenth century, the self-made men.[4] Probably more relevant than his childhood experience was the role the papers played in the course of Harnett's career.[5] The only autobiographical statement that survives is the oft-quoted interview from the *New York News.*[6] Most contemporary reviews of his work appeared in the papers.[7] Anecdotes about Harnett's phenomenal style, such as those relating to his near-arrest on counterfeiting charges for painting currency, were also featured in the papers.[8] Since newspaper reviews and articles were potential patrons' main sources of information about the artist and his work, Harnett's success ultimately lay with the newspapers.[9] Even today, almost everything

By the 1870s, newspapers had regained their position, lost earlier in the century to magazines and books, as the primary bearer of ideas.[14] The sheer number of papers available was staggering and continued to grow. Between 1870 and 1880, the number of titles nearly doubled.[15] The aggregate circulation for the nation in 1880 climbed to over 3.5 million per day—greater than anywhere else in the world.[16] The profusion of mass-marketed, inexpensive papers was possible because the popular press was able to draw upon a large reading public. The democratic system boasted widespread opportunities for education, and investment in education yielded literacy.[17] Harnett's paintings of newspapers were part of an educational phenomenon: pictures incorporating words proliferated during the late nineteenth century, the first time that a broad base of people in America could read and write.[18]

While the growth of the press depended on widespread literacy, newspapers in turn became one of the instruments of education. As the papers emerged from domination by political parties, they became one of the most important interpreters of and guides to the rapidly changing world. In 1880, Dr. J. M. Gregory maintained that "the free press [was] the necessary complement of the free school." "Americans live, work and think through the newspaper," which Gregory claimed was "the best index of American life."[19] Another writer noted that the press had come to rank "with the schools, the churches, and the libraries as an educating and elevating influence in society."[20]

Early in his career, Harnett assembled a completely new kind of tabletop still life, frequently incorporating a folded newspaper. As casually arranged as these compositions appear at first, Harnett calculated the placement of each object, and the newspapers are no exception. Although the papers look as if they have been read, he carefully manipulated them so that in many cases part, but never all, of the masthead remains visible.

The early newspaper pictures that include mugs and pipes have been called "bachelor's" still lifes,[21] an allusion to the solitary male activities they imply.[22] It has been suggested as well that their popularity reflected the growing taste among Harnett's patrons for Old Master still lifes.[23] Although valid to a point, these observations do not account for the significance of newspapers within Harnett's work. Even though mugs and especially pipes were attributes of the bachelor, or at least of men, the newspaper was no longer. Papers increasingly depended upon advertising to remain financially viable and consequently were geared to the broadest possible readership. Recognizing that women controlled more and more of the household finances, editors and business managers made substantial attempts to appeal to female readers and advertised products and services of particular interest to women.[24] Through newspapers such as the *New York Herald,* the paper that earned more from advertising than any other[25] (and the one Harnett represented most often), the spirit, if not the physical presence, of women subtly intruded into previously exclusive male domains. Futhermore, reading a newspaper could not be considered a strictly solitary activity. Harnett's paintings describe a daily ritual—looking over the news from the outside world in the privacy of one's own home. The purpose of the newspaper, however, remained undeniably social even when it was read alone, so taking in the day's news was arguably both private and social.

In these bachelor's still lifes, such as *A Man's Table Reversed* of 1877 (pl. 7), one senses palpable activity conveyed by common objects: tobacco spills out of a favorite pipe, a cracker and crumbs litter the table, and an earthenware beer mug rests by a creased newspaper. Just as American portrait and landscape paintings have been considered still lifes,[26] Harnett's innovative tabletops may be viewed as genre scenes, paintings that tell a story about everyday life. While genre pictures include people, Harnett's pictures recount a familiar story with still-life models alone. The newspaper's reader—the lead, yet unportrayed, character—appears to have stepped away momentarily or to be seated just out of sight.

Even when the banner of a paper is not visible and we do not know the original owner of a picture, the newspaper still lifes tell us something about Harnett's early career and audience. Since Harnett painted a good number of such pictures and supported himself by selling his work, he must have found a ready market for them. The purchasers of these paintings must have been—or wished to give the impression that they were—literate newspaper readers. And the plot thickens considerably when the banner of a newspaper—and therefore the character of the paper and, by extension, of the unseen reader—can be discerned, especially as he may have been the owner of the painting.

When a banner is partially revealed, Harnett usually showed enough of it so that his contemporaries, who would been more familiar with the masthead typefaces and logos than we are today, would have had little trouble recognizing the paper.[27] The titles Harnett painted most frequently in the 1870s and in 1880 were among the most popular in New York—the *Times, Sun,* and *Herald*—and in Philadelphia—the *Times* and *Public Ledger.*[28] We know little about the original owners of most of Harnett's small, early paintings, and even when the first owner can be identified and we know the picture was painted for him, the city of the painted newspaper does not necessarily indicate where he lived. For example, a painting presumably done for Dennis Gale, an art dealer who lived and worked in Philadelphia, includes

Fig. 98. William M. Harnett, *Solace*, 1878. Oil on canvas, 12¼ x 10¼ in. Private collection

the *New York Herald* (fig. 32). Harnett himself lived in Philadelphia at this time, but he painted more papers from New York—they must have been easier to sell.

The *Herald,* featured in Gale's painting and in so many others, such as *Solace* of 1878 (fig. 98), was Harnett's favorite newspaper. The *Herald* conformed to a type—the eastern, big-city, nationally known paper—but it also maintained its own special character, which would have been widely appreciated when it appeared in Harnett's paintings. One of the first cheap newspapers with mass appeal, by 1870 the *Herald* was known for its adventurous and energetic coverage of national and world events. Along with the news, the *Herald* covered Wall Street, the arts, sports,

society and shipping events, and local crusades for civic improvement. The paper favored the Democrats but most often appeared to be above partisanship. In the 1870s, circulation reached 150,000, and the *Herald* enjoyed a distinguished reputation coast to coast.[29] Unlike many other papers, the *Herald* devoted its entire front page to advertisements. The obvious ties the newspaper held to the world of commerce must have been not only acceptable to its readership but indeed part of its attraction, particularly for readers who were actively engaged in wholesale and retail businesses, as were many of Harnett's patrons.[30]

At the end of the 1870s, Harnett also began to depict foreign newspapers in his paintings. Once

Fig. 99. William M. Harnett, *Still Life with Violin,* 1886. Oil on canvas, 20 x 24 in. The New Britain Museum of American Art, Conn., Grace Judd Landers Fund

Fig. 100. William M. Harnett, *Still Life with the Toledo Blade,* 1886. Oil on canvas, 22⅛ x 26³⁄₁₆ in.
The Toledo Museum of Art, Ohio, Gift of Mr. and Mrs. Roy Rike

abroad, in the early 1880s, he continued to include them, as in *Still Life with "Le Figaro"* and *Munich Still Life,* both of 1882 (pls. 23, 24). From 1883 until the end of his career, however, Harnett executed far fewer still lifes with folded newspapers, both in absolute numbers and in relation to his exploration of other motifs.

When Harnett did paint this subject after 1883, the pictures tend to be larger than before, such as *Still Life with Violin* of 1886,[31] *Ease* of 1887, and *Emblems of Peace* of 1890 (fig. 99, pls. 41, 46). These later works sometimes show an American paper from outside the New York–Philadelphia area, as in *Still Life with the*

Toledo Blade of 1886 and *The Cincinnati Enquirer* of 1888 (figs. 100, 14). While not all the early provenances of the late newspaper paintings are known, *Ease, Toledo Blade,* and *Emblems of Peace* were purchased by wealthy, self-made businessmen: James Terry Abbe, Isaac Newton Reed, and Charles T. Shean, respectively. Some of Harnett's patrons would have found newspaper subjects particularly appropriate because of their connections to the business. Abbe, who commissioned *Ease,* was president of the company that published the *Springfield Daily Union,* and a George Reed, who may have been related to Isaac, was the managing editor of the Toledo paper. Even though it is not always possible to identify which paintings they owned, several of Harnett's other patrons and their friends—Peter Samuel Dooner, Henry Bentley, Monroe Smith, and Henry A. Rowan[32]—also had ties to the newspaper business, which would have made Harnett's pictures particularly attractive to them.

While the circumstances of each commission varied, that of the *Toledo Blade* is particularly well documented and may throw light on why, beyond any psychological appeal the subject might have had, a patron would have wanted a painting that features a newspaper. Reed hailed from Toledo and was a prominent member of his profession, the wholesale, and later retail, drug trade.[33] He probably asked Harnett to include the *Blade* to indicate his hometown and, if a member of his family was its managing editor, his personal connection to the paper. But the *Toledo Blade* stood for much more than that. Under editor David Locke, who joined the staff in 1865, the paper was transformed from a respected local organ into a publication of national repute.[34] By the time Harnett painted it, the *Blade* was at the peak of its influence. Although Toledo's population was only a little over fifty thousand in 1886, hundreds of thousands of readers all over the country knew and closely followed the weekly edition of the *Blade*.[35] Since the rest of the nation presumably knew about and thought more highly of Toledo because it was the home of the paper, Reed's commission was also a declaration of civic and regional pride. Not surprisingly, the installation of Harnett's painting in Reed's drugstore for all Toledo to see was duly reported; a writer, perhaps for the *Blade* itself, deemed it a picture "well worth seeing" and concluded that it represented "the highest triumph of artistic genius. . . approaching the actual—in the perfect reproduction of the subject presented."[36]

Although Harnett painted fewer folded newspaper pictures late in his career, he executed several works that show a single hanging object, often accompanied by a clipping, such as *The Faithful Colt* of 1890 (pl. 48). Trompe-l'oeil painting is most successful when still-life objects are rendered as if parallel to the picture plane, within a shallow space, and against a flat background—a formula Harnett employed with great skill. His clippings appear to be pasted onto the background of the picture; their apparent proximity emphasizes the shallowness of the pictorial space, and their apparent flatness reinforces the vertical background plane. Since Harnett could paint them so convincingly, they add to the overall trompe-l'oeil effect. Although none of the clippings is legible, viewers inevitably associated the unreadable text with the juxtaposed object. A reporter writing about *The Old Violin* of 1886 (pl. 37) insisted that the completely illegible clipping referred to the artist.[37] This compulsion to connect the object with illegible text added to viewers' fascination with the painting and encouraged them to use their imagination to invent a text for the clipping, thus inventing their own meaning for the picture.

Harnett devoted much of his considerable talent to painting newspapers, and the contemporary understanding and acceptance of the place they held would have created an intended and unavoidable content in his work. Since word of Harnett's virtuosity spread mainly through the papers, the artist became famous, in part, for painting the medium that promoted him. Favorable reviews must have encouraged him to continue to paint newspapers, and his patrons, especially those tied to the newspaper business, must have been encouraged to purchase or commission the works. Although on first "reading," Harnett's use of newspaper seems exclusively formal and deceptively simple, the story he tells with his pages and clippings proves extensive and complex. His pictures of folded papers are a type of genre painting in which the patrons are the main character; while not actually portrayed, they are suggested and defined by the objects that are represented. The still lifes with illegible clippings, especially when paired with a single object, could be interpreted uniquely by every viewer. The meaning of Harnett's work has largely been ignored for a century. This brief study of but one aspect of the artist's subject matter suggests that others be explored because, as expressive as the newspapers are, presumably they tell only part of the story.

NOTES

I would like to thank John Wilmerding, Doreen Bolger, and Thayer Tolles Mickel for their generous assistance and encouragement during the preparation of this essay.

1. "Painted Like Real Things: The Man Whose Pictures Are a Wonder and a Puzzle," interview in *New York News,* probably 1889 or 1890, quoted in Alfred Franken-stein, *After the Hunt: William Harnett and Other American Still Life Painters, 1870–1900,* rev. ed. (Berkeley and Los Angeles: University of California Press, 1969), p. 55.

2. See Barbara Groseclose, "Politics and American Genre Painting of the Nineteenth Century," *Antiques* 120 (November 1981), p. 1214; and David Cassedy and Gail Shrott, *William Sidney Mount: Works in the Collection of the Museums at Stony Brook,* exhib. cat. (Stony Brook, N.Y.: Museums at Stony Brook, 1983), pp. 61, 63. See also *The Newspaper in American Art,* exhib. cat. (San Diego: Fine Arts Gallery of San Diego, 1965), unpaginated.

3. "My father died in Philadelphia when I was a little boy, and I was obliged to do something to help support my mother and the children. My first work was selling newspapers" ("Painted Like Real Things," quoted in Frankenstein, *After the Hunt,* p. 29). One of Harnett's patrons, Charles T. Shean, a hotel proprietor from Springfield, Mass., earned his living as a newsboy until a wealthy man offered him a position as a bootblack at an important hotel. Newsboys became a frequent subject of sentimental mid- and late-nineteenth-century genre painting and poetry.

4. The subtitle of the interview "Painted Like Real Things" reinforces this idea: "How He Began and the Success He Has Met With—Poverty Forced Him to Earn a Living in the Line in Which He Excels." On self-made men, see E. Anthony Rotundo, "Learning about Manhood: Gender Ideals and the Middle-Class Family in Nineteenth-Century America," in J. A. Mangan and James Walvin, eds., *Manliness and Morality: Middle-Class Masculinity in Britain and America, 1800–1940* (New York: St. Martin's Press, 1987), pp. 35–51.

5. See John Tebbel, *The Compact History of the American Newspaper,* rev. ed. (New York: Hawthorn Books, 1969), pp. 125–26.

6. "Painted Like Real Things." The newspaper interview in question-and-answer form was invented in 1859, when Horace Greeley traveled to Utah to interview Brigham Young for the *New-York Daily Tribune* (Tebbel, *Compact History,* p. 109).

7. See William H. Gerdts, "The Artist's Public Face: Lifetime Exhibitions and Critical Reception," pp. 87–98.

8. "Painted Like Real Things," quoted in Frankenstein, *After the Hunt,* p. 56.

9. Harnett made a point of reminding his public of the notices he had received in the popular press, saying "One of them [the paintings of money] was exhibited in this city, and had attracted several notices from the daily newspapers" (ibid.).

10. When *The Old Violin* (pl. 37) was exhibited in 1886 at the Thirteenth Cincinnati Industrial Exposition, its trompe-l'oeil technique caused a sensation that was extensively covered in the press. Three enthusiastic reviews of the painting were reprinted in a brochure (Blemly scrapbook, Alfred Frankenstein Papers, Archives of American Art, Smithsonian Instution, Washington, D.C., microfilm, roll 1374, frames 279–82) that announces the sale of the lithograph after *The Old Violin* published by F. Tuchfarber Co. Each reviewer specifically refers to Harnett's extraordinary rendering of the clipping. Clearly, Tuchfarber believed the notices that appeared in the press would be the most effective promotion for his print.

11. See Daniel E. Sutherland, *The Expansion of Everyday Life, 1860–1876* (New York: Harper & Row, 1989), pp. xi–xiii.

12. "Painted Like Real Things," quoted in Frankenstein, *After the Hunt,* p. 55.

13. This idea is clearly related and greatly indebted to David M. Lubin's discussion of Harnett's trompe-l'oeil painting as an attempt to revivify old-fashioned values by revivifying the objects of the past ("Trompe l'Oeil Painting and Commodity Display in Late-Nineteenth-Century America," paper delivered at the International Convention of the American Studies Association and the Canadian Association for American Studies, Toronto,

November 2–5, 1989). Lubin's thesis, however, deals only with old objects in Harnett's paintings.

14. Tebbel, *Compact History,* p. 125.

15. S. N. D. North, *History and Present Condition of the Newspaper and Periodical Press of the United States, with a Catalogue of the Publications of the Census Year,* prepared for the Department of the Interior, Census Office (Washington, D.C.: Government Printing Office, 1884), p. 58. The population during the same period increased by a third.

16. Ibid., p. 75.

17. In 1840, the rate of illiteracy for the total population twenty years old and over was 22 percent; for the population ten years old and over, by 1880 it was 17 percent, and by 1900, 10.7 percent (U.S. Bureau of the Census, *Historical Statistics of the United States, Colonial Times to 1970,* pt. 1 [Washington, D.C.: Government Printing Office, 1975], pp. 365, 382).

18. See Robert F. Chirico, "Language and Imagery in Late Nineteenth-Century Trompe l'Oeil," *Arts Magazine* 59, no. 7 (March 1985), p. 113; and Barbara Novak, *American Painting of the Nineteenth Century: Realism, Idealism, and the American Experience,* 2nd ed. (New York: Harper & Row, 1979), pp. 225, 226.

19. Dr. J. M. Gregory, "The American Newspaper and American Education," *Journal of Social Science* 12 (December 1880), pp. 63, 62, 61.

20. North, *History and Present Condition,* p. 52.

21. Frankenstein, *After the Hunt,* p. 42.

22. See William H. Gerdts, *Painters of the Humble Truth: Masterpieces of American Still Life, 1801–1939,* exhib. cat., Philbrook Art Center, Tulsa, Okla. (Columbia, Mo., and London: University of Missouri Press, 1981), pp. 155–56.

23. Ibid., p. 158.

24. See Sidney Kobre, *The Yellow Press and Gilded Age Journalism* ([Tallahassee]: Florida State University, 1964), pp. 18–20.

25. See Frank Luther Mott, *American Journalism: A History of Newspapers in the United States through 250 Years, 1690 to 1940* (New York: Macmillan Co., 1941), p. 420.

26. "Much American art . . . can in fact be seen as still life, whether a portrait by Copley or a landscape by Lane" (Novak, *American Painting,* p. 221).

27. Harnett often included a date on his newspapers so that many of them can be identified to the day, but no corollation has emerged between the subject of any painting and that day's news.

28. Harnett was more selective than might first appear. It should be remembered that at this time New York alone had twenty-nine daily newspapers and Philadelphia had twenty-four (North, *History and Present Condition,* p. 77).

29. Kobre, *Yellow Press,* pp. 81, 83, 85–86; and Mott, p. 420.

30. See Doreen Bolger, "The Patrons of the Artist: Emblems of Commerce and Culture," pp. 73–85.

31. *Still Life with Violin* includes the Philadelphia *Times.*

32. Bolger, "Patrons of the Artist."

33. See Susan E. Strickler, *The Toledo Museum of Art: American Paintings* (Toledo, Ohio: Toledo Museum of Art, 1979), p. 57. The painting is inscribed on the reverse: *PAINTED TO ORDER / FOR I. N. REED. / OF TOLEDO. / OHIO. / 1886 / W^m. M. Harnett.*

34. See John M. Harrison, *The Blade of Toledo: The First 150 Years* (Toledo: Toledo Blade Co., 1985), p. 82.

35. Ibid., pp. 112, 85.

36. "A Fine Picture," quoted in Frankenstein, *After the Hunt,* p. 7.

37. The review reads, in part: "In the lower left corner is an envelope bearing upon its face the artist's name, and above this, a newspaper clipping containing a complimentary allusion to the work" (from a brochure for *The Old Violin* lithograph, Blemly scrapbook, frame 282).

"JOB LOT CHEAP"

Books, Bindings, and the Old Bookseller

ANDREW WALKER

In 1878, two years before leaving Philadelphia for six years of study abroad, William Michael Harnett painted *Job Lot Cheap* (pl. 9). The title refers to an early mercantile practice in which a large assortment of goods is sold as a single unit to reduce unwanted or out-of-date stock quickly and profitably. Used books are the discarded merchandise in *Job Lot Cheap*. The colorful pile of handcrafted and machine-bound volumes is heaped on top of a book-peddler's table.[1] Harnett's precise rendering of the textures of leather, cloth, and paper is substantial and convincing. The torn page that extends over the edge of the table, a common device in still-life painting, reinforces the viewer's sense of involvement. Across the front of the wooden table are torn green, blue, and yellow publishers' labels. In the lower left corner, haphazardly written on the inside cover of an old book, is a notice announcing the sale.

One naturally wonders if the scattered volumes are painted versions of books actually owned by Harnett. Many of the old Latin and German vellum-bound volumes auctioned at the 1893 sale of the contents of his studio were described in the accompanying catalogue as "One of Mr. Harnett's famous models" or "A favorite model." Even more suggestive are the ten lots of untitled old books that are described as "Used as models."[2] Aside from this provocative association, however, little empirical data exist to situate Harnett's picture within the broader social and economic milieu in which it was produced.[3]

After completing *Job Lot Cheap*, Harnett sent a photograph of it to his friend Edward Taylor Snow and wrote on the reverse: *To E. T. Snow, thanks for the idea, Yours Truly, William M. Harnett*.[4] The painting was later sold to Byron Nugent, a wealthy dry-goods

merchant in Saint Louis. In later years, Snow became an art dealer in Philadelphia and helped shape Harnett's artistic reputation, but in 1878 he was working for the large Philadelphia dry-goods firm Cooper and Conard.[5] Could Snow's "idea" have been that a large-scale painting about books and possessions would be attractive to a businessman such as Nugent? But would a modern merchant who was helping to transform America's consumer economy purchase a painting that celebrates a business practice that was already outdated? While *Job Lot Cheap* certainly reflects the enthusiasm of the late-nineteenth-century merchant class for collecting valuable objects,[6] it also suggests the period's changing attitudes toward the appearance, display, and marketing of books. In *Job Lot Cheap,* the overall presentation is a metaphor for a creative use of the past in order to deflect, and even heal, during a period of complex economic and social change.[7]

Most of the book spines in *Job Lot Cheap* are blurred and illegible. By virtue of accessibility and formal arrangement, only four titles are clear: Homer's *Odyssey, Cyclopaedia Americana/Vol. II, Arabian Nights,* and a light blue, torn paperback translation of *Forty-five Guardsmen* (1848) by Dumas *père*. These volumes represent distinct categories of literature that would have served as the foundation of a respectable home library for America's growing reading public at the time. Beginning in the 1870s, appropriate shelf lists for the middle-class household were a topic of increasing interest. Popular monthly magazines such as *Scribner's* and *Lippincott's* printed book reviews to help the "average" reader make suitable purchases. But more important to book publishers and distributors was the establishment of criteria for the library.

Fig. 101. William M. Harnett, *Job Lot Cheap* (detail, pl. 9)

The February 2, 1878, issue of the trade journal *Publisher's Weekly* outlined its version of the mission of "The Home Library":

> The standard library['s] . . . purpose is not to make money, but to make men. The broader a man is the more is his enjoyment; and no man should feel at his ease until he has accumulated about him some reasonable representation of the great authors who appeal to every person of average intelligence.[8]

The approved categories included books of general knowledge, religious classics, Shakespeare, the best American and English poets, selections of Europe's contemporary masters, books on popular science, natural histories, and children's stories.

The four volumes in the center of the composition represent several of these categories. The 1850 edition of *Encyclopaedia Americana,* for example, contained general knowledge about the arts, sciences, politics, history, and biography.[9] The *Odyssey* and its companion, the *Illiad,* were often included in the World's Greatest Literature lists printed in booksellers' journals during the 1880s.[10] Dumas's *Forty-five Guardsmen* was considered a masterpiece of contemporary French literature and was included in both the affordable

Parlour and Seaside Library series.[11] The *Arabian Nights* was widely translated and popular among all age groups throughout the nineteenth century.[12]

During the last quarter of the century, the successful development of bookbinding machines revolutionized the trade by answering the increased demand for inexpensive books.[13] One of the new printing machines was capable of transferring a roll of paper into a completely bound and finished book "at the rate of 5,000 copies an hour" (fig. 102).[14] Writings on bookbinding published between 1880 and 1900 ranged from business journals such as *American Bookmaker,* which kept specialized labor and consumer groups informed about changes in the trade, to polemical treatises published privately or in expensive art journals aimed at wealthy book collectors.[15] *American Bookmaker* championed mass-produced books as the answer to new consumer demands.

> Books for mountain and sea-side resorts, books for loiterers and loungers at watering-places, books for those who "go a-fishing,["] handbooks for tourists. . . . These are the golden days of the paper cover, the limp leather, the flexible cloth, the "pocket-book" form and the tuck attachment.[16]

On the other hand, *Art Amateur,* a magazine published largely for connoisseurs and collectors, praised the exquisite handcrafted bindings of the Middle Ages and Renaissance as models for the modern bibliophile and criticized machine-bound books as aesthetically and morally inferior.[17]

All kinds of book bindings—leather, cloth, and paper—are represented in *Job Lot Cheap.* Any sense of the differences in the materials is lessened by the

Fig. 102. "New Book Perfecting and Printing Machine," *American Bookmaker: A Journal of Technical Art and Information* 5 (November 1887), p. 180

NEW BOOK PERFECTING AND PRINTING MACHINE.

equalizing effects of age. Worn leather edges and ripped paper covers eased the class-oriented conflicts that surrounded books and bookmaking. In the painting, age becomes a symbol of sorts that extends from the book titles, to the bindings, to the very nature of consumer display.

The wooden surface on top of which the books are piled is an antiquarian bookseller's table, a type of peddler's display that was essentially obsolete at the time the painting was executed. Earlier in the century, the peddler had been perceived as a trickster,[18] a popular literary character whose distrusted magical powers lured unsuspecting buyers and encouraged frivolous purchases.[19] After the Civil War, he was seen as a grave character versed in the book lore of all cultures.[20] His store or bookstall was typically cluttered with unkempt folios and octavos. A drawing by Edwin Austin Abbey represents one view of the

Fig. 103. William M. Harnett, *Job Lot Cheap* (detail, pl. 9)

mysterious secondhand bookshop (fig. 104). Heaped in a box in the foreground are used and torn books priced at five cents each. For the growing numbers of middle-class shoppers in the 1870s and 1880s, however, the bookseller was not a trickster but a wise wizard whose power to persuade buyers was less socially threatening because of the moral and intellectual value of his product.

As a subject of poems, paintings, and even personal reminiscences, the seller of old books grew in strength in the 1890s. In 1891, William Brotherhead, once an antiquarian bookseller himself, published *Forty Years among the Old Booksellers of Philadelphia,* in which he characterized the bookshop as intellectually stimulating and the bookseller as a learned man and therefore more than a general tradesman.[21] In paintings, however, Harnett and his contemporary John Frederick Peto chose to depict the bookstall without its peddler. In his *Job Lot Cheap,* completed after 1900 (fig. 105),[22] Peto hints at the old man's presence using the fragment of a torn sign announcing

Dealer in Books tacked to the open door. While Harnett's picture invites us to walk up and touch the books, Peto's emphasizes distance. The well-thumbed, untitled volumes are visible only through a window.

The seller of old books was a powerful symbol because of changes in the marketing of books and other consumer goods at the time. Beginning in the 1870s, both the retail stores of large publishing houses and the book divisions of department stores began challenging the old bookstalls and street vendors. "Ballade of the Old Bookseller," a poem published in an 1888 edition of John Wanamaker and Company's monthly *Book News,* underscores the nostalgic meaning that surrounded this type of peddler:[23]

> He sits alone, a dirt-grimed man,
> With portly tomes and dust around,
> And piles of learning's store doth scan,
> With books from ceiling high to ground.
> In chaos grand, without a plan,
> Old authors lie; and by the mound
> *He* sits alone, a dirt-grimed man
> Midst portly tomes and dust around.[24]

The new professional bookseller began following trends that would further revolutionize methods of commodity display. Stacks of products arranged in clean, evenly lit spaces became a standard marketing practice. The American Book Association's display at the Philadelphia Centennial Exposition of 1876 illustrates the new trend (fig. 106). The books are ordered by size in rows, and the tables are stacked with editions in such a way that any semblance of disorder is absent. By the 1890s, the book peddler had all but disappeared from the competitive market. The disarray of books in Harnett's painting signaled a practice made obsolete by a more modern and democratic system of merchandising and shopping.

Merchants such as Byron Nugent and John Wanamaker replaced the peddler evoked in *Job Lot Cheap.* In their department stores, they initiated a new system of selling goods that used common-sense advertising, creative display methods, and, above all, standardized pricing to attract middle-class shoppers.[25] B. Nugent and Brother was one of the largest and most innovative department stores.[26] Each year, the firm issued a catalogue that pictured views of interiors and special store displays, which Nugent hoped would entice passersby.[27]

Wanamaker shared Nugent's modern views on advertising and product display. In 1879, as Harnett was painting *Job Lot Cheap,* John Wanamaker and Company was moving toward an orderliness of display, even of books, such as that recorded in the Centennial stereograph. Wanamaker initiated the practice of selling books in department stores in 1877, a year after he opened his Grand Depot store in Philadelphia.[28] "A 'book department'" he wrote,"may

Fig. 104. Edwin Austin Abbey, "Over the Counter, Spectacles on Nose, Old Richard Stooped," in John Townsend Trowbridge, *The Book of Gold and Other Poems* (New York: Harper & Bros., 1878), frontispiece

"OVER THE COUNTER, SPECTACLES ON NOSE, OLD RICHARD STOOPED."

Fig. 105. John F. Peto, *Job Lot Cheap,* after 1900. Oil on canvas, 30 x 40⅛ in.
The Fine Arts Museums of San Francisco, Gift of Mr. and Mrs. John D. Rockefeller 3rd (1979.7.81)

be a bookstore that creates readers, that puts books where busy people can catch glimpses of radiant spheres within this world of everyday duties."[29] Each year, rare, foreign, and popular titles were added to the general inventory of the store. By 1882, a bookstore had been made a separate department on the first floor, and Wanamaker's monthly journal *Book News* began publication.[30] On busy days it was estimated that the sale of books brought in nearly one-tenth of all the store's receipts. By 1887, John Wanamaker and Company was doing the largest retail book business in the United States.[31] An early-twentieth-century advertisement shows that the store continued to display old volumes, neatly stacked, one upon the other (fig. 107).

Fig. 106. *American Book Association Centennial Display,* 1876. Stereograph.
Centennial Photographic Co., Philadelphia.
Historical Society of Pennsylvania, Philadelphia

Fig. 107. "The Wanamaker Bookstore, on the Main Floor," *A Friendly Guide to the Wanamaker Store*
(Philadelphia: John Wanamaker, 1917), p. 15

Wanamaker's "one-price system" was carried from Philadelphia to Saint Louis and beyond.[32] This novel approach to marketing and constructing consumer desire, however, threatened to displace the individual, specialized merchant.[33] The economic shift from specialty shops to corporate structures is fundamental to the meaning of Harnett's picture. The books in *Job Lot Cheap* represent the increased availability of literature to a wider audience, while the bindings suggest the trappings of the upper classes of society. Harnett made the image nostalgic by depicting old books in a display that consciously evokes the metaphor of the early peddler. On one level, nostalgia defused and even denied jarring economic change for the patron, Byron Nugent, who helped bring about that change. But the nostalgia of the painting was also a reminder of how superior the modern system of shopping was at giant department stores that catered to thousands of middle-class consumers. *Job Lot Cheap* pays homage to a business practice vanquished by its owner.

Notes

I would like to acknowledge Elizabeth Johns, David Brigham, and Sylvia Yount, all at the University of Pennsylvania.

1. See Alfred Frankenstein, *After the Hunt: William Harnett and Other American Still Life Painters, 1870–1900,* rev. ed. (Berkeley and Los Angeles: University of California Press, 1969), p. 47.

2. *The Wm. Michael Harnett Collection: His Own Reserved Paintings, Models and Studio Furnishings,* sale cat., Stan. V. Henkels at Thos. Birch's Sons, Auctioneers, Philadelphia, February 23–24, 1893, p. 23, no. 385; p. 24, nos. 391, 405–14.

3. See Alfred Frankenstein, *The Reality of Appearance: The Trompe l'Oeil Tradition in American Painting,* exhib. cat., University Art Museum, Berkeley ([Greenwich, Conn.]: New York Graphic Society, 1970), p. 62; and John Wilmerding, *Important Information Inside: The Art of John F. Peto and the Idea of Still-Life Painting in Nineteenth-Century America,* exhib. cat., National Gallery of Art, Washington, D.C. (New York: Harper & Row, 1983), pp. 129–30.

4. Frankenstein, *After the Hunt,* p. 47.

5. Between 1878 and 1893, Snow is known to have worked for two prominent Philadelphia dry-goods firms, Cooper & Conard and John Wanamaker & Co. In 1887, he left a managerial position at Cooper & Conard to take a job in the wholesale department at Wanamaker's (see E. T. Snow, Late Manager of the Wholesale Department of Cooper & Conard's, "John Wanamaker, Wholesale Department, Market, Chestnut and City Hall Square," printed announcement, E. Taylor Snow Papers, Historical Society of Pennsylvania, Philadelphia).

6. See William H. Gerdts, *Painters of the Humble Truth: Masterpieces of American Still Life, 1801–1939,* exhib.

cat., Philbrook Art Center, Tulsa, Okla. (Columbia, Mo., and London: University of Missouri Press, 1981), p. 155.

7. Three sources have structured my conceptual framework: Janet Wolff, *The Social Production of Art* (New York: St. Martin's Press, 1981); Raymond Williams, "Base and Superstructure in Marxist Cultural Theory," in *Problems in Materialism and Culture: Selected Essays* (London: Verso Editions & NLB, 1980), pp. 31–49; and Jean Baudrillard, "Consumer Society," in *Jean Baudrillard: Selected Writings,* ed. Mark Poster (Stanford: Stanford University Press, 1988), pp. 29–56.

8. "The Home Library," *Publisher's Weekly* 13 (February 2, 1878), p. 154.

9. Francis Lieber, ed., *Encyclopaedia Americana: A Popular Dictionary of Arts, Sciences, Literature, History, Politics and Biography, a New Edition; Including a Copious Collection of Original Articles in American Biography, On the Basis of the Seventh Edition of the German Conversations-Lexicon* (Philadelphia: Lea & Blanchard, 1850). After the Civil War, the market for encyclopedias of all sorts expanded as publishers and editors tried to keep abreast of the rapid changes in technology, the natural sciences, and politics. *The American Cyclopaedia, The Columbian Cyclopaedia, The Encyclopaedia Britannica,* and *Chambers's Encyclopaedia* were some of the more popular references intended for a broad, middle-class readership. See "Chambers' Encyclopaedia," *Book News* 6 (May 1888), p. 407; and "A Few English Cyclopaedias," *Book News* 7 (April 1889), p. 243.

10. "Sir John Lubbock's List of One Hundred Books," *Book News* 4 (April 1886), pp. 230–31; and "The Best Hundred Books," *Book News* 6 (April 1888), p. 354.

11. Douglas Munro, *Alexandre Dumas Père: A Bibliography of Works Translated into English to 1910* (New York

and London: Garland Publishing, 1978), pp. 131–34. By the 1870s, editions of the books shown in *Job Lot Cheap* were available in what were termed "Cheap Libraries" issued by the various publishing houses from lists supplied by Harper's in New York and Lippincott's in Philadelphia. See "The Cheap Libraries," *Publisher's Weekly* 12 (October 6, 1877), pp. 396–97; "Cheap Books," *Lippincott's Magazine* 25 (May 1880), pp. 641–42; and "Seaside Library, Quarto Edition," *Book News* 2 (November 1883), p. 55.

12. Christopher M. Murphy, "A Brief Look at Illustrated Translations of the *Arabian Nights*," in Kay Hardy Campbell et al., *The 1001 Nights: Critical Essays and Annotated Bibliography* (Cambridge, Mass.: Dar Mahjar, 1983), pp. 86–99. Sources from the nineteenth century include "The People of the Arabian Nights," *Living Age,* 3rd ser., no. 71 (August 6, 1859), pp. 327–42; and "The Arabian Nights," *Cornhill Magazine* 32 (December 1875), pp. 711–32. For a broad survey of the reception of the *Arabian Nights* in the nineteenth century, see Peter L. Caracciolo, ed., *The* Arabian Nights *in English Literature: Studies in the Reception of* The Thousand and One Nights *into British Culture* (London: Macmillan Press, 1988).

13. See *Bookbinding in America, 1680–1910: From the Collection of Frederick E. Maser* (Bryn Mawr, Pa.: Bryn Mawr College Library, 1983); Joseph W. Rogers, "The Rise of American Edition Binding," in Hellmut Lehmann-Haupt, ed., *Bookbinding in America: Three Essays* (Portland, Maine: Southworth-Anthoensen Press, 1941), pp. 179–85; and Lewis A. Coser, Charles Kadushin, and Walter W. Powell, *Books: The Culture and Commerce of Publishing* (New York: Basic Books, 1982), pp. 21–22.

14. "New Book Perfecting and Printing Machine," *American Bookmaker: A Journal of Technical Art and Information* 5 (November 1887), p. 180.

15. *American Bookmaker* began publication in July 1885.

For books and journals representing the point of view of wealthy connoisseurs and collectors, see William Matthews, *Modern Bookbinding Practically Considered* (New York: Grolier Club, 1889); Brander Matthews, *Bookbindings Old and New: Notes of a Book-Lover* (New York and London: Macmillan & Co., 1895); M. Mauris, "Mediaeval Bookbinding," *Art Journal,* n.s. 40 (April 1878), pp. 106–12; and "The Art of Bookbinding," *Art Amateur* 7 (September 1882), pp. 74–75.

16. "Books in Summer Suits," *American Bookmaker* 5 (July 1887), p. 6.

17. Theodore Child, "Artistic Book-Binding: I," *Art Amateur* 11 (October 1884), pp. 109–10; and "Artistic Bookbinding: II," *Art Amateur* 11 (November 1884), p. 133.

18. See Barbara Babcock-Abrahams, "'A Tolerated Margin of Mess': The Trickster and His Tales Reconsidered," *Journal of the Folklore Institute* 11 (March 1975), pp. 147–86.

19. See Jackson Lears, "Beyond Veblen: Rethinking Consumer Culture in America," in Simon J. Bronner, ed., *Consuming Visions: Accumulation and Display of Goods in America, 1880–1920* (New York and London: W. W. Norton & Co., 1989), p. 78.

20. "Book Talk and Tattle," *American Bookmaker* 5 (August 1887), p. 51.

21. W. Brotherhead, *Forty Years among the Old Booksellers of Philadelphia, with Bibliographical Remarks* (Philadelphia: A. P. Brotherhead, 1891). See also William Loring Andrews, *The Old Booksellers of New York and Other Papers* (New York: William Loring Andrews, 1895), p. 4.

22. On Peto's painting, see Frankenstein, *Reality of*

Appearance, p. 100; and Wilmerding, *Important Information Inside,* pp. 129–30.

23. By "nostalgic" I mean a socially constructed fiction that edits history in order to mediate the present, not an elusive state of mind. For a provocative study of the sociology of nostalgia, see Fred Davis, *Yearning for Yesterday: A Sociology of Nostalgia* (New York: Free Press, 1979).

24. "Ballade of the Old Bookseller," *Book News* 6 (June 1888), p. 448. Other poems with similar nostalgic appeals appeared frequently in *Book News.* See "Books and Bindings," *Book News* 6 (September 1887), p. 14; "How a Bibliomaniac Binds His Books," *Book News* 6 (February 1888), p. 272; and "A Ballad of Olde Bookes," *Book News* 7 (April 1889), p. 245.

25. New modes of advertising during the late nineteenth century were significant and highly complex. See T. J. Jackson Lears, "From Salvation to Self-Realization: Advertising and the Therapeutic Roots of Consumer Culture, 1880–1930," in Richard Wightman Fox and T. J. Jackson Lears, eds., *The Culture of Consumption: Critical Essays in American History, 1880–1980* (New York: Pantheon Books, 1983), pp. 1–38; and Jean-Christophe Agnew, "The Threshold of Exchange: Speculations on the Market," *Radical History Review* 21 (Fall 1979), pp. 99–118.

26. I am grateful to Doreen Bolger for sharing important biographical data on Nugent. See also John M. Leonard, *The Book of St. Louisans: A Biographical Dictionary of Leading Living Men of the City of St. Louis* (St. Louis: St. Louis Republic, 1906), p. 438; and "Byron Nugent Will Be Buried Today," *St. Louis Globe Democrat,* April 5, 1908, p. 1.

27. See, for example, "Recent Trade Catalogues," *Dry Goods Economist* 46, no. 2470 (November 21, 1891),

p. 22; and "Nugent's Catalogue for '92–'93," *Dry Goods Economist* 47, no. 2511 (September 3, 1892), p. 40. Store displays were of central importance to commercial dry-goods houses. Many treatises were written to guide window dressers and display designers. See, for example, George S. Cole, *A Complete Dictionary of Dry Goods and History of Silk, Linen, Wool and other Fibrous Substances, Including a Full Explanation of the Modern Processes of Spinning, Dyeing and Weaving, With an Appendix Containing a Treatise on Window Trimming* (Chicago: W. B. Conkey Co., 1892). For important interpretations of the cultural implications of store display, see Stuart Culver, "What Manikins Want: *The Wonderful Wizard of Oz* and *The Art of Decorating Dry Goods Windows*," *Representations* 21 (Winter 1988), pp. 97–116; and William Leach, "Strategists of Display and the Production of Desire," in Bronner, *Consuming Visions,* pp. 99–132.

28. See *Catalogue of Goods at the Wanamaker Grand Depot, Thirteenth Street and the New City Hall* (Philadelphia: John Wanamaker: [1877]), p. 10; Herbert Adams Gibbons, *John Wanamaker,* 2 vols. (New York and London: Harper & Bros., 1926), 1, pp. 195–211; and *Golden Book of the Wanamaker Stores: Jubilee Year, 1861–1911* ([Philadelphia]: John Wanamaker, 1911), p. 78.

29. "Books in a General Store," *Book News* 5 (February 1887), p. 187.

30. See Gibbons, *John Wanamaker,* 1, p. 202; "John Wanamaker—Bookseller," *Publisher's Weekly* 102 (December 16, 1922), pp. 2105–6; and *Golden Book,* p. 75.

31. Gibbons, *John Wanamaker,* 1, p. 202.

32. "Haggling or One-Price?" *Book News* 4 (November 1885), p. 59.

33. Gibbons, *John Wanamaker,* 1, pp. 177–78.

COMMODIFIED DISPLAYS

▼

The Bric-a-Brac Still Lifes

SYLVIA YOUNT

Throughout his career, William Michael Harnett produced a number of still-life paintings depicting bric-a-brac, which, in the currency of the day, encompassed antique metalwork, ceramics, and glasswork as well as mass-produced artistic objects. The taste for bric-a-brac increased in the postbellum decades as newly monied Americans rummaged through bazaars and shops at home and abroad in search of "old curiosities of artistic character."[1] As original objets d'art were of limited availability, reproductions—both direct replicas and interpretations inspired by antique forms—achieved a commensurate popularity.[2]

This American taste for the collecting of eclectic bric-a-brac was engendered, in part, by the Aesthetic movement, which sparked interest in the cultures and decorative arts of diverse periods and locales and directed attention to notions of aesthetic quality and design.[3] Aestheticism, which sprang from the English Reform movement of the 1850s and 1860s, began to flourish in America after the 1876 Philadelphia Centennial Exposition, where thousands of American producers and consumers were introduced to objects from around the world (fig. 108).

American manufacturers were quick to respond to the widespread desire for aesthetic products and began to mass-produce goods for the broader consumer population. Whereas wealthier collectors from the leisure class were often driven to acquire unique antique objects, the middle-class consumer discovered artistic merit in manufactured reproductions, seemingly valuing them as much as the genuine articles. Thus, collections of bric-a-brac, formed for purposes of display, filled the parlors and dining rooms of comfortable homes and extravagant mansions alike (fig. 109). Even American artists were not immune to the bric-a-brac craze, and many amassed large collections that

they displayed in their fashionable studios. Harnett, an avid collector of bric-a-brac, began to acquire objects for use as studio props as early as 1874 and collected most vigorously during and after his sojourn in Europe, from about 1880 until his death in 1892. His interest in bric-a-brac may have been stimulated by the displays at the Philadelphia Centennial, where he also could have seen one of the sumptuous *Objects of Art from the Louvre* (The Metropolitan Museum of Art, New York) by the well-known French painter of still life, Blaise Desgoffe.[4]

The extent of Harnett's interest in bric-a-brac is apparent both in the great number of objects sold in

Fig. 108. "The Centennial: Bronze and Lacquer Work in the Japanese Department, Main Building," *Harper's Weekly,* August 12, 1876, p. 660

Opposite: William M. Harnett, *A Study Table* (detail, pl. 26)

Fig. 109. *Mr. H. G. Marquand's Dining Room* [Newport, R.I.], in *Artistic Houses: Being a Series of Interior Views
of a number of the Most Beautiful and Celebrated Homes in the United States,* 2 vols.
(New York: D. Appleton & Co., 1883–84), 2, pt. 1, following p. 84

his 1893 estate sale and in his membership in the Old
Curiosity Club, a New York group of amateur collectors. At Harnett's death, the contents of his studio
included over three hundred "miscellaneous articles"
in addition to paintings, armor and weaponry, and
musical instruments.[5] The miscellaneous category
included bronze and brass objects, Eastern and
Western china, pottery, glass, tapestries, and embroi-
dered textiles—goods the artist depicted throughout
his career.

The Old Curiosity Club, which held weekly
meetings at the Old Curiosity Shop, an antiques
establishment on Third Avenue near Nineteenth Street,
provided Harnett with a forum in which to explore
bric-a-brac collecting. Organized about 1891, the club
counted as its members jewelers, goldsmiths, engravers, ivory workers, painters, sculptors, and wealthy
businessmen and professionals, including Alfred
Trumble, editor and proprietor of *The Collector,* "A
Current Record of Art, Bibliography, Antiquarianism,

Etc."[6] (Trumble and Harnett had been acquaintances
since their student days.)[7] Ostensibly, the cohesion of
the club derived as much from the shared artistic
interests of its members as from their activities as
collectors of bric-a-brac and other specialties.

Still Life for William Ignatius Blemly of about
1877 (fig. 110) and *The Chinese Vase* of that year
(Brady Galleries, Inc., South Burlington, Vt.) suggest
Harnett's early collecting habits. With their depictions
of objets d'art, these paintings testify to the artist's
move away from the tradition of fruit still lifes. In both
works, manufactured "exotic" vases—an Egyptian- or
Pompeian-inspired design in the first painting, a
Chinese one in the second—are used as foils to the
products of nature. Because of Harnett's financial
difficulties at the time, these objects were probably
inexpensive reproductions of antiques that were
widely circulated, or they may have been items he
borrowed, perhaps from the curio cabinet at the
Pennsylvania Academy of the Fine Arts.[8]

Fig. 110. William M. Harnett, *Still Life for William Ignatius Blemly,* ca. 1877. Oil on canvas, 12½ x 8 in. Courtesy of Richard York Gallery, New York

Fig. 111. William M. Harnett, *Still Life with Portrait by
Raphael,* 1878. Oil on canvas, 28¼ x 34½ in.
Collection of Mr. and Mrs. Henry B. Holt

In 1878, Harnett produced two paintings for the
wealthy Philadelphia dry-goods and textile merchant
William Hazleton Folwell, *Still Life with Bric-a-Brac*
and *Still Life with Portrait by Raphael* (figs. 9, 111).[9]
Together, these works represent the eclectic bric-a-
brac collections of both artist and patron, which
included both mass-produced goods and antiques.
Still Life with Portrait by Raphael shows carefully
arranged objects, including books, a violin, a Lekythos-
style Greek vase, and a framed oil copy of Raphael's
Portrait of Bindo Altoviti—all owned by Harnett
except the prominently placed vase, which belonged
to Folwell.[10] The standardized gold ornamental pattern
on the vase and the absence of the handle and fig-
urative decoration traditionally found on this type of
ancient ware reveal its status as a reproduction. This
plaster vase also appears in *Still Life with Bric-a-Brac,*
along with fourteen other objects owned by Folwell,

Fig. 112. Photograph of objects in William M. Harnett's *Still Life with Bric-a-Brac* (fig. 9). Fogg Art Museum,
Harvard University, Cambridge, Mass., Friends of the Fogg Art Museum Fund

ranging from an assortment of vessels and an Eastern-style saber to a rare book and a bronze bust of Minerva (fig. 112). Many of the models portrayed, including English and French china, a "Persian bronze lampstand," and an "olive wood candlestick from Palestine," appear to be reproductions.[11]

It would seem Harnett's still lifes appealed to patrons who had a taste for bric-a-brac and an interest in "culture" in general—thus the references to literature, music, and art. But these images not only document and glorify a patron's wealth and collecting accomplishments,[12] they also raise questions about the relationship between the late-nineteenth-century market for aesthetic objects and middle-class consumption. Executed while frenzied collecting was on the rise, the paintings speak to the tastes and habits of the artist and his newly monied merchant-patrons, who seemed to value a copy as much as an original. Harnett and his patron Folwell certainly did own some rare aesthetic objects, but they and other contemporary collectors accepted the artistic quality of the reproductions that they exhibited side by side with antiques.

After his departure for Europe, Harnett continued collecting and painting eclectic bric-a-brac, as evidenced by two small still lifes, *Reminiscences of Olden Time* (fig. 113) and *Ye Knights of Old,* both of about 1881 and executed in the artist's miniaturistic style.[13] These works, known only through photographs, show armor and weapons, vases, tankards, Japanese lacquer, snuff boxes, repoussé plaques, vellum-bound books, and rich embroideries. As was true of many of the objects Harnett had collected previously, some of these appear to be reproductions rather than antiques.

Harnett's still lifes also suggest the contemporary taste for collecting bric-a-brac from East and West and for displaying such objects in harmonious arrangements. The Aesthetic movement in America coincided with a general interest in the classical world and medieval Europe and a passion for Japanese culture. Aesthetic tastemakers encouraged the collecting of objects from such diverse cultures to create artistic displays. The middle-class public, however, rarely gained a full historical understanding of either Eastern or Western objects or styles. Indeed, untutored consumers were encouraged to view the history and style of eclectic aesthetic objects collectively under the rubric "olden time."

Harnett's early still lifes of bric-a-brac differ markedly from some of his later compositions in that they are significantly less cluttered and rendered in a harshly linear fashion, with sharp contrasts of color and texture. Further, the appearance of the majority of bric-a-brac in these works suggests a quality of newness, which may be read as a sign of mass production. This taste for manufactured goods, therefore, might well be ascribed not only to Harnett's merchant-patrons but to the artist himself.

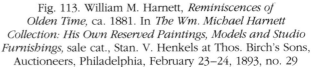

Fig. 113. William M. Harnett, *Reminiscences of Olden Time,* ca. 1881. In *The Wm. Michael Harnett Collection: His Own Reserved Paintings, Models and Studio Furnishings,* sale cat., Stan. V. Henkels at Thos. Birch's Sons, Auctioneers, Philadelphia, February 23–24, 1893, no. 29

The collecting and display of mass-produced goods may have been connected with the wide availability and marketing of art objects to the middle class through department and jewelry stores.[14] Recognizing the lucrative market for aesthetic objects, manufacturers distributed their products to retailers across the country.[15] Both of Philadelphia's major department stores—Strawbridge and Clothier, and John Wanamaker and Company—operated bric-a-brac departments or counters.[16] Folwell's commissioning of a painting of his bric-a-brac collection, which included objects readily available in popular emporia, implies that such an image was understood to be more than a display of wealth or prestige. As a merchant involved in new modes of commodity presentation, Folwell's professional enterprise was validated through his still life, which evokes the contemporary fashion of "artistic" merchandise display and advertising advanced by department stores.[17]

An 1885 advertisement for Wanamaker and Brown, a Philadelphia men's store, elucidates the issue of art as a commodity (fig. 114). Entitled "Monomaniacs," the illustration depicts a man of some wealth admiring his

---

Fig. 114. "Monomaniacs," *Philadelphia Inquirer* 112 (June 9, 1885), p. 8

bric-a-brac collection. Addressed to a certain class of consumers (the same class that patronized Harnett), the advertisement examines the habits of the collector—of ceramics or clothes. Likewise responding to the interests of its middle-class readership, *Lippincott's Magazine* frequently addressed the phenomenon of collecting and its inherent relationship to consumption. "The Collecting Mania" cartoon of 1882 examines six forms the collecting craze took for those of some means (fig. 115). Much as in the Wanamaker and Brown advertisement, bric-a-brac collecting is depicted as a "masculine" pursuit in the person of an elegantly self-satisfied and discerning gentleman admiring his possessions in a room that displays the characteristic horror vacui of the period.

This lighthearted poke at bric-a-brac collecting acquired an angry, critical edge in a *Lippincott's* editorial of one year later, a piece that suggests there was more than one perception of the bric-a-brac collector at the end of the nineteenth century.[18] Attacking the collector motivated by profit and fashion—or "lust of ownership"—the author of "Beauty versus Bric-à-Brac" distinguishes between a "genuine lover of beauty" and a "capable and successful 'bric-à-brac' collector."[19] The latter is identified as a member of the "well-to-do class" whose concern lies not with the intrinsic beauty of an object but with the rareness or uniqueness that dictates its market value. Conversely, a true lover of beauty, by implication a member of the middle or upper middle class, is not swayed by rarity and thus would more readily purchase a reproduction. Accordingly, Harnett and his merchant-patron would be viewed as representative of true lovers of beauty who chose to collect and display reproductions alongside rare antiques.

Harnett's bric-a-brac still lifes illuminate the collecting habits and tastes of American middle-class consumers during the Aesthetic era. Their collections—comprised of antiques, contemporary copies, and Aesthetic reinterpretations—were proudly displayed and represented as harmonious arrangements, implying that few distinctions were made between the aesthetic value of the manufactured replica and that of the genuine article. To this end, Harnett's images may be read as visual narratives that connect the marketplace with the dissemination and consumption of artistic goods in late-nineteenth-century America.

Fig. 115. "The Collecting Mania," *Lippincott's Magazine* 29 (January 1882), p. 112

AN INNOCENT LOVE OF CARDS.

ARDENT PURSUIT OF STAMPS.

STAND AND DELIVER—YOUR AUTOGRAPH.

THE SWEETEST THING IN OLD CHINA.

A CRITICAL TASTE IN BRIC-À-BRAC.

THE RULING PASSION STRONGEST ON RENT-DAY.

Notes

▾

I would like to thank Thayer Tolles Mickel and Doreen Bolger for providing some of the archival material utilized in this essay. In addition, I am grateful to Elizabeth Johns and Andrew Walker for their insightful comments.

1. *The Compact Edition of the Oxford English Dictionary,* s.v. "Bric-à-brac."

2. My use of the term *reproduction* is drawn from Walter Benjamin's seminal 1936 essay, "The Work of Art in the Age of Mechanical Reproduction," in Harry Zohn, trans., and Hannah Arendt, ed., *Illuminations* (New York: Harcourt, Brace & World, 1968), pp. 219–53. According to Benjamin, the genuine "original" differs from the copy in its uniqueness and historical authority, or "aura."

3. For a comprehensive study of the American Aesthetic movement, see Doreen Bolger Burke et al., *In Pursuit of Beauty: Americans and the Aesthetic Movement,* exhib. cat. (New York: Metropolitan Museum of Art, 1986).

4. On Desgoffe, see William H. Gerdts, "The Bric-a-Brac Still Life," *Antiques* 100 (November 1971), pp. 746–47.

5. *The Wm. Michael Harnett Collection: His Own Reserved Paintings, Models and Studio Furnishings,* sale cat., Stan. V. Henkels at Thos. Birch's Sons, Auctioneers, Philadelphia, February 23–24, 1893.

6. The eleven original members of the club were Trumble; businessmen Samuel Goodwin, Guido Foster,

and Robert Fullerton (the antiques and picture dealer who owned the Old Curiosity Shop); the Reverend Waldo Messaros, a Baptist minister; and artists Harnett, Edward Clemens, Max Eglau, Robert Cushing, and Fritz and Guido Kaldenberg (see "Last of the Grewsome Old Curiosity Club: A Company of Jolly Art Lovers Broken Up by the King of Terrors, undated [ca. 1894] and otherwise unidentified article, Blemly scrapbook, Alfred Frankenstein Papers, Archives of American Art, Smithsonian Institution, Washington, D.C., microfilm, roll 1374, frame 357).

7. Trumble discussed his friendship with Harnett on the occasion of the painter's death ("The Awakening of the Giant," *Collector* 4 [October 1, 1893], pp. 293–94).

8. I am grateful to Thayer Tolles Mickel for suggesting to me Harnett's possible use of the "Cabinet of Materials of Costume, of Ceramic Wares, of Ornamented Metals, and of Arms and Armor" at the Pennsylvania Academy.

9. See Gerdts, "Bric-a-Brac Still Life," pp. 744–48. In *Still Life with Portrait by Raphael,* Folwell's name appears on an envelope sandwiched between two small books at the right.

10. See *Wm. Michael Harnett Collection.* Lot 37 (p. 8) is listed as "Oil Painting Old Master. Portrait of Raphael."

11. Fogg Art Museum, Harvard University, Cambridge, Mass., curatorial files. See also Alfred Frankenstein, *After*

the Hunt: William Harnett and Other American Still Life Painters, 1870–1900, rev. ed. (Berkeley and Los Angeles: University of California Press, 1969), p. 46. Elsewhere, Frankenstein suggests that a number of the objects are reproductions (see Frankenstein to Mr. Kuhn, San Francisco *Chronicle,* June 19, 1948, p. 1, in which he notes that the two-handled vase "seems to be a Wedgwood copy of the Portland vase," Fogg Art Museum, curatorial files).

12. See Gerdts, "Bric-a-Brac Still Life," pp. 744–48.

13. The paintings are reproduced in *Wm. Michael Harnett Collection,* opposite pp. 7, 8.

14. Arguing that "art goes hand-in-hand with commerce," John Wanamaker was the first to feature aesthetically pleasing displays of merchandise in the department store (see *Golden Book of the Wanamaker Stores: Jubilee Year, 1861–1911* [(Philadelphia): John Wanamaker, 1911], pp. 245, 247). In 1881, Wanamaker opened an art gallery in the Philadelphia store for the exhibition and sale of paintings and art objects (see Joseph H. Appel, *The Business Biography of John Wanamaker, Founder and Builder: America's Merchant Pioneer from 1861 to 1922* [New York: Macmillan Co., 1930], p. 105).

15. For a discussion of the artistic production of the large commercial factories and the so-called art potteries operating throughout the United States during the Aesthetic era, see Alice Cooney Frelinghuysen, "Aesthetic Forms in Ceramics and Glass," in *In Pursuit of Beauty,* pp. 200–51; and Dianne H. Pilgrim, "Decorative Art: The Domestic Environment," in *The American Renaissance: 1876–1917,* exhib. cat. (New York: Brooklyn Museum, 1979), p. 137.

16. On Strawbridge & Clothier, see the late-nineteenth-century store plan currently on exhibition in the store in Philadelphia. The bric-a-brac counter was located on the first floor near the main entrance, in between "laces and dress trimmings" and "notions." For Wanamaker's, see Appel, *Business Biography,* p. 67; Herbert Adams Gibbons, *John Wanamaker,* 2 vols. (New York and London: Harper & Bros., 1926), 2, p. 196; and *Golden Book,* pp. 204, 210.

17. The second of Wanamaker's seven points of "store-keeping" states: "The vast area of space allotted to the many kinds of merchandise displayed made it seem more like a museum than a store" (see Appel, *Business Biography,* p. 92). For a discussion of Wanamaker's artistic merchandising and advertising, see *Golden Book,* pp. 183–226. Although little information exists regarding Folwell's own dry-goods establishment, it may be assumed that he was aware of his local colleague's methods.

18. "Beauty versus Bric-à-Brac," *Lippincott's Magazine* 31 (February 1883), pp. 202–6. I am indebted to Andrew Walker for bringing both *Lippincott's* features to my attention.

19. Ibid., pp. 203, 202.

GRAVE COUNSEL
▾
Harnett and Vanitas

CHAD MANDELES

While William Michael Harnett has long been esteemed for his seemingly effortless technique and the formal elegance of his pictorial designs, the underlying meanings of his paintings have gone largely unnoticed. Despite the risks inherent in any iconographic interpretation, there are, nevertheless, compelling reasons for arguing that symbolic content is a vital force in Harnett's oeuvre. It can be argued that Harnett brought to his paintings not only a dexterous hand but an allegorical frame of mind, vivid with nuance and comic insight. Indeed, in some of his pictures, the sophisticated formal arrangement and illusionistic technique actually seem to heighten the expression of symbolic meaning.

Even within the confines of a single theme, Harnett's work assumes a remarkable variety of forms. The theme of vanitas, a meditation on the vanity of human life and achievement, preoccupied Harnett from very early in his career. His fascination with this subject—compounded, if not actually instilled, by his Irish-Catholic background—is not limited to his early pictures of skulls but figures more widely in his oeuvre and in more surprising ways than has been commonly supposed. Although Harnett's vanitas paintings initially conveyed a grim and unpromising picture of the end of life, over the years his message became increasingly hopeful, open to the possibility that even death could be redeemed by faith in resurrection.

Naturally enough, Harnett at first gave countenance to the theme of vanitas with the human skull, a traditional symbol of mortality. He may have been inspired by Evert Collier's *Vanitas* of 1662 (fig. 116), which Harnett could well have seen at the Metropolitan Museum of Art in the early 1870s.[1] As in the Dutch painting, the musical instrument, sheet music, and

books in Harnett's *Mortality and Immortality* of 1876 (pl. 3) allude to the vanity of human effort, while the flower and guttered candle symbolize transience. Both artists represented the violin as useless: Collier by laying the bow between the strings and the waist of the instrument; Harnett, as Barbara Groseclose thoughtfully observed, by placing the violin "with touching finality atop the bow."[2] In Harnett's composition, the sharply illuminated page of the fanned book stands perfectly upright, inviting us to consider its existence

Fig. 116. Evert Collier, *Vanitas*, 1662. Oil on wood, 37 x 44⅛ in. The Metropolitan Museum of Art, New York, Purchase, 1871

Fig. 117. William M. Harnett, *To This Favor—A Thought from Shakespeare*, 1879. Oil on canvas, 24 x 20 in.
Courtesy of Berry-Hill Galleries, New York

as part of the transient, perishable world, not only because of its curiously transfixed appearance—which posits a reader who opened the text and then abruptly departed—but also because of its placement next to the left canine of the ominous and ravenous skull. The inference seems clear: an unseen yet implied human presence has suddenly left off his reading, probably for the last time.

A similar moralizing message is expressed in *Memento Mori*—*"To This Favour"* and *To This Favor—A Thought from Shakespeare,* both of 1879 (pl. 12, fig. 117), in which the viewer once again finds the combination of a skull, an extinguished candle, and books, to which is added, in the former work, an hourglass. Inscribed on the inside cover of a torn book in *Memento Mori* and on a ragged sheet of paper in *To This Favor* is an apt and revealing quotation from Shakespeare's *Hamlet* (act 5, scene 1): "Now get you to my lady's chamber, and tell her, let her paint an inch thick, to this favor she must come." To be sure, even the endeavors of Shakespeare are made to seem no more enduring than the paper on which they are printed, for the presentation of his celebrated words on a dangling cover and a tattered page have the ironic

effect of reminding the viewer of the fugacity of wisdom and fame.

This type of symbolic program is far less explicit in other works by Harnett. In *Job Lot Cheap* of 1878 (pl. 9), Harnett combined, rather unexpectedly, the concept of books as emblems of the vanity of human achievement and learning, as seen in Jan Davidsz. de Heem's *Still Life with Books* of 1628 (fig. 118), with the vernacular charm of a contemporary secondhand bookstall.[3] The sign *Job Lot Cheap,* which appears in the lower left, is written, as if in diluted black ink, on the inside cover of an old dismembered book that leans against the side of the crate. This message stands as an expression of mutability and a reproach to human vanity and, in conjunction with the printed notice *Just Publishe[d]*, which is pasted to the opposite side of the crate, represents a mixture of wit and irony that appears frequently in Harnett's oeuvre. One writer acknowledged Harnett's humor and underscored the painting's ironic twist: "That is a fine group of rare old books, that the painter has subtitled facetiously: 'Job Lot, cheap.' Some of them are very valuable works that have been loaned for this purpose."[4] The two notices and the books, in

Fig. 118. Jan Davidsz. de Heem, *Still Life with Books,* 1628. Oil on wood, 14¼ x 19⅛ in. Mauritshuis, The Hague

particular those that are "rare" and "valuable," provided Harnett with an overt means of reminding the viewer of the rise and fall of literary achievement and of the notion that even the kingdom of learning ultimately comes to nothing.

It follows that a single discarded volume of the *Cyclopaedia Americana* is found not only wedged in amid the pile of books but moored between a worn copy of the *Odyssey* and a fancy edition of the *Arabian Nights*. In the studied haphazardness of *Job Lot Cheap,* these books are—by their very nature, not to mention their central position—near the heart of Harnett's true subject. The *Arabian Nights* boasts a lush green cover scrolled with an ornate design, but however rich its imprint, this once-admired book has been taken from a bookcase and relegated to a secondhand bookstand, and even its original authors are no longer known. Indeed, in Harnett's time it was generally believed that the *Arabian Nights* was no more the original conception of a single or known author than the *Odyssey* was the handiwork of an oral poet named Homer. These books, rather than being mere discards, become statements of the inexorable fate of human learning and cultural achievement. As such, they exhibit the fate of many cultures past and present, of the East and the West. Even a masterpiece once ascribed to the great Homer has been consigned to the job lot, and we are forced to recognize that the reputation of the Greek epic poet, whose time-honored efforts scaled the heights of fame and success, is now assailed by doubts and, like the heap of books on the crate, will slowly turn to dust. Neither periods of history nor places nor individuals are exempt.

The detached book cover used for the *Job Lot Cheap* sign signals the last course in the cycle of the mutability of literature. This battered casualty has a frayed corner, worn edges, and brown age spots; it also has the number 25 inscribed in its corner, as if to suggest that the secondhand book dealer had previously conceded its saleability only at a bargain rate. The anonymity of this volume complements the unknown authorship of the *Arabian Nights,* as well as that of the less-distinguished volumes assembled on the flat top of the crate, and seems to presage the inevitable collapse of books and learning into literary desolation.

Less jocose in tone than *Job Lot Cheap* but not without its ironic jests is Harnett's *Bard of Avon* (fig. 119), also of 1878, which may be seen as both a pictorial elegy to Shakespeare and a wry commentary on the vanity of fame. Harnett placed a bust of the revered author in an improbable spot atop two books. The book on the bottom of this assembly is *Shakespeare's Tragedies/Illustrated,* and on top of it is a volume with a partially obscured title, presumably a reference to the author's *Comedies,* which would complete the modal balance of comedy and tragedy on which Shakespeare's bust, not to say his very reputation, might be said to rest. The compass of the Bard's genius is extended by a third book, *Shakespeare's Sonnets,* which leans diagonally against the base of the sculpture at the left.

The terrestrial globe (fig. 120), partially concealed by the left shoulder of the bust on the right, may be a punning reference to the Globe Theatre, where Shakespeare's plays were staged. A suitably theatrical setting is suggested by the heavy maroon curtain behind this ensemble. The bright illumination on the bust might be seen as casting Shakespeare in the spotlight, or limelight, of global fame.[5] Moreover, the notion of his everlasting fame is promoted by the very existence of the bust portrait. In contrast to the skull that symbolizes extinction in Harnett's memento-mori paintings, the well-preserved bust in *Bard of Avon,* in which mortal flesh and bone have been turned to a semblance of stone, suggests survival. Indeed, the image of the Bard basking in glory is what one would expect from a painting called *A Tribute to Shakespeare*—the title of a Harnett shown in 1892 at

Fig. 119. William M. Harnett, *Bard of Avon,* 1878. Oil on canvas, 29½ x 19½ in. Courtesy of Hirschl & Adler Galleries, Inc., New York

Earle's Galleries in Philadelphia that was probably *Bard of Avon.*[6]

Further consideration suggests, however, that the name of Shakespeare—so familiar and so widely honored—would have been particularly useful to an artist concerned with the mutability of human life and worldly affairs. *Bard of Avon* may be seen as another ironic spoof in which Harnett addressed the vanity of fame, appropriating the image of Shakespeare to symbolize "the bubble reputation" (*As You Like It,* act 2, scene 7). While the picture may praise the Bard on one hand, it proceeds audaciously on the other to

Fig. 120. William M. Harnett, *Bard of Avon* (detail, fig. 119)

question the assertion of enduring fame that it purport-edly represents.

Not surprisingly, it has been suggested that the globe behind the bust—which shows the contours of Africa, Arabia, and India—"refers to the worldwide spread of the dramatist's reputation."[7] Harnett did go to some lengths to describe each of these areas, but it could not have been for the express purpose of charting the vastness of Shakespeare's fame, for Afri-can and Arabic versions of his works did not appear until the twentieth century. Indeed, not only are the British Isles and the Continent hidden behind the Bard's left shoulder, but North America would be entirely lost from sight in an unobstructed view of the globe. The globe in Harnett's painting may thus be a cryptic jest parodying the limitations and—given Shakespeare's mythic stature in America—the uncertainty of fame.

The mocking quality of the globe is further amplified when its traditional role as a symbol of the vanity of worldly concerns is taken into account, the role it plays in Collier's *Vanitas*. Also, as in Collier's picture, the quill pen, presumably the Bard's own, is not accompanied by an inkwell. This poignant image represents the idea of the cessation of activity that results from death, and, accordingly, the maroon curtain is pulled aside to reveal nothing but darkness. *Bard of Avon* may be seen, then, as a reminder of the temporal nature of even the most honored earthly achievements. If Harnett was struck by the over-whelming reverence for Shakespeare in America, then so ripe in the wake of the 1864 tricentennial celebration of the Bard's birth, it is also clear that he decided not to follow the party line. He may have deliberately chosen Shakespeare as the object of this rumination, using the Bard's unparalleled fame to emphasize that not even he merits exemption from oblivion.

The theme of mortality is developed further in *The Social Club* of 1879 (pl. 16). This picture, which art critic Clarence Cook dismissed as an example of "merely external painting,"[8] is much more than a literal-minded and parochial vision of the smoker's world. A deeper, moralizing message can be dis-cerned that hints at the transience of human existence and the ephemeral nature of earthly pleasures. The pipes and matches on the marble tabletop are pre-sented as if they were a collection of requiescent objects, left abandoned for an indeterminate period. Although the "social club" may be called to order yet again, no live sparks or wisps of smoke—devices common in Harnett's art—were employed to suggest persons who had suddenly disappeared from sight.

In Harnett's day, scenes of smoking were not only redolent of worldly pleasures but also urged medita-tion on the vanity of human pursuits, much as they had in the seventeenth century.[9] Nowhere is the relation between tobacco and vanity more obvious than in a

seventeenth-century emblem by Francis Quarles, whose works were reissued throughout the nineteenth cen-tury. In an 1861 edition of *Quarles' Emblems*, a putto sitting on a cloud of smoke, contentedly puffing a pipe (fig. 121), invites us to consider the following:

Come, burst your spleens with laughter to behold
A new-found vanity, which days of old
Ne'er knew: a vanity that has beset
The world, and made more slaves than Mahomet:
That has condemn'd us to the servile yoke
Of slavery, and made us slaves to smoke.
But stay, why tax I thus our modern times,
For new-born follies, and for new-born crimes?
Are we sole guilty, and the first age free?
No, they were smok'd and slav'd as well as we:
What's sweet-lipt honour's blast, but smoke?
What's treasure,
But very smoke?
And what more smoke than pleasure?[10]

Fig. 121. Francis Quarles,
"Emblem IV," in *Quarles' Emblems*
(London: James Nisbet & Co., 1861), p. 80

The Social Club includes signs that correspond directly to this allegorical theme. Although the label in the wooden cigar box is partially hidden by the stem of one of the clay pipes, Harnett provided us with a clear view of the first seven letters, which read *FLORDEL,* or "flower of" in Spanish. While Harnett may have chosen this trademark because he had a similar cigar box at hand, the flower, being short-lived, was a familiar emblem of transience. In Lilly Martin Spencer's *We Both Must Fade* of 1869 (fig. 122), for example, the youthful-looking woman, wearing a rich satin and lace dress, gazes upon a flower that has begun to droop and lose some of its petals.

The significance of the proper noun on the inner label, *FLORDEL[FUMAR],* is stressed by the clay pipe in the foreground.[11] Propped against the cigar box with the end of its stem framed by the oval design of the label, this pipe points directly to the brand name, which strengthens the symbolic allusions to transience and the vanity of life by referring not only to flowers (*flor*) but also, covertly, to smoke (*fumar*), which quickly fades. Just as the pipes and tobacco draw attention to the brevity of life and the transience of worldly gratifications, so the linguistic allusions to flowers and smoke serve the same end.

The complete name on the inner label, *FLORDEL[FUMAR] DE L. BA[...]UETE H[A]BANA,* conveys further illusory overtones. In what might be characterized as a kind of commercial trompe l'oeil, American cigar manufacturers in the 1870s frequently adopted Spanish brand names with an eye to fooling the consumer.[12] Indeed, when the painted box is inspected, one finds the remnant of a United States Internal Revenue Stamp but no sign of the Customs Stamp that would have been reserved for a box of imported cigars.[13] Thus, to the extent that Harnett would have us confuse a domestic for an imported cigar or vice versa, the use of the Spanish brand name can be seen as an outgrowth of his allegorical intentions. Whether the cigar is domestic or foreign, real or imaginary, the Spanish brand name Flor del Fumar echoes the symbolic consonance of the pipes and tobacco and leaves little doubt that the pleasures of smoking are illusive and open to question.

The subject of vanitas also figures profoundly in *A Study Table* of 1882 (pl. 26), painted while Harnett was in Munich.[14] There is in the picture, however, evidence of a change of attitude: the artist is not entirely given over to the unpromising end of life but seems purposefully engaged in raising the prospects of resurrection—an outlook that would continue to inform his work, as it does that of seventeenth-century Dutch still-life painters.[15] As are so many of Harnett's vanitas paintings, both early and late, *A Study Table* is seasoned with revelations of vanity that can be apprehended through the senses. The musical instruments and sheet music, ivory tobacco box, and tankard

Fig. 122. Lilly Martin Spencer, *We Both Must Fade* (*Mrs. Fithian*), 1869. Oil on canvas, 71⅝ x 53¾ in. National Museum of American Art, Smithsonian Institution, Washington, D.C., Museum Purchase

allude to sensory pleasures. In keeping with a well-established iconographic tradition, the iron helmet and worn books may be seen as reflections of the vanity of learning, wealth, and power. Although these symbolic allusions are presented in recondite form, they are, as in Harnett's earlier vanitas paintings, much enhanced by the artist's illusionistic style. The wonderfully tactile old books, cracked flute, and dented tankard, which all bear witness to the effects of time and hard use, are rendered with an irrepressible realism that appeals directly to the viewer. Harnett dangled these motifs before us, making them reach out in a gesture that is precarious and foreboding.

Harnett endeavored to extend the traditional iconographic scheme in *A Study Table* by substituting a medieval helmet for the human skull. As an expression of vanity, the helmet, once the property of a proud knight, now sits in an empty posture of nobility near the crown of the composition and is relegated to a shadowy region on the far side of the heap. We are reminded that neither wealth nor power offers any protection from death, a point that is underscored by the dimly seen vase of daisies in the background at left. Tellingly, the flowers are in bud rather than fully developed, emphasizing the notion of the passage of time and seasonal change and hinting at the latent possibility of redemption.[16]

The titles on the books and sheet music in *A Study Table* also bespeak the hope of resurrection. As a counterbalance to the main pyramidal group, Harnett presented the sheet music from François-Adrien Boïeldieu's *La Dame blanche* and Miguel de Cervantes Saavedra's *Don Quixote/Tome IV*. In addition, there is a volume entitled *Dante Alighieri* half-buried at the core of the pile, and near the apex of the aggregation is the large book *Biblia sacra*. The title of Boïeldieu's opera refers to a woman whose ghost, it is believed, lives on in the castle of Avenel. And, the idea of life after death, with respect to Christian notions of salvation, is expressed in the opening paragraph of book 4 of *Don Quixote:*

> It is in vain to expect uniformity in the affairs of this life; the whole seems rather to be in a course of perpetual change. The seasons from year to year run in their appointed circle—spring is succeeded by summer, summer by autumn, and autumn by winter, which is again followed by the season of renovation; and thus they perform their everlasting round. But man's mortal career has no such renewal: from infancy to age it hastens onward to its end, and to the beginning of that state which has neither change nor termination.[17]

It is impossible to think of Dante without recalling his allegorical journey through hell, purgatory, and paradise in *The Divine Comedy,* and Harnett may have included the volume *Dante Alighieri* because he had this mediating vision in mind. While Dante reaches paradise in his poem and gains worldly immortality in the bargain, we are perhaps intended to recognize that in the cosmic scheme of things, his good fortune will be short-lived. One may further surmise that the copy of *Biblia sacra* several steps above the Dante is meant to convey the proper route to immortality. Appropriately, in Christian formulation, daisies allude to the innocence of the Christ child.[18] In Harnett's painting, the daisies are on the verge of blooming, perhaps in anticipation of the childhood of Christ, the season of innocence that is the first step on the path to Christian salvation.

Harnett again employed the associative power of the written message in *The Old Cupboard Door* of 1889 (pl. 45), one of his last and most monumental works. In a composition stocked with the paraphernalia of a typical vanitas picture—old books, musical instruments, sheet music, a statuette, a shell, a rose, a candlestick, and snuffers—are several texts that reflect the allegorical theme of the painting. Affixed crookedly to the cupboard door, for instance, is a sheet of music with passages from Thomas Moore's "Dernière Rose d'été" and Vincenzo Bellini's tragic opera *Norma,* which both deal with death in one form or another. Overhead, in the collection *30 Petits Morceaux,* is the aria "Che farò senza Euridice?" from Christoph Gluck's *Orfeo ed Euridice*, an opera fraught with dolorous overtones of death.

The allusion to Orpheus is made all the more emphatic by Bacchus's presence and the imprint of a lyre on the hanging cover of a volume entitled *Shakspere*—the nethermost element in the composition. According to myth, it was because of Orpheus's enchanting playing of the lyre that Eurydice was allowed to return from Hades, even though she ultimately fell back to the netherworld when, against his word, Orpheus turned to look at her before crossing the Styx. But in contrast to the mythological account, Gluck's tale ends on a happy note: Orpheus's untimely display of affection is treated as a test of faith, which he passes, and in consequence Amor restores Eurydice to life and her adoring husband. Thus, for Harnett, Gluck's opera may have embodied the idea of resurrection, for it invokes the mixture of gloom and hope that had already begun to occupy his attention by the early 1880s.

This focus on the theme of death does not mean *The Old Cupboard Door* is free of humor. Even here, there is in the title *30 Petits Morceaux* a rather wicked pun. As the ancient story goes, after Orpheus failed in his attempt to rescue Eurydice from the underworld, "his grief for his wife was so great that he scorned the Thracian women, and they in revenge tore him to pieces in their Bacchic feasts."[19] It is not clear from the mythological record in just how many parts Orpheus ended up, but Harnett may have tendered "thirty little pieces" as his unofficial estimate.

Just above and to the right of the book *Shakspere* is a copy of *Don Quixote* standing slightly askew near the front edge of the shelf. It is not Cervantes's *Don Quixote/Tome IV,* which had figured so felicitously in *A Study Table,* but, as its loose frontispiece proclaims, a Spanish edition of Cervantes's novel entitled *Vida, y Hechos del Ingenioso Cavallero Don Quixote*. The title appropriately occupies a prominent position in the center of the shelf, insofar as Harnett set up a dialogue between the objects on the right and those on the left. The first word, *vida* ("life"), seems to invite reflection upon the symbols of earthly life on the left, which include various representations of the arts of mankind—music (bow and violin), art (bronze statuette), and literature (books)—and the turban shell as an object of natural beauty. The man-made beauty of the statuette is complemented by the beauty of the common shell, whose rough exterior has been stripped by human hands to reveal its mother-of-pearl interior and then polished.[20] The picture of the good life is represented by the joyful image of Bacchus, whose cup, it would seem, hath runneth over.

This idea is even more striking in that Bacchus is merely a statuette— and, to paraphrase Magritte, it is not a statuette but only a painting of one. If the figure of Bacchus appears slightly inebriated, it is not from real wine but from an imaginary concoction, a vintage as illusory as the pleasures of earthly life. By the turn of Bacchus's head, the viewer's gaze returns to the frontispiece of Cervantes's book and toward the region of death on the right. There, with the word *hechos*, the "exploits" of Don Quixote can be seen slipping quite literally into shadow and obscurity. Like the dangling cover of *Shakspere*—not to mention Eurydice, whose fate hangs on Orpheus's lyre, printed upon it—the loose leaves of the Cervantes are at risk and, by implication, so is the future of Don Quixote's adventures. It is appropriate to note that the gallant exploits of Cervantes's mad protagonist are themselves only illusory. As we move farther to the right, the inevitability of death is indicated by the rose that has lost a petal and, much more emphatically, by the age-old symbol of a candle that has long since been snuffed out.

In *The Old Cupboard Door*, Harnett confronted the actual and the tangible, assimilating the various textures of our lives into the framework of his picture. The shallow, restricted space of the composition and its illusionistically projecting shelf, which appears conjoined to the viewer's world, further heighten the sense of reality in the painting. *The Old Cupboard Door* suggests the five senses, the means by which we perceive the everyday world. The books, which we come to know through reading, and the corner of the sheet music, which we can see through the well-oiled, translucent tambourine, allude to sight; the bow resting against the tambourine, to touch; the cup of wine held high by the bronze figure of Bacchus, to taste and touch; the rose, to smell; and the musical instruments and sheet music, to hearing. Moreover, as real and present as the assembly of elements may appear and as pleasant as the sensate experience may seem, the viewer is left in doubt about the importance of these objects.

Despite Harnett's attention here, as elsewhere, to the look and feel of the visible world, he brings us to a consideration of the cupboard door as a plane that mediates between the visible and worldly and the invisible and spiritual; between that which explicitly reaches out to us and that which implicitly lies beyond our grasp. The hopefulness of the composition's upward movement, its suggestion of spiritual ascent, culminates in the key at the upper right. Separated from the rest of the assembly, this key is perhaps intended to be recognized as the key that unlocks the "truth" behind the picture's illusions. This motif suggests that something lies beyond the formal and prescribed limits of Harnett's painting, and by grasping the key we may be allowed to seek further, to inquire, by an act of the imagination that turns the lock, into the nature of this unseen order. In so doing, we enlarge the dimensions of the picture beyond the surface to include the dark recesses of the cupboard and, in the process, move from a finite world of visual appearance to an infinite, cosmic realm of transcendent imagination. Surely we are allowed to consider the possibility that the key is emblematic of one of Saint Peter's keys of heaven—not the key of excommunication, but that of absolution. Such an allusion would complement the reference to Orpheus in the sheet music to the left of the key, for in Harnett's time this pagan thaumaturgist was also understood as a symbol of Christ.[21]

The Old Cupboard Door, then, is another instance of Harnett's recurring interest in the theme of vanitas balanced with the possibility of spiritual rescue. And while we have considered only a selection of Harnett's visual statements on the subject, it seems apparent that vanitas not only gripped his attention from early on but never relaxed its hold. Of course, *Job Lot Cheap, A Study Table*, and *The Old Cupboard Door* also manifest the strong illusionism that was a Harnett trademark. For all his careful attention to appearances in his work, it would seem the artist was continually concerned with the delicate and tenuous relationship between the aesthetics and the symbolism of illusion. We may suppose that his ability to compel and orchestrate notice was conducted by an intense spirit that was philosophic, religiously devout, and blessed with a full measure of wit and good humor. We may further surmise that rather than deposing meaning, Harnett's attempts at creating illusions of reality were frequently compounded by revelations of the vanity and illusory nature of earthly existence.

Notes

I am grateful to Dr. Mark D. Mandeles and Laura Mandeles for their generous and helpful comments on my essay.

1. The painting *Vanitas,* now thought to be by Collier, is attributed to Caesar van Everdingen in *Catalogue of the Pictures in the Metropolitan Museum of Art, No. 681 Fifth Avenue, in the City of New York* ([New York]: Metropolitan Museum of Art, 1872), p. 33, no. 65.

2. Barbara S. Groseclose, "Vanity and the Artist: Some Still-Life Paintings by William Michael Harnett," *American Art Journal* 19, no. 1 (1987), p. 54.

3. My approach to *Job Lot Cheap* converges on several points with the work of Barbara B. Millhouse, president of Reynolda House, Museum of American Art, Winston-Salem. I wish to thank Mrs. Millhouse for allowing me to consult galleys of her catalogue entry on *Job Lot Cheap,* which appears in Charles C. Eldredge and Barbara B. Millhouse, *American Originals: Selections from Reynolda House, Museum of American Art,* exhib. cat., American Federation of Arts (New York: Abbeville Press, 1990), pp. 82–84.

4. Clipping from an unidentified and undated newspaper, Blemly scrapbook, Alfred Frankenstein Papers, Archives of American Art, Smithsonian Institution, Washington, D.C., microfilm, roll 1374, frame 335.

5. See Theodore Fuchs, *Stage Lighting* (Boston: Little, Brown & Co., 1929), p. 42. For more on the history of limelight, see Brian Legge, "Stage Lighting in the Nineteenth Century," *Tabs* 26, no. 3 (September 1968), p. 19.

6. *Paintings of the Late W. M. Harnett on Exhibition,*

exhib. cat. (Philadelphia: Earle's Galleries, 1892), no. 10.

7. "An American Survey: Paintings from Two Centuries," *Kennedy Quarterly* 7 (March 1967), p. 48.

8. [Clarence Cook], "Academy of Design: Fifty-fourth Annual Exhibition," *New-York Daily Tribune,* April 26, 1879, p. 5.

9. For example, a popular seventeenth-century song attributed to George Wither that draws on the relation between tobacco and vanity was widely known in the late nineteenth century. Versions and variations of the song, which was sometimes called "Tobacco Is an Indian Weed," can be found in, for example, E. R. Billings, *Tobacco: Its History, Varieties, Culture, Manufacture and Commerce, with an account of its various modes of use, from its first discovery until now* (Hartford, Conn.: American Publishing Co., 1875), p. 100. The relation between tobacco and vanity also appears in a host of contemporary poems, including Robert Eden Brown's "My Havana Cigar," which was published in the Philadelphia *Play-Bill* 2, no. 1 (August 1, 1876), unpaginated.

10. [Francis Quarles], *Quarles' Emblems* (London: James Nisbet & Co., 1861), pp. 81–82.

11. Billings seems to confirm the existence of such a brand but does not make its point of origin clear: "It is a common thing here [America] to see a man ask in a cigar store for a *Flor del Fumar,* a *Figaro,* or an *Espanola.* . . . These are not the names which designate the size, but are the names of the manufactories. In Havana, were a man to ask for a *Flor del Fumar,* the dealer would ask him what size he wanted" (*Tobacco,* p. 262). If Harnett used an actual cigar box as his model, he nevertheless chose to include a box with this particu-

lar—and suggestive—brand name from a pool of tens of thousands of different cigar brands, both domestic and foreign, then on the American market.

12. Billings summarized the ploy and its shortcomings: "All the cigars made in the United States are invariably put up in imitation Havana boxes, with imitation Havana labels and brands. It is doubtful, however, whether this transparent device deceives anybody" (ibid., p. 261).

13. Customs stamps, which were first issued in 1866, "were used to indicate that import taxes were paid on foreign cigars when they were brought into the country" (Tony Hyman, *Handbook of American Cigar Boxes*, exhib. cat. [Elmira, N.Y.: Arnot Art Museum, 1979], p. 71). Leonard Buckley, Assistant Foreman, Product Design and Engraving Division, Department of the Treasury, Washington, D.C., has tentatively identified the torn blue Internal Revenue Stamp in *The Social Club* as a "50 cigar, 25 cent, tax paid stamp of the First Series, under the Act of July 20, 1868 as amended" (memorandum to the author, July 9, 1990). In attempting to sort out the issue of the stamp in Harnett's painting, I should like to acknowledge the expertise and patient assistance of Mr. Buckley and Margaret Phelan, Intern, Office of the Curator, Department of the Treasury.

14. See also my entry on *A Study Table* in Paul D. Schweizer, ed., *Masterworks of American Art from the Munson-Williams-Proctor Institute* (New York: Harry N. Abrams, 1989), p. 84.

15. See Ingvar Bergström, *Dutch Still-Life Painting in the Seventeenth Century*, trans. Christina Hedström and Gerald Taylor (New York: Thomas Yoseloff, 1956), p. 154.

16. The connection between flowers, seasons, and the symbolism of resurrection is treated in F. Edward Hulme, *Bards and Blossoms; or, the Poetry, History, and Associations of Flowers* (London: Marcus Ward & Co.; Belfast: Royal Ulster Works, 1877), p. 153.

17. Miguel de Cervantes Saavedra, *Adventures of Don Quixote de la Mancha,* trans. Charles Jarvis (New York: John Wurtele Lovell, 1880), 2nd pt., bk. 4, chap. 53, p. 691.

18. See George Ferguson, *Signs and Symbols in Christian Art* (New York: Oxford University Press, 1975), p. 30. On the daisy as a symbol of "the innocence of the Christ Child," see Wilhelm von Schadow's *Artist's Children* of 1830 in *German Masters of the Nineteenth Century: Paintings and Drawings from the Federal Republic of Germany,* exhib. cat. (New York: Metropolitan Museum of Art, 1981), p. 194.

19. Clara Erskine Clement, *A Handbook of Legendary and Mythological Art* (Boston and New York: Houghton Mifflin Co., 1881), p. 473.

20. I am indebted to Walter Sage, Senior Scientific Assistant, American Museum of Natural History, New York, for kindly identifying this shell for me.

21. See Charles Browne, *Symbolism: A Lecture, delivered on behalf of the Stoke Newington and Hackney Church Association, at the Schoolroom of S. Matthias, Stoke Newington* (1855; London: Joseph Masters, 1865), pp. 9–10. Browne's discussion of the relation of Orpheus to Christ is quoted in its entirety in W. and G. Audsley, *Handbook of Christian Symbolism* (London: Day & Son, [1865]), p. 36. See also F. Edward Hulme, *The History, Principles and Practice of Symbolism in Christian Art* (London: Swan Sonnenschein & Co., 1891), p. 42.

LITERARY REFERENCES IN HARNETT'S STILL-LIFE PAINTINGS

JUDY L. LARSON

William Michael Harnett's dazzling technical virtuosity and captivating visual effects have distracted scholars and viewers from pursuing subtler and more profound levels of meaning in his paintings. Yet Harnett's familiar models—the stubby candle in its holder, the blue-and-white Delft jar, the much-played violin, and the vellum-bound, dog-eared books—appear with such frequency and propinquity that patterns seem to emerge. Since Harnett left few explanations of his work, it is impossible to form a single interpretation of these patterns. Nevertheless, his meanings are most immediately apparent in his antiquarian interest in literature, either about the Middle Ages or evocative of its virtues. Harnett's literary allusions take the form of painted books, broadsides, sheet music, and busts of authors, from ancient Greece to the Middle Ages and the Renaissance, from Gothic novels to Romantic operas. Approximately fifty legible book and song titles appear in Harnett's known oeuvre, and almost all are united by themes of courtly love, chivalry, death, and resurrection.[1] Taken as a whole, these novels, tattered incunabula, and familiar songs and arias express the noble spirit of mankind within the edifying framework of medieval faith, love, and honor.

Harnett was a devout Roman Catholic educated in a parochial Catholic school. He belonged the Catholic Philopatrian Literary Institute, which gave him access to a circulating library of books on topics ranging from theology to politics.[2] He was probably familiar with nineteenth-century English and Continental medievalist movements that sought to restore the primacy of Catholicism. Kenelm Henry Digby, an influential leader of English medievalists, believed that if man were to rise above vulgar worldly conceits, he must return to simple medieval Christianity. Digby glorified the culture and values of the Middle Ages, which he believed "were ages of highest grace to men; ages of faith; ages when all Europe was Catholic . . . ages of vast and beneficent intelligence . . . ages of the highest civic virtue . . . ages of the noblest art . . . ages of more than mortal heroism."[3] Digby's romantic awe for the Middle Ages influenced a generation of writers and artists, including William Wordsworth, William Morris, Edward Burne-Jones, and John Ruskin.

It is not known how Harnett became familiar with the history, literature, and theology of the Middle Ages, but Ruskin would be an educated guess.[4] During the Aesthetic movement in America, from roughly 1876 to the turn of the century, Ruskin's theories gained even greater popularity. He coined the term *medievalism* to define a style of Gothic-inspired architecture, but the word soon came to encompass any revival of the culture and values of the Middle Ages. Ruskin's writings also stimulated an Amerian fascination with the nostalgic revival of everyday objects from the past. The Aesthetic movement fostered respect for the fine craftsmanship found in works of the Middle Ages and inspired a revival of interest in the medieval notions of integrity and an appreciation of beauty.

Harnett's impulse toward medievalism might seem strangely out of context in late-nineteenth-century America. The nation was, after all, founded on Puritan theology, not Catholicism; it was a democratic, rather than an aristocratic, society; its economy was based on capitalism rather than feudalism. Harnett, however, did not try to re-create a medieval setting in his paintings; rather, he suggested the era and the workings of the medieval mind. His still lifes set on the tops of desks and tables evoke private spaces for contemplation and meditation. These are quiet places of individual study or spiritual retreat. Harnett created a medieval ambience by using old-world objects such as a knight's helmet, fancy iron hinges, paneled walls, and rich textiles. Most important, he used books, ballads, and arias whose narratives venerate love, honor, and faith—values held in high esteem in the Middle Ages. Harnett chose widely read authors, such as Dante, Shakespeare, and Cervantes, as well as popular novels and well-known arias. Embedded in these stories are complex themes that enhance the meanings of his compositions.

In Harnett's still-life paintings, the theme of love deals with courtly love, a codified behavior system that allowed men and women to rise above mere sexual desire and enter into a spiritual union, a perfect love. Chivalry was the structured deportment of honor. It too allowed mankind to rise above the human condition, to escape from the chaos and immorality of the vulgar world. Finally, faith provided the hope of resurrection and eternal life. The Catholic church was the embodiment of faith and served as the foundation of a well-ordered world. Like the English medievalists, Harnett did not address the contradictions and artificiality of these concepts. Instead, he used medieval themes to distinguish characteristics of the nineteenth century from those of the fifth through the fifteenth. He seemed to express, with regret, that modern man had lost his sense of love, honor, and faith.

Dante Alighieri's fourteenth-century *Divine Comedy,* a paradigm of medieval culture and values, is the

Fig. 123. William M. Harnett, *Still Life with Tankard,* 1885. Oil on wood, 16½ x 21⅛ in. Harriet and Mortimer Spiller Collection, Buffalo, N.Y.

primary nexus of Harnett's literary focus. It is a poem about the transience of worldly things, the inevitability of death, and the certainty of resurrection and eternal life. Dante removed the barrier of earthly time and clearly revealed the connection between human deeds and eternity. *The Divine Comedy,* therefore, also served as a theodicy, a defense of God's goodness and omnipotence in the face of evil. Harnett found in Dante a literary equivalent for the visual emblems of vanitas, which, like Dante's journey, reveal that life is fleeting.[5] The epic poem also deals with the medieval concept of courtly love, an unquestioning devotion to an unattainable ideal. Dante and Beatrice are exemplary lovers who transcend the mundane world through the purity of spiritual, rather than physical, union. Dante's love for Beatrice enables him to accept the divine revelation of God and ultimately leads him to salvation.

Dante's image and works become a dominant motif in Harnett's still-life paintings after the artist's arrival in Europe in 1880. Harnett had included a book by Dante in *Music and Literature* of 1878 (pl. 10), but European travel and study seem to have fostered a more profound exploration of *The Divine Comedy* and of other literary references. Particularly from his Munich paintings forward, there is a richness of texture, a new multiplicity of ideas, and an intricate interweaving of new literary references with his old favorites. *A Study Table* of 1882 (pl. 26) exemplifies the new complexity in Harnett's compositions. The painting depicts a chaotic arrangement of books, sheet music, instruments, textiles, and other objects. The volumes include *Dante Alighieri, Don Quixote/Tome IV, Biblia sacra,* and *Andreae Vallensis.* The themes of courtly love, chivalry, and faith are represented by the first three references. The fourth is a seventeenth-century book on church law by André Delvaux. In *A Study Table,* Harnett acknowledged the medieval distinction between the contemplative and the active life. The contemplative life is represented by literature and theology; the active, by politics and law. By choosing a book on church law, Harnett also may have been nostalgically looking back to medieval society, which unified Christian faith with all aspects of life, wedding secular law and papal authority. The sheet music for *La Dame blanche* by François-Adrien Boïeldieu completes the thematic cycle of love, honor, and faith. The opera is based on the novels *Guy Mannering* (1815) and *The Monastery* (1820) by Sir Walter Scott. The heroine of the opera masquerades as a ghost who supposedly haunts a Gothic pile in Scotland. Harnett's choice of this music cover, with its clear reference to a spectral lady, offers a mystic vision of the hereafter.

In Harnett's still lifes, Dante's *Divine Comedy*—*Inferno, Purgatory,* and *Paradise*—is usually paired with other books in such a way as to suggest the artist's familiarity with the origins and influences of the

Fig. 124. William M. Harnett, *Professor's Old Friends,* 1891. Oil on canvas, 27 x 33¼ in. William A. Farnsworth Library and Art Museum, Rockland, Maine

literature of courtly love. In *Munich Still Life* of 1882 (pl. 24) Dante is combined with an unidentified volume of Ovid, the Roman poet whose writings were one of the sources for Dante's epic. In *Still Life with Tankard* of 1885 (fig. 123), Harnett paired Dante with Petrarch by depicting the *Purgatorio* and a volume called *Vie Petrarch.* Both Dante and Petrarch adored unattainable women—Beatrice and Laura—and both devoted a large portion of their writings to their courtly loves. In *Professor's Old Friends* of 1891 (fig. 124), Harnett replaced Petrarch with Geoffrey Chaucer, whose fourteenth-century translation of the *Roman de la rose* (*Romaunt of the Rose*) served as an English handbook on courtly love. Chaucer, who had read Dante and Petrarch, serves as a link between Continental and English literary conventions of love. Beginning with Chaucer, the English literature of courtly love was kept alive, from the Elizabethan poets and playwrights to the nineteenth-century Gothic novelists.

Harnett's paintings include ballads and legends from the Middle Ages and adaptations of period songs. The genesis of courtly literature is found in the poems of the troubadours, poet-musicians who celebrated the conventions of courtly love and chivalry in their songs. The tale of Saint Kevin, which appears as a piece of nineteenth-century sheet music in *Still Life—Violin and Music* of 1888 (pl. 43), is based on a sixth-century Irish legend about Kathleen, a young girl who follows her beloved saint to the cliffs of Glendalough. Kevin, who has vowed to live alone on an island, throws Kathleen over the cliffs. At the end of the song, her ghost returns to "glide, / Smiling, o'er the fatal tide!"[6]

Fig. 125. Infrared photograph of William M. Harnett's *Still Life with Bust of Dante* (pl. 27)

The inclusion of the sheet music is another of Harnett's many references to the spiritual realm of the afterlife.[7]

"The Fair Rosamund" is a well-known tragic ballad that Harnett may have been referring to in many of his still lifes by including a nineteenth-century sheet of music entitled "Rosamund." Although several writers have assumed that the title refers to a work by Franz Schubert (D. 797), this cannot be confirmed by the painting, which does not show a complete title page or recognizable stanzas of music. It is therefore possible that the reference alludes to the Rosamund of medieval legend. According to the tale, the twelfth-century King Henry II keeps his beautiful young concubine, Rosamund, in a protective bower so that his wife, Eleanor of Aquitaine, will not harm her. The jealous queen, however, finds the girl and offers her a choice—to take her own life or be killed. She chooses suicide. Rosamund was a favorite subject of the English Pre-Raphaelites and the heroine of the play *Rosamund* (1860) by the nineteenth-century English poet and critic Algernon Charles Swinburne. As a literary character, she represents the emptiness of worldly values.

Her tragic story reflects the medieval sense of the fragility of the world, in which all things are subject to death and decay. Rosamund's only way to immortalize both love and beauty is to die in youth.

The sheet music "Rosamund" is included among the books and objects in *Still Life with Bust of Dante* of 1883 (pl. 27).[8] On what appears to be a cabinet in a gentleman's study are heaped a bust of Dante, a medieval helmet, a dented keyed bugle, and a group of books, including a tattered copy of Dante's *Divine Comedy,* its shabby cover hanging rather precariously over the edge of the cabinet. The helmet takes on an eerie appearance and plays the role of an actual skull, which Harnett incorporated into earlier paintings. It is also part of the panoply of a knight and is thus emblematic of chivalry. There are about a dozen books—some bound in vellum, some in calf, some in paper wrappers—including *Dante Alighieri* and *Juliette.* The marquis de Sade's *Histoire de Juliette* (1797), a book of erotica about an amoral woman, is an apt symbol for a vanitas about excessive sexual desire.[9] Perhaps Harnett included *Juliette* as a prurient reference to Dante's description of the second ring of hell, which is reserved for those who fall prey to carnal lust, or he may have wanted to focus the viewer's attention on the differences between lust and love by contrasting Juliette with Dante's pure and godly Beatrice.[10] Rosamund, the third heroine referred to in the painting, also acts as a foil for Beatrice, as it is Rosamund's adulterous affair with Henry II that results in her sacrifice of her own life. Rosamund values the worldly aspects of love and beauty; Beatrice values the spiritual.

Harnett often created a dialectic in his paintings by juxtaposing antithetical objects. In *Still Life with Bust of Dante,* the knight's helmet is a symbol of action, bravery, and honor. Seventeenth-century Dutch still-life painters often used armor as a vanitas symbol—weapons and armor are no defense against death. On the other hand, books, part of the paraphernalia of a scholar, are symbols of learning and wisdom.[11] In the painting, the world of deeds and action is balanced with that of quiet meditation. Both boldness and wisdom were venerated in medieval society. In a broader context, the knight represents courage and action, or the tangible domain of the body. The scholar embodies wisdom and contemplation, or the intangible realm of the soul. In the Middle Ages, man was defined by this duality, which is also the basis for Christianity; mortal man may know God because man also has a spiritual nature.

The theme of Christian salvation appears throughout Harnett's literary references. The juxtaposition of books and vanitas objects suggests that earthly life is a preparation for life in the hereafter. Harnett's message offers the hope of salvation, which in turn engenders faith and encourages action—a viewpoint taken directly from medieval Christianity. In *Still Life with Bust of Dante,* Harnett underscored this message by including a rampant lion in the decoration of the background panel (fig. 125). This heraldic emblem symbolized resurrection in medieval iconography. Having established the concept of the dual nature of man, Harnett turns the viewer's attention toward resurrection—the moment body and soul are reunited in eternal life.

William Shakespeare appears to have been another of Harnett's favorite authors. Shakespeare's view of a world that is orderly and moral, one in which death is certain but not fearsome, is compatible with Harnett's philosophy. At times Harnett's references to Shakespeare are general——a bust, a broadside of a play, a book of sonnets. Often, as in *Still Life* of 1888 (fig. 74), Harnett carefully selected specific Shakespearian works. Here, *King Richard III,* a story about absolute corruption, is pitted against *Romeo and Juliet,* a tale of innocence and love.

In *My Gems* of 1888 (fig. 126), one volume contains both *Hamlet* and *Troilus and Cressida.* The first

is a classic portrayal of revenge. The protagonist's mother, Gertrude, is a weak-willed woman who has married her husband's murderer. Her lack of fidelity and Hamlet's sense of loyalty create a source of conflict in the play. The second is a story Shakespeare adapted from Chaucer. In Chaucer's poem, Troilus is a strong and noble hero, the model of chivalric loyalty. This, however, is not quite the character portrayed by Shakespeare. In his play, Troilus, son of the king of Troy, has fallen in love with the fickle Cressida. The pair having been separated by war, Cressida is unfaithful to Troilus, and as the play unfolds, their relationship disintegrates into one of distrust and bitterness. Neither character evinces moral courage or fortitude, and the story ends in disillusionment. *My Gems* also includes sheet music from Verdi's opera *Rigoletto,* which concerns similar issues of fidelity. Gilda's generous and forgiving spirit acts as a foil to the selfish nature of the duke and to her own father's insensitivity and all-consuming desire for revenge. Both *Rigoletto* and *Troilus and Cressida* expose the frailty of human faith. Harnett, like the nineteenth-century medievalists, may

Fig 126. William M. Harnett, *My Gems,* 1888. Oil on wood, 18 x 14 in. National Gallery of Art, Washington, D.C., Gift of the Avalon Foundation (1985.64.98)

have viewed his own age as lacking nobility and high ideals. Almost as a commentary on the human folly of unfaithfulness, he placed a sheet of music falling over the edge of the table so that its title can be read as a caption for the painting: *Hélas, Quelle Douleur*.[12]

In two nearly identical compositions—*Music* of 1886 (pl. 38) and *Still Life* of 1887 (Mr. and Mrs. Meyer P. Potamkin)—Harnett depicted a volume of Shakespeare's plays that includes *Romeo and Juliet, Hamlet, The Comedy of Errors, Richard III,* and *Twelfth Night.* This selection of tragedies and comedies is united by the common themes of power, love, and loss. On the dangling cover of the volume in *Music* is an emblem that consists of a lute, which is a symbol of lovers, crisscrossed by a sword and a horn, attributes of the muse of tragedy. The implication would seem to be that love is crosscut by tragedy. The name Ben Jonson appears above and below the emblem, as if this volume were at some point part of his personal library. A playwright and friend of Shakespeare's, Jonson also dealt with the theme of the foibles of man. It is no coincidence that the imprint on the book is 1598 and that the date flanking the emblem is 1605. In 1598, Jonson was imprisoned for murder, and he converted to Catholicism while serving his sentence. In 1605, he voluntarily returned to prison to join his collaborators George Chapman and John Marston, who had been jailed for offending James I. Thus the dates Harnett chose mark Jonson's embracing of Catholicism and his performing of an honorable deed of chivalry—both acts that would have been regarded as meaningful by nineteenth-century medievalists.

Music also contains several books and printed documents that further enrich the viewer's understanding. Returning to the theme of the active versus the contemplative life, Harnett included Torquato Tasso's *Jerusalem Delivered* (1575) and Homer's *Iliad* and *Odyssey.* All three works represent the allegorical journey of man through life, and all include complementary heroes who stand for boldness and wisdom. *Jerusalem Delivered* is a story about an army (man) striving to conquer Jerusalem (felicity). Rinaldo is the active figure, the warrior; Godfrey embodies the thinking, intellectual man. In order to conquer the city, a walled fortress in a rugged and mountainous setting, the two must work together. This dichotomy is also evident in the *Iliad* and the *Odyssey.* In the first, the Greek hero Achilles is a strong, courageous warrior. Odysseus, on the other hand, is a contemplative, solitary man whose strength lies in his intellect. One hero is not deemed superior to the other; both embody the notion of chivalry.

The contents of the pile of printed papers in *Music* symbolically underscores the artist's message of love, faith, and salvation. In the stack is the sheet music for Edmond Servel's "Séparation," a romantic song about parted lovers; a page of plainsong titled "Benedictio

Fig. 127. William M. Harnett, *Philadelphia Letter, Books, and Writing Plume*, 1879. Oil on canvas, 17½ x 25 in. Private collection

fontis"; and the lower corner of a print showing a sandled foot and the tip of a sword. It is possible that the engraving is the frontispiece for *Jerusalem Delivered,* which shows the archangel Michael and Godfrey watching the Crusaders storm the walls of Jerusalem. The frontispiece portrays the moment when, through divine intervention, deeds and faith coalesce and victory is given to the righteous. Another symbol for salvation is found in the "Benedictio fontis," a medieval plainsong that was sung or chanted during the sacrament of baptism.[13] Symbolizing life, death, and resurrection, baptism embodies the medieval tripartite notion of the cycle of life. To the right is a rolled piece of sheet music for *Ave Maria.* This too addresses medieval theology, in that the veneration of Mary began in the Middle Ages. The exaggerated admiration of women in courtly tradition parallels the religious cult of the Virgin.

The chivalry of the Middle Ages was accorded special attention in Harnett's literary references. He often chose novels with heroes who are brave, honorable, and bound by a sense of duty. The qualities cultivated by medieval knights lived on in the romantic works of nineteenth-century novelists such as Sir Walter Scott, one of Harnett's favorites. In *Philadelphia Letter, Books, and Writing Plume* of 1879 (fig. 127), Harnett included Scott's novel *The Betrothed* (1825). Set during the reign of Henry II, following the First Crusade to the Holy Land, the story is a complex interweaving of many characters, sacred oaths, honor, and unrequited love. At some point each of the principal characters makes a decision honoring the chivalric code, decisions that often require the sacrifice of happiness or life itself. The novel focuses on the intrinsic value of honor, a theme that occupied Harnett as well.

Another of Harnett's favorite writers of historic romances was the English novelist Jane Porter. In *Latakia II* of 1880 (fig. 128), Harnett depicted one volume of her *Scottish Chiefs* (1810), a story set during the thirteenth century that records the noble efforts of Scotsmen in their struggle for independence. The hero, Sir William Wallace, is a good and true Christian knight who defends his king and country, shows mercy to his enemies, and protects women. An equally chivalric gentleman is the hero of Porter's *Thaddeus of Warsaw* (1803), which appears in Harnett's *Materials for a Leisure Hour* of 1879 (Thyssen-Bornemisza Collection). This story is set in the eighteenth century, but Thaddeus's wisdom and generosity are inspired by the idealized values of the aristocracy of medieval Europe. His sense of noblesse oblige, fairness, intelligence, and

refined manners befit a nobleman. Both novels glorify honor and bravery, concepts associated with the Middle Ages.

Harnett's strongest call for the virtues of chivalry is found in his numerous references to Miguel de Cervantes Saavedra and his masterpiece, *Don Quixote de la Mancha* (1605; part 2, 1615). Don Quixote, an aging gentleman who has read too many chivalric romances, determines that he too must fight for the right. His shortcomings and misadventures are laughable at first, yet his determination and selflessness strike a sympathetic chord in the reader, who grows to respect Don Quixote's idealism and his sense of honor and duty. His squire, Sancho Panza, provides an effective contrast to Don Quixote's visionary strivings. Sancho appraises the world with a practical eye, yet his judgments are never the wiser for it.

Don Quixote appears as early as 1878 in Harnett's *Music and Literature* (pl. 10), and the artist used the

Fig. 128. William M. Harnett, *Latakia II,* 1880. Oil on canvas, 11 x 15 in. Private collection

Fig. 129. William M. Harnett, *The Smoker's Companions,*
1878. Oil on wood, 9 x 12 in.
Courtesy of Kennedy Galleries, Inc., New York

novel in many other paintings. Even the windmill design on the Delft jar that appears again and again in his still lifes may be emblematic of Don Quixote's famous jousting scene, serving as a supportive reference to the notion of chivalry. A parody on chivalry that borrows heavily from *Don Quixote* was created by Samuel Butler in his poem *Hudibras* (3 parts; 1663, 1664, 1678), which appears in Harnett's *Smoker's Companions* of 1878 (fig. 129). Sir Hudibras and his squire, Ralpho, set out to reform an evil world. In this duo, Ralpho represents divine inspiration, relying on revelation to find his way; Sir Hudibras represents the intellect by making practical, cognitive decisions.

Both *Don Quixote* and *Hudibras* raise the issue of the duality of the ideal versus the actual, or the visionary versus the practical, issues that affected Americans at the close of the nineteenth century. Charles Darwin, Thomas Henry Huxley, and Herbert Spencer were contemporaries of Harnett's who advocated a quantitative, logical world and the verification of facts. Many theologians saw no compatability between faith and science, and, even worse, believed that scientific achievements threatened a loss of faith. The men of faith, like the medievalists, were the visionaries. Their reaction to the dilemmas of modern man was to look back to a simpler, purer faith found in medieval Christianity. Harnett's still-life paintings, with their references to love, faith, and honor, reveal his interest in redirecting his contemporaries' attention toward these medieval virtues.

Harnett again turned to the issue of faith in two nearly identical paintings—*Still Life with Letter to*

Thomas B. Clarke and *Still Life with Letter to Dennis Gale,* both of 1879 (pl. 15, fig. 32). Gale was an Englishman, and as a nod in the direction of his nationality Harnett included books by two British authors, a copy of *Hudibras* and a volume identified as *Wordsworth's Works.* The other, nearly identical painting was done for New Yorker Thomas Benedict Clarke, and in it Harnett substituted an American work—John Greenleaf Whittier's *Poems*—for Wordsworth and *Shakespeare* for *Hudibras.* Harnett very rarely cited American authors, but in this notable exception he chose a Quaker poet whose reputation was based on his humanitarian views. Whittier, like Wordsworth, lamented the loss of faith in nineteenth-century society. In his famous poem "The Panorama" (1856), Whittier describes the decline of America, a nation that has given in to "Its lust of gold, its strife for place and power; / Its lack of manhood, honor, reverence, truth." Harnett may have chosen Whittier because he shared his profound faith in God. "The Panorama" concludes by suggesting Americans need to rekindle their faith, a faith that made men "steadfast, manly, just, / True to the faith your fathers left in trust."[14]

Another American author represented in Harnett's still-life paintings is Longfellow, which offers further evidence of the artist's focus on themes of faith and salvation. A book of Longfellow's poems is included among the objects in Harnett's *Emblems of Peace* of 1890 (pl. 46), which also includes volumes by Tasso and Dante. Longfellow spent a good part of his career translating the works of Dante into English. After that accomplishment, he considered his trilogy "Cristus: A Mystery" his most ambitious work. The second part of the poem, "The Golden Legend," is based on a twelfth-century troubadour's song "Der Arme Heinrich," which chronicles the self-sacrificing love of Elsie for Prince Henry. Longfellow believed that the Christian faith of the Middle Ages was the unifying force of that culture. Harnett may have incorporated Longfellow as a literary reference because of the poet's suggestion that modern man had lost the power of a strong Christian faith.

In 1887, Harnett painted *Ease* (pl. 41), commissioned by the wealthy American James Terry Abbe. Some of the book titles are new for Harnett and may have been incorporated at the patron's request.[15] To the left of the composition is a stack of books that includes the first volume of William Cullen Bryant's *Popular History of the United States* (1876). In the preface, Bryant explains that he was inspired to write the book because he felt the nation needed to know about slavery.

We stand therefore at a point in our annals where the whole duration of slavery in our country from the beginning to the end, lies before us as on a chart; and certainly no history of our Republic can now be regarded as complete which should fail to carry the reader through the various stages of its existence, from its silent and stealthy origin to the stormy period in which the world saw its death-struggle, and recognized in its fall the sentence of eternal justice.[16]

Resting atop Bryant's *History* is a volume entitled *Scott's Poetical Works.* The Bible is the large foundational book at the bottom of the stack; Harnett may have placed it there to convey the concept that faith is a basis for both history and culture.

In a contemporary review of *Ease,* a reporter claimed that "the light-brown leather book . . . is the old account book of Thomas Noble, once governor of Indiana (and the grandfather of Mr. Tyner, Mr. Abbe's partner), and contains the record of 'Black Tom's and Sarah's children'—Black Tom having been a slave of Mr. Noble in Kentucky and one of the originals of Mrs. Stowe's 'Uncle Tom.'"[17] Harriet Beecher Stowe's famous *Uncle Tom's Cabin* (1852) stirred the emotions of Northerners against slavery and kindled a moral spirit of outrage that united the Union. This reference to slavery may suggest the politics of Abbe, a staunch Republican and probable supporter of the Emancipation Proclamation.

Harnett seems to have used still-life painting as a vehicle for commenting on the values of his era. His career spanned a period in American culture that experienced many potentially threatening changes. Harnett viewed greed and a lack of honor as the disturbing characteristics of modern man and called for a return to faith and a sense of duty. In the last decades of the nineteenth century there were still lingering memories of the Civil War, a grim conflict that pitted brother against brother in a decidedly unchivalric manner. After the war, many Americans moved into the western territories, but the frontier as an opportunity for adventure and derring-do had nearly disappeared. The stirrings of the feminist movement were already apparent, as women sought equality in lieu of veneration. There were fewer and fewer opportunities for men or women to act in a courtly and chivalric manner. Harnett and the larger movement of which he was a part revived the literature and themes of the Middle Ages in a nostalgic effort toward reclaiming values that seemed at odds with the modern world.

Perhaps Harnett can best be characterized as a late-nineteenth-century Don Quixote who used still-life painting as a conduit for his personal lamentations on the folly of man. Ruskin advocated that great art revealed great spirituality in its creator. From what is known about Harnett's private life, it seems he took his Catholic faith seriously, and his art does reveal a deeply spiritual man. It also appears he was familiar with the novels, plays, poems, and operas alluded to in his paintings. The consistency of his references indicates he chose and grouped them with precision. This is not to claim that every painting contains personal testimony nor that every book in his paintings is charged with a specific meaning. A pervasive theme, however, can be found in his literary allusions to life, death, and eternity. The underlying message seems to be that faith alone should shape and inform the culture and values of modern society. It is tempting to wonder if Harnett had read Ruskin's assessment of modern man in which he protests that the weary sadness of contemporary life is revealed in "jaded intellect, and uncomfortableness of soul and body." The Middle Ages were not dark; it is modern man who claims this darkness of heart, and the profoundest reason for it is "our want of faith."[18]

NOTES

I am most appreciative of Dr. David Helsa and Dr. Cristine Levenduski, both of Emory University, for their help in reading and offering suggestions for this essay.

1. From the inventory of Harnett's estate, it is evident the books he owned reflected his wide-ranging interests—from law to medicine to theology to classical poetry and much more. However, only a handful of his personal books are actually incorporated into his compositions. Harnett often repeated a familiar binding but changed the title or invented a place or date of publication. For a list of the books in his estate, see *The Wm. Michael Harnett Collection: His Own Reserved Paintings, Models and Studio Furnishings,* sale cat., Stan. V. Henkels at Thos. Birch's Sons, Auctioneers, Philadelphia, February 23–24, 1893, pp. 23–24.

2. I wish to thank Edward Suarez, manager of the Catholic Philopatrian Literary Institute, Philadelphia, who allowed me to examine what remains of the library books and to read through the minutes of early meetings in search of book, serial, and newspaper titles.

3. [Kenelm Henry Digby], *Mores Catholici; or, Ages of Faith,* 11 vols. (London: n.p., 1831–42), 1, pp. 2–3, quoted in Kevin L. Morris, *The Image of the Middle Ages in Romantic and Victorian Literature* (London: Croom Helm, 1984), p. 111. Digby's other important medievalist work was *The Broad Stone of Honour; or, Rules for the Gentlemen of England* (London: n.p., 1822, revised 1823, 1826–29 [*The Broad Stone of Honour; or, The True Sense and Practice of Chivalry*], 1844–48, 1876–77, 1883).

4. See *Comments of John Ruskin on the Divina Commedia,* comp. George P. Huntington (Boston and New York: Houghton Mifflin & Co., 1903).

5. For a discussion of vanitas and Harnett, see Chad Mandeles, "William Michael Harnett's *The Old Cupboard Door* and the Tradition of *Vanitas,*" *American Art Journal* 18, no. 3 (1986), pp. 51–62; and Barbara S. Groseclose, "Vanity and the Artist: Some Still-Life Paintings by William Michael Harnett," *American Art Journal* 19, no. 1 (1987), pp. 51–59.

6. *Moore's Irish Melodies,* rev. ed. (Boston: Oliver Ditson & Co., 1893), p. 82.

7. A journey into the afterlife or an encounter with a spirit, apparition, or ghost is a common theme in Harnett's literary references. Dante and Odysseus visit the realm of the afterlife. The book *Fantomes* in *The Imperial Eagle* (*Still Life with Bust of Dante*) of 1883 (fig. 141) refers to ghosts. Shakespeare's Hamlet and Richard III come upon ghosts, as does Scott's Eveline in *The Betrothed.* Boïeldieu's White Lady pretends to be a ghost, and in Giacomo Meyerbeer's *Dinorah,* or *Le Pardon de Ploërmel,* included in Harnett's *Still Life* of 1885 (pl. 35), the young maiden left at the altar is mistaken for one.

8. Only the last two letters of the name Rosamund are visible on the flat sheet music in the High Museum version of *Still Life with Bust of Dante,* but in *The Imperial Eagle,* its variant, the rolled sheet music clearly reads *ROSA[MUND]*.

9. In *The Imperial Eagle,* the book *Fantomes* has replaced *Juliette.* The volume may be a reference to Victor Hugo's poem "Fantomes," which was published in the collection *Les Orientales* (1829). "Fantomes" concerns a beautiful young woman who cares only about parties and ball gowns. She gets a chill and dies but is periodically allowed to return as a ghost dancing, a pleasure she had so loved in life. It is impossible to tell if Harnett meant the Hugo poem, but its theme is certainly appropriate.

10. Denis de Rougemont makes an interesting connection between the writings of the marquis de Sade and courtly love in *Passion and Society,* trans. Montgomery Belgion (London: Faber & Faber, 1941). He observes (p. 212) that the writings of the marquis de Sade "issued from the intolerable tension of a mind that sustained *its life* with this contradiction [of love and sensation] by undergoing sensuality and yet yearning for the courtly ideal. That is where the Marquis obtained his material, and it is also what supplied the motive power of his rebellion. Sade admired the poetry of Petrarch, as he remarks in his *Crimes de l'amour. . . .* [Petrarch] was unaware of woman as 'a means.' Sade, a product of the eighteenth century, was only too conscious of the monotonous tyranny which the 'means' exerted."

11. Peter Eikemeier claims that seventeenth-century Dutch painters were less than innovative in their use of books in still lifes. "In paintings of the seventeenth century it is true that books were regarded as vehicles of spiritual merit, but this was contrasted with universal warnings against the piling up of empty knowledge and a false use of reading. Reading is of service in this life, in this world or in the next, and should not become an end in itself; as a recreation and pastime it was completely despised" (my translation; see "Bücher in Bildern," offprint from *De Arte et Libris: Festschrift Erasmus, 1934–1984* [Amsterdam: Erasmus Antiquariaat en Boekhandel, 1984], p. 67).

12. Actual copies of "Hélas, Quelle Douleur" (Alas, what sadness) have not been located. Alfred Frankenstein, however, identified the piece as the work of Servel (*After the Hunt: William Harnett and Other American Still Life Painters, 1870–1900,* rev. ed. [Berkeley and Los Angeles: University of California Press, 1969], p. 41). A religious chorus by Louis-Emmanuel Jadin begins with these words, but it does not appear to match Harnett's score. I wish to thank Pierre Vidal, Bibliothèque Nationale, Paris,

for this information. The same piece of music appears in *Still Life* of 1888, where Harnett also seems to be using it as a commentary. In *My Gems* the wickedness of Richard III and Rigoletto acts as a foil to the purity of Romeo and Juliet and of Gilda, and Harnett may have been expressing the same regret for man's loss of faith and honor.

13. Although not all the words on the sheet music are visible, a full translation would read: "Truly meet it is and just, truly right and wholesome for the soul, to sound forth Thy praise, O Lord, in every time, but more festively on this night when Christ our Paschal Lamb was sacrificed" (*The Masses of Holy Week and the Easter Vigil,* arranged by Godfrey L. Diekmann, O.S.B., 2nd ed. [Collegeville, Minn.: Liturgical Press, 1957], p. 169). The salvation theme is underscored by the reference to a sacrament performed at Easter.

14. *The Complete Poetical Works of John Greenleaf Whittier* (Boston and New York: Houghton Mifflin & Co., 1894), pp. 324, 326.

15. I would like to thank Doreen Bolger for sharing information on the patronage of Abbe.

16. William Cullen Bryant and Sydney Howard Gay, *A Popular History of the United States, from the First Discovery of the Western Hemisphere by the Northmen, to the End of the First Century of the Union of the States,* 4 vols. (New York: Scribner, Armstrong & Co., 1876–81), 1, p. viii.

17. "A Fine Still-Life Painting," *Springfield Daily Republican,* November 7, 1887, p. 6.

18. *The Works of John Ruskin,* ed. E. T. Cook and Alexander Wedderburn, 39 vols. (London: George Allen; New York: Longmans, Green & Co., 1903–12), 5, pp. 321, 322, quoted in Morris, *Image of the Middle Ages,* p. 203.

AFTER THE HUNT

ELIZABETH JANE CONNELL

William Michael Harnett's quartet of paintings entitled *After the Hunt* (pls. 28, 29, 33, 34) are among his most celebrated works. The first three versions, painted in Munich (two in 1883 and one in 1884), are the artistic culmination of his Bavarian experience. The fourth version, painted in 1885 in Paris and exhibited at the Salon that year, was destined for lasting fame as a saloon attraction in New York.

The four monumental works are still lifes of antique hunting gear and small game hung upon old wooden doors that have elaborate hinges. All the objects are meticulously rendered using sophisticated trompe-l'oeil techniques. Beginning with an inventory of hat, hunting horn, gun, game bag, sword, and upland game birds and adding or rearranging objects, Harnett created increasingly grand and complex compositions. The first and second versions are nearly identical; their fan-shaped orchestrations of gear and catch are visually secured by the long diagonal of the gun. The second version is distinguished, in part, from the first by the ventral presentation of the mallard drake. Notable additions to the third version are antlers, an alpenstock, and a hare; and to the fourth, a horseshoe, a pistol, a key, and a flask. The last two versions include decorative hinges of increased scale, and the compositions are characterized by an X-shaped format.

Harnett's hunting subjects display an air of Continental sophistication and connoisseurship and speak of masculine leisure and retreat, of wealth and elegance. The hunting equipment is of European origin, following the taste of fashionable collectors of antique bric-a-brac. Echoes of seventeenth-century Dutch masterpieces, nineteenth-century German genre and still-life paintings, and contemporary European photographs can be observed. Traditions of nineteenth-century American still-life painting and prints also resound in these pictures, and a certain late Victorian penchant for reflection and reverie is evoked in the dark tonalities and precisely detailed accounts of age and wear.

Harnett's *After the Hunt* paintings are steeped in the pictorial still-life traditions of Northern European game pieces. While in Munich, he could have studied such examples as Jacopo de' Barbari's *Still Life with Partridge, Iron Gauntlets, and Crossbow Bolt* (fig. 130).[1] Painted in Germany in 1504 and considered the earliest extant trompe-l'oeil easel picture, this work manifests many characteristics found in Harnett's game still lifes: the sharp relief of objects hung against a wood-grained surface; the calculated balance of volume, silhouette, and color; and the concentration on diverse textures and reflective properties. In addition, Jacopo's combination of dead game and armor alludes to battle and the hunt as proper pursuits of a nobleman. Like Jacopo's implements, Harnett's hunting horn, sword, and pistol are not used to hunt the game with which they are associated in his compositions. Instead of being an accurate record of a particular event, Harnett's paintings evoke a more broadly conceived aura of the hunt. Wealthy gentlemen, his intended patrons, would recognize and admire these references to the success of their sporting exploits.

Painters of such souvenirs or trophies of the hunt flourished in the second half of the seventeenth century, particularly in Holland and Flanders. Specialists such as Cornelis Lelienbergh described a variety of hunting implements in a vertical format, with a game bird or hare suspended above a table or shelf. Concurrently, Melchior d'Hondecoeter, William Gowe Ferguson, and Jan Baptist Weenix were concerned

---

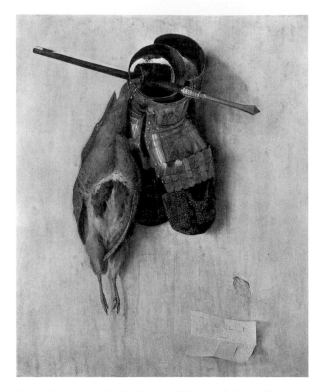

Fig. 130. Jacopo de' Barbari, *Still Life with Partridge, Iron Gauntlets, and Crossbow Bolt,* 1504. 20⅜ x 16⅝ in. Bayerisches Staatsgemäldesammlungen, Munich

and David Neal. The Viennese-born Eibl, who studied under the enormously influential Wilhelm von Diez at the Academy in Munich, was best known for his elaborate and often decorative still lifes of dead game. Neal, one of the first Americans to gain prominence painting in the Munich style, was an accomplished portraitist and history and still-life painter who excelled at the illusionistic techniques for which his teacher, Karl von Piloty, was acclaimed.

The hunting pictures of Eibl and Neal—for example, Eibl's *Still Life with Wild Game* of 1875 (Wallraf-Richartz Museum, Cologne) and Neal's *After the Hunt (Retour de chasse)* of 1870 (fig. 132)—depict dramatically lit interiors with tables, chairs, and floors laden with illusionistically rendered game, hunting gear, and bric-a-brac. Based on a special type produced in Munich and Vienna, these large-scale still lifes recall some of the more elaborate Dutch Baroque game pieces in composition and technique. With their lavish display of man-made objects, they also emulate the *pronkstilleven* that originated in Holland and Flanders. Harnett likewise aspired toward the luxurious in his works. He collected the kinds of antiques and reproduction antiques his wealthy patrons enjoyed and frequently used these objects as subjects in his paintings after 1880.[2] In the *After the Hunt* series, he incorporated such rarities as a shotgun decorated with a carved stag, an inlaid wheel-lock rifle, a flintlock

with developing game pieces utilizing trompe-l'oeil devices and techniques. Their works usually depict birds and accessories, such as lures, horns, and falconry equipment, hung before a monochrome background, wood wall, or niche that seems to recede behind the picture plane rather than project forward into the viewer's space. A variant of this type of game piece is the trompe-l'oeil still life of hunting gear painted on a larger canvas to accommodate more elaborate hunting implements, including traps and, later, rifles, swords, and other accessories. Despite the increase in size, there is a certain solemnity in a work such as *Still Life—Bird Hunting Instruments* (fig. 131), painted about 1670 by the best-known practitioner of the genre, Johannes Leemans. The intimate quality of this painting, the arrangement of objects in an ordered state of repose, and the brooding, coloristic restraint, which recalls Dutch tonal paintings of the 1630s and 1640s, are all evoked in Harnett's *After the Hunt* series.

By the time Harnett arrived in Germany, the influence of seventeenth-century Dutch art was well established, especially in Munich and Düsseldorf, the major German art centers. Still-life painting, which did not have a strong tradition in early-nineteenth-century Munich, became increasingly popular by the third quarter of the century through the work of Ludwig Eibl

Fig. 131. Johannes Leemans, *Still Life—Bird Hunting Instruments,* ca. 1670. Oil on canvas, 40 x 39⅛ in. Seattle Art Museum, Purchase Fund (64.30)

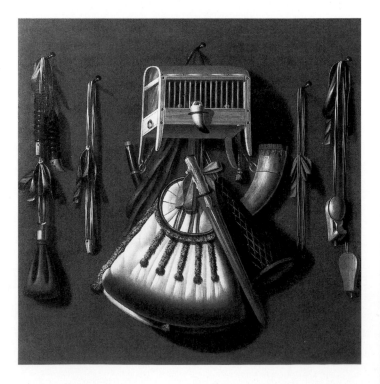

Fig. 132. David Neal, *After the Hunt* (*Retour de chasse*), 1870. Oil on canvas, 62 x 46 in.
Los Angeles County Museum of Art, Gift of Mr. and Mrs. Will Richeson

pistol with applied silver elements, and a lion-headed hunting sword.[3]

During his stay abroad, Harnett also may have been impressed by the work of other regional still-life painters, such as Johann Wilhelm Preyer of Düsseldorf. Harnett had embraced Preyer's *feinmalerei* technique before departing for Europe. However, the specific compositional devices and motifs of Harnett's pictures were more likely derived from nineteenth-century German genre painting. Optimistic, human-interest themes portrayed with absolute fidelity to nature were cultivated to near perfection in Germany in works that were highly prized by wealthy collectors in Europe and America. Among the many masters of genre painting probably known to Harnett were Franz von Defregger, Eduard Grützner, and Moritz von Schwind of Munich; Johann Peter Hasenclever of Düsseldorf; and Ludwig Knaus of Berlin.[4]

Interior scenes with still-life vignettes abound in the oeuvres of these artists. The repertoire of hunt and battle accessories hung on walls was well established, accessible, and perpetuated throughout the century. The arrangement of guns and game bag topped by a

Fig. 134. Franz von Defregger, *Spechbacher and His Son Andreas,* 1869. Oil on canvas, 37¾ x 48⅜ in. Tiroler Landesmuseum Ferdinandeum, Innsbruck

Fig. 133. Moritz von Schwind, *The Visit,* ca. 1855. Oil on canvas, 28⅜ x 20⅛ in. Bayerisches Staatsgemäldesammlungen, Munich

feathered Tyrolean hat, found in Schwind's *Visit* of about 1855 (fig. 133), for example, is a forerunner of the basic compositions of Harnett's hunting pictures. The hunting gear, heroic statuary, and world map are accoutrements of a gentleman's domain, in this case infiltrated by an inquisitive feminine presence. In Defregger's *Spechbacher and His Son Andreas* of 1869 (fig. 134), the flush of revolutionary fervor is invoked by the prominent placement of guns and sword hung from a stag's antlers on a farmhouse wall. These elements embody the story of the rise of the Tyroleans against Austria in which Andreas, the son of their leader Spechbacher, volunteers as the movement's youngest recruit. In contrast, Harnett isolated symbolic still-life motifs from any narrative context and enlarged the objects to life size, investing them with an iconic presence.

In addition to the inventory of motifs that genre and still-life painting provided, there were ample counterparts in European photography from the mid-1850s onward. Harnett and other painters were attracted to the stark realism of the photographic image and sought to achieve similar verisimilitude in their illusionistic pictures. Photographers, in turn, admired Northern European paintings and wished to create works that would be aesthetically and symbolically equal or superior. In particular, they emulated Dutch still lifes and a variety of sporting prints.

Compositions of groups of small game, birds, or waterfowl, hanging alone or in tandem with hunting gear, culinary paraphernalia, and bric-a-brac, were a speciality of nineteenth-century photographers such as the Alsatian Adolphe Braun, the Frenchmen Charles-Phillipe-Auguste Carey and Louise Laffon, and the British photographers Francis Edmond Currey,

William Lake Price, and Dr. Hugh Welch Diamond. Braun's game pieces most closely approximate Harnett's *After the Hunt* pictures in their grandeur of conception and scale and in their remarkable similarity of subject and composition (figs. 82, 83). It is probable that the game still lifes and other themes pioneered by Braun were available in Munich for Harnett to study.[5] Works by the other photographers—especially the complex meditations on mortality by Dr. Diamond—were also possible inspirations for Harnett. In the photograph *Still Life* of the 1850s (fig. 135), a dead hare is suspended at center among cascading brocaded draperies, elaborate vases filled with flowers, a game bag, a powder horn, a shoe, and other worldly excesses that constitute a provocative Victorian vision of the traditional vanitas theme.

While Harnett's *After the Hunt* series relies heavily on European antecedents, the works are not without precedent in America. Hanging still lifes first became popular in the 1850s through prints by Currier and Ives after game pieces by Arthur Fitzwilliam Tait. In the mid-1870s, L. Prang and Company published a series of "Dining-Room Pictures" that included game pieces of waterfowl hanging in front of a neutral background (fig. 92). These chromolithographs, reproduced from paintings by George N. Cass and G. Bossett, were destined to decorate many a Victorian dining room and parlor. Harnett was probably also familiar with the game pieces of Philadelphia artist John Archibald Woodside, Sr., and he was certainly acquainted with the hanging-fowl and dead-game pictures of Pittsburgh's George Hetzel, for Harnett and Hetzel are known to have shared a friendship with Henry Lea Tatnall, a Wilmington, Delaware, businessman turned painter.[6] The motif of the hanging-game still life was also absorbed into popular American photography, as seen in the work of John C. Browne (fig. 136).

In these and other nineteenth-century works, American artists generally showed a preference for trompe-l'oeil still life that seems to project from the picture plane into the viewer's space, whereas the Europeans, especially the Dutch, more frequently chose to portray the catch of the day on a table or in

Fig. 135. Dr. Hugh Welch Diamond, *Still Life,* 1850s. Royal Photographic Society of Great Britain, London

Fig. 136. John C. Browne, *Delaware Water Gap,*
October 1880. Photograph.
Library Company of Philadelphia

retains a sporty arabesque of tail feathers and a stiffly groomed comb. The bird conveys a dignified air, its piercing eye meeting the viewer's with a look of disdain. Tufts of down, caught in splinters of the plank wall, speak of the freshness of the kill, and a feather seemingly stuck in the frame lures the viewer in for a closer look.

More solemn and less visceral than *Plucked Clean* is Harnett's *Merganser* of 1883 (fig. 138), painted when the artist began the *After the Hunt* series. Unlike the flippant rooster, the subject of this picture has succumbed with the graceful poise of a ballerina. Balance is accomplished by the placement of the feet, which are extended at right angles, and by the vertical seam of wood planks that stitch together the tail, leg, and wing at equidistant points. In addition, there is a decorative quality in this work: Harnett delighted in depicting the undulating folds and scallops of the underwing; the silhouetted rhythms of dark wing against light breast and light wing against dark wall;

Fig. 137. Nikolaus Gysis, *Still Life with Hen,* 1881.
Oil on canvas, 24¼ x 15½ in. Bayerisches
Staatsgemäldesammlungen, Munich

a niche—illusionistically behind the picture plane. In their hanging-game still lifes, European painters were more prone to indulge in the ornate and decorative and to delight in the particular contortions of death: the flair of a wing spread to full span, the drama of shadows playing boldly upon a wall, the complexity of a clawed foot bound by knots and loops of string or ribbon. American artists, on the other hand, were more factual and straightforward and tended to produce game pieces of greater austerity, using simple lines and controlled symmetry. In the *After the Hunt* pictures, the European Baroque is tempered by a purposeful American clarity; rarely does virtuosity or embellishment overpower the inherent storytelling nature of the still-life objects.

Harnett's own preludes to *After the Hunt* were painted in Munich and are relatively few. These works depict single, isolated dead animals rendered with illusionistic finesse and exactitude. The subject of his first hanging, or vertical, still life, *Plucked Clean* of 1882 (pl. 25), is the suspended corpse of a rooster. (A later variant is *For Sunday's Dinner* of 1888 [pl. 42].) *Plucked Clean* is probably modeled after Nikolaus Gysis's *Still Life with Hen* (fig. 137), painted in Munich in 1881, though Harnett's picture does not exude the same level of grotesque physiognomy and pungent death and defeathering. Instead, it takes on a narrative aspect, colored by a wry sense of humor not unlike that of the German genre painters. The rooster, despite its stretched body and taut and bloodied skin,

Fig. 138. William M. Harnett, *Merganser,* 1883. Oil on canvas, 34⅛ x 20½ in.
San Diego Museum of Art

the soft loop of string juxtaposed with the sharp claw of a webbed foot.[7]

In 1883, Harnett probably exhibited a picture of a dead hare at the Munich Academy, where it reportedly drew admiring crowds.[8] The hare in that painting may have served as the model, if not the inspiration, for those that appear in the third and fourth versions of *After the Hunt.* Certainly the hare in the fourth version is nearly identical, though in mirror image, to that in another variant, *Trophy of the Hunt* (pl. 36), painted in 1885, which depicts in clinical detail a single bloody-nosed hare strung by one foot from a nail driven into a door. *Trophy of the Hunt* invites storytelling, and there is beauty in its perfect symmetry. The hare is framed between the straps of the hinges. The composition is further balanced on either side by a rivet and a ring; the diameter of the ring equals that of the decorative holes of the hinges. The near hind foot of the hare, extended at a right angle to the top horizontal strap, is counterbalanced by the animal's ears. Narrative allegorical possibilities are many: old rivets are replaced by new; some nails are unused while others have splintered the wood and enlarged the nail holes by frequent use; blood and rust stain the door; and the freshness of the kill is echoed in the new wood exposed by a recently broken hinge strap.

These early individual experiments, in which the artist chose objects for their narrative potential, calculated delicate balancing acts, and studied shapes and textures in mellow light, lay the groundwork for the challenging complexities of the *After the Hunt* series. Starkly isolated objects imbued with an iconic quality did not draw Harnett's attention again until his return from Europe in 1886, when revolvers, pipes, horseshoes, and chickens became subjects of special interest.

In what is probably the first version of *After the Hunt* (pl. 28), a game bag, shotgun, powder horn, hunting horn, and partridge are hung from a single point near the top of a wooden door, and the layered arrangement is crowned with a Tyrolean hat.[9] Adjacent to this group of objects hangs a string of upland birds, including a partridge and a mallard drake. Perhaps to introduce a hint of animation into this otherwise languid grouping, the artist positioned a sheaf of grain so that it seems to blossom from the bell of the hunting horn. The hilt of the sword emerges from behind the game bag, the carved lion in its handle appearing to snarl in the direction of the key plate.

This collection of hunting gear and catch fans outward from the topmost point and is held in place by the symmetry of two triangles—one created by the door hinges and key plate, the other by three rivets. The intersection of the triangles forms a diamond pattern, which is approximately repeated and emphasized in the shape and position of the game bag. In this controlled system of design, no object imposes itself upon the integrity of another; each is given its full measure of space and light. Textures of leather, felt, iron, and down are recorded with absolute clarity. The patina of wood, the sheen of bone and ivory, the polish of brass, and the iridescence of feathers are all equally celebrated. The diagonals of gun, gun strap, sword hilt, and sheaf of grain are played against the circles and curves of hat, coiled hunting horn, powder horn, cascading feathers, open wings, and decorative hinges. While the gravitational pull of limp and rigid objects hung on a door is fully realized, the otherwise sobering tone of the subject is counteracted by the lift of the upturned horn.

Beyond the visual spectrum of design and detail, the picture is tantalizingly ambiguous and emotionally compelling. The effect of a trompe-l'oeil deception is usually short-lived, even momentary. In the hands of this master, however, the power of deception is sustained by such ploys as concealing the exact place and manner in which the still-life objects are hung. The viewer, whose curiosity has been piqued, tends to read the objects as levitating slightly before the surface of the door. Common knowledge of the history or function of each object is supported by personal memories and associations, which further enhance the viewer's experience of the composition.

The second version of *After the Hunt* (pl. 29), is a sophisticated refinement of the initial work. Notably, the mallard drake has been turned around to expose a light expanse of breast and the underside of one wing. In a subtle yet dynamic change, the cord of the powder horn now overlaps the large coil of the hunting horn instead of lying behind it, an adjustment that allows for the outward curve of the powder horn and increases the perception of three-dimensionality. These artful revisions point to the probability that, of the two 1883 versions, the second was an attempt to perfect the original concept.

All the objects project in strong relief from the brooding darkness of the green door. Harnett said he wanted his models "to have the mellowing effect of age . . . the rich effect that age and usage gives."[10] He defined use and wear in the dented brass surface of the hunting horn, expressed time in the rust stains of hinges and key plate, and articulated age and distinction in the detail of a running stag carved on the gunstock. Solemn and still, the objects hang in nostalgic reverie, commemorating times gone by.

The contemplative nature of the first and second versions is equally, though differently, observed in the third, painted in 1884 (pl. 33). Here, on a slightly larger scale, Harnett introduced new objects and a more complex format. A similar door supports a stag's antlers, a wheel-lock rifle crossed with an alpenstock, a powder horn, a larger hunting horn than in the earlier versions, and the now-familiar Tyrolean hat, game bag, and sword. Behind the antlers hang a pigeon and a hare, and below, a partridge is suspended by a string in the angle formed by the rifle and alpenstock. This time, the sword points upward, its hilt in the lower portion of the composition, the carved lion fixing its gaze on the axe-wielding warrior that forms the key plate. This arrangement of objects is framed by massive hinges whose straps extend across the width of the canvas.

The result is more ponderous, but its effect is no less ponderable. The dominant X-form at the center of the composition is more staunchly geometric and rigid in its symmetry than it is in the more fluid earlier versions. The objects are somewhat larger and consume more of the canvas. The dead animals are strung up more visibly and vividly, yet an expression of gentleness and even compassion is present. Mellow golden light illuminates the objects. The thick, soft fur of the hare is meant to be admired; no blood stains are recorded. The animal's stance suggests its vitality at full run rather than lifeless rigidity. The birds are captured seemingly in mid-flight. The animals are treated with the same respect as the rifle. No excitement of the chase or anticipation of a feast is suggested. Full of silence, the picture is a venerable emblem of the hunt and its elegant accessories.

Quite in contrast to the suspended animation of the third version and the somber, restrained tenor of the first two is the aggressive vitality of the fourth *After the Hunt,* in which Harnett pulled out all the stops (pl. 34). In 1885, the artist left Munich and traveled to Paris to "refer the question of [his] ability as a painter to a higher court," by which he meant the Salon.[11] He spent three months completing this last of the *After the Hunt* pictures, the version that made the unusual journey from Salon to saloon. The canvas is the largest of them all, measuring ten inches wider and more than fourteen inches higher than the first, and the palette is brighter. A horseshoe, pistol, key, and flask have been added to the inventory of objects, and the cross formation of the composition has been doubled. Objects radiate outward from the hat like spokes from the hub of a wheel. As always, Harnett maintained control: diagonals run parallel to one another; horizontal stability is provided by long hinge straps; and the horseshoe and flask mark the endpoints of the central vertical axis.

The picture is highly charged with animation, humor, and wonder. The dead animals are whimsically choreographed: a partridge executes a perfect upside-down pirouette at center stage, within the circumference of the hunting horn, while below, its mate imitates the stance in mirror image. The hare, still the bloodied, clinical specimen of *Trophy of the Hunt,* is now positioned with its foot poised as if to spin the hunting horn like a wheel of fortune. And what of the marvels of gravity? The alpenstock floats unaccount-

ably while the sword is mysteriously held in place. And how is the angle of the rifle maintained? "In painting from still life I do not closely imitate nature. Many points I leave out and many I add. Some models are only suggestions."[12] As Harnett himself said, he often made aesthetic judgments for the sake of his composition.[13]

In each picture in the series, objects are imbued with symbolic qualities. In the fourth version, the horseshoe hangs in a traditional good-luck position, at the top of the door. The blood of the hare mingles with rust stains, and a broken hinge succumbs to time and use. This picture, like the others, represents layers of time: the past, suggested by antique bric-a-brac, weathered doors, and broken hinges; and the present, immediately following the capture, when the blood still moves in the animal's veins. But only this final version offers a further dimension of time—the future. A key, shiny from use, hangs in tempting proximity to the keyhole, inviting the viewer to contemplate unlocking the door and to imagine what lies beyond such poignant encounters with mortality.

Harnett certainly hoped the fourth *After the Hunt*—his greatest virtuoso effort—would be the ticket to his future success in Europe. But however grand or well positioned on the Salon's walls it may have been, the picture was not sold.[14] Harnett left Paris almost immediately, returning to New York in 1886. The first version of *After the Hunt* remained with Adolph Loewi of Regensburg.[15] The second and third versions were purchased by patrons Francis Charles Sessions of Columbus, Ohio, and Monroe Smith of Philadelphia, respectively. These pictures remained in private hands until long after Harnett's death.[16] The fourth *After the Hunt* was bought by New Yorker Theodore Stewart, who installed it in his Warren Street saloon. The painting was framed in a shadow box, protected by a railing, and specially lighted. It achieved immediate notoriety. "There is on Warren Street," wrote a reporter for the *Star,* "a famous lunch and liquor place, whose glory is a panel picture of large size named 'After the Hunt.'"[17]

The fame of this last *After the Hunt* spread to the art community, and it became a prototype for many successive hanging game and other vertical still lifes. Harnett's technical expertise inspired an entire American school of trompe-l'oeil painting in the late nineteenth century that continued into the early 1920s. Skilled practitioners Richard La Barre Goodwin, George Cope, Alexander Pope, John Frederick Peto, Jefferson David Chalfant, and Charles Meurer produced many remarkable still lifes with game, fishing equipment, or military paraphernalia hung upon a door. Nevertheless, Harnett's *After the Hunt* pictures—the first three versions as much as the fourth—remain unsurpassed in their unity and elegance of design, skill of execution, and depth of psychological power.

NOTES

Special thanks to my colleagues Marc Simpson and Sally Mills of the Fine Arts Museums of San Francisco; Clyde Singer of the Butler Institute of American Art; and Doreen Bolger, Kathie Bennewitz, and Jane Myers of the Amon Carter Museum, for their patient, friendly, and enthusiastic research assistance. Thanks as well to Linda Ayers of the Wadsworth Atheneum and Jennifer Savelle of the Honolulu Academy of Arts. I am also indebted to Naomi Rosenblum of Parsons School of Design and Becky Simmons of the International Museum of Photography at George Eastman House for their insights regarding the photographs of Adolphe Braun. Without the assistance of Daniel M. Galbreath, Columbus Museum of Art trustee and eminent hunter, and that of the late Leonid Tarassuk, Senior Research Associate, Department of Arms and Armor, The Metropolitan Museum of Art, I would not have had the good fortune of having detailed analysis and identification of the game and antique arms portrayed by Harnett.

1. During Harnett's sojourn in Munich, this important still life was housed in the gallery at Augsburg, thirty-five miles to the northwest. In 1909, the painting became part of the collections of the Alte Pinakothek, Munich (see Erich Steingräber, *The Alte Pinakothek, Munich* [London: Scala/Philip Wilson, 1985], p. 6; and Ernst Buchner, *Alte Pinakothek, Munich* [Munich: Carl Gerber, 1938], p. 13).

2. See *The Wm. Michael Harnett Collection: His Own Reserved Paintings, Models and Studio Furnishings,* sale cat., Stan. V. Henkels at Thos. Birch's Sons, Auctioneers, Philadelphia, February 23–24, 1893.

3. The decorated shotgun that appears in the first and second versions of *After the Hunt* is a double-barrel, muzzle-loading model dating from the mid-nineteenth century. In the third version, Harnett depicted a wheel-lock hunting and target rifle of late Baroque design decorated with wood inlay and a carved stag. The rifle is probably German and may be dated about 1740. Although by 1700 most Europeans considered the wheel-lock outdated and preferred the flintlock rifle, the wheel-lock continued to be used in Germany and Austria. A nearly identical rifle with mother-of-pearl inlay is depicted in the fourth *After the Hunt.* On its side plate, Harnett incorporated the name *TRIEVT,* the initials *J* and *E,* and the date *1710.* Trient, or Trent, is not found in standard gunmakers' directories. When this type of firearm is signed at all, the signature is usually located on the barrel or lock rather than on the side plate. The date, which may be considered early for such a gun, is perhaps a fabrication of Harnett's, meant to emphasize and enhance a feeling of antiquity in the picture. The fourth version also includes a flintlock pistol with applied silver decoration of a parrot's head. The pistol dates from the late eighteenth century and is probably German, Austrian, or Bohemian. All four hunt pictures depict a mid-nineteenth-century lion-headed hunting or navel dirk—a type of short, straight sword. Also included in the four pictures are powder horns and hunting horns that probably date from the late eighteenth or the nineteenth century. I am grateful to the late Leonid Tarassuk for his expert assistance in identifying these objects.

4. For the influence of German genre painting on the art of Harnett, see especially William H. Gerdts and Russell Burke, *American Still-Life Painting* (New York, Washington, and London: Praeger Publishers, 1971), p. 142; and William H. Gerdts, "On the Tabletop: Europe and America," *Art in America* 60, no. 5 (September–October 1972), pp. 62–69.

5. See Douglas R. Nickel, "Harnett and Photography," pp. 179–82.

6. See "Recollections of Henry Lea Tatnall (1829–1885) by His Son Henry Lea Tatnall, Jr.," Henry Lea Tatnall Papers, Historical Society of Delaware, Wilmington, pp. 12–13.

7. Very similar in composition, though somewhat less elegant, is Harnett's *Mallard Drake Hanging* of 1883 (National Gallery of Canada, Ottawa).

8. Alfred Frankenstein, *After the Hunt: William Harnett and Other American Still Life Painters, 1870–1900,* rev. ed. (Berkeley and Los Angeles: University of California Press, 1969), p. 69.

9. The picture at Kennedy Galleries (formerly in the collection of the Amon Carter Museum) is generally considered the first of the series, though no reason is given in the many sources in which this version and the second are mentioned. Frankenstein initially ranked the Kennedy Galleries picture as the second version (see *After the Hunt,* p. x), but reversed his opinion in a 1973 letter to Hirschl & Adler Galleries (quoted, in part, in *The Art of Collecting,* exhib. cat. [New York: Hirschl & Adler Galleries, 1984], p. 29), noting the picture's smaller size and simpler composition.

10. "Painted Like Real Things: The Man Whose Pictures Are a Wonder and a Puzzle," interview in *New York News,* probably 1889 or 1890, quoted in Frankenstein, *After the Hunt,* p. 55.

11. Ibid.

12. Ibid.

13. Referring specifically to the fourth *After the Hunt,* Harnett said, "Take for instance the handle of the old sword. . . . The ivory has a particularly mellow tint. Had I chosen a sword with an ivory handle of a different tint the tone of the picture would have been ruined" (ibid.).

14. American still-life painting in general received little attention in Salon reviews (see Lois Marie Fink, *American Art at the Nineteenth-Century Paris Salons* [Washington, D.C.: National Museum of American Art, Smithsonian Institution, 1990], p. 251. On comments about Harnett's work in the Salon exhibition, see Frankenstein, *After the Hunt,* p. 70.

15. Loewi is mentioned as the owner in *Wm. Michael Harnett Collection,* p. 8, no. 40. The painting was rediscovered in Munich in 1968.

16. The frame (which is thought to be the original) of the Sessions picture bears a paper label that reads: *Earles' Galleries and Looking Glass Warerooms, 816 Chestnut Street, Philadelphia.* This suggests Earle's may have sold the painting or at least provided the frame. This version of *After the Hunt* remained with the Sessions family until it was bequeathed to the Columbus Museum of Art, Ohio, in 1919. The Smith picture was exhibited at Earle's in fall 1892 in the memorial show *Paintings of the Late W. M. Harnett on Exhibition* (no. 32). The Butler Institute of American Art, Youngstown, Ohio, acquired the painting from the estate of Monroe Smith through the Downtown Gallery, New York, in 1954.

17. "Art's Counterfeiting: Some Notable Examples of Deceiving the Eyes by Pictures," *Star* (New York), December 30, 1885, p. 6.

HARNETT AND MUSIC

Many a Touching Melody

MARC SIMPSON

It is a commonplace that music is the most abstract of the arts. While literature, painting, and architecture, for example, have traditionally seemed imbedded in the world of objects, music has hovered in the realm of the spiritual.[1] William Michael Harnett, fascinated with the surface aspects of things and living in an intensely materialistic age, was evidently susceptible nevertheless to the emotional powers of music.[2] Throughout his career, specific musical instruments recur in his paintings as prominent, even heroic, characters. Likewise, pieces of music that would have been familiar to his late-nineteenth-century audience appear continually, establishing the tone and atmosphere of his works. Fully a quarter of Harnett's known paintings, and virtually all of his most ambitious ones, touch upon music.

Harnett was an amateur musician who played the flute. He probably read music, rather than simply played by ear, since he sometimes performed duets with his friend and biographer Edward Taylor Snow,[3] and his generally faithful transcriptions of printed music show a respect for and understanding of the specific meanings of musical signs. While he was living in New York in the 1870s, Harnett's neighbors were members of the Manhattan Band, whose playing, according to the artist James Edward Kelly, "seemed to soothe and inspire him—or perhaps drive him—to extra effort."[4] Further, the catalogue to Harnett's estate sale indicates that he possessed a fairly large collection of musical instruments, many acquired in Europe (fig. 139).[5] He must have kept the majority of these for props rather than performance, since in his paintings they sometimes display eccentricities in assembly that a musician would not perpetrate.[6] But his misstrung violins and out-of-alignment clarinets are exceptions; Harnett usually paid faithful attention to the form and structure of his instruments.[7]

Other than these scant testimonies there are almost no extant documents concerning Harnett's musical life, either regarding his attendance at concerts or operas or his participation in instrumental or choral ensembles.[8] Only the many pages of sheet music portrayed in his paintings—bindings with bold display type and detached pages, principally from collections of melodies suitable for flute or violin—provide clues concerning his taste in music.[9]

It is in these depictions of sheet music that Harnett manifests some of his most startling accomplishments, ranging from the purely technical manipulation of paint, so as to suggest light falling on printed paper, to the development of an iconographic program, wherein the choice of melodies demonstrably shades the subtle meanings of his compositions. In addition, Harnett's depictions of music are so faithful to such details as key, meter, and melodic progression that they reproduce staves fully capable of conveying musical messages rather than, as in his paintings of letters and newspapers, merely a texture of black on white.[10] His music is thus playable, and the few measures he provided are usually sufficient to reveal the entire melody to the consciousness of the musically literate viewer.[11] In this manner the artist crossed the line separating illusion from reality and, by adding the sense of sound to the normal silence of paintings, accomplished true synaesthesia.[12] The paintings of music are thus simultaneously Harnett's nearest approaches to reality and his most abstract creations.

From beginning to end of his short career, from *Mortality and Immortality* of 1876 to *Professor's Old Friends* of 1891, Harnett painted tabletop still-life paintings showing music and musical instruments. The objects in such works rarely exist in a vacuum; their nature and combination more often suggest a space (study or library, for instance) and an atmosphere

Fig. 139. *William M. Harnett's Musical Instruments,* in *The Wm. Michael Harnett Collection: His Own Reserved Paintings, Models and Studio Furnishings,* sale cat., Stan. V. Henkels at Thos. Birch's Sons, Auctioneers, Philadelphia, February 23–24, 1893, opposite p. 10

(luxury or penury) that extend beyond the limits of the canvas. In his tabletop compositions involving music, Harnett conjured up one space more frequently than any other: a masculine, scholarly, bohemian study filled with well-thumbed texts, musical instruments, and curious objects in a state of casual disorder. By virtue of its intimacy and informality and through the implication of its privacy, this space can be identified as the artist's (or, with a small leap of imagination, the viewer's) own. For nearly all of his career, whether he was physically in Philadelphia, Munich, Paris, or New York, Harnett returned to this imaginary room as his subject.

Harnett baldly announced the space as a realm for the contemplation of life's most basic mysteries in one of his earliest works, *Mortality and Immortality* (pl. 3). A violin and bow rest on sheet music to the right, while to the left a pile of books provides the base for a toothful skull whose empty eye sockets stare at the

viewer.[13] A vanitas interpretation of the work is inevitable.[14] The crucial issue involves the interpretation of the skull: is this death's head a pessimistic warning of the futility of human endeavor or a physical fact contrasted with the spiritual achievements of music and literature?[15] Harnett provided a double-edged clue in the music that he chose to portray, an arrangement in D major for two treble instruments of "Con te li prendi" (Take them with you) from the opera *Norma* (1831) by Vincenzo Bellini.[16]

The opera was immensely popular in New York and would have been well known to much of Harnett's audience.[17] Its plot revolves around the illicit love of the Druid high-priestess Norma for the Roman proconsul Pollione. Norma, referring to her two illegitimate children, sings "Con te li prendi" with Adalgisa, a young priestess who, unaware of Norma's love for Pollione, has sought to be released from her vows so that she can elope with him to Italy.[18] The two women, caught in confessions of sacrilegious and sexual betrayal, seek to comfort and sacrifice for each other. The duet embodies noble aspirations, and its revelations move the characters to righteous actions—Adalgisa to a reaffirmation of her religious vows and Norma to public confession ending, in best nineteenth-century fashion as regards a fallen woman, in death.[19] Thus, one reading of "Con te li prendi" suggests that death will indeed take, or prevail over, music and literature. Equally plausible, however, is the interpretation that music and literature will triumph over the grave. After all, this optimistic message is the import of the present title of the painting as well as of the title—*Life and Death*—of a work, probably this very picture, that was included in the 1892 Earle's Galleries exhibition.[20] For, if the skull stands for mortality or death, then the books and music clearly symbolize immortality or life. It seems that, at least in this early painting, Harnett did not completely control the iconographic elements of his composition.

Two years later Harnett again used music to affirm the contemplative nature of his still-life realm. *Music and Literature* (probably the work also known as *After a Hard Night's Study*) of 1878 (pl. 10) is one of the artist's most ambitious early paintings.[21] A clutter of books, a nearly spent candle in a brass stick, and a spattered inkwell and pen bear witness to a student's long night of solitary study. The student, having now abandoned his desk, apparently turned to music between his readings, for a disassembled flute made of ebony with an ivory head and silvered keys lies to the left. The carefully detailed crack in the head joint identifies this as a specific instrument, presumably the artist's own, since it will travel with him over the course of his career.[22] The flute rests on top of a fairly difficult set of variations in 3/8 time in the key of A major on themes from Giuseppe Verdi's *La Traviata* (1853).[23] The visible measures elaborate the melody from the love duet of Alfredo and the dying Violetta, "Parigi, o cara" (We shall leave Paris, oh dear one). Evidently, the night of study has been interspersed with melancholy ruminations about mortality and the transience of romantic love.

The presence of Harnett's own instrument has encouraged one scholar to read the painting as "a self-portrait of Harnett the flutist" that conveys "the commonality of music, art and literature, which have been brought together in a conceptual corner of his life."[24] Indeed, music and musical instruments had a well-respected place in the studios of many artists during Harnett's era. Numerous self-portraits, genre interiors, and photographs showing his colleagues' studios testify to the easy mingling of the arts that often took place in the painter's realm.[25] Notably absent from Harnett's oeuvre in this regard, however, are overt references to painting. Paints, brushes, palettes, easels, drawings—the stuff of the studio—simply do not appear in his work.[26] It is almost as if he did not want to bring up the visual arts and thus to suggest that the visions before the viewer were actual paintings—an anxiety of influence with a twist.

During Harnett's sojourn in Europe, from 1880 to 1886, musical instruments played a role in many of his paintings. In a few, such as *Münchener Bote* of 1881 (Yale University Art Gallery, New Haven), *Still Life with Horn* of 1883, and the four versions of *After the Hunt* of 1883 to 1885 (pls. 28, 29, 33, 34), musical instruments are liberated from the urban garret and instead accompany the accoutrements of hunting and country life. Brass horns coexist with arms, food, drink, newspapers, and smoking paraphernalia. Sheet music does not appear in these works; the instruments are for calling and signaling, not for the art of music. Yet these paintings will prove crucial to Harnett's later career, for it is in them that he first experiments with the composition that will bring him his greatest fame: a single object suspended before a door or panel.

For the most part, however, Harnett continued during this period to explore the student's world of *Music and Literature*. The luxury and number of props increase, as does the elaborateness of their presentation. Antique and modern lamps,[27] figural candlesticks, increasingly old and rare-looking books—souvenirs of raids into European antique and curio shops—make their appearance. But, as in the earlier American works, the intermingled pursuits of knowledge and cultural enlightenment dominate the scene.

A Study Table of 1882 (pl. 26) is the largest and most ambitious of these European paintings now known.[28] Nestled among the books, helmet, lamp, and fabrics is a stringed instrument (probably the "Roman mandolin" featured in his estate sale) and Harnett's flute, with its lower section perched precariously on a fanned book. Sheet music drapes over the edge of the table revealing both the cover of an arrangement of tunes from François-Adrien Boïeldieu's *La Dame blanche* (1825)[29] and, in 3/8 time and A major, another variation of "Parigi, o cara" from *La Traviata*. Variations on this aria will recur in several paintings of these years—understandably, Harnett has taken his flute and some favorite music to Europe.

The music shown in *A Study Table* does not readily sustain the vanitas interpretation now often associated with this picture. "Parigi, o cara" is a duet of reconciliation and clarification. Violetta is admittedly at death's door, but peace and transcendence are the promise of Verdi's music, not eternal condemnation for an immoral and luxury ridden life. More determinedly optimistic still is Boïeldieu's *La Dame blanche*. The work is opéra comique at its most fluent and graceful, the music light and virtuosic, the story a delightful concoction of mistaken identities, concealed treasure, and, amid Gothic trappings, the triumph of romantic love.[30]

Fig. 140. William M. Harnett, *Student's Writing Table,* 1882. Oil on canvas, 11½ x 15 in.
Philadelphia Museum of Art, The Albert M. Greenfield and Elizabeth Greenfield Collection

In 1882, Harnett or one of his patrons evidently thought enough of the painting for him to produce a near replica on a much smaller scale, *Student's Writing Table* (fig. 140).[31] Many of the artist's known still-life paintings of musical instruments from his European period were developed on this miniaturizing model. The shift in scale is of dramatic importance, imposing on the viewer's response a magical concentration of energy and resolution. Through miniaturization, the viewer attains an understanding of, and hence power over, the entire scene instantaneously rather than arriving at that knowledge through a study of the parts, as most often happens in the real world (or in paintings on a life scale). To see or, better, to hold one of these precious panels in the hand is to grasp a radically comprehensible vision.[32]

Several of Harnett's works from these years show such an increased elaboration of subject that the space is transformed from that of the scholar's desk into the collector's showcase. In these paintings he does not allow the viewer to imagine that the objects are for use; arrangements are perched upon cabinets, with no place for the student to draw up a chair and actually read the books or play the instruments. In works such as *Still Life with Bust of Dante* and *The Imperial Eagle* (*Still Life with Bust of Dante*), both of 1883 (pl. 27, fig. 141), the choice of instrument complements the staged quality. Emphasizing the element of display, their musical centerpiece is a showy keyed bugle, an instrument popular in the early nineteenth century.[33] Harnett has portrayed music even more elaborate than previous examples (though none of it

Fig. 141. William M. Harnett, *The Imperial Eagle* (*Still Life with Bust of Dante*), 1883. Oil on canvas, 10¼ x 13¾ in. Private collection

suitable for solo bugle),[34] including a cover that probably belongs to Franz Schubert's incidental music to *Rosamund* (1823; D. 797), an unidentified piano piece in D-flat major, and, to the far left, a roll of music that reveals just enough of its title page to demonstrate that it is a piece for nine players. The various elements of these works imply accumulation rather than immediate use. Significantly, these are among the earliest still lifes in which Harnett closed off the background with carved woodwork instead of a neutral atmosphere; here starts the road to the late trompe-l'oeil shelf pictures wherein treasured objects are strongly and boldly displayed without thought of utility.

Among the richest of these precious European panels, and the painting with which he made a well-received debut at the Royal Academy of Arts in London, *Still Life* of 1885 (pl. 35) combines Harnett's flute with a Roman lamp, old books, the often-painted inkwell and pen, and pages from the benediction of a 1680 Roman missal.[35] The modern music that hangs over the edge of the cabinet, partially obscured by the sheets of the "Benedictio cervi" and the cover of the *Traviata* variations that rest over it, reveals the melody from the central section of the aria "O possente magia" (Oh powerful magic) from Giacomo Meyerbeer's *Dinorah,* or *Le Pardon de Ploërmel* (1859).[36] After singing of how he shall be richer than a king by finding a cursed treasure, the Breton goatherd Hoël remembers his beloved Dinorah and claims that he wants the treasure not for himself but for her. This passage is followed immediately by Hoël's reaffirmation that he shall soon be richer "than a monarch on his throne." Thus Harnett isolated this brief moment of selflessness trapped by Hoël's all too human greed. In the end, the story concludes happily for all.

Following his return to the United States, Harnett produced a proliferation of musical still lifes. The majority of these works return the viewer to the scholar's den, but the two largest are clear evocations of a rich collector's library, with carpet-draped cabinets and a welter of objects. The earlier of these is *Music* of 1886 (pl. 38). Commissioned by the saloon owner Theodore Stewart, it follows the general design of Harnett's European works and includes many familiar props—violin and bow (the violin cannot be played, since one string is snapped and curls springily in the air), Roman lamp, visored helmet, blue-and-white Dutch jar, Turkish rug, vellum-bound books (one with the impress of a lute, trumpet, and sword intermeshed), and Gregorian neumes ("Benedictio fontis"), all displayed atop a paneled cabinet.

If many of the objects are familiar from the preceding European works, the sheet music displayed in *Music* is new to Harnett's paintings. There are two covers, one of which appears to be *Mélodies* collected by Edmond Servel,[37] and a sheet of music with at least two selections on it—Servel's *Séparation* (about 1869; 6/8, G major)[38] and Thomas Moore's "'Tis the Last Rose of Summer" (3/4, F major).[39] Both are sentimental ballads of consciously overwrought emotion. *Séparation,* with lyrics by Delambre, tells the tale of a village couple about to part, though only for a while, and closes with the plaint, "Ah! reviens hâte toi si tu m'aimes toujours" (Oh, come back soon if you love me as always). "'Tis the Last Rose of Summer" consists of three stanzas of pathetic feeling in which the narrator, finding a lone rose, plucks and scatters its petals and, in maudlin self-absorption, hopes that death will likewise pluck him when friendships have gone:

> So soon may *I* follow,
> When friendships decay,
> And from Love's shining circle
> The gems drop away!
> When true hearts lie wither'd,
> And fond ones are flown,
> Oh! who would inhabit
> This bleak world alone?[40]

The tune that Moore chose for the lyric, and that Harnett portrayed, is the sentimental and aptly named "Groves of Blarney."

This is the first of several instances in which works by Servel and Moore, in varying arrangements, will appear in Harnett's paintings. While it is tempting to ascribe a face value to the artist's choice of these tunes, thus labeling him a bathetic sentimentalist, the roll of music for Franz Schubert's *Ave Maria* in *Music* cautions against the assumption. The inclusion of such a pious, sacred melody in a work commis-

sioned to hang in a saloon betrays a glimmer of the ironic wit that enlivens many of Harnett's later works.

An even more elaborate library picture followed in 1887 with James Terry Abbe's commission of *Ease* (pl. 41), the only one of the known tabletop still lifes to show both the flute (its head atypically angled downward) and violin (also atypically placed, in a standing position). The only music depicted is a stained folio that hangs over the edge of the table, revealing a melody for treble solo in 4/4 time and B-flat major. A newspaper covers most of the staves, yet a few measures of triplet figures and the cadenza are enough to reveal the closing of "Vi ravviso, o luoghi ameni" (Oh remembrance of scenes long vanished) from Vincenzo Bellini's *La Sonnambula* (1831).[41]

Among Harnett's later tabletop still lifes, *Music* and *Ease* are unusual in both ambition and scale—they are very full pictures, and the objects are depicted life size. The effect is startling. Newspaper writers counted *Music* "among the artistic wonders of New York" and marveled at its impression of reality.[42]

> Notwithstanding the perfection of [*After the Hunt*], the picture called "Music" is almost equally remarkable. . . . The effect is so realistic that one scarcely restrains himself from reaching out his hand to take up the music. The fiddle looks as though it needed only the hand of a master to make it respond to the touch.[43]

As gratifying as the praise of his work must have been for Harnett (there can be no stronger compliment paid to a trompe-l'oeil picture than proclaiming it irresistibly lures the hand), the financial reward would have been no less important. According to one account, Stewart paid a very respectable three thousand dollars for *Music,*[44] and *Ease* likewise provoked attention and a healthy fee.[45]

If *Music* and *Ease* were clear evocations of a rich man's library, most of Harnett's works during these years in New York were, on the contrary, small and restrained returns to the scholar's study. Two nearly identical still lifes of a violin, a roll of sheet music, books, a pipe, a salt-glaze pitcher, and a newspaper earned Harnett acclaim in Philadelphia and Toledo, Ohio.[46] Another series of spare and elegant works from these years includes either Harnett's flute or a piccolo at center: *The Last Rose of Summer* of 1886 (fig. 142), *La Flûte Enchantée* of 1887 (fig. 143), and *My Gems* and *Still Life,* both of 1888 (figs. 126, 74).[47] The last of these paintings includes a piccolo, the cover of *Rigoletto,* and the music for "Hélas, Quelle Douleur" (coupled on a sheet with an unidentified piece in 2/4 and C major). Of the known paintings including piccolos, it seems likely that *Still Life* was the picture mentioned in the catalogue of Harnett's estate sale: "68 Piccolo Painted in the picture exhibited at Cincinnati."[48] If so, this may be the work exhibited

Fig. 142. William M. Harnett, *The Last Rose of Summer,* 1886. Oil on canvas, 24 x 20⅛ in. Cincinnati Art Museum, The Edwin and Virginia Irwin Memorial

Fig. 143.   William M. Harnett, *La Flûte Enchantée,* 1887. Oil on wood, 14 x 12 in.
Courtesy of Hirschl & Adler Galleries, Inc., New York

as *The Student's Den* at the 1888 Cincinnati Centennial Exposition, where *Ease* was also on display. The two would have made artful pendants: the large canvas displaying a rich collector's library, the modest panel showing a poor student's study.

It is in the student's den that Harnett set one of the most fully resolved tabletop still lifes of his late career, *Emblems of Peace* of 1890 (pl. 46). Despite Harnett's title, the work contains no obvious references to the military, inviting speculation about personal matters. The artist's health was precarious at this time, with one hospital stay from December 1888 to February 1889 and another in March, a therapeutic trip to German spas in the summer and early fall, and then yet a further hospital stay in December. After such a year, the opportunity to work once again with the flute, Dutch jar, and meerschaum pipe—Harnett's companions during his productive years—may have prompted his gratitude for a return to routine and somewhat better health. They might very well be "emblems," that is, symbolic signs, of a personal peace.

The music in *Emblems of Peace* is "Papageno's Song" from Wolfgang Amadeus Mozart's *Magic Flute* (1791).[49] One of the few pieces of eighteenth-century music shown in Harnett's paintings, the aria is sung at the charming moment when the audience first sees the bird-catcher, Papageno, "a happy man" who plans to use his net and pipes to catch a wife.[50] Frankenstein reported that Harnett became engaged during 1891 or 1892.[51] Could the inclusion of the Mozart, unusual for Harnett, be a sign that the artist had met the woman who turned his thoughts to marriage?

One conclusion seems clear: the tabletop still lifes with music seek to impress by their erudition. Their very titles, with repeated nouns of learning, such as "study," "student," and "professor,"[52] and honorific adjectives of age reinforce the notion of scholarly tradition. Popular examples of music and literature, mail and objects from foreign lands, allude to cultural pursuits. In 1860, Ralph Waldo Emerson defined culture as "the suggestion from certain best thoughts, that a man has a range of affinities . . . acquaintance with the world, with men of merit, with classes of society, with travel, with eminent persons, and with the high resources of philosophy, art, and religion: books, travel, society, solitude."[53] And Harnett asserted his cultural aspirations through means other than his models. Culture, which Emerson called "the word of ambition at the present day," entailed "a catholicity, a power to see with a free and disengaged look every object."[54] This seems as fair a description of Harnett's seemingly objective style as one could frame in words.

When Harnett returned to New York following his years of study abroad, he was immensely popular due to Theodore Stewart's acquisition and prominent display of the fourth version of *After the Hunt*, executed in Paris in 1885.[55] Earlier, his tabletop still lifes had been praised for their realistic color and texture. But with the trompe-l'oeil *After the Hunt*, the artist apparently found the means to bewitch viewers, convincing one and all that his painted illusions were the things themselves. Having been largely ignored by the principal art critics of his day and detached from the better circles of his colleagues, Harnett understandably returned to the attention-getting trompe-l'oeil format periodically over the next seven years, producing the paintings that gained him the most renown and by which he is best known today.

One of the earliest of these American trompe-l'oeil pictures is *The Old Violin* of 1886 (pl. 37).[56] The painting is simple in its components, elegant in its presentation. Its base is a worn plank door just over three feet tall. Nails stud the upper third of the planks. From the topmost nail, just to the left of center, an old violin hangs from a loop of twine, its ruddy hue serving to project it from the grayish green of the door.[57] A bow is suspended from a nail to the right. Three pieces of paper are attached to the door, though what supports them is not evident.

All of this is illusion, but the transcription so closely meets expectations of reality, and the whole is so convincingly ordered, that perception and knowledge continually challenge each other. *The Old Violin* succeeded in stirring disbelief from its earliest public appearance, in Cincinnati in 1886:

> A painting has been added to the Art Gallery, which has created a furore. . . . An old gentleman stood and gazed at it last night, through his spectacles, and finally said: "By Jove, I would like to play on that violin," enthusiastically judging that many a touching melody had been wafted from its well resined strings.[58]

The folio of music hanging beneath the violin shows two pieces for solo treble instrument, and both are touching melodies indeed. At the top, untitled, is "Vi ravviso, o luoghi ameni" from Bellini's *La Sonnambula*, the tune seen in *Ease*, again in 4/4 and B-flat major but now set an octave lower; beneath it is "Hélas, Quelle Douleur" in 2/4 and G major and set an octave lower than it is in *My Gems*. This transposition sets the melodies into the throaty, resonant range of the violin and seems particularly apt for "Vi ravviso," the cavatina sung by Count Rodolpho:

> Oh remembrance of scenes long vanish'd,
> Soft enchantment long lost and banish'd,
> Where my childhood serenely glided,
> Where the joyous moments flew;
> Oh how peaceful have ye abided,
> While those days naught can renew![59]

Unlike the tabletop still lifes, in which the music was most often buried beneath other pieces of paper, in

The Poor Musician's Ode.

TO HIS OLD VIOLIN.

Torn
Worn
Oppress'd I mourn
Bad
Sad
Three-quarters mad
Money gone
Credit none
Duns at door
Half a score
Wife in lain
Twins again
Others ailing
Nurse a railing
Billy hooping
Be-ides poor Joe
With festered toe
Come then, my fiddle
Come, my time-worn friend
With gay and brilliant sounds
Some sweet thought transient solace land,
Thy polished neck in close embrace
I clasp, while joy illumes my face
When o'er the strings I draw my bow,
My drooping spirits pant to rise,
A lively strain I touch, and lo !
I seem to mount above the skies,
There on Fancy's wing I soar,
Heedless of the duns at door;
Oblivious all ! I feel my woes no more !
But skip o'er the strings
As my old fiddle s'ngs,
"Cheerily O ! merrily go
"PRESTO ! good master.
"You very well know
"I will find music,
"If you will find bow.
"From E up to alt, to G down below,"
Fatigued, I pause to change the time
For some *Adagio*, solemn and sublime.
With graceful action moves the sinuous arm ;
My heart responsive to the soothing charm,
Throbs equally; whilst every healtu corroding care
Lies prostrate, vanquished by the soft mellifluous air
Anon.more plaintive grown, my eyes with tears o'erflow
And risignation mild, soon smooth my wrinkled brow,
Reedy Hautb·y may sque·k, wailing Flauto may squall
The Serp·nt may grunt and the Trombone may bawl
But my Poll,*my old Fiddle's the prince of them all
Could e'n Dryden return thy praise to rehearse
His ode to Cecilia would seem ragged verse,
Now in thy case, in flannel warm to lie
Till call'd again to pipe thy master's eye.
* Apollo.

Fig. 144. "The Poor Musician's Ode: To His Old Violin,"
American Art Journal 30 (March 8, 1879), p. 294

a violin (fig. 144). In both poem and painting, the violin becomes the vehicle for escaping life's troubles. By making the sentiment-laden tunes so clear and the violin so commanding, Harnett set the imagination trembling. Yet, on entirely another level, with his astounding technique and the elegant touch of the letter postmarked in Paris, he gave fair warning that things in his works are not nearly as simple and unsophisticated as they seem.

Two years later Harnett returned to the theme of the suspended violin in *Still Life—Violin and Music* of 1888 (pl. 43). Working again in life scale, the painter expanded and complicated the scene depicted in *The Old Violin*. By shifting the tonality of the background from dark to light, he created one of the most striking and luminous canvases of his entire career. The inset frame of the cabinet, which is only implied in the earlier work, is now visible, creating a double rectangle around the door that imposes formality upon the composition. Harnett prevented any rigidity, however, by variegating the colors of the borders, scuffing the edges of the wood, carving the date 1888 into the lower right corner, and detailing the hardware—hinges and matchbox on the left, lock and staple on the right.

The center of the composition is also more complicated. To the violin, music, and bow hanging on the door in *The Old Violin,* Harnett added a piccolo, a horseshoe in good-luck position, a calling card, and a hasp to lock the cabinet. The rounded shapes of—or contained in—these objects echo the circular ornaments of the hinges and the violin, setting up a dynamism that draws attention over the entire canvas. Most important, Harnett put the entire composition in motion by swinging the door open slightly. He thus created a very difficult problem for himself, pushing the illusionistic backdrop of the composition beyond the picture plane at the right. He amplified the complexity further by having the piccolo and horseshoe hang at yet other angles in relation to the plank door. The strong light coming from the left creates prominent shadows that are difficult to calculate and render. With a confidence approaching *sprezzatura,* Harnett conquered all these optical difficulties without calling attention to the virtuosity involved. And he expended all this effort on seemingly humble objects. The combination of factors—exaggerated poverty revealed through extreme realism—borders on the incongruous and, therefore, on the humorous.[60]

The music hanging behind the violin in *Still Life—Violin and Music* reveals a similar incongruity, reinforcing Harnett's wit. "Saint Kevin" (4/4, D major) comes from Thomas Moore's fourth volume of *Irish Melodies* (1811). Harnett's painted edition faithfully conveys the original score, including the keyboard introduction and Moore's explanatory note: *This ballad is founded upon one of th[e many stories related of*

The Old Violin it is fully visible and life size, seemingly just used, the tune still hanging in the air.

The artist imbued the work with a sense of nostalgia—the painting's title, the sentimental tunes, and the violin itself, worn from use and dusted with rosin from the scraping of the bow. This yearning for the past is in accord with "The Poor Musician's Ode: To His Old Violin," a poem printed in the shape of

Saint Kevin, whose bed in the rock is to be seen at Glenda]lough, a most gloomy and romantic spot in the county [of Wicklow].[61] It also identifies the American publisher: *Published by J. J. DALY 419 Grand Street N.Y.* John J. Daly was at this address from 1852 to 1869.[62] The plate number at the bottom left, *336:2,* indicates that Daly issued "Saint Kevin" on two sheets, probably in late 1868.[63] So Harnett portrayed music that had been published twenty years earlier; even in his choice of sheet music, he leaned toward the worn and time-stained.

This telling of Saint Kevin's tale provides, as Moore wrote of Irish music in general, "that unaccountable mixture of gloom and levity."[64] While its five stanzas detail the sexual torment and murderous release of the young saint, the specific language used in retelling the story is wholly ironic, revealing through its tone the opposition between the author's statement and his meaning. The saint flees from the devoted Kathleen (whose eyes were "of most unholy blue!") to find rest on the rocks above the waves of Glendalough, but Kathleen follows him ("Ah! the good Saint little knew / What that wily sex can do"). When he awakens, he finds her beside him, and "Sternly from his bed he starts, / And with rude, repulsive shock, / Hurls her from the beetling rock." He immediately regrets his haste, wishing "'Heav'n rest her soul!'" At this, "Round the Lake light music stole; / And her ghost was seen to glide, / Smiling, oe'r the fatal tide!"[65] Confirming Moore's lighthearted approach to this tale of passion and murder, the tune, a reel known in other places as "The Brown Irish Girl," and its strumming accompaniment establish the essentially jolly nature of the music just played on the old violin.

The following year Harnett once more expanded the scope of the cupboard-door still life. For *The Old Cupboard Door* of 1889 (pl. 45), he stepped back again to reveal not only the cupboard door and its embrasure but a goodly section of the surrounding plaster at the top and a mass-produced wainscoting at the bottom. A shelf stretches beneath the door, filled with books and items of virtu. Paradoxically, these objects seal the door more effectively than its elaborate lock and key—only by sweeping them away could one open it.

The violin is again a crucial element in the composition, but it occupies a scant sixth of the canvas. Its bow is propped insecurely on the shelf. The picture also includes the first known instance of Harnett's painting of a tambourine. This instrument, with its dance associations, is at first glance an odd adjunct to the other items of the student-collector. One does not readily conjure up an image of a lone scholar picking up the tambourine and beating out a swift tattoo in order to further his contemplation of literature or an objet d'art. Rather, the tambourine is a social instrument, meant to provide pulse and rhythmic accents while the rest of an ensemble produces the melody and harmony. But in New York during the late 1880s, in part thanks to the popularity of flamenco dancers and singers such as La Carmencita, the instrument would also have carried a strong hint of Spain. Could this be Harnett's way of noting the Spanish element in the social and studio life of fashionable New York artists such as William Merritt Chase, a world to which Harnett apparently did not have access? The prominent display of a Spanish edition of Cervantes's *Don Quixote* on the shelf beneath the tambourine bolsters this suggestion.[66]

Two sheet-music covers also hang from separate nails, each a French collection of melodies and short pieces. One sheet is beginning to separate from its binding and reveals a few measures of Christoph Gluck's *Orfeo ed Euridice* (1762), probably Orfeo's "Che farò senza Euridice?"[67] Tacked up at an angle and partially hidden by the translucent head of the tambourine, another sheet reveals two familiar tunes: Moore's "Air Irlandais—Dernière Rose d'été" (3/4, F major), marked as the seventh selection of the compilation, and "Con te li prendi" from *Norma* (4/4, G major), cast as a solo rather than the D major duet in *Mortality and Immortality*. A full-blown rose dropping its petals and a bronze statuette identified as the Roman god Bacchus in Harnett's estate sale (a god that Pollione in *Norma* may have worshiped) complement the selections.[68]

The Old Cupboard Door is one of Harnett's fullest and most visually complex paintings.[69] The welter of individualized objects draws the viewer's attention over the entire surface of the canvas. The distinctive diagonal planking of the door and the ornate hardware and ogee molding guarantee that the background will attract the eye if an object does not. Yet Harnett imposed unity through his careful choice of color and the palpable atmosphere, arrived at through the consistent direction of the light and the uniform softening of textures. It is only in terms of the design that there is no center, no principal focus. This is a radical departure both from Harnett's earlier trompe-l'oeil paintings, such as the centralized compositions of *After the Hunt,* and from the compositional strategies of most American painters of the 1880s.[70] Hidden within his unassertive technique and the apparently random arrangement of humble objects, Harnett created a daring composition that pushes in the direction of (though via wildly different means) the overall decorative effects of twentieth-century abstractions.

Three years after *The Old Cupboard Door,* Harnett returned to the cupboard format with *Old Models* of 1892 (pl. 49), reportedly his final painting. Slightly smaller and far simpler than its predecessor, *Old Models* brings together a keyed bugle (a less elaborate instrument than the one he painted in Europe), the Dutch jar, three books and a pamphlet, sheet music (the cover of *50 M[él]odies Pour Violin* and the music

[3/4, F major] for Moore's "'Tis the Last Rose of Summer"), and violin and bow. The cupboard door, consisting of three planks, is hinged to a straight molding that is in turn set into a plain wall of vertical boards. For all this relative simplification, the painting is ambitious and accomplished.[71] The elegiac note of Moore's song about a beauty too pure to exist alone aptly twines around this last work of Harnett's short life.

With the tabletop still lifes, one could posit a space and purpose implied by the collected objects—generally a library or study. The imaginary room for Harnett's trompe-l'oeil doors and cupboards is more difficult to imagine. They seem interior due to the wall treatment and the objects depicted. But neither kitchen, parlor, library, chamber, nor any other room of a house provides a ready context for the plank doors and fine objects. Nor do office, stable, or barn suggest themselves as viable locales. Paradoxically, the very paintings that most tempt one's belief in the reality of the painted objects deny the opportunity to put them easily into a context. They become arrangements, willed into place solely by the artist's caprice. It is in this artifice, these arrangements that exist for no plausible purpose beyond that of being painted, that Harnett ceased to depict the garret study and instead revealed himself to be portraying the artist's studio.

Harnett's paintings of music and musical instruments reveal a great deal about him. Along with the rest of his oeuvre they are, of course, testaments to his uncanny skill with paint and to his ambitious use of that skill in replicating an impression of reality. A chronological review of the musical still lifes unveils the artist's progressively greater control over his technical means and the challenges to which he put them as he moved toward the compositional complexity of such works as *Still Life—Violin and Music* or *The Old Cupboard Door*. But the musical paintings in particular also enrich our view of Harnett the man. The imaginary space he constructed for these pictures is the arena of the scholar and student, and to some degree it seems he tried to situate himself in this idealized world. With their commingling of music, literature, travel, and religion, these works repeatedly demonstrate his cultural aspirations. Moreover, it is through his use of music to enrich the meanings of his work that Harnett most clearly demonstrated his wit and intellect, stretching the very limits of his art and shattering with many a touching melody the accustomed silence of painting.

NOTES

I would like to thank Thayer Tolles Mickel, Doreen Bolger, and the staff of the Music Library, University of California, Berkeley, for their assistance in locating material for this essay. Alfred Frankenstein and Carol Oja concentrated considerable attention on Harnett's use of musical themes; their works, cited below, provided the foundation for much of this paper. In addition, Professor Oja was markedly generous with thoughts and information. Sally Mills, Catherine Johnson, Derrick Cartwright, and Gerald Smith, all of the Fine Arts Museums of San Francisco, have been models of assistance and collegiality. I would also like to thank Henry Adams, Nelson-Atkins Museum, Kansas City; Alan Fausel, Frick Art Museum, Pittsburgh; Judy L. Larson, High Museum of Art, Atlanta; and Joan O'Connor, San Francisco Conservatory of Music, for aid and good will above the call the duty.

1. "Fine music does not inspire great thoughts so much as deep emotions," wrote editor George William Curtis ("Editor's Easy Chair," *Harper's New Monthly Magazine* 44 [February 1872], p. 458).

2. In the words of conductor Theodore Thomas, "The Americans are certainly a music-loving people. They are peculiarly susceptible to the sensuous charm of tone. . . . The incessant pressure of work which every American feels, prevents the men from paying much attention to music, but as the country advances in age and begins to acquire some of the repose which age brings, there will come possibilities of development which cannot now be estimated" ("Musical Possibilities in America," *Scribner's Monthly* 21 [March 1881], p. 777). Writing in 1883—about the time Harnett's fabulously realistic still-life paintings were becoming known—the critic Marianna Griswold Van Rensselaer saw Americans' respect for the emotive, ideal nature of music as compensation for the materialism of their era: "This our nineteenth century is commonly esteemed a prosaic, a material, an unimaginative age. Compared with foregoing periods, it is called blind to beauty and careless of ideals. . . . There is one great opposing fact of such importance that by itself alone it calls for at least a partial reversal of the verdict we pass upon ourselves as children of a nonartistic time. This fact is the place that music—most unpractical, most unprosaic, most ideal of the arts—has held in nineteenth-century life" ("'Parsifal' at Baireuth," *Harper's New Monthly Magazine* 66 [March 1883], p. 540).

3. See Alfred Frankenstein, *After the Hunt: William Harnett and Other American Still Life Painters, 1870–*

1900, rev. ed. (Berkeley and Los Angeles: University of California Press, 1969), p. 41.

4. James Edward Kelly, quoted in Frankenstein, *After the Hunt,* p. 38.

5. *The Wm. Michael Harnett Collection: His Own Reserved Paintings, Models and Studio Furnishings,* sale cat., Stan. V. Henkels at Thos. Birch's Sons, Auctioneers, Philadelphia, February 23–24, 1893, p. 9, nos. 45, 46, 50; p. 10, nos. 55½–64; p. 11, nos. 65–68, and ills.). See also E. Taylor Snow, "William Michael Harnett, A Philadelphia Catholic Artist," *American Catholic Historical Researches* 10 (April 1893), p. 75.

6. Harnett generally depicted violins with the strings attached to the incorrect tuning pegs, which Frankenstein concluded was a matter of innocent mistake rather than meaningful manipulation (*After the Hunt,* p. 41). Similarly, Harnett painted clarinets with the mouthpieces backward, with the reed positioned over the fingerholes, which would render the instrument virtually unplayable.

7. I assert this in spite of testimony to the contrary contained in the often-quoted interview in the *New York News,* which is our longest autobiographical statement: "In painting from still life I do not closely imitate nature. Many points I leave out and many I add. Some models are only suggestions. Take the flute in one of the accompanying illustrations. The flute that served as a model is not exactly like the one in the picture. The ivory was not on the flute at all, and the silver effects for the keys and bands I got from a bright silver dollar" ("Painted Like Real Things: The Man Whose Pictures Are a Wonder and a Puzzle," interview in *New York News,* probably 1889 or 1890, quoted in Frankenstein, *After the Hunt,* p. 55). The description of the flute in the catalogue from the sale of Harnett's studio effects, however, reveals the ivory head and silver keys that the artist denies (*Wm. Michael Harnett Collection,* p. 10, no. 62).

8. There is one playbill in the Blemly scrapbook (Alfred Frankenstein Papers, Archives of American Art, Smithsonian Institution, Washington, D.C., microfilm, roll 1374, frame 358) that relates to Harnett's probable attendance at a performance of Gilbert and Sullivan's *Der Mikado; oder, Ein Tag in Titipu* at the Stadt Theater in Carlsbad, Germany, on July 26, 1889 (Frankenstein, *After the Hunt,* p. 91). A perusal of volumes 10 to 15 of George C. D. Odell's *Annals of the New York Stage,*

15 vols. (New York: Columbia University Press, 1927–49), presents the plethora of options that Harnett faced while in New York.

9. Many of the pieces shown are either arias from popular operas or salon pieces. While there were eleven lots of music in Harnett's estate sale (*Wm. Michael Harnett Collection,* p. 22, nos. 303–13), they were not itemized. The majority of the spare sheets he portrayed were apparently taken from such collections as *50 Mélodies pour violon, 100 Mélodies célèbres transcrites pour violon,* and *30 Petits Morceaux,* covers that he depicted in *Old Models* and *The Old Cupboard Door.* Sadly, these collections have proven both ephemeral and elusive; I have been unable to locate copies. A survey of Adolph Hofmeister's *Handbuch der Musikalischen Literatur,* 19 vols. (Leipzig: Friedrich Hofmeister, n.d.) and Franz Pazdírek's *Universal-Handbuch der Musikliteratur aller Zeiten und Völker,* 34 vols. (Vienna: Pazdírek & Co., [1904–10]), however, reveals the prevalence of such compilations. According to Frankenstein, who generally disparaged a search for meaning in the artist's work, "Harnett's painted sheet-music is also entirely a matter of texture, but there is reason to believe that he originally bought much of the music he depicted for his own use as an amateur flutist. He probably read very few of the books that appear in his canvases, having acquired them solely as studio props; his painted music, on the other hand, provides us with unintended clues to his tastes and activities in this art" (*After the Hunt,* pp. 40–41).

10. The only other instances in Harnett's oeuvre when language is conveyed so precisely (presuming that music can be classified as a language) are his depictions of money and handwritten letters and envelopes. The money portrayals are straightforward and convey a degree of information, but the replica is ultimately non-negotiable—it cannot serve as legal tender. In this connection, the modern artist J. S. G. Boggs has charged boldly into the puzzle of worth and values (see Lawrence Weschler, "Bogg's Bills," in *Shapinsky's Karma, Bogg's Bills, and Other True-Life Tales* [San Francisco: North Point Press, 1988], pp. 178–260). In Harnett's depictions of correspondence, scraps of information and partial sentences are most often there to be deciphered, but the presumed intent of the original—clear communication—is thwarted.

11. Among the known paintings that include music, only *Still Life* of 1890 (fig. 29) and *A Bachelor's Friends* of

1891 (Kennedy Galleries, Inc., New York) contain legible scores that are not playable.

12. Thomas Eakins later approached the same effect in *The Concert Singer* of 1892 (Philadelphia Museum of Art) in which, in addition to depicting the physiognomy of the singing Weda Cook, he also carved into the painting's frame the melody of "O Rest in the Lord" from Felix Mendelssohn's *Elijah* (see Elizabeth Johns, *Thomas Eakins: The Heroism of Modern Life* [Princeton: Princeton University Press, 1983], p. 139). For an interesting discussion of music in painting, see Robert F. Chirico, "Some Reflections of Sound and Silence in the Visual Arts," *Arts Magazine* 56, no. 8 (April 1982), p. 103; and Edward Lockspeiser, *Music and Painting: A Study in Comparative Ideas from Turner to Schoenberg* (New York: Harper & Row, 1973).

13. Except for the skull, Harnett's composition bears a reasonable similarity in content and tone to contemporary French realist still-life paintings, such as François Bonvin's *Still Life with Violin, Sheet Music, and a Rose* of 1870 (The Fine Arts Museums of San Francisco).

14 . Scholars have long recognized that this work initiates the painted memento mori in the American nineteenth-century still-life tradition, the earliest of Harnett's many thematic innovations (see, for example, William H. Gerdts and Russell Burke, *American Still-Life Painting* [New York, Washington, and London: Praeger Publishers, 1971], p. 134; and Chad Mandeles, "William Michael Harnett's *The Old Cupboard Door* and the Tradition of *Vanitas,*" *American Art Journal* 18, no. 3 [1986], pp. 51–62). According to Carol J. Oja, it also appears to be the first American still life to portray instrument and music together ("The Still-Life Paintings of William Michael Harnett [Their Reflections upon Nineteenth-Century American Musical Culture]," *Musical Quarterly* 63 [October 1977], p. 505).

15. One scholar has recently written, "The implication is that man's creative achievements, like his mortal existence, come to nothing" (Barbara S. Groseclose, "Vanity and the Artist: Some Still-Life Paintings by William Michael Harnett," *American Art Journal* 19, no. 1 [1987], p. 54). Others, however, have noted that despite the presence of the skull, the painting's message is "that although man may perish bodily, his works will live on" (Gerdts and Burke, *American Still-Life Painting,* p. 134).

16. Identified by Frankenstein, *After the Hunt,* p. 41. See

also Carol Jean Oja, "Musical Subjects in the Paintings of William Michael Harnett" (master's thesis, University of Iowa, 1976), pp. 39–40.

17. Irving Sablosky testifies to the popularity of *Norma* and other Bellini operas in New York in the nineteenth century in *What They Heard: Music in America, 1852–1881* (Baton Rouge and London: Louisiana State University Press, 1986), pp. 25, 44, 190. In addition to any number of performances (see, for example, "The Italian Opera at the Academy: Debut of Palmieri," *American Art Journal* 26 [October 7, 1876], p. 5), the omnipresence of the work can be demonstrated by the fact that *Norma* was often the standard used to compare other operatic roles (see "Italian Opera," *American Art Journal* 24 [February 5, 1876], pp. 28–29, contrasting Donizetti's *Lucrezia Borgia* with *Norma*).

18. Only after giving her permission does Norma learn that Adalgisa's planned seducer is Pollione, her own secret husband and father of her children. When Norma learns of Pollione's betrayal, she reveals her own transgressions and begs that her children be taken with Adalgisa to Rome, singing "Con te li prendi." Adalgisa, in response, swears to renounce Pollione and to kindle his love for Norma. Pollione follows Adalgisa into a sacred precinct and is sentenced to death. Norma would help him escape on the condition that he renounce Adalgisa, but he refuses. Norma then publicly confesses her love for him and is condemned to be burned. At last, Pollione again feels his love for Norma and joins her on the pyre; united, they die.

19. For a discussion of the fallen woman in nineteenth-century art, with a particular emphasis on England, see Linda Nochlin, "Lost and *Found*: Once More the Fallen Woman," in *Women, Art, and Power and Other Essays* (New York: Harper & Row, 1988), pp. 57–85.

20. *Paintings of the Late W. M. Harnett on Exhibition,* exhib. cat. (Philadelphia: Earle's Galleries, 1892), no. 6.

21. The painting appears as an illustration with the title *Music and Literature* in an untitled clipping from an unidentified and undated newspaper in the Blemly scrapbook (frame 339) and has been so known since the Albright-Knox acquired the painting in 1941. The work is the basis for E. Taylor Snow's design (fig. 149) on the cover of James S. Earle & Sons 1892 catalogue (*Paintings of the Late W. M. Harnett on Exhibition*). The title *Music and Literature,* however, is not listed as one of the works in the show. Since the other portions of Snow's design are based on works exhibited, it stands to reason that *Music and Literature* was there but under another name—*After a Hard Night's Study* is the most logical possibility, especially since we know it showed a flute. In *Wm. Michael Harnett Collection,* the entry for no. 62 (p. 10) reads: "Ebony Flute Ivory mouth-piece; silver-plated keys. Mr. Harnett's oldest model, painted in his first large canvas, 'After a Hard Night's Study,' considered one of his best groupings. Owned by a collector in this city." The collector referred to was William Folwell (see "Trade in Philadelphia," *Dry Goods Economist* 47 [November 12, 1892], p. 38; and Frankenstein, *After the Hunt,* p. 45). It seems likely that *Music and Literature* was also the large work exhibited in 1878 at the National Academy of Design, "No. 115 *After a Hard Night's Work,*" for which Harnett asked the relatively high price of $600 (see Maria Naylor, ed. and comp., *The National Academy of Design Exhibition Record, 1861–1900,* 2 vols. [New York: Kennedy Galleries, 1973], 1, p. 394).

22. Snow apparently purchased the flute from the estate sale, as Frankenstein wrote in 1948 of visiting the home of Snow's daughter and seeing it along with six other objects from the studio in her possession (Whitney Museum of American Art Papers, microfilmed by the Archives of American Art, roll N664, frame 708).

23. Identified by Frankenstein, *After the Hunt,* p. 48. *La Traviata,* first produced in 1853, tells the story by Dumas *fils* of Alfredo Germont's love for the courtesan Violetta Valery, the lady of camellias. Ill with consumption but in love for the first time in her life, Violetta leaves Paris to live in the country with Alfredo. Alfredo's father, however, begs Violetta to break off her relationship with Alfredo since its scandal endangers his daughter's engagement. Violetta agrees and, without explanation, returns to Paris. Wounded and embittered by her apparent fickleness, Alfredo publicly insults her and, as a result, is challenged to a duel and disowned. Only afterward does he learn the reason for Violetta's sacrifice; he returns to find her dying.

24. Celia Betsky, "American Musical Paintings, 1865–1910," in *The Art of Music: American Paintings and Musical Instruments, 1770–1910,* exhib. cat. (Clinton, N.Y.: Fred L. Emerson Gallery, Hamilton College, 1984), pp. 60, 62.

25. For works in the American tradition, see Thomas Hovenden's *Self-Portrait of the Artist in His Studio* of 1875

(Yale University Art Gallery, New Haven), Dennis Miller Bunker's *Guitar Player* (also called *Bohemia*) of 1885 (private collection), William Merritt Chase's *In the Studio* of 1892 (Mr. and Mrs. Arthur G. Altschul), Jefferson David Chalfant's *Interrupted Musicale* of about 1895 (private collection), Winslow Homer's *Studio* of 1867 (The Metropolitan Museum of Art, New York), and Stacy Tolman's *Musicale* of 1887 (The Brooklyn Museum). A photograph from about 1885 of John Frederick Peto's studio (Shelburne Museum, Vt.) shows an extreme example of mingling, though it should be noted that Peto made his living as a musician after about 1889. It is telling in this regard that in a photograph from the 1870s showing Harnett and Peto, the latter holds a violin and bow while Harnett holds a pipe and small book (illustrated in John Wilmerding, *Important Information Inside: The Art of John F. Peto and the Idea of Still-Life Painting in Nineteenth-Century America*, exhib. cat., National Gallery of Art, Washington, D.C. [New York: Harper & Row, 1983], p. 18). For a recent and richly illustrated guide to the European tradition, see Pierre Georgel and Anne-Marie Lecoq, *La Peinture dans la peinture* (Paris: Adam Biro, 1987).

26. The principal exception to this is *Still Life with Portrait by Raphael* of 1878 (fig. 111), perhaps the painting that was exhibited at Earle's Galleries in 1892 as *An Artist's Table* (*Paintings of the Late W. M. Harnett*, no. 12). In addition to books, a tan vase, a letter, and a violin, the composition also includes a reduced copy, in a distinctly 1870s frame, of Raphael's portrait *Bindo Altoviti* of about 1515 (National Gallery of Art, Washington, D.C.). For much of the nineteenth century, the Raphael was on view in Munich's Alte Pinakothek with the title *Self-Portrait*. Frankenstein (*After the Hunt*, p. 46) noted that an "old master portrait of Raphael" was included in Harnett's estate sale (see *Wm. Michael Harnett Collection*, p. 8, no. 37, "Oil Painting Old Master. Portrait of Raphael").

27. The lamp most often seen appears to be identical to the Student and Astral Lamp developed by Knapp Manufacturing Co., New York, in the mid-1870s, which was praised for its superior light and safety (see *Watson's Art Journal* 24 [December 4, 1875], p. 75, ill.; and "A Novelty," *Watson's Art Journal* 24 [December 11, 1875], p. 85).

28. Even larger and more crowded was *George Fryer's Still Life* of 1884 (46 x 56 in.), known today only through a nineteenth-century photograph (see Frankenstein, *After the Hunt*, pl. 57, pp. 68, 71, 176).

29. Identified by Oja, "Musical Subjects," pp. 40–41; see also Chad Mandeles, "William Michael Harnett (1848–92), *A Study Table*," in Paul D. Schweizer, ed., *Masterworks of American Art from the Munson-Williams-Proctor Institute* (New York: Harry N. Abrams, 1989), pp. 84, 224, no. 36, n. 6. *La Dame blanche* was markedly popular in the 1870s. In 1875, a New York critic claimed it "compares favorably with the best kindred works of the present day and generation" ("Herr Wachtel in 'Dame Blanche,'" *Watson's Art Journal* 24 [November 6, 1875], p. 20); and the opéra comique of Paris planned on opening its 1877 season with the work ("News Nutshell," *American Art Journal* 27 [July 7, 1877], p. 153).

30. The story, set in Scotland in 1759, derives from Sir Walter Scott's *Guy Mannering* (1815) and *The Monastery* (1820). It tells of how Julien of Avenel, rightful heir to the counts of Avenel (but knowing nothing of his birthright and believing himself to be a simple soldier named Georges Brown), comes into his own through the good will of his tenants and the intercession of the orphan, Anna, and the old nurse, Marguerite. The White Lady is both a statue, where the fortune of the Avenels is hidden, and a legendary spirit reputed to appear when the Avenel family is threatened. No spirit appears on stage; the revelations and plot resolutions brought about by the White Lady are the actions of Anna in disguise. Human enterprise and happy coincidence bring Julien and Anna together amid general rejoicing (see *The Simon and Schuster Book of the Opera* [New York: Simon & Schuster, 1977], pp. 148–49).

31. The larger version of the work was apparently sold in Germany, where it remained until 1956. Mandeles (*"A Study Table,"* p. 223, no. 36, n. 1) was the first to note that the illustration and size information in Frankenstein's *After the Hunt* (pl. 56) purporting to refer to *A Study Table* at the Munson-Williams-Proctor Institute Museum of Art, Utica, N.Y., did not match the actual painting. Frankenstein was aware of the error and intended to correct it in the third, never printed, edition of *After the Hunt* (Frankenstein to Edward H. Dwight, Director, Munson-Williams-Proctor Institute Museum of Art, July 21 and August 9, 1970, Munson-Williams-Proctor Institute files). The work illustrated in Frankenstein was a smaller version, with variations, of the Utica painting. Once in the collection of Irving H. Vogel, it is now in the

Philadelphia Museum of Art (fig. 140). The situation is complicated by the existence of at least two small copies, clearly by another hand, of this smaller painting—one in the Philadelphia Museum of Art and the other in a private collection (Frankenstein to Dwight and to one-time owner Mrs. John Gerrard, March 29, April 23, July 16, 1970, ibid.).

32. In 1962, the French philosopher and anthropologist Claude Lévi-Strauss observed: "What is the virtue of reduction either of scale or in the number of properties? It seems to result from a sort of reversal in the process of understanding. To understand a real object in its totality we always tend to work from its parts. The resistance it offers us is overcome by dividing it. Reduction in scale reverses this situation. Being smaller, the object as a whole seems less formidable. By being quantitatively diminished, it seems to us qualitatively simplified. . . . In the case of miniatures, in contrast to what happens when we try to understand an object or living creature of real dimensions, knowledge of the whole precedes knowl-edge of the parts. . . . In other words, the intrinsic value of a small-scale model is that it compensates for the renunciation of sensible dimensions by the acquisition of intelligible dimensions" (*The Savage Mind* [Chicago: University of Chicago Press, 1966], pp. 23–24).

33. For a rich discussion of the invention and early history of the keyed bugle (also called a Kent bugle), see "An Historical Sketch," *American Art Journal* 27 (July 28, 1877), pp. 167–68. See also Clifford Bevan, *The Tuba Family* (London: Faber & Faber, 1978), pp. 57–59; and Oja, "Musical Subjects," pp. 33–35.

34. Indeed, Clarence Cook wrote that the closely related cornet was "that most unsuitable instrument for any room, public or private" ("Home and Society: Some Old-Fashioned Things Worth Reviving," *Scribner's Monthly* 22 [May 1881], p. 147). Lawrence W. Levine has compiled several marvelously wicked quotations from the *New York Times* of 1880 decrying brass instruments of all kinds (*Highbrow/Lowbrow: The Emergence of Cultural Hierarchy in America* [Cambridge, Mass., and London: Harvard University Press, 1988], p. 165).

35. *Still Life* was acquired before the opening of the London exhibition by the Royal Academician George Richmond (see "Painted Like Real Things," quoted in Frankenstein, *After the Hunt*, p. 55; and Frankenstein *After the Hunt*, pp. 70, 71, 177; see also "Harnett's Body

Here!" *Times* [Philadelphia], November 1, 1892, p. 1). Favorable reviews of the work include "Royal Academy: Third Notice," *Times* (London), May 25, 1885, p. 4. A close copy of this work, now at the Yale University Art Gallery, New Haven, has been identified with the Richmond painting.

36. The story of the opera tells of how, on the day before their marriage, the Breton goatherd Hoël and the lovely Dinorah are driven apart by the destruction of Dinorah's family home. Hoël, fearing poverty, leaves the village to search for a hidden treasure that carries a curse—he who first lays hands on it will die within a year. Meanwhile, Dinorah, having no word of him, loses her mind and wanders throughout the countryside. Hoël, who is so anxious for the treasure that he is willing to trick a comrade into bringing the curse upon himself, sings "O possente magia" at the moment he believes his plans are about to be fulfilled. Eventually Hoël and Dinorah are brought together, Hoël abandons the search for the treasure in order to rescue her, she recovers her sanity, and the two are married.

37. Servel (active 1863–79) was a French composer and arranger who, though little known today, published a significant number of songs and collections of melodies.

38. Misspelled, in the painting, as "Seperation." Edmond Servel, *Séparation* (Paris: Alfred Skelmer & Cie, [1869]). I am deeply grateful to Judy L. Larson for sharing with me the sheet music to *Séparation*.

39. Moore (1779–1852) was an Irish poet who set folk tales and his own lyrics to traditional Irish melodies. His works were exceedingly popular in the United States at the end of the nineteenth century: the centennial of his birth provoked many concerts in 1879, and in 1880 a memorial with bronze bust was placed in New York's Central Park ("The Poet of Ireland," *American Art Journal* 33 [June 26, 1880], pp. 129–32).

40. *A Selection of Irish Melodies; with Symphonies and Accompaniments by Sir John Stevenson: and Characteris-tic Words by Thomas Moore*, 5th no. (London: J. Power, n.d.), p. 14. "'Tis the Last Rose of Summer" was a popular tune, as witnessed by its appearance in sheet music and on concert programs. See, for example, the scorn with which one critic greeted the work of another: "Mlle. Tietjens has been somewhat astonished at Americans, and especially disgusted with some of the

critics. . . and with good cause. . . . The *Times* man heard her sing the 'Last Rose of Summer,' and criticised it as 'Home, Sweet Home'" (*Watson's Art Journal* 24 [October 30, 1875], p. 3). See also the notice of the Battery Park concert held by Crook's Amateur Band on August 26, 1881, which included the song played on solo tuba (*American Art Journal* 35 [September 3, 1881], p. 371).

41. I would not have been able to identify this tune were it not for Henry Adams, who conveyed Stephen Addis's (University of Kansas, Lawrence) observation concerning *The Old Violin* to me.

42. Clipping from an unidentified and undated source, Frankenstein Papers, roll 2398, frame 720. We know Harnett was pleased with this work because the following year he made a close variant of it (Mr. and Mrs. Meyer P. Potamkin), at just over half size, for his family.

43. "Queer Art Illusions: Some of the Many Methods Employed to Produce Them," clipping from an unidentified and undated newspaper, Blemly scrapbook, frame 327.

44. "Theodore Stewart's Collection," clipping from an unidentified and undated newspaper, Blemly scrapbook, frame 328.

45. "A Fine Still-Life Painting," *Springfield Daily Republican*, November 7, 1887, p. 6. See also Frankenstein, *After the Hunt*, pp. 83–84, 178.

46. These were *Still Life with Violin* and *Still Life with the Toledo Blade*, both of 1886 (figs. 99, 100). The first was purchased for Peter Samuel Dooner's Hotel in Philadelphia, and the second was commissioned by druggist Isaac Newton Reed of Toledo, Ohio. Dooner's inn was the site of much music- and merry-making. According to one history of the establishment, the best male chorus of the city met there—the Kelly Street choir, formed by members of the Kelly Street Business Men's Association (Christopher Morley and T. A. Daly, *The House of Dooner: The Last of the Friendly Inns* [Philadelphia: David McKay Co., 1928], pp. 26–27).

47. These works range in size from 14 by 12 inches to about 24 by 20 inches, holding a place midway between Harnett's miniature and life-size productions. The largest and earliest of the group, *The Last Rose of Summer,* shows an unrolled sheet of music containing Schubert's

Ave Maria (4/4, B-flat major) and "La Dernière Rose d'été" (3/4, E major). This combination, though in a different guise, also appears in *Music*. In *La Flûte Enchantée,* the crack on the flute has progressed—it now extends from the first joint through the airhole and a bit beyond. The music includes a blue cover of melodies from *La Traviata,* a sheet from a missal, and the music to "Papageno's Song" from Wolfgang Amadeus Mozart's *Magic Flute* (1791), labeled in French *La Flûte Enchantée/Chanson de Friseleur* (2/4, G major). *My Gems,* apparently the second painting Harnett made in 1888, shows several of the same characters as *La Flûte Enchantée*. Rather than his flute, however, Harnett depicted an ivory-headed piccolo. The music he chose includes a cover for a selection from Verdi's *Rigoletto* (1851) and another folio of melodies for treble instrument, the face of which shows an unidentified tune (3/4, F major) and, marked as *No. 42,* Servel's "Hélas, Quelle Douleur" (2/4, G major). Identified by Frankenstein (*After the Hunt,* p. 41).

48. *Wm. Michael Harnett Collection,* p. 11, no. 68.

49. Identified by Frankenstein, *After the Hunt,* p. 180; and Oja, "Musical Subjects," p. 40.

50. Harnett used the piece only once before, three years earlier in *La Flûte Enchantée* (see Note 47), though the sheet of music is apparently from a different collection since here it is the second piece on the page and labeled *No. 37.*

51. Frankenstein, *After the Hunt,* p. 93. His fiancée remains an almost complete mystery. Frankenstein records that her name was Enright, she lived in New York, and she received a portion of Harnett's estate, but he was not able to trace her further.

52. As, for example, the last tabletop still life of his career, *Professor's Old Friends* of 1891 (fig. 124), which includes a clarinet, music, and books.

53. Ralph Waldo Emerson, "Culture," in *Ralph Waldo Emerson: Essays and Lectures* (New York: Library of America, 1983), pp. 1018, 1019.

54. Ibid., pp. 1015, 1017.

55. One of the earliest known notices about the painting reads: "If any of my readers should be in the vicinity of

8 Warren Street, drop in at Theodore Stewart's and look at a very remarkable picture there, called 'After the Hunt,' by William H. [*sic*] Harnett, a young New York artist, now living in Paris. This really marvelous production seemed to attract little or no attention in France, but here it is not only making a profound sensation, but the gifted painter's fortune is assured by this one effort. Hundreds of ladies and gentlemen visit the place daily, and a prominent millionaire of this city has offered $15,000 for a copy" ("'Jeems Pipes' Pipings: From My Attic Room, 23 Union Square," *American Art Journal* 44 [January 23, 1886], p. 231).

56. Thanks to the chromolithograph (fig. 147) manufactured and distributed by Frank Tuchfarber, the earliest owner of the painting, *The Old Violin* is probably Harnett's most widely recognized work. The chromolithographs, both on glass and paper, were widely advertised (see, for example, *Harper's Magazine Advertiser* 75 [June 1887], p. 317) and distributed. They, in turn, were often copied. For an extended discussion, see Frankenstein, *After the Hunt*, pp. 73–78.

57. For a discussion of the instrument, see Oja, "Musical Subjects," pp. 28–32, 51–54.

58. Clipping from an 1886 Cincinnati newspaper (otherwise unidentified), Blemly scrapbook, frame 281.

59. Vincenzo Bellini, *La Sonnambula*, libretto by Felice Romani, English version by Natalia MacFarren (New York: G. Schirmer, 1901), p. 55.

60. Albert Ten Eyck Gardner, one of the few early scholars to appreciate Harnett's quiet humor, wrote that this painting has "an entertaining and humorous aspect of a rare kind: the painter is playing an optical joke upon the viewer, not by the representation of a comic subject but by sheer technical dexterity" ("Harnett's *Music and Good Luck*," *Metropolitan Museum of Art Bulletin* 22 [January 1964], p. 160).

61. Thomas Moore, *A Selection of Irish Melodies*, 4th no. (London: J. Power, [1811]), p. 82.

62. Harry Dichter and Elliott Shapiro, *Early American Sheet Music: Its Lure and Its Lore, 1768–1889* (New York: R. R. Bowker Co., 1941), p. 183.

63. D. W. Krummel, professor of Library Science and Music, University of Illinois at Urbana-Champaign, to Laurence Libin, curator in the Department of Musical Instruments, November 6, 1975, The Metropolitan Museum of Art, curatorial files.

64. "The Irish Melodies," in *Moore's Irish Melodies*, rev. ed. (Boston: Oliver Ditson & Co., 1893), p. viii.

65. Ibid., p. 82.

66. On La Carmencita, see James Lomax and Richard Ormond, *John Singer Sargent and The Edwardian Age*, exhib. cat. (Leeds: Leeds Art Gallery, 1979), pp. 50–51. The tambourine was a rarely used symbol of carnal love in sixteenth-century Italy (A. P. de Mirimonde, "Les Vanités à personnages et à instruments de musique," *Gazette des Beaux-Arts* 92 [October 1978], p. 116).

67. Christoph Gluck, *Orfeo ed Euridice*, libretto by Ranieri De' Calzabigi (Milan: G. Ricordi, n.d.), pp. 120–23. The full opera was not especially well known in New York: "Last Friday the Academy of Music was comfortably filled . . . with a legion of amateurs anxious to hear the first performance in New York, and so far as we know, the first in this country, of Gluck's 'Orpheus and Eurydice.'" The work was popular in Paris, however, and portions of it were apparently well known in the United States ("Gluck's 'Orpheus and Eurydice' at the Academy of Music," *American Art Journal* 44 [January 16, 1886], p. 214).

68. *Wm. Michael Harnett Collection*, p. 12, no. 83.

69. Mandeles has proposed a complementary complexity of meaning for the work, exploring both the possibility of reading the painting as a vanitas and as an allegory of the senses ("Harnett's *Old Cupboard Door*," pp. 51–62).

70. Not even Harnett's rack paintings, such as *Mr. Hulings' Rack Picture* of 1888 (pl. 44), so effectively disperse the focus over nearly the entire surface. The rational explanation of what is being portrayed in the letter rack is partly responsible for this. Joseph Decker's *Pears* of about 1885 (private collection) and John Haberle's *Bachelor's Drawer* of 1890–94 (The Metropolitan Museum of Art, New York) explore the same manner of composition.

71. Harnett reportedly intended it for the Chicago World's Columbian Exposition of 1893.

CHRONOLOGY

▼

THAYER TOLLES MICKEL

1848

August 10. Born in Clonakilty, County Cork, Ireland, to William, a shoemaker, and Honora ("Hannah") Holland Harnett (1821–1891), a seamstress. Siblings Patrick (1847–1873), a saddlemaker; and Anne (1863–1898), Margaret (1853–1921), and Ella (1860–1923), all seamstresses

About 1849

Emigrates with family to Philadelphia

1850s

Attends St. Mary's Parochial School, Zane Street Grammar School, and/or Filbert Street Grammar School

Early 1860s

Helps support family by selling newspapers and, later, by working as an errand boy

Father dies, reportedly drowned in Delaware River

1865

Begins work as an engraver of steel, copper, wood, and, later, silver

1866

Attends antique classes at the Pennsylvania Academy of the Fine Arts

1868

October 24. Takes oath of allegiance to the United States

1869

Moves to New York

Early 1870s

Employed at Wood & Hughes until 1872, engraving monograms and patterns on table silver. Also works for Tiffany & Co.

1870

Registers for one year at the Cooper Union for the Advancement of Science and Art

1872

Registers at the Antique School of the National Academy of Design; enrolled until 1876

1874

Registers for one year at the Life School of the National Academy

September. Completes first known oil, *Paint Tube and Grapes* (fig. 58)

1875

April 8–May 20. Exhibits *Fruit* at the National Academy (*Catalogue of the Fiftieth Annual Exhibition of the National Academy of Design, 1875,* no. 160)

Gives up engraving as a profession but continues to produce pieces for friends

Studio at 104 East Eleventh Street

Studies briefly with portraitist Thomas Jensen

September–October. Exhibits *Muscatel Grapes* at the Louisville Industrial Exposition (*Catalogue of Paintings, Natural History and Ladies' Department,* no. 191)

November 29–December 11. Exhibits *Basket of Fruit* at the Brooklyn Art Association (*Catalogue of Pictures Exhibited at Their Fall Exhibition . . . ,* no. 6)

Opposite: William M. Harnett, *Still-Life—Violin and Music* (detail, pl. 43)

1876

March 28–May. Exhibits *A Lunch* at the National Academy (*Catalogue of the Fifty-first Annual Exhibition of the National Academy of Design,* no. 130)

April 24–May 6. Exhibits two works entitled *Fruit* at the Brooklyn Art Association (*Catalogue of Pictures Exhibited at Their Spring Exhibition . . . ,* nos. 428, 429)

Resides at 806 South Thirteenth Street, Philadelphia, with mother and sister, Ella

Studio at Wistar House, 400 Locust Street

Autumn. Attends life classes at the Pennsylvania Academy

May 10–November 10. Exhibits *Fruit* at the Philadelphia Centennial Exposition (*International Exhibition, 1876. Official Catalogue, Department of Art,* no. 195)

December 4–16. Exhibits *Fruit* at the Brooklyn Art Association (*Catalogue of Pictures Exhibited at Their Fall Exhibition . . . ,* no. 8)

Late 1870s

Friendship with John Frederick Peto (fig. 145), fellow student at the Pennsylvania Academy

Visits artist Henry Lea Tatnall at his home and studio in Wilmington, Del.

1877

February–March. Attends antique classes at the Pennsylvania Academy

April 2–May. Exhibits *Lunch* and *Fruit* at the National Academy (*Illustrated Catalogue of the Fifty-second Annual Exhibition,* nos. 113, 632)

Spring. Exhibits *A Study Table* and *Fruit* at the Pennsylvania Academy (*Catalogue of the Forty-eighth Annual Exhibition of the Pennsylvania Academy of the Fine Arts,* nos. 93, 396)

August 7–September 22. *Materials for a Quiet Evening; Mynheer's Lunch; Books, Inkstand, Coin, etc.; Pendant;* and *Materials for a Leisure Hour* (owned by Dennis Gale) exhibited in San Francisco (*Catalogue of Art Department of the Twelfth Industrial Exhibition, Held under the Auspices of the Mechanics' Institute,* nos. 81, 161, 256, 257, 357)

1878

April 2–June 1. Exhibits *After a Hard Night's Work, Jakes' Solace,* and *A Bad Counterfeit—Panel* at the National Academy (*Catalogue of the Fifty-third Annual Exhibition of the National Academy of Design,* nos. 115, 165, 201)

April 22–June 2. Exhibits *An Evening's Comfort* at the

Fig. 145. *John F. Peto in His Studio,* mid-1880s. Glass-plate photograph. Joy Peto Smiley and Blossom S. Bejarano

Pennsylvania Academy (*Catalogue of the Forty-ninth Annual Exhibition of the Pennsylvania Academy of the Fine Arts,* no. 273)

April. Exhibits *Bachelor's Comfort* with the Philadelphia Society of Artists at the Pennsylvania Academy

Exhibits painting of peaches at Earle's Galleries, Philadelphia

September–October. Exhibits *An Evening's Comfort* at the Louisville Industrial Exposition (*Louisville Industrial Exposition: Catalogues of Paintings and Statuary, 1878,* no. 234)

1879

April 1–May 31. Exhibits *The Social Club* (pl. 16) at the National Academy (*Catalogue of the Fifty-fourth Annual Exhibition of the National Academy of Design,* no. 44)

April 28–June 8. Exhibits *Thieves in the Pantry* (fig. 23)

at the Pennsylvania Academy (*Catalogue of the Fiftieth Annual Exhibition of the Pennsylvania Academy of the Fine Arts*, no. 3)

September 10–October 13. Exhibits *The Smoker's Solace* and *Still Life* at the Cincinnati Industrial Exposition

November 1–December 1. Exhibits *After Supper* and *Still Life* (owned by Lewis Wiener) with the Philadelphia Society of Artists at the Pennsylvania Academy (*Illustrated Catalogue of the First Annual Exhibition of the Philadelphia Society of Artists, held at the Pennsylvania Academy of the Fine Arts, Cor. Broad and Cherry Streets, Philadelphia*, nos. 43, 98)

November 17–December. Exhibits *Bric-a-Brac* and *Smoker's Companions* at the Seventh Regiment New Armory Fair, New York (*Catalogue of the Loan Art Exhibition, Consisting of Choice Examples of the Modern Foreign and American Schools of Painting, Rare Etchings, Engravings and Other Art Works . . .*, nos. 155, 195A)

1880

Sale of paintings provides for European study trip

Arrives in London by October 30

1881

Spends six months working for patron in Frankfort

Works briefly in Paris(?)

Resides in Munich

March 22–May 14. Exhibits *Still Life* at the National Academy (*Catalogue of the Fifty-sixth Annual Exhibition of the National Academy of Design*, no. 371)

April 4–May 29. Exhibits *Materials for a Leisure Hour* and *Still Life* (*Bank Notes, Coin, etc.*) at the Pennsylvania Academy (*Pennsylvania Academy of the Fine Arts. Catalogue of the Fifty-second Annual Exhibition*, nos. 92, 97)

October. Application for admission to the Munich Academy rejected

Becomes artist member of the Kunstverein and participates in weekly exhibits through 1884

1882

March 27–May 13. Exhibits *Still Life* at the National Academy (*Catalogue of the Fifty–seventh Annual Exhibition of the National Academy of Design*, no. 304)

August. Exhibits *Table with Books, Sheet Music, and Musical Instruments* with the Kunstverein

October–November. Exhibits two works entitled *Still Life* at the National Academy (*Catalogue of the Special Autumn Exhibition of the National Academy of Design*, nos. 122, 211)

1883

April 2–May 12. Exhibits two works entitled *Still Life* and two entitled *Fruit* at the National Academy (*Catalogue of the Fifty-eighth Annual Exhibition of the National Academy of Design*, nos. 292, 369, 625, 677)

July 18–October 15. Exhibits *Still Life* at the Munich Glaspalast (*Illustrirter Katalog der Internationalen Kunstausstellung in Konigl. Glaspalaste in München 1883*, no. 773)

September 5–October 20. *Consolation* (owned by Norton Quincy Pope) exhibited in Chicago (*Eleventh Annual Chicago Inter-State Industrial Exposition*, no. 212)

October 16–November 27. Exhibits *A Royal Dessert* in Boston (*Museum of Fine Arts: Catalogue of the Fourth Annual Exhibition of Contemporary American Art . . .*, no. 125)

November. *Still Life* (owned by Mary R. Kase) exhibited at the Essex Art Association, Newark, N.J. (*First Loan Exhibition*, no. 106)

December 28–January 12, 1884. *Still Life* exhibited in New York (*The Private Collection of Paintings by Exclusively American Artists Owned by Thomas B. Clarke at the American Art Galleries, Madison Square . . .*, no. 50)

1884

August 16–October 25. Exhibits *Still Life* and *A Library Table* (owned by George Henry Moore) in Louisville (*Illustrated Catalogue of the Art Gallery of the Southern Exposition*, nos. 313, 335)

November 8–28. Exhibits *Still Life* at the National Academy (*Catalogue of the Autumn Exhibition of the National Academy of Design*, no. 137)

December 8–19. Exhibits *Still Life* at the Brooklyn Art Association (*Catalogue of Oil Paintings, Brooklyn Art Association, December, 1884*, no. 114)

Exhibits a painting of a hanging rabbit, probably *After the Hunt* (pl. 33), with the Kunstverein

1885

Resides at 7, rue Tortaque, Paris

May–June. Exhibits *Trophée de chasse* (pl. 34) at the Salon (*Catalogue illustré de Salon*, no. 1227)

May–June. Exhibits *Still Life* (pl. 35) in London (*The Exhibition of the Royal Academy of Arts, MDCCCLXXXV: The One Hundred and Seventeenth*, no. 860)

Fig. 146. *The Hanway Street Gallery of Fine Arts.*
Photograph. E. Taylor Snow Papers,
Historical Society of Pennsylvania, Philadelphia

Summer. Resides at 32 Hanway Street, London
(fig. 146)

1886

Returns to the United States

Resides at 28 East Fourteenth Street, New York

Theodore Stewart purchases *After the Hunt* (pl. 34) for
$4,000 and hangs it in his saloon at 8 Warren Street,
New York.

April 5–May 15. Exhibits *Still Life* at the National
Academy (*Catalogue of the Sixty-first Annual Exhibition
of the National Academy of Design*, no. 450)

September 1–October 9. Exhibits *Still Life, After a
Smoke,* and *The Old Violin* (pl. 37) in the Thirteenth
Cincinnati Industrial Exposition (*Official Illustrated
Catalogue of the Art Department . . . ,* nos. 346, 360,
unnumbered)

1887

March 10–12. Exhibits *Still Life* in New York (*Union
League Club Exhibition of Paintings . . . ,* no. 35)

September 1–October 15. Exhibits *Still Life* (owned by
George Ingraham Seney) and *The Old Violin* at the
Second Minneapolis Industrial Exposition

1888

May 28–June. Exhibits *Suspended* in the first annual of
the Art Institute of Chicago

July 4–November 8. Exhibits *Ease* (pl. 41; owned by

Fig. 147. *The Old Violin.* Chromolithograph after the painting by
William M. Harnett. F. Tuchfarber Co., Cincinnati, 1887.
Amon Carter Museum, Fort Worth

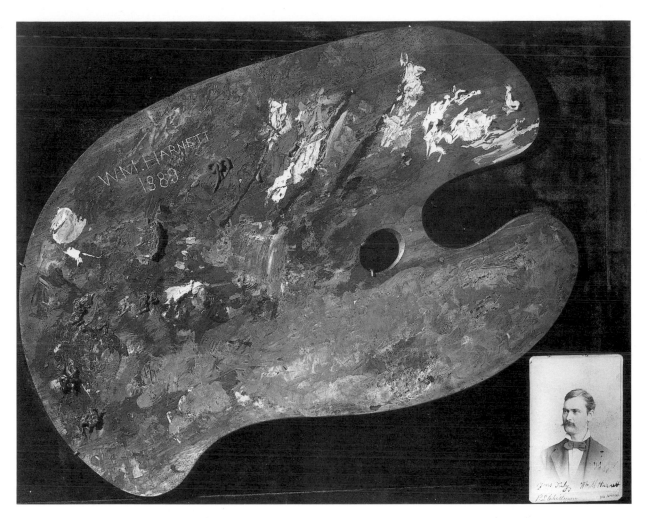

Fig. 148. *Palette*. Signed and dated: *W. M. Harnett. 1889.* The Manney Collection

James Terry Abbe) and *The Student's Den* in Cincinnati (*Catalogue of Paintings in the Art Gallery of the Cincinnati Centennial Exposition*, nos. 74, 75)

October–November. *Still Life* (owned by Joseph Fulton Humphrey) exhibited at the *Art Loan Exhibition for the Benefit of the Bellevue Sanitarium, Colorado Springs*, no. 113

November–December. Exhibits *For Sunday's Dinner* (pl. 42) and *Recreation* at the National Academy (*Catalogue of the Seventh Autumn Exhibition of the National Academy of Design*, nos. 44, 454)

December 11. Admitted to St. Francis Hospital, New York, for over two months

December. *For Sunday's Dinner* (pl. 42) exhibited at John Wanamaker & Co., Philadelphia

1889

February. *Mighty Monarchs* (owned by Edwin C. Ray)

exhibited at the members' annual, New York Athletic Club

February 1–March 1. Exhibits *An Evening Comfort* in Springfield, Mass. (*Twelfth Annual Exhibition, Gill's Art Rooms*, no. 50)

February 22. Discharged from St. Francis Hospital

March 9. Admitted to St. Francis Hospital

March 16. Discharged from St. Francis Hospital

Summer. Second trip to Europe

Takes cure for rheumatism at Carlsbad and Wiesbaden

August 21–September 28. Exhibits *Colossales Glück* (fig. 71) at the Fourth Industrial Exposition, Minneapolis

November–December. Exhibits *Still Life* at the National Academy (*Catalogue of the Eighth Autumn Exhibition of the National Academy of Design*, no. 232)

December 5. Admitted to New York Hospital

Fig. 149. Edward Taylor Snow, *Paintings of the Late
W. M. Harnett on Exhibition,* exhib. cat.
(Philadelphia: Earle's Galleries, 1892), cover.
Joy Peto Smiley and Blossom S. Bejarano

December 24. Discharged from New York Hospital

About 1889

Interviewed by *New York News*

1890

Resides at 132 East Sixteenth Street; studio at 1227
Broadway, New York

December. Exhibits *Emblems of Peace* (pl. 46) and *The
Faithful Colt* (pl. 48) at Black, Starr & Frost, New York

1891

February 2–28. Exhibits *Emblems of Peace* in Springfield,
Mass. (*Gill's Fourteenth Annual Exhibition of American
Paintings,* no. 54)

April 6–May 16. Exhibits *A Bachelor's Friend* at the
National Academy (*National Academy of Design
Catalogue: Sixty-sixth Annual Exhibition,* no. 256)

Mother dies; buried September 14 at Cathedral Cemetery,
Philadelphia

1892

Autumn. Takes cure for rheumatism at Hot Springs,
Ark.

October 27. Admitted to New York Hospital

October 29, 9:55 P.M. Dies at New York Hospital

November 2. Requiem Mass at St. Augustine's Church,
Philadelphia, with Charles and Joseph McCann, A. A.
Ryan, James McCloskey as pallbearers. Buried at
Cathedral Cemetery

Ella M. Harnett named administratrix of artist's estate,
valued at $2,500

November. Memorial exhibition (fig. 149) at Earle's
Galleries, Philadelphia

1893

February 23–24. Estate sale at Thos. Birch's Sons,
Philadelphia

SELECTED BIBLIOGRAPHY

Archival Material

Alfred H. Barr, Jr., Papers. Museum of Modern Art, New York. Microfilmed by the Archives of American Art, Smithsonian Institution, Washington, D.C.

Cooper Union for the Advancement of Science and Art, New York. Archives.

Downtown Gallery Papers. Archives of American Art.

Albert Duveen (firm) Papers. Archives of American Art.

Alfred Frankenstein Papers (includes Blemly scrapbook). Archives of American Art.

National Academy of Design, New York. Archives.

Pennsylvania Academy of the Fine Arts, Philadelphia. Archives.

E. Taylor Snow Papers. Historical Society of Pennsylvania, Philadelphia.

Henry Lea Tatnall Papers. Historical Society of Delaware, Wilmington.

Whitney Museum of American Art Papers. Whitney Museum of American Art, New York. Microfilmed by the Archives of American Art.

Books and Catalogues

Adams, Philip R., and Dwight, Edward H. *Still Life Painting since 1470*. Exhib. cat. Milwaukee: Milwaukee Art Institute; Cincinnati: Cincinnati Art Museum, 1956.

American Painting, 1865–1905. Exhib. cat. Toronto: Art Gallery of Toronto, 1961.

American Paintings from the Manoogian Collection. Exhib. cat. Washington, D.C.: National Gallery of Art, 1989.

American Still-Life Paintings, 1820–1920. Exhib. cat. New York: Victor D. Spark, 1946.

Art of Collecting. Exhib. cat. New York: Hirschl & Adler Galleries, 1984.

Baigell, Matthew. *A Concise History of American Painting and Sculpture*. New York and Toronto: Harper & Row, 1984.

Battersby, Martin. *Trompe l'Oeil: The Eye Deceived*. New York: St. Martin's Press, 1974.

Betsky, Celia. "American Musical Paintings, 1865–1910." In *The Art of Music: American Musical Paintings and Musical Instruments, 1770–1910*. Exhib. cat. Clinton, N.Y.: Fred L. Emerson Gallery, Hamilton College, 1984.

Born, Wolfgang. *Still-Life Painting in America*. New York: Oxford University Press, 1947.

Burke, Doreen Bolger. *American Paintings in the Metropolitan Museum of Art*. Vol. 3, *A Catalogue of Works by Artists Born between 1846 and 1864*. Edited by Kathleen Luhrs. New York: Metropolitan Museum of Art, 1980.

Caffin, Charles H. *American Masters of Painting*. New York: Doubleday, Page & Co., 1902.

Campbell, John H., and Dougherty, Daniel J. *History of the Society of the Friendly Sons of St. Patrick for the Relief of Emigrants from Ireland of Philadelphia*. Philadelphia: Friendly Sons of St. Patrick, 1952.

Chambers, Bruce W. *Old Money: American Trompe l'Oeil Images of Currency*. Exhib. cat. New York: Berry-Hill Galleries, 1988.

Chew, Paul A., ed. *Penn's Promise: Still Life Painting in Pennsylvania, 1795–1930*. Exhib. cat. Greensburg, Pa.: Westmoreland Museum of Art, 1988.

Dars, Célestine. *Images of Deception: The Art of Trompe l'Oeil*. Oxford: Phaidon, 1979.

Early American Genre and Still-Life Paintings. Exhib. cat. New York: Victor D. Spark, 1941.

Eldredge, Charles C., and Millhouse, Barbara B. *American Originals: Selections from Reynolda House, Museum of American Art*. Exhib. cat. New York: Abbeville Press, 1990.

Enault, Louis. *Paris-Salon, 1885*. 2 vols. Paris: E. Bernard & Cie, 1885.

Frankenstein, Alfred. *John F. Peto*. Exhib. cat. Brooklyn: Brooklyn Museum and Brooklyn Institute of Arts and Sciences, 1950.

————.*After the Hunt: William Harnett and Other American Still Life Painters, 1870–1900*. Berkeley and Los Angeles: University of California Press, 1953. Rev. ed. 1969.

————."William Michael Harnett" and "John Frederick Peto." In *The 150th Anniversary Exhibition*. Exhib. cat. Philadelphia: Pennsylvania Academy of the Fine Arts, 1955.

————.*The Reality of Appearance: The Trompe l'Oeil Tradition in American Painting*. Exhib. cat. [Greenwich, Conn.]: New York Graphic Society, 1970.

Gerdts, William H. *Nature's Bounty and Man's Delight: American Nineteenth-Century Still-Life Painting*. Exhib. cat. Newark, N.J.: Newark Museum, 1958.

————.*A Century of American Still-Life Painting, 1813–1913*. Exhib. cat. New York: American Federation of Arts, 1967.

————.*Painters of the Humble Truth: Masterpieces of American Still Life, 1801–1939*. Exhib. cat. Columbia, Mo., and London: University of Missouri Press, 1981.

Gerdts, William H., and Burke, Russell. *American Still-Life Painting*. New York, Washington, and London: Praeger Publishers, 1971.

Goodrich, Lloyd. *Art of the United States, 1670–1966*. Exhib. cat. New York: Whitney Museum of American Art, 1966.

Graham, F. Lanier. *Three Centuries of American Painting*. Exhib. cat. San Francisco: M. H. de Young Memorial Museum and California Palace of the Legion of Honor, 1971.

Harnett Centennial Exhibition. New York: Downtown Gallery, 1948.

Hartley, Marsden. *On Art by Marsden Hartley*. Edited by Gail R. Scott. New York: Horizon Press, 1982.

Hellerstedt, Kahren Jones; Moore, Joanne B.; Rosenthal, Ellen M.; and Wells, Louise F. *Clayton: The Pittsburgh Home of Henry Clay Frick, Art and Furnishings*. Pittsburgh: Helen Clay Frick Foundation, 1988.

Howat, John K., and Spassky, Natalie. *Nineteenth-Century America: Paintings and Sculpture*. Exhib. cat. New York: Metropolitan Museum of Art, 1970.

Howat, John K.; Spassky, Natalie; and Davis, Mary. *The Heritage of American Art: Paintings from the Collection of the Metropolitan Museum of Art*. Exhib. cat. New York: American Federation of Arts, 1976.

Illusionism and Trompe l'Oeil. Exhib. cat. San Francisco: California Palace of the Legion of Honor, 1949.

Inness, George, Jr. *Life, Art, and Letters of George Inness*. New York: Century Co., 1917.

In This Academy: The Pennsylvania Academy of the Fine Arts, 1805–1976. Exhib. cat. Philadelphia: Pennsylvania Academy of the Fine Arts, 1976.

Larkin, Oliver, W. *Art and Life in America*. New York: Rinehart & Co., 1949.

Lubin, David. "A Manly Art: Late Nineteenth-Century Trompe l'Oeil Painting and the Manufacture of Masculinity." In *The Material Culture of Gender/The Gender of Material Culture*. Winterthur Museum and W. W. Norton, forthcoming.

McDougall, Walt. *This Is the Life!* New York: Alfred A. Knopf, 1926.

McElroy, Guy C. *Facing History: The Black Image in American Art, 1710–1940*. Exhib. cat. San Francisco: Bedford Arts Publishers, 1990.

Mandeles, Chad. "William Michael Harnett (1848–92), *A Study Table*." In Paul D. Schweizer, ed., *Masterworks of American Art from the Munson-Williams-Proctor Institute*. New York: Harry N. Abrams, 1989.

Mastai, M. L. d'Otrange. *Illusion in Art: Trompe l'Oeil, A History of Pictorial Illusionism*. New York: Abaris Books, 1975.

Miller, Dorothy C., and Barr, Alfred H., Jr., eds. *American Realists and Magic Realists*. Exhib. cat. New York: Museum of Modern Art, 1943.

Milman, Miriam. *Trompe l'Oeil Painting: The Illusions of Reality*. New York: Rizzoli, 1982.

More Than Meets the Eye: The Art of Trompe l'Oeil. Exhib. cat. Columbus, Ohio: Columbus Museum of Art, 1986.

Morley, Christopher, and Daly, T. A. *The House of Dooner: The Last of the Friendly Inns*. Philadelphia: David McKay Co., 1928.

"Nature-Vivre" by William M. Harnett. Exhib. cat. New York: Downtown Gallery, 1939.

Novak, Barbara. *American Painting of the Nineteenth Century: Realism, Idealism, and the American Experience*. New York, Washington, and London: Praeger Publishers, 1969.

Old and New "Trompe l'Oeil." Exhib. cat. New York: Julien Levy Gallery, 1938.

The Painters of Still Life. Exhib. cat. Hartford, Conn.: Wadsworth Atheneum, 1938.

Paintings of the Late W. M. Harnett on Exhibition. Exhib. cat. Philadelphia: Earle's Galleries, 1892.

Philadelphia: Three Centuries of American Art. Exhib. cat. Philadelphia: Pennsylvania Academy of the Fine Arts, 1976.

Quick, Michael; Ruhmer, Eberhard; and West, Richard V. *Munich and American Realism in the Nineteenth Century*. Exhib. cat. Sacramento: E. B. Crocker Art Gallery, 1978.

Reality and Deception. Exhib. cat. Los Angeles: University of Southern California, 1974.

Rediscoveries in American Painting. Exhib. cat. Cincinnati Art Museum, 1955.

The Reminiscent Object: Paintings by William Michael Harnett, John Frederick Peto and John Haberle. Exhib. cat. La Jolla: La Jolla Museum of Art; Santa Barbara: Santa Barbara Museum of Art, 1965.

[Rich, Theodore D.]. *Theodore Stewart.* [New York: L'Artiste Publishing Co., 1888].

Richardson, Edgar P. *Painting in America: The Story of 450 Years.* New York: Thomas Y. Crowell Co., 1956.

————.*American Art: An Exhibition from the Collection of Mr. and Mrs. John D. Rockefeller 3rd.* Exhib. cat. San Francisco: Fine Arts Museums of San Francisco, 1976.

Sill, Gertrude Grace. *John Haberle: Master of Illusion.* Exhib. cat. Springfield, Mass.: Museum of Fine Arts, 1985.

Sterling, Charles. *Still Life Painting from Antiquity to the Present Time.* New York: Universe Books; Paris: Editions Pierre Tisne, 1959.

Thirty Paintings of Early America. Exhib. cat. New York: College Art Association, 1935.

Trois siècles d'art aux Etats-Unis. Exhib. cat. Paris: Editions des Musées Nationaux.

Troyen, Carol, "William Michael Harnett, *The Faithful Colt,* 1890." In Theodore E. Stebbins, Jr., Carol Troyen, and Trevor J. Fairbrother, *A New World: Masterpieces of American Painting, 1760–1910.* Exhib. cat. Boston: Museum of Fine Arts, 1983.

Wilmerding, John, *American Art.* Harmondsworth, England: Penguin Books, 1976.

————.*Important Information Inside: The Art of John F. Peto and the Idea of Still-Life Painting in Nineteenth-Century America.* Exhib. cat. New York: Harper & Row, 1983.

Wilmerding, John; Ayres, Linda; and Powell, Earl A. *An American Perspective: Nineteenth-Century Art from the Collection of Jo Ann and Julian Ganz, Jr.* Exhib. cat. Washington, D.C.: National Gallery of Art, 1981.

The Wm. Michael Harnett Collection: His Own Reserved Paintings, Models and Studio Furnishings. Sale cat. Philadelphia: Stan. V. Henkels at Thos. Birch's Sons, Auctioneers, 1893.

Newspapers

"The Academy Exhibition." *New York Times,* April 21, 1878, p. 6.

"Art and Artists." *Chicago Tribune,* September 16, 1883, p. 10.

"The Art Gallery." *Cincinnati Commercial Gazette,* September 16, 1886, n.p.

"Art Loses a Master: William M. Harnett, the Painter of 'Still Life,' Dead in New York." *North American* (Philadelphia), November 1, 1892, p. 1.

"Artist Harnett Dead: The Well-Known Still-Life Painter Dies in Hospital." *New York Times,* October 31, 1892, p. 3.

"Art's Counterfeiting: Some Notable Examples of Deceiving the Eyes by Pictures." *Star* (New York), December 30, 1885, p. 6.

"At the Exposition." *Louisville Courier-Journal,* September 14, 1875, n.p.

"At the Exposition Building." *St. Paul and Minneapolis Pioneer Press,* October 12, 1887, pp. 1–2.

"Auspiciously Opened." *St. Paul and Minneapolis Pioneer Press,* September 1, 1887, p. 8.

Blemly, Wm. I. "Honor to Whom Honor Is Due." *World* (New York), August 14, 1887, p. 5.

"The Churches: Pictures at the Exposition Furnish Material for a Sermon." *Minneapolis Tribune,* September 12, 1887, p. 5.

[Cook, Clarence]. "Academy of Design: Fifty-fourth Annual Exhibition." *New-York Daily Tribune,* April 26, 1879, p. 5.

"The Eastern Art Collection." *San Francisco News Letter and California Advertiser,* September 1, 1877, p. 5.

"Fine Arts." *New York Mail,* April 1, 1878, p. 4.

"Fine Arts: National Academy of Design, Special Autumn Exhibition." *New-York Daily Tribune,* October 21, 1882, p. 5.

"The Fine Arts: The Artists' Reception." *Daily Evening Telegraph* (Philadelphia), April 2, 1878, p. 8.

"A Fine Still-Life Painting." *Springfield Daily Republican,* November 7, 1887, p. 6.

Flexner, James Thomas. "Uncommon Commonplace." *New York Times,* September 13, 1953, sect. 7, p. 7.

Frankenstein, Alfred. "Around the Art Galleries: The Strange Case of True Art and the Counterfeit Money." *San Francisco Chronicle,* April 21, 1940, "This World" sect., p. 28.

————."Art and Music: The Full Story behind a Guggenheim Award and an Artist Named Harnett." *San Francisco Chronicle,* May 4, 1947, "This World" sect., pp. 24, 26.

————."The Harnett Story." *San Francisco Chronicle,* August 29, 1948, pp. 9, 11; September 5, 1948, "This World" sect., cover, pp. 19, 21.

————."Bay Area Art 'Find': An 1887 Harnett Painting." *San Francisco Chronicle,* September 21, 1971, p. 33.

————."Instrumental in Rediscovery: Harnett Biographer Tells Story of Painting." *Fort Worth Star-Telegram,* March 5, 1972, pp. 1, 3.

————."'Merganser Duck': Still and Truthful."*San Diego Union,* November 19, 1972, sect. E, pp. 1, 8.

"Harnett: How George Hulings Lost His Fiddle."*Evening Item*(Philadelphia), June 11, 1895, p. 1.

"Harnett's Body Here!" *Times* (Philadelphia), November 1, 1892, p. 1.

"Harnett's Name Forged." *Times* (Philadelphia), May 23, 1893, p. 2.

"In the Domain of Art: A Last Glance around the Autumn Academy Display." *New York Herald,* December 9, 1888, p. 19.

Jackson, Joseph Henry. "Solving the Mystery of the Artist with Two Styles—Hard and Soft." *San Francisco Chronicle,* September 13, 1953, "This World" sect., pp. 14, 16.

"Kunst." *New Yorker Staats-Zeitung und Herald,* November 25, 1888, p. 4.

"Loan Exhibition." *Weekly Gazette: Colorado Springs,* October 20, 1888, p. 3.

"The National Academy." *Sun* (New York), April 13, 1879, p. 2.

"National Academy of Design: Close of the Annual Exhibition. *New York Times,* June 1, 1879, p. 2.

"Original Paintings: A Sale by Messrs. James S. Earle and Sons." *North American* (Philadelphia), April 27, 1878, p. 1.

"Paintings at the Academy." *New York Times,* November 26, 1889, p. 5.

"Paintings Left by Artist Harnett." *World* (New York), November 1, 1892, p. 10.

"Recent Deaths: A Famous Still-Life Painter." *Boston Evening Transcript,* November 1, 1892.

"Royal Academy: Third Notice." *Times* (London), May 25, 1885, p. 4.

"Theater, Kunst und Wissenschaft." *Münchner Neueste Nachrichten und Münchner Anzeiger,* July 6, 1883, n.p.

"William M. Harnett." *New York Herald,* October 30, 1892, p. 25.

"William M. Harnett." *New York Recorder,* November 1, 1892, p. 3.

"William M. Harnett." *Public Ledger*(Philadelphia), October 31, 1892, p. 2.

"William M. Harnett." *Star* (New York), October 31, 1892, p. 3.

"William M. Harnett Dead: Demise of a Well-Known Painter of 'Still Life' Subjects." *Evening Bulletin* (Philadelphia), October 31, 1892, p. 6.

"A Wonderland." *Cincinnati Enquirer,* September 19, 1886, p. 12.

Periodicals

"Art Notes." *Art Journal* 8 (November 1882), pp. 349–50.

Barry, Roxana. "Plane Truths: Nineteenth-Century American Trompe l'Oeil Painting." *Art and Antiques*4 (September–October 1981), pp. 100–107.

Baur, John I. H. Review of *After the Hunt: William Harnett and Other American Still Life Painters, 1870–1900* by Alfred Frankenstein. *College Art Journal* 13 (Spring 1954), pp. 242–44.

Bolger, Doreen. "Cards and Letters from His Friends: *Mr. Hulings' Rack Picture* by William Michael Harnett." *American Art Journal* 22, no. 2 (1990), pp. 4–32.

Born, Wolfgang. "William M. Harnett: Bachelor Artist." *Magazine of Art* 39 (October 1946), pp. 248–54.

Bragazzi, Olive. "The Story behind the Rediscovery of William Harnett and John Peto by Edith Halpert and Alfred Frankenstein." *American Art Journal* 16, no. 2 (Spring 1984), pp. 51–65.

Chirico, Robert F. "Some Reflections on Sound and Silence in the Visual Arts." *Arts Magazine*56, no. 8 (April 1982), pp. 101–5.

————."Language and Imagery in Late Nineteenth-Century Trompe l'Oeil." *Arts Magazine* 59, no. 7 (March 1985), pp. 110–14.

Cogswell, Louisa Trumbull. "Art in Boston." *Arcadia* 1 (December 1, 1892), pp. 305–6.

Cook, Clarence [?]. "The National Academy of Design: The Autumn Exhibition." *Studio,* n.s. [1], no. 7 (November 8, 1884), pp. 79–82.

"'Emblems of Peace' by William M. Harnett." *Springfield Museum of Fine Arts Bulletin* 4, no. 9 (June 1938), unpaginated.

Frankenstein, Alfred. "'After the Hunt'—and After." *Bulletin of the California Palace of the Legion of Honor* 6 [September 1948], unpaginated.

————."Harnett: One Century." *Art News*47, no. 5 (September 1948), pp. 14–17, 52–53.

————."Harnett, True and False." *Art Bulletin* 31 (March 1949), pp. 38–56.

————."New Harnett Discoveries." *Magazine of Art* 44 (February 1951), pp. 62–66.

————."Harnett, Peto, Haberle: The Three Nineteenth Century Still-Life Artists Make a Striking Show at La Jolla." *Artforum* 4, no. 2 (October 1965), pp. 27–33.

————."The American Nineteenth Century, Part 2: Saloon

Salons." *Art News* 67, no. 5 (September 1968), pp. 44–47, 64.

———."Mr. Hulings' Rack Picture." *Auction* 2, no. 6 (February 1969), pp. 6–9.

———."The Reality of Appearance." *Art Gallery* 13, no. 6 (March 1970), pp. 23–28.

———."Yankee Rhyparography."*Art News* 69, no.1 (March 1970), pp. 50–53, 75–76.

———."Exhibition Preview: The Reality of Appearance." *Art in America* 58, no. 2 (March–April 1970), pp. 94–99.

———."Harnett's *Front Face*," *Auction* 4, no. 3 (November 1970), pp. 48, 51.

———."Fooling the Eye." *Artforum* 12, no. 9 (May 1974), pp. 32–35.

———."Illusion and Reality." *Horizon* 22, no. 7 (July 1979), pp. 24–31.

"Frankenstein Gets Guggenheim." *Art Digest* 21, no. 15 (May 1, 1947), p. 10.

Gardner, Albert Ten Eyck. "Harnett's *Music and Good Luck*." *Metropolitan Museum of Art Bulletin* 22 (January 1964), pp. 156–65.

Gerdts, William H. "A Trio of Violins." *Art Quarterly* 22 (Winter 1959), pp. 370–83.

———."The Bric-a-Brac Still Life." *Antiques* 100 (November 1971), pp. 744–48.

———."On the Tabletop: Europe and America." *Art in America* 60, no. 5 (September–October 1972), pp. 62–69.

Goodrich, Lloyd. "Notes: Harnett and Peto, A Note on Style." *Art Bulletin* 31 (March 1949), pp. 57–58.

Groseclose, Barbara S. "Vanity and the Artist: Some Still-Life Paintings by William Michael Harnett." *American Art Journal* 19, no. 1 (1987), pp. 51–59.

Halpert, Edith Gregor. "The Harnett Tradition." *Art Digest* 28, no. 1 (October 1, 1953), p. 23.

"Harnett Resurrected from the Shadows." *Art Digest* 13, no. 15 (May 1, 1939), p. 7.

"An Interesting Letter." *Sketch Book* 1, no. 7 (July 1883), pp. 76–77.

"'Jeems Pipes' Pipings: From My Attic Room, 23 Union Square." *American Art Journal* 44 (January 23, 1886), p. 231.

"Letters: John I. H. Baur and Olive Bragazzi." *American Art Journal* 17, no. 1 (Winter 1985), p. 93.

Mandeles, Chad. "William Michael Harnett's *The Old Cupboard Door* and the Tradition of *Vanitas*." *American Art Journal* 18, no. 3 (1986), pp. 51–62.

"Mr. Gill's Annual Sale." *Collector* 2 (May 15, 1891), p. 164.

"A Notable Art Center." *Progressive Springfield* 2, no. 1 (June 1891), pp. 2–6.

Nygren, Edward J. "The Almighty Dollar: Money as a Theme in American Painting." *Winterthur Portfolio* 23 (Summer–Autumn 1988), pp. 129–50.

Oja, Carol. "The Still-Life Paintings of William Michael Harnett (Their Reflections upon Nineteenth-Century American Musical Culture)." *Musical Quarterly* 63 (October 1977), pp. 505–23.

Roditi, Edouard. "William Harnett: American Necromantic." *View* 5, no. 4 (November 1945), pp. 9, 19–20.

Snow, E. Taylor. "William Michael Harnett, A Philadelphia Catholic Artist." *American Catholic Historical Researches* 10 (April 1893), pp. 74–76.

———."William Michael Harnett, A Philadelphia Catholic Artist." *Griffin's Journal* 21 (April 1893), p. [1].

"The Society of American Artists: Ninth Exhibition." *Studio*, n.s. 2, no. 12 (June 1887), pp. 209–17.

Sozanski, Edward J. "Sleight of Hand from a Master Illusionist." *Antiques World* 3, no. 5 (March 1981), pp. 44–49.

Staiti, Paul. "William Harnett." *Mount Holyoke College Art Museum* 4, no. 1 (Fall 1980), pp. 1–4.

"Trade in Philadelphia." *Dry Goods Economist* 47, no. 2521 (November 12, 1892), p. 38.

[Trumble, Alfred]. "The Awakening of the Giant." *Collector* 4 (October 1, 1893), pp. 293–94.

Weinberg, H. Barbara. "Thomas B. Clarke: Foremost Patron of American Art from 1872 to 1899." *American Art Journal* 8, no. 1 (May 1976), pp. 52–83.

White, Frank Linstow. "Art Notes." *Epoch* 8 (December 12, 1890), p. 300.

Unpublished Material

Chamberlin-Hellman, Maria. "Thomas Eakins as a Teacher." Ph.D. diss., Columbia University, 1981.

Lubin, David M. "Trompe l'Oeil Painting and Commodity Display in Late-Nineteenth-Century America." Paper delivered at the International Convention of the American Studies Association and the Canadian Association for American Studies, Toronto, November 2–5, 1989.

Oja, Carol J. "Musical Subjects in the Paintings of William Michael Harnett." Master's thesis, University of Iowa, 1976.

Tepfer, Diane. "Edith Gregor Halpert and the Downtown Gallery Downtown, 1926–1940: A Study in American Art Patronage." Ph.D. diss., University of Michigan, 1989.

INDEX

▼

Additional photograph credits:

Fig. 1. Sotheby's

Fig. 7. Geoffrey Clements

Figs. 8, 16. Amon Carter Museum

Fig. 20. Geoffrey Clements

Fig. 27. Frick Art Reference Library

Fig. 28. The Metropolitan Museum of Art

Fig. 29. Lockwood Hoehl

Fig. 31. Historical Society of Pennsylvania

Fig. 34. Courtesy of Gerold Wunderlich & Co., Inc., New York

Fig. 41. Colin McRae

Fig. 43. Courtesy of the Connecticut Valley Historical Museum, Springfield, Mass.

Fig. 49. Geoffrey Clements

Fig. 53. Amon Carter Museum

Fig. 55. Joseph Szaszfai

Figs. 61, 63. Amon Carter Museum

Fig. 69. ©All Rights Reserved

Figs. 73, 75, 76, 78, 79. The Metropolitan Museum of Art

Fig. 84. Amon Carter Museum

Fig. 98. Geoffrey Clements

Fig. 99. E. Irving Blomstrann

Frontispiece p. 232, Amon Carter Museum

Fig. 101. Amon Carter Museum

Fig. 102. Harlan Hatcher Graduate Library, University of Michigan

Fig. 103. Amon Carter Museum

Fig. 104. Rare Book and Manuscript Library, Columbia University, New York

Fig. 107. Free Library of Philadelphia

Fig. 108. Marc Meachem

Fig. 109. Thomas J. Watson Library, The Metropolitan Museum of Art, photograph by David Allison

Fig. 113. Frick Art Reference Library

Figs. 114, 115. Van Pelt-Dietrich Library Center, University of Pennsylvania

Figs. 117, 119, 120. Helga Photo Studio

Fig. 121. Arents Collection, The New York Public Library, Astor, Lenox, and Tilden Foundations

Fig. 125. High Museum of Art, Atlanta

Fig. 139. Frick Art Reference Library

Fig. 143. Helga Photo Studio

Fig. 144. Microfilm collections, Harold B. Lee Library, Brigham Young University

Fig. 148. Helga Photo Studio

Pl. 3. Henry Nelson

Pl. 22. Julius Lowy Frame & Restoring Company, Inc.

Pl. 42. Photograph ©1988, All Rights Reserved

Pl. 45. Derek Greaves

Pl. 47. Photograph ©1991, All Rights Reserved